US-CHINA RELATIONS
In the OBAMA ADMINISTRATION:
FACING SHARED CHALLENGES

JOHN MILLIGAN-WHYTE
DAI MIN

CENTER *FOR* AMERICA-CHINA PARTNERSHIP

New School Press' Ltd's books can be purchased for educational, business or sales promotional use. For ordering details, please contact:

New School Press Ltd

244 5th Avenue, Suite 2356
New York, NY 10001-7604 USA
Tel: (212) 302 1890

Website: www.CenterACP.com
Email: info@centeracp.com

ISBN(13): 978-0-9822803-7-9
ISBN: 0-9822803-7-8

First Edition
Library of Congress's cataloging-in-publication data available.

By John Milligan-Whyte and Dai Min in America-China Partnership Book Series:

- A White Paper for The Presidents Of America And China
- China & America's Emerging Partnership: *A New Realistic Perspective*
- New China Business Strategies: *Chinese & American Companies As Global Partners*
- China & America's Responsibilities in Mankind's Future
- China & America's New Economic Partnership: *The Success of Economic and Moral Authority*
- The New School of China America Relations
- Being China: *The Meaning of Deng Xiaoping*

Dedication

This book is dedicated to those on the road to war and catastrophe who might come to understand and take the road less traveled.

Acknowledgements

This book is the work of billions of people dead, living and unborn. We thank each of you who help discover what we are and can be.

John Milligan-Whyte, Chairman of Whyte DaiMin Investments Limited, is the co-host of the ChinaSmartMagazine.com podcasts and *Collaboration of Civilizations* television series. He is author of a column on US-China relations in *People's Daily*, which calls him the "new Edgar Snow" and "21st century Kissinger." In 2009 *China Daily* recognized the Center for America China Partnership that he co-founded in New York in 2005 as "the first American think tank to combine and integrate American and Chinese perspectives providing a complete answer for America and China's success in the 21st century." He is the author of five books in the America China Partnership Book Series published in 2009 and 2010 that created the "New School of America China Relations" summarized in A *White Paper for the Presidents of America and China* used in President Hu Jintao's preparation for meetings with President Obama. This book, originally titled *China and America's Leadership in Peaceful Coexistence*, is the first by an American author since 1989 to be translated and published in China by the Central Party School, which titled it in Mandarin: *China-Us Relations in the Obama Administration: Facing Common Challenges.* He was selected as a participant in the Inaugural Meeting of New Champions by the Managing Editor of the Harvard Business Review and Chairman of the World Economic Forum and was elected with 12,534 votes the first non-Chinese winner of the Outstanding China Business Leader Social Responsibility Award from the China Business Leaders' Summit sponsored by the CPC Central Committee, State Council Information Office, *China News and Red Flag* magazine. From 1992 to 2008 he was Chairman of CORE Capital Ltd and a director of currency trading software, broadcasting, WiFi, e-Smart technology, Internet, reinsurance and hedge fund companies.

From 1984 to 2008 he was a founding partner of Milligan-Whyte & Smith, which became a World Economic Forum member in 1992 and was co-recipient of the *International Financial Law Review's* Asian M&A Deal of the Year Award in 2002 for its role in the first and most successful foreign acquisition by a Chinese state owned company.

He is an Honorary Research Professor at Beijing University, Senior Advisor to the Venture Capital Research Center at China's Renmin University, Guest Professor at China's University of International Business & Economy, a Fellow of the International Center for Legal Studies in Strasburg, Austria, and received a B.A (Honors) in Political Philosophy, LL.B and LL.M degrees from the University of Toronto, Queen's Law School, Osgoode Hall

Law School, continuing legal education at Harvard Law School and executive education at Harvard Business School.

Dai Min, President of Whyte DaiMin Investments Limited, is co-host and executive producer of the ChinaSmartMagazine.com and the *Collaboration of Civilizations* television Series, co-author of a *People's Daily* column on US-China relations and eight books in the *China America Partnership Book Series* recognized in 2009 by the Chinese Academy of Social Sciences as creating a "New School of China America Relations." She cofounded the Center for America China Partnership in 2005 and America-China Partnership Foundation in 2008 in New York and is Chairman of AmeriChina Finance Ltd, which represents leading technology firms in China, and a director of foreign currency software trading and media companies.

She won the national contest in the performing arts in China in 1978 and was a lyric soprano with China's National Opera & Dance Company before working at the United Nations in New York, on Wall Street as a currency trader, an advisor to ABB and Obermeyer on developing business in China, and advising Chinese and American companies on business development.

She is the granddaughter of General Dai Fengxiang, one of the earliest highranking generals to support Sun Yat-sun to overthrow the Qing Dynasty and establish the Republic of China. She was educated in China, Germany, England and America and is an Honorary Research Professor at Beijing University, Honorary Advisor to the Beijing University Education Foundation and initiated The China Insurance Industry Executive Leadership Program in conjunction with the Wharton School of University of Pennsylvania, China Renmin University and XL Capital.

Table of Contents

Book 2

CHINA & AMERICA'S LEADERSHIP IN PEACEFUL COEXISTENCE

CHINA'S EXCEPTIONALISM: THE DREAM OF A HARMONIOUS SOCIETY AND WORLD

Chapter 1: STRATEGIC CONVERGENCE OF THE INTERESTS OF AMERICA AND CHINA IN ASIA

Chapter 2: THE CHALLENGE OF LIVING UP TO THE EXALTED JUSTICE
AND BENEVOLENCE OF A HARMONIOUS SOCIETY

AMERICAN EXCEPTIONALISM: THE DREAM OF THE UNIVERSALITY OF HUMAN RIGHTS AND EXALTED JUSTICE

Chapter 3: THE CHALLENGE OF LIVING UP TO THE AMERICAN
IDEALS OF EXALTED JUSTICE AND BENEVOLENCE

Chapter 4: WILL PEOPLE PERISH FROM THE EARTH?

LEADING 2008 AMERICAN PRESIDENTIAL CANDIDATES' FOREIGN POLICY PERSPECTIVES

Chapter 5: WHAT GOVERNMENT ARE THE AMERICAN PEOPLE CAPABLE OF IN THE 21ST CENTURY?

CONVENTIONAL AMERICAN PRINCIPLES OF CONFLICT BASED POLICY ON CHINA

Chapter 6: THE LIMITS OF AMERICAN MILITARY AUTHORITY

Chapter 7: THE LIMITS OF CONVENTIONAL AMERICAN PRINCIPLES OF CONFLICT BASED CHINA POLICY

Chapter 8: THE LIMITATIONS OF CONVENTIONAL AMERICAN PRINCIPLES OF CONFLICT BASED ASIAN POLICY ANALYSIS

Combining the Moral Authority of American and Chinese Exceptionalisms in a Harmonious World

Chapter 11: THE MORAL AUTHORITY OF HUMAN RIGHTS IN A HARMONIOUS
WORLD MODEL

Chapter 12: AMERICA'S CHOICE OF FAILURE OR SUCCESS

Summary

The 21st century's fundamental foreign policy, defense strategy and scientific research issue is the prevention of human extinction which we refer to as "the fundamental issue". Current human thought processes are propelling us to extinction as the proliferation of species lethal weapons and science enables individuals or a nation or nations to accidentally or deliberately destroy our species. Conventional American foreign policy analyses are not focused on preventing our extinction.

China's Central Party School Publishing House has translated and is publishing *China & America's Responsibilities in Mankind's Future* in Mandarin. We refer to it as Book I. It translated and published *China & America's Leadership in Peaceful Coexistence* in 2010 giving it the name in Mandarin used in this English edition *China-US Relations in the Obama Administration: Facing Shared Challenges*. We refer to these as Books 1 and 2 because they are interrelated. These are the only two books by an American think tank that the China's Central Party School has translated and published in China since 1989. They present a plan for the solution to what we term the "Human Extinction Challenge" in "The Age of Species Lethal Weapons and Science" and for the creation of an international system suited to the 21st century's needs. The plan moves beyond the fallible tactics of America's War on Terror, which looks for the opponents with a war of terror, that attempts to detect and police dangerous individuals and nations. The plan examines how the Human Extinction Challenge can be managed successfully and then solved. The plan formulates an agenda for the 21st century and is a guide for detecting and neutralizing the dangerous causes of extinction in human nature.

The Human Extinction Challenge is "the New School" in which mankind must learn and adapt quickly. Creating immediate and long-term solutions requires that solving the Human Extinction Challenge becomes mankind's "New School" because conventional perspectives are not and cannot solve it. The "New School's perspectives" are summarized in chapter 1 of Book 1 and examined in the America-China Partnership Book Series. Adding the New School's perspectives to conventional American perspectives is essential and will prove beneficial to mankind. One of the New School's perspectives is that America and China must be permanent genuine win-win partners. Senior Researchers at the Chinese Academy of Social Science indicated in 2008 that *China & America's Emerging Partnership: A New Realistic Perspective* and *New China Business Strategies: Chinese and American Companies as Global Partners* present a win-win mindset and strategies that provide a complete answer for America and China's success in the 21st century and "establishes a New School of America-China relations. American foreign affairs and economic scholars have been unable to transcend their traditional zero-sum game mindset and strategies on US-China relations." The Chinese Academy of Social Science is an institution directly under the State Council and the highest academic research organization in philosophy and the social sciences and a national center for comprehensive studies in China. The State Council is China's highest executive and administrative body.

China and America's Responsibilities in Mankind's Future examines why and how the new international system and defense systems that are essential for solving to solve the Human Extinction Challenge can only be based on moral authority and the laws of physics that human beings innately obey. Its two-part thesis is that only if:

1. China and America combine their military, economic and moral authority as win-win partners rather than zero sum game competitors, can mankind's current sole superpower

and emerging mega superpower create a 21st century inter-national system capable of policing and then pacifying 192 diverse nations and the 6.5 billion individuals in mankind.

2. China and America's partnership also leads a Manhattan II Project combining mankind's most able minds in the interrelated new fields of research required, can the solution to the Human Extinction Challenge can be found. This requires mankind's understanding and using the power of philosophy, genetics and physics of "moral authority" to create new defense systems and evolutionary leap in human nature required.

China-US Relations in the Obama Administration: Facing Shared Challenges advances a three-part thesis

1. Deng Xiaoping is one of the world's leading 21st century foreign policy and defense strategist.
2. America and China must redefine their current zero sum game confrontational engagements and become committed global partners with shared new win-win mindsets and strategies. This would allow the alignment and fulfillment of their common needs for economic success propesperity and their national security.
3. China has established the sound proof foundation for America's new economic development, foreign policies and defense strategies in the 21st century. This is based on the Principles of Peaceful Coexistence.

Chapters 1, 2 and 3 examine China's and America's convergent strategies in the context of the fundamental issue. Chapters 4 and 5 examine the vision of the four presidents who prevented America's failure and the policies of Deng Xiaoping who prevented China's failure. We will also compare their takes on foreign policy of the leading candidates seeking to be America's 44th president. Chapters 6, 7, and 8 examine America's conventional foreign policy and defense strategies. Chapters 9, 10 and 11 examine the charisma of China and America's partnership's leadership in implementing the Principles of Peaceful Coexistence among over 192 nations comprising 6.5 billion people in 7 or 8 civilizations.

The Foundations of Economic and National Security and Moral Authority

Deng Xiaoping made prosperity and peace China's top priorities. He also envisioned that China's main goal will be seeking a harmonious world. Since 1978, three generations of Chinese leaders have successfully implemented the Principles of Peaceful Coexistence as the basis of China's economic development, foreign policy and defense strategies as well as overcome the Principles of Conflict.

The Principles of Peaceful Coexistence are:

1. Mutual respect for the sovereignty and territorial integrity,
2. Mutual nonaggression,
3. Non-interference in each other's internal affairs,
4. Equality and mutual benefits, and

China's Premier Zhou Enlai first set forth the Principles of Peaceful Coexistence in a talk with an Indian delegation during the inter-governmental negotiations from December 1953 to April 1954. Premier Zhou Enlai and Prime Minister Nehru, no doubt influenced by Gandhi, pioneered the Principles of Peaceful Coexistence in a 1954 communiqué. They have been practiced by China since 1979. According to the Chinese, they "have been adopted in many other international documents and have become widely accepted as norms for relations between countries."

China, the most populous country in the world, has pioneered the implementation of the Principles of Peaceful Coexistence in its policies. The Principles of Peaceful Coexistence are the only possible sustainable foundation that will generate and facilitate a successful 21st century international system.

The Principles of Peaceful Coexistence are embodied, though less so than in China, in the United Nations' Charter. But, the United Nations is perceived by many as not being effective in realizing the goals laid out in its Charter. The UN must therefore be allowed to implement those goals successfully through the partnership of America and China as we envision it in chapter 11 of Book 2.

Conventional zero sum game strategies in place in the UN's other 191 member states' policies generally operate under the Principles of Conflict. The conventional zero sum mindset including the Principles of Conflict is common in America's policies toward China. The Principles of Conflict cannot protect America's security in the 21st century. This conventional zero sum mindset operating under the Principles of Conflict is not solving the fundamental issue or the related foreign policy problems threatening America.

Many American policymakers, scholars, and opinion leaders do not yet thoroughly see, the opportunities for America's economic success and security that the foundation of China's development provides for America's success and survival in the 21st century. The genius for peace and global implementation of the Principles of Peaceful Coexistence are what we term "China's Exceptionalism."

The Principles of Conflict we formulated and examined in chapter 2 of Book 1 are:

1. The Fairness Hypocrisy
2. "Believe and Behave as I do" Intolerance
3. "Do as I say, Not as I Do Hypocrisy"
4. "Do as I Say Arrogance"
5. "We are Better Than You" Arrogance
6. "My Country is Right or Wrong" Bias
7. The tendency for Conflict, Power and Harming Others

Chapter 1 of Book 1 examines why the Principles of Peaceful Coexistence must replace the Principles of Conflict and conventional perspectives:

Extinction is an objective criterion. It ends prejudices and disputes. In that sense, our extinction would create a lasting peace. But it is "the peace of the grave." Is our species capable of any other peace but in the Age of Species Lethal Weapons and Science?

The New School's perspective is that the Human Extinction Challenge entails a unique combination of high probability and catastrophic risks that cannot be ignored or successfully dealt with using "might is right" statesmanship and the "Principles of Conflict." Therefore, the Human Extinction Challenge must be managed using the Principles of Peaceful Coexistence, under which "right is might" statesmanship and solutions presented in the Manhattan II Project, We must learn how to "make all bad men good and good men great" because in our lifetimes anyone can commit suicidal murder on a massive scale, or even human species suicide. Suicidal persons with lethal weapons can do so, just as suicide bombers today kill individuals, which is examined in chapter 4 of Book 1.

The Human Extinction Challenge can only be solved in the short term by better managing human behavior using moral authority and in the long term with new defense systems and the remaking of human nature. It is essential that a successful partnership of America and China be based on the Principles of Peaceful Coexistence. That is possible because China and India pioneered the Principles of Peaceful Coexistence in 1953-1954, and Deng Xiaoping and his successors have made them the basis of China's foreign policies and defense strategies since 1978....

Deng Xiaoping, commented frequently that foreigners did not believe him when he said China remained committed to peaceful coexistence with all nations. We have also observed that many Americans do not believe that China sincerely wants to live up to the requirements of peaceful coexistence with America. The concept of a peaceful rise of a major power is not part of America's or Europe's histories. But it is part of modern China's history.

Currently, American reactions to the rapid phenomenon of China's economic development are shock, hostility and confusion. On their end, the Chinese have been unable to express their desire for peaceful coexistence with America, in ways that Americans can understand. But the Chinese's desire for peace is a sincere endeavor. The real danger is that Americans do not want to yet accept that the Chinese in fact sincerely want and pursue a peaceful coexistence. There are fundamental cultural differences, as well as dangerous perceptive and communicative gaps that make it difficult for Americans to accept China's success. It seems to contradict America's national pride and deep yearning for ideological and geopolitical hegemony.

At an even deeper level, the Chinese's view that their success can be win-win for China and America is incomprehensible to the type of zero sum mindset that is part of and is facilitated by Americans' Rights Society and Rule of Law culture. This is examined in *China & America's Emerging Partnership: A New Realistic Perspective* and *New China Business Strategies: Chinese and American Companies as Global Partners*. Americans tend to think and feel: How can we win, if China does not lose? But, China's desire for economic growth and peaceful coexistence are consistent with China's "win-win" Consensus Democracy and Permission Society. China's current leaders think how can we succeed if the Americans do not succeed too?

The Principles of Conflict are entrenched in human nature. The Chinese experiment with the Principles of Peaceful Coexistence fit the requirements for China's economic development. Deng Xiaoping recognized that China's domestic and foreign policies should not be built on the assumption, on which Mao Zedong operated, that America or Russia will deliberately start a new world war in the Age of Species Lethal Weapons. Deng Xiaoping was however correct to suggest that America and the USSR only avoided a nuclear war by the extraordinarily able leadership in 1962. Deng Xiaoping recognized the "new logic" of nuclear nations' peaceful coexistence. President Kennedy did the same, and called it "the new face of war." War in the Age of Species Lethal Weapons and Science is unwinnable.

China's Principles of Peaceful Coexistence, exhibited in the real world of international relations by 30 years of evidence constitutes an extraordinary achievement. China's foreign policy and defense strategies have overcome the Principles of Conflict in human nature.

Now comes the question: Which will triumph in the Age of Species Lethal Weapons and Science:

1. Human nature as it is, as developed before Mankind's New School of the Human Extinction Challenge, or
2. Human nature as it must become in order for us to continue to exist and prosper?

To continue to exist, we must change. We must evolve quickly or fail as a species. It is fortunate for America that Chinese leaders have produced and implemented the Principles of Peaceful Coexistence. Their growth rates are so much higher than ours. Therefore, we must align our success with theirs.

China's prosperity depends on America's ability to remain at peace with China. On their end, Americans also need prosperity. Our common challenge is that the Principles of Conflict are not consistent with America's, China's or indeed the world's prosperity in the Age of Species Lethal Weapons and Science. To succeed in this century, America must align its mindset and strategies with those on which Chinese have based their policies.

America's conventional policies and strategies toward China are impacted by our species' innate flaws that we refer to collectively as the "Principles of Conflict."

The Principles of Conflict have been the defining features of human nature and international relations. Fortunately, China's leaders are trying, with their goal of a harmonious world, to rise above them.

America's leaders, scholars and people must reinforce this attempt to evolve beyond the flaws of human nature which will destroy us if we do move away from them.

The Principles of Conflict are not a sound basis for American policymaking, in the Age of Species Lethal Weapons and Science. Foreign policies based on the Principles of Conflict are an example of a nation moved by exalted justice and benevolence that President Washington recommended to the American people. The Principles of Peaceful Coexistence are such an example. In contrast, the Principles of Conflict are not the formulae for lasting peace that President Kennedy believed were essential after the Cuban Missile Crisis. Books 1 and 2 examine the fundamental question of our future: Will Americans choose the Principles of Peaceful Coexistence or the Principles of Conflict?

America and China are currently pursuing goals of prosperity and peace but are taking leading roles in the international system with different mindsets, priorities and strategies. America's leading role is implementing the Principles of Conflict and China's is implementing the Principles of Peaceful Coexistence. Conventional American policymakers seem not to recognize or understand this very different role China is performing. They inherently China to operate according to the Principles of Conflict. They expect China to have the goals of obtaining ideological and military hegemony. Based on that assumption, China and America are in conflict. However, China has recognized that there are far greater advantages in seeking economic development which requires peace without the employment of ideological or military hegemony. Thus China has realized that hegemony is not worth pursuing and that because China does not seek it, it will become a leading nation. This is due to the combination of China's population size, abilities, and economic development, as well as the moral authority of its adherence to the

Principles of Peaceful Coexistence.

America has made the imposition of its ideals and the preservation of its superpower status and hegemony its priorities. As a result, America is facing profound and complex military crises. Simultaneously, it is confronted with the largest national debt in the world and it is the epicenter of a financial crisis. But by employing such strategies, America's crisis endangers China as well.

However, the fact remains and American policymakers must recognize it: China has made prosperity and peace its priorities rather than seeking superpower hegemony. As a result, it has been enjoying economic development and peace.

To achieve the economic and national security that America requires, it must make prosperity and peace its primary goals, and base its foreign policies on the Principles of Peaceful Coexistence. Like China, America must evolve beyond the Principles of Conflict. Books1 and 2 and the New School make that point. Why have conventional American policymakers not previously recognized and accepted that reality?

America became the world's sole superpower late in the 20th century following its development over the last two centuries. This past success shapes Americans perspectives of the world. They feel that America is the best nation. That is understandable, and hopefully it will continue. But, China has been the world's largest, wealthiest, and most innovative nation for 48 of the last 50 centuries and is reemerging as an economic superpower not interested in the irrationality and futility of war in the 21st century.

How will Americans' perspectives of themselves, enable them to accept the emergence of 22% of mankind from poverty and failure? How are Americans going to resist or align their success with the developing nations of China, India, the Middle East, Russia, Venezuela, and others?

America is the richest and China is the 100th poorest country in the world. The Chinese are 22% and Americans are 5.6% of the over

6.5 billion people on Earth. America's civilization and its values are 4 centuries old and China's are 50 centuries old.

As laudable as America's Ideals and many aspects of its government are, they are not the only principles mankind can be governed by. The European Enlightenment and America's evolution have played increasing roles in the 17th, through the 20th centuries. Nowadays, China's modernization, growing wealth, and world view will play a critical role in the 21st century's international arena. Americans did not anticipate and refuse to accept China's peaceful development. America will play a new role in the 21st century in international affairs than it did in the 20th century. For that to happen, Americans must adjust to this emerging reality rather than misalign America's future success against obvious global trends.

As genuine global partners committed to the Principles of Peaceful Coexistence, American and Chinese administrations can act together as the dominant guardians of the world. When American policymakers are not using the Principles of Conflict and collaborate rather than compete with, the two states will be more stable and will not trigger a war in which they take sides with rival factions in client states. Only if they are successful partners will each nation have the moral, economic, and military authority to say to and succesfuly persuade unstable nations that peace is mandatory. The ability to police and pacify the world requires the combined moral, economic and military authority of America and China. That reality must become the focus of policy making, in America and China.

The reasons for China and America to become partners in policing the world and pacifying its malcontents are as compelling as America's and China's differences. Their successful partnership is an all too novel example of the peaceful collaboration a "Rights Society," "Majority Rule Democracy" and "Rule of Law Society" and China as a "Permission Society," a "Consensus Democracy" and a Rule by Law Society" that have both embraced capitalism in different ways. This new conceptual framework is formulated and examined in *China & America's Emerging Partnership: A New Realistic Perspective.*

The New School's perspective is that China is the "balancer" of the instability of some leaders that Majority Rule Democracies can produce. Rather than a unipolar world of American leadership or a bipolar world of American and Chinese the focus of domestic and foreign policy debate must be collaboration of the two. That collaboration must occur because international systems based on the Principles of Conflict will inevitably lead to clashes of nations. Only if America and China synchronize their economic, geopolitical and security interests can they prevent wars that destabilize regions and, implicitly, the global economy. If the world's superpower and emerging superpower cannot engage in a committed partnership in the management of development under the Principles of Peaceful Coexistence, there will not be peace achieved. *China US Relations in the Obama Administration: Facing Shared Challenges* builds upon the logic and empirical foundations of the New School's perspectives presented in Book 1.

In order to help transcend the cultural, conceptual, and perceptive gaps between America and China, we analyze the striking similarities between the advice of George Washington and Deng Xiaoping and John F. Kennedy to their nations. President Washington's advice emphasized morality and religion, avoiding foreign debts and foreign conflicts, and giving to the world the example of a people always guided by justice and fairness. Deng Xiaoping's advice emphasized ideals and discipline as well seeking prosperity and peace, rather than world hegemony. His advice was that China should promote the example of a society pursuing the goal of a harmonious world. We examine the striking similarities between John F. Kennedy's and Deng Xiaoping's speeches, because they both recognized the requirement of achieving genuine, lasting peace by finding peaceful solutions to conflicts between nations.

The New School's perspectives are examined in chapter 1 of

Book 1 and include the idea that restoring America's leadership among other nations and finding solutions to America's security dangers is paramount to changing America's conventional goals. We strongly believe that such strategies are inconsistent with both America's *ideals* and *economic and national security*. In the terminology the New School uses is: America's conventional foreign policy goals and defense strategies do not adequately exemplify and therefore protect America's "moral, economic or military authority."

Although China's policymakers recognized as early as 1978 that the Principles of Conflict cannot protect China's security and ideals, American policymakers remain focused on America's 20th century foreign policy traditions strictly operating on the Principles of Conflicts. As we emphasize, as a result, America is not correctly, addressing the 21st century's fundamental issues or the related foreign policy and defense problems, in the increasingly unstable international system. It is essential but challenging for conventional American policymakers to:

1. Change America's foreign policy goals and related defense strategies unless they accept that America's success and security require a partnership aligning America and China's successes; and
2. Create the new defense systems world's survival is contingent on, which can only be developed and deployed by
3. Implementing the new agenda and new plan capable of securing peace and prosperity
4. Create the new international system operating on the Principles of Peaceful Coexistence that adequately respects the diversity of mankind and simultaneously fulfills the requirements of our survival.

The New School's perspective is also that America's success and security can only be protected if America lives up to its ideals. The

Principles of Peaceful Coexistence have moral authority while the Principles of Conflict have immoral authority. The Principles of Peaceful Coexistence correspond to President Washington's Farewell Advice to the American people while the Principles of Conflict do not.

President Washington's Farewell Address, in 1796, as well as President Lincoln's final public address in 1865, and President Kennedy's last speeches in 1963, are fundamentally alike in addressing the needs of America. President Washington facilitated the unification of the American people after a successful revolutionary war. President Lincoln sought to reunite people who had fought in a civil war. President Roosevelt understood that America's national security depended on its being capacity to become successful in a world war. President Kennedy understood the need to achieve lasting and genuine peace and to be with diversity among nations.

President Washington understood the necessity of America's being an example of exalted justice while cultivating harmony with all nations. President Lincoln understood the necessity of creating "a righteous and speedy peace" among Americans with diverse opinions after a civil war. President Franklin Roosevelt understood that America's security depended on America's having progressive economic and social policies. President Kennedy understood that America's security necessitated a "genuine peace and lasting peace" among mankind.

However, conservative and authoritarian factions emerged, led by a president who described himself as "neoconservative." President George W. Bush's administration implemented illiberal unprogressive policies and engaged in a military conflict that were profoundly damaging. The results have created a widespread recognition among the American people that they must "restore" the respect they had previously earned in the world.

Unfair policies and violent military strategies lacking moral authority will not allow America to obtain the economic and national security it requires and deserves. America can only obtain this security through collaboration with other nations and by being an example of a nation behaving in a just and fair way. The results of the policies of America's 43rd president made the need for different policies self-evident enough for Americans to select a 44th president with very different ideals.

In the New School's perspective, that is an encouraging indication of the good character of the American people, which is so profoundly important in mankind's fate. However, there are powerful factions among the American people that will oppose the search for peace in the Age of Species Lethal Weapons and Science. However, peace, if sought, can be achieved. There is more collaboration than conflict among the world's peoples. As the ratio of collaboration to conflict increases with the vision of the 44th president ultimately conflict will succumb to collaboration.

But, the Age of Species Lethal Weapons and Science is an alarming, relentless and unforgiving test of the American system of government that was specifically designed to cope with the Principles of Conflict. The American people's challenges in achieving economic and national security in the 18th century's strikingly different international context are very different from those Americans are confronting with in the 21st century.

President Kennedy was one of America's four greatest presidents who kept America from destruction in the Age of Species Lethal Weapons and Science He realized that a genuine peace could not be "a Pax Americana" secured by the use of weapons. He realized that the survival of mankind was the fundamental issue in the Age of Species Lethal Weapons and Science. He did not state this compelling reality in those words. But he made it clear in his public speeches after the Cuban Missile Crisis, including the one he intended to give on the day he was assassinated, that he realized and understood that human progress had made conventional American policies inevitably fatal.

Human creativity has changed the "face of war" as President

Kennedy said. The New School's perspective is that human creativity must therefore change "the face of peace." Those presented in the America-China Partnership Book Series urge human creativity to focus its power in the "new school of the Human Extinction Challenge" .

Our gene pool has powerful instincts to survive. But not all of us care if either they or we as a species survive. Some things are perceived to be worth dying for. For the profoundly malcontent, as suicide bombers demonstrate on a daily basis, death can sometimes be perceived as a solution. We are caught in the horror of an Age in which a single individual can make this ultimate decision And that is the core of the Human Extinction Challenge that Books 1 and 2 address.

This partnership is also required to solve the Human Extinction Challenges that results from pollution and global warming as examined in chapter 16 of *America & China's Emerging Partnership: A New Realistic Perspective and America & China's New Economic Partnership.*

The American and Chinese people have a responsibility to themselves and mankind to produce. The Chinese have recognized and responded to that responsibility by taking leadership and implementing the Principles of Peaceful Coexistence since 1978. If 300 million Americans cannot or will not change, who among the other nations will?

Gandhi was correct in pointing out that moral authority rather than military and economic authority is the most powerful force in the Age of Species Lethal Weapons and Science. The use of military authority with moral authority can awaken and inspire enlightenment in human beings because of its potency. If we are able to use the power of moral authority, we will solve the fundamental issue and amend the defects in human nature.

The Human Extinction Challenge is unavoidable but perhaps not a compelling new theory that will *eliminate or enlighten all of us.* After at least 4 billion years we have reached the test of coping with the consequences of human nature and the dangers of knowledge similar to those that Adam and Eve faced in the Bible. President Washington put it this way in his Farewell Address which is the core theme of Books 1 and 2:

"Observe good faith & justice towards all nations. Cultivate harmony with all. *Religion and morality enjoin this conduct; and can it be that good policy does not equally enjoin it?* It will be worthy of a free, enlightened, and, in no distant period a great nation, to give to mankind the magnanimous and too novel example of a people always guided by an exalted justice & benevolence. Who can doubt that in the course of time and things the fruits of such a plan would richly repay any temporary advantages which might be lost by a steady adherence to it? Can it be that Providence has not connected the permanent felicity of a nation with its virtue? The experiment, at least, is recommended by every sentiment which ennobles human nature. *Alas! Is it rendered impossible by its vices?*" (Emphasis added)

The Age of Species Lethal Weapons and Science is a test of man's values and viability. The New School's perspective is that it is "good policy" that makes America observe good faith towards all nations. Good policy requires it. This earth might ironically still a "Garden of Eden" compared to what we might make it. How extraordinary it is to be alive and have a role among the people who will be responsible for the success or failure of mankind. Do you choose to succeed or fail?

Deng Xiaoping understood the ramifications of "the new face of war". As a philosopher and statesman with a predisposition for peace he changed the face of war. He did so by implementing consensus for his country's decision to make the Principles of Peaceful Coexistence China's policy Xiaoping's and, implicitly, China's decision was brilliant and successful. Taking the less travelled road of the Principles Peaceful Coexistence saved China from collapse and created prosperity and peace. Consequently, China remains a example of a country that cultivates harmony among in the world.

If America and China do *not both* observe good faith to wards all nations both civilizations will perish as the Principles of Conflict take seed, in an environment of bad faith, injustice, and conflict.

There is something wonderful in the atrocity of the Human Extinction Challenge. It demands we choose a road less traveled as America's four greatest presidents urged and as China's leaders chose. We are confident that mankind will choose to implement the Principles of Peaceful Coexistence and support the breakthroughs needed to survive.

Human nature respects moral authority and the laws of physics. Mankind will find solutions to the Human Extinction Challenge within the power of moral authority. What we all need will become obvious *only when* we realize we must find it.

Introduction to the Realism of the Principles of Peaceful Coexistence

Americans hoped that China would quickly adopt their political and economic model, which they see as the best in the world. Eventually, with the implementation of the plan blueprinted in our books, this might be possible. Americans also assume that it is necessary to America's security interests for other nations to agree with it and follow it closely. For the reasons examined in *China & America's Emerging Partnership: A New Realistic Perspective*, these hopes are unrealistic when applied to China. It is not in either country's interests for China to copy America's political and economic models. However, conventional American foreign policy evangelizes and typically tries to impose America's ideals by using economic and military authority when only moral authority is realistic.

China's 1949 revolution rejected America's model. Its staggering economic success makes it unlikely that the Chinese will adopt America's political and economic models unless they become successful partners.

Why would China adopt foreign-born strategies when its own

approaches and tactics are working well for the Chinese? If America and China are not partners, why would the Chinese government adopt America's ideals and Constitutional Majority Rule Political System? Americans did not change their ways when the former Soviet Union, was hostile to them. Neither will the 1.5 billion Chinese. For the reasons examined in Books 1 and 2 American policies and strategies based on the Principles of Conflict, are self-defeating.

The success of China's political vision makes the copying of European Enlightenment or American strategies less of a priority than continuing to implement China's successful political model and priorities of achieving prosperity and peace. After two centuries of political instability, and many attempts to reject foreign rule it has been successful with its culture and political system. The Chinese have embraced "capitalism with Chinese characteristics," and China has been rapidly developing as a result of that. Robert Zoellick, the American Deputy Secretary of State sought to persuade China to adopt America's Ideals. He took the unpersuasive "responsible stakeholder" approach examined in Chapter 7 of Book 2. In 2008 he finally admitted that: "It is sometimes hard to change successful models. It is prototypically American to say 'This worked well but now you have to change it.'" This candid statement is a public admission of the wisdom of China's way. It is a growing enlightenment that is facilitated by "the American cultural revolution" caused by "the worst financial crisis in 100 years." What Zoellick admitted as "prototypically American" is what we refer to as the "Amerientric" perspective.

Many observers currently term China's government "undemocratic" and America's "democratic." Even in the context of that terminology a permanent genuine partnership between these countries is essential. Trade war, Cold War or armed conflicts between a "Rights Society" and "Permission Society," are not suitable foreign policy outcomes or a "lens" through which the 21st century's emerging realities should be viewed.

The relative abilities of Rights and Permission Societies to provide their citizens with prosperous government will determine the appeal of the alternate approaches to government. Because China has been developing rapidly with what is viewed as an "undemocratic" government, and because war is an unsuccessful way to change China, a genuine partnership is essential for the two states to remain at peace. Genuine partnership and the Principles of Peaceful Coexistence will work. Conflict, competition, containment, and the clash of civilizations will not.

But, are the American people and their leaders capable of allowing Americans to accept the necessity of being peaceful partners with the Chinese? This key question requires great attention that it has not yet received. It is a question of whether America is capable of peace in the 21st century.

America's and China's alternate models of government reflect the diversity of one or multi-party systems among other nations.

The emerging international system will have to contain a spectrum of diverse governments and economic systems. The New School's perspective is that this emerging international system, if it is to be successful, will have to be a sincere alliance among democratic and non-democratic states, and must be based on the Principles of Peaceful Coexistence.

China's and America's partnership will be an important example of collaboration between two powerful "democratic" and "undemocratic" states with different cultures but similar needs for prosperity and peace. the success of this partnership will inspire and stabilize most of other nations, This partnership will also help America and China to stabilize and rebuild failed states safely.

Most nations are majority-rule-democracies like America, but some are not, and likely cannot become stable majority-rule-democracies any time soon. America's imposition of democracy on Japan after World War II, and the overthrowing of governments in other nations is not a sound template for political reform in the 21st century which is why American attempts to transplant American-style democracy using military authority have failed. But, these stories are useful as examples of what will not work which can open the discussion to alternate approaches.

If Americans wish to see their ideals thrive among 192 nations, they must ensure that these Ideals are sustainable and allow for economic progress. If America is in economic decline it will lack the "moral and economic authority," and over time the "military authority" to present the merits of America's Rights Society Model or sustain that model in America.

The American Rights Society Model has merits that both the Chinese leadership and the Chinese people admire. It also has some features they think are unsuitable to their culture. Chinese remember, for example, that Americans were the only one of eight foreign powers in the 19th and 20th centuries that built schools and hospitals in China. They Chinese are moved by such examples of "the right spirit," which Americans see as part of their identity. The Chinese are still extremely close to their agrarian roots. Like farmers in America, they are serious and have great energy and courage. The "character" of the American and Chinese people make them excellent potential partners if both have "the right spirit" of kindness rather than the wrong lifestyle of selfishness and greed.

If America, as a Rights Society, is aligned in a successful economic and geopolitical partnership with China's Permission Society, the American Model will be fairly judged by nations using the Permission Society Model or who have a culturally blighted understanding of a Rights Society Model.

China's Exceptionalism: The Dream of a Harmonious Society and World

Chapter 1

Strategic Convergence of the Interests of America and China

Overview

Americans must replace the Principles of Conflict with the Principles of Peaceful Coexistence which have been successfully implemented Chinese economic and foreign policies 30 years. Americans must undergo the same change that China made in making prosperity and peace its priorities and abandoning those of evangelization and hegemony. That is an interesting challenge: are Americans capable of making prosperity and peace national priorities instead of hegemony?

Deng Xiaoping is America's Most Enlightened 21st Century Foreign Policy Strategist

A smart American foreign policy will align America's and China's goals. China hopes that America's new presidents will accept a genuine, global partnership. China has been preparing for this partnership for 30 years. Deng Xiaoping's genius and the aspirations of the Chinese people made prosperity and peace China's goals

Deng Xiaoping is both America's and China's greatest 21st century policy strategist because the Principles of Peaceful Coexistence that he implemented are the template for a successful partnership and for human survival in the Age of Species Lethal Weapons and Science.

This partnership is America's smart foreign policy because it aligns America's success with China's. But it is also the unexpected answer for conventional America foreign policymakers. The key issue in America's and China's relationship in the 21st century is whether American and the, character of the American people will be able to choose this foreign policy. The purposes of the books in the America & China Partnership's series, the Center for America-China Partnership, and New School of America-China Relations are to address this key issue and create the blueprints for the only relationship that is in both country's mutual interests. By explaining how the partnership will work, we attempt to stimulate its creation and successful operation.

America's policymakers, scholars and people using a win-win mindset rather than a zero sum game mindset is one of the many enormous challenges facing its people and leaders. America's conventional mindset cannot preserve America's security in the 21st century. This is an era of the "Collaboration of Rights and Permission Societies Era," which began with the founding of the United Nations after America created the Age of Species Lethal Weapons and Science in 1945.

Strategic Convergence of America and China' s interests

Zhang Yunling is the Director of APEC Policy Research at the Chinese Academy of Social Sciences and Professor at the Institute of Asia-Pacific Studies. Tang Shiping is an Associate Research Fellow and Deputy Director at the Center for Regional Security Studies at the Chinese Academy of Social Sciences. In 2005, they argued that:

Because economic development is considered the only way to tackle all the pressing challenges that China is facing and will face, China's grand strategy must serve the central purpose of development. Therefore, the central objective of China's grand strategy in the past two decades – a strategy that may well last to 2050 – can be captured in just one phrase: to secure and shape a security, economic, and political environment that is conducive to China concentrating on its economic, social and political development. [1]

America's new "grand strategy" should be exactly what Zhang Yunling and Tang Shiping conceptualize as China's grand strategy. American policymakers can merely insert the word "America" where the word "China" occurs in China's strategy. America's grand strategy should be:

To serve the central purpose of development. Therefore, the central objective of America's grand strategy in the past two decades – a strategy that may well last to 2050 – can be captured in just one phrase: to secure and shape a security, economic, and political environment that is conducive to America concentrating on its economic, social and political development.

Zhang Yunling and Tang Shiping, in discussing China's Regional Strategy, stated:

Because the United States remains at the center of China's strategic calculus, the first external factor that is going to influence the future of China's regional strategy is U.S. long-term strategic intentions toward China and how Washington views China's interaction with regional countries. What the United States is doing, plans to do, or even is rumored to do will influence China's behavior.

In dealing with the United States, however, China faces a conundrum that cannot be easily overcome. Because there will always be voices inside the United States arguing that China will become an inevitable foe, and some, looking through the zero-sum prism, will continue to view any perceived or real increase of Chinese influence in the region as at least potentially detrimental to U.S. interests, China faces a difficult balancing act in dealing with regional states but reassuring Washington. If China actively participates in regional affairs and norms, some in the United States will take it as a sign that China is aiming to challenge U.S. dominance. At the same time, international politics is becoming more regional, and this again puts China in a difficult situation.

There are three possible scenarios for how the U.S.-China relationship may evolve in a regional context. The first scenario is that even though many regional initiatives (for instance, the ARF and ASEAN Plus Three, or APT) were not originally China's idea, China has begun to actively participate in them for fear of being left out. As China increases its involvement in these bodies, the United States may deem that China and other Asian states are trying to exclude the United States from the region. Second, there are some regional programs that did evolve from China's initiatives, but these initiatives were actually designed to assure regional states of China's benign intentions (e.g., ASEAN-China FTA, and the recent ARF Security Policy Conference). Nonetheless, because these initiatives originated with China, they arouse U.S. suspicions. Finally, there are initiatives (e.g., SCO) that are designed to limit U.S. influence. The problem is that the United States will pay attention only to its exclusion, even though the SCO is a stabilizing force.

On the other hand, over the years China has come to recognize that regional states are more qualified to comment on the "China threat" because of their geographical proximity and relatively smaller size (thus they are more vulnerable and sensitive), yet it is exactly in these countries that the China threat theory is losing its audience. On the contrary, the global hegemony, the United States, tends to exaggerate other countries' capabilities and hostility, as it did in the case of the Soviet Union and Japan. Accordingly, China should pay less attention to rhetoric about the China threat coming out from the United States. This, in turn, causes many Chinese analysts to argue that China should pay more attention to working with regional states and putting the region in good order rather than appeasing the "Blue Team" in the United States. The rationale is that as long as regional states do not consider China a clear and present danger, and China and regional states can manage the region well, the United States will be hard pressed to forge a containment coalition. This means that regional states are becoming more important to China, and the weight of the United States in China's strategic calculus may face a reevaluation.

With the United States taking active measures to prevent or even contain China's rise, and China becoming less attentive to U.S. concerns when it believes it is acting together with regional states, both situations have potential to increase the mutual suspicion between the two countries, resulting in a classic security dilemma. This security dilemma will add yet another dimension of uncertainty to bilateral relations.[2]

Because economic development is considered the only way to tackle all the pressing challenges that China is facing and will face, China's grand strategy must serve the central purpose of development. Therefore, the central objective of China's grand strategy in the past two decades – a strategy that may well last to 2050 – can be captured in just one phrase: to secure and shape a security, economic, and political environment that is conducive to China concentrating on its economic, social and political development. [3]

Zhang Yunling and Tang Shipping comment:

Until the late 1990s, may observers would have agreed that China was still searching for a coherent national identity and was not sure of its proper role in the Asian region. Today, we can perhaps argue that China has largely completed its painful search for a national identity, thus becoming more confident of its relationships and its position in the region. Today, China no longer sees itself as a country facing imminent external danger or on the verge of internal implosion. Instead, it sees itself as a country with resources for managing its grand transformation and a growing ability to shape its environment. One would expect that as long as China's optimistic assessment of its external environment and its self-identity as a responsible great power continue to hold, China's current grand and regional strategies will also continue. If this is so, the world and the region can take a more relaxed posture toward the 'fourth rise of China' and behave accordingly, and this will in turn reinforce the domestic support for China's current grand and regional strategies. In the end, the future of the Asia-Pacific region depended not only upon China's choice of strategy, but also upon the strategy of other countries in the region, including the United States.[4]

Wang Jisi is Dean of the School of International Studies at Beijing University and Director of the Institution of International Studies at the Central Party School of the Communist Party of China. Unlike American experts, who speculate on China as examined in chapters 7 and 8 of Book 2, Wang Jisi is in a position to know actual Chinese on about America. What is noteworthy is that, unlike that of his American counterparts, his perspective or comments are focused on economic and moral authority rather than military authority, which is an obsession among American scholars of China's development and intentions.

China would like a cooperative partnership with America and has adopted policies facilitating cooperation with America. In 2005, in an article in *Foreign Affairs* titled "Searching for Stability with America" Wang Jisi stated:

After 9/11

The United States is currently the only country with the capacity and the ambition to exercise global primacy, and it will remain so for a long time to come. This means that the United States is the country that can exert the greatest strategic pressure on China. Although in recent years Beijing has refrained from identifying Washington as an adversary or criticizing its 'hegemonism' – a pejorative Chinese code world for U.S. dominance – many Chinese still view the United States as a major threat to their nation's security and domestic stability.

Yet the United States is a global leader in economics, education, culture, technology and science. China, therefore, must maintain a close relationship with the United States if its modernization efforts are to succeed. Indeed, a cooperative partnership with Washington is of primary importance to Beijing, where economic prosperity and social stability are now top concerns.

Fortunately, greater cooperation with China is also in the United States' interests – especially since the attacks of September 11, 2001. The United States now needs China's help on issues such as counter-terrorism, nonproliferation, the reconstruction of Iraq, and the maintenance of stability in the Middle East. More and more, Washington has also started to seek China's cooperation in fields such as trade and finance, despite increased friction over currency exchange rates, intellectual property rights, and the textile trade.

Although there is room for further improvement in the relationship, the framework of basic stability established since September 11 should be sustainable. At least for the next several years, Washington will not regard Beijing as its main security threat, and China will avoid antagonizing the United States.

The Lonely Superpower

To understand the forces that govern U.S. – Chinese relations, it helps first to understand U.S. power and Washington's current global strategy. Here is a Chinese view: in the long term, the decline of U.S. primacy and the subsequent transition to a multipolar world are inevitable; but in the short term, Washington's power is unlikely to decline, and its position in world affairs is unlikely to change....

The Chinese-U.S. relationship remains beset by more profound differences than any other bilateral relationship between major powers in the world today. It is an extremely complex and highly paradoxical unity of opposites. It is not a relationship of confrontation and rivalry for primacy, as the U.S. – Soviet relationship was during the Cold War, but it does contain some of the same characteristics. In its pattern of interactions, it is a relationship between equals. But the tremendous gap between the two countries in national power and international status and the fundamental differences between their political systems and ideology have prevented the United States from viewing China as a peer. China's political, economic, social, and diplomatic influences on the United States are far smaller than the United

State's influences on China. It is thus only natural that in their exchanges, the United States should take the offensive role and China the defensive one.

In terms of state-to-state affairs, China and the United States cannot hope to establish truly friendly relations. Yet the countries should be able to build friendly ties on nongovernmental and individual levels. Like all relations between states, the Chinese-U.S. relationship is fundamentally based on interests. But it also involves more intense love-hate feelings than do the majority of state-to-state ties. The positive and negative factors in the links between China and the United States are closely interwoven and often run into one another.

As this complex dynamic suggests, trying to view the US-China relationship in traditional zero-sum terms is a mistake and will not guide policy well; indeed, such a simplistic view may threaten both countries' national interests. Black-and-white analyses inevitably fail to capture the nuances and complexities of the situation. If, for instance, the United States really aimed to hamper China's economic modernization – as the University of Chicago's John Mearsheimer has argued should be done – China would not be the only one to suffer. Many U.S. enterprises in China would lose the returns on their investments, and the American people would no longer be able to buy inexpensive high-quality Chinese products. On the other hand, although American's motives for developing economic and trade ties with China may be to help themselves, these ties have also helped China, spurring its economic prosperity and technological advancement.

This prosperity and advancement will naturally strengthen China's military power – something that worries the United States. Indeed, this issue represents a paradox at the heart of Washington's long-term strategy toward Beijing. Unless China's economy collapses, its defense spending will continue to rise. Washington should recognize, however, that the important question is not how much China spends on its national defense but where it aims its military machine, which is still only a fraction of the size of the United States' own forces. The best way to reduce tensions is through candid and comprehensive strategic conversation; for this reason, military-to-military exchanges should be resumed.

China faces a similar paradox: only a U.S. economic decline would reduce Washington's strength (including its military muscle) and ease the strategic pressure on Beijing. Such a slide, however, would also harm China's economy. In addition, the increased U.S. sense of insecurity that might result could have other consequences that would not necessarily benefit China. If, for example, Washington's influence in the Middle East diminished, this could lead to instability there that might threaten China's oil supplies. Similarly, increased religious fundamentalism and terrorism in Central and South Asia could threaten China's own security, especially along its western borders, where ethnic relations have become tense and separatist tendencies remain a danger.

The potential China-U.S. conflict over energy supplies can be seen in a similar light. Each country should be sensitive to the other's energy needs and security interests worldwide. China is currently purchasing oil from countries such as Venezuela and Sudan, whose relations with the United States are far from amicable. In the meantime, Washington is not thought to be eying Central Asian oil fields near China's border. Both Beijing and Washington should try to make sure that the other side understands its intentions and should explore ways to cooperate on energy issues through joint projects, such as building nuclear power plants in China.

History has already proved that the United States is not China's permanent enemy. Nor does China want the United States to see it as a foe. Deng Xiaoping's prediction that 'things will be all right when Sino-U.S. relations eventually improve' was a fair assessment based on China's long-term interests. To be sure, aspirations cannot replace reality. The improvement of Chinese-U.S. relations will be slow, conditional and limited and could even be reversed in the case of certain provocations (such as a Taiwanese declaration of independence). It is precisely for this reason that the thorny issues in the bilateral relationship must be handled delicately, and a stable new framework established to prevent troubles from disrupting an international environment favorable for building prosperous societies. China's leadership is set on achieving such prosperity by the middle of the twenty-first century; with Washington's cooperation, there is little to stand in its way.[5]

As time goes on with China's focus on prosperity, peace and harmony, and the Chinese state becomes simultaneously less concerned about American obsessions with hegemony bringing America into conflict with China In 2007, Wang Jisi stated in an article in *Global Asia* titled "America in Asia: How much does China Care?" :

> China does care about what the US is doing diplomatically and militarily in Asia, but China's regional concerns, seen in a broader context, are manageable. Other urgent issues, especially nontraditional security concerns that have their roots in domestic problems, are more pressing.
>
> To be sure, growing Chinese material power is lending more confidence and leverage to its diplomacy, which is increasingly mature and proactive. While it is reasonable to assume that China's international stature is being enhanced at the expense of the US it is not necessarily China's intention, or in its interest, to compete directly for "spheres of influence." Mutual trust at strategic levels is still lacking between the two countries. Consequently, it is worthwhile for other Asian powers to assume that they must keep a balance, and indeed play a role between these two giants. However, it may not be advisable to base their foreign policies on the presumption that China and the US are moving in the direction of becoming long-term strategic rivals similar to the US-Soviet relationship in the Cold War years. All other Asian countries, along with China and the US, should see themselves as "stakeholders" in hedging against possible turbulence and disequilibrium.[6]

Wang Jisi discussed the increasing focus of Chinese policymakers on economic matters in geopolitical rivalry. He makes this point by noting a contrast between two bestselling books in China in 2007 which became popular among Chinese intellectuals, and a bestseller in China ten years ago. Wang Jisi states:

> One is a translation of *Confessions of an Economic Hit Man* by John Perkins. In the book Perkins describes his work as a highly paid professional helping US intelligence agencies and

multinationals cajole and blackmail foreign leaders into serving American interests, and how the US, according to him, cheated poor countries around the globe out of trillions of dollars by lending them more money than they could possibly repay in order to take over their economies.

The other book, *Huobi Zhanzheng* (Currency Wars) is by Song Hongbing, a Chinese who was educated in America in the 1990's and formerly worked for American financial institutions. In his book, Song tells numerous stories of how international capital dominates the United States and other countries, manipulating politics, creating financial crises, and controlling global wealth. According to Song, the financial history of the world is simply a tale of conspiracies seeking domination and the uneven distribution of wealth in favor of the rich. He concludes that China should be prepared to fight "bloodless wars" waged by evil forces like the US Federal Reserve aimed at destroying China's economy.

Compare these two books with a bestseller in China 10 years ago – *The China That Can Say No: The Political and Sentimental Choice in the Post-Cold War Era*. Written by several young Chinese intellectuals at a time when tensions were flaring up across the Taiwan Strait, the book demonstrates how these scholars became disillusioned and angered by America's international behavior, especially its sympathy toward Taiwan, American attacks on China's human rights record after Tiananmen and the US-Japan alliance supposedly aimed against China....the generation of *The China That Can Say No* expressed vehement nationalistic feelings based almost solely on their reading of China's official media.[7]

Wang Jisi stated:

China's political elites today have gained a much deeper and more sophisticated understanding of the United States, owing to enormously increased international exposure and experience. More interestingly, with a much larger and more open economy and a fast-changing society, China's focus on the US is moving away from traditional security concerns like US-Taiwan relations and the US military presence in the western Pacific to issues that are more relevant to China's domestic agenda, including financial security, energy procurement, environmental protection, climate change, the trade balance, intellectual property rights, product quality and safety, and so on. These concerns are more global than regional in nature.

Perceptions of US Power

A deeper understanding of the United States and the new focus on nontraditional security issues, however, does not necessarily bring about increased trust. On almost every issue, the Chinese harbor suspicions that the US has malignant plans to restrain the growth of China's power and to take advantage of its vulnerabilities. In terms of climate change, for instance, a conventional view is that Western countries, having polluted the air in their long process of industrialization are attempting to slow China's economic growth by pressing it to reduce carbon emissions. In the same light, the United States is viewed as trying to trap China into appreciating the value of the Renminbi on the one hand, while depreciating the US dollar on the other, so as to maintain its dominance in the international monetary system. In energy security, it is believed that the US deliberately keeps oil prices high and tries to deprive China of cheaper oil from countries like Sudan by demonizing China's policy toward Africa. Hence the popularity of Confessions *of an Economic Hit Man and Currency Wars*.

As China reaches out for trade, investment, and natural resources, its influence and interests have extended to Europe, Africa and South America. In China's geopolitical and geoeconomic perceptions, Asia is redefined to include, importantly, Central Asia and the Russian Far East, in addition to East Asia and South Asia.[8]

To the degree that these perceptions are correct, American policies are neither stealthy nor effective, and must be corrected. Containment, however subtle, eventually becomes transparent, ineffective and unrealistic. It endangers American economic and national security interests.

Wang Jisi stated:

Against the backdrop of its own expanding global interests, China views the power and role of the US first in global terms. Despite widely shared impressions and hopes in China that Washington's global influence has been severely damaged by the quagmire in Iraq and the tainted US image in many parts of the world, strategic planning in Beijing is not based on an assessment of a weakened US at present or any time soon. Rather, the emphasis is on the continued growth of US capabilities, especially its "hard power," to influence world affairs. Despite concerns about its shaky mortgage market, the robust US economy is widening its gap with the economies of Japan and the European Union, and its technological edge over other powers is still considerable. US military expenditures have expanded, and the US remains the only country that can actually project power into any corner of the world. American cultural products continue to dwarf all their competitors in the world market.[9]

Wang Jisi stated that the "lie low" approach of Deng Xiaoping is very prevalent among leading Chinese strategic thinkers:

There are plenty of reasons, therefore, for Chinese strategists to conclude that US power is expanding not only globally but regionally in an effort to circumscribe China's international space. Frankly, not many insightful Chinese thinkers are thrilled by international commentaries noting that the size of the Chinese economy is catching up with the US, that in the next one or two decades China will become a "superpower" vying with America for dominance in Asia and that the so-called "Beijing Consensus," or the Chinese model of development, is appealing to other developing countries who would like to cast aside the free market economic model often referred to as the Washington Consensus.

Notably, leading Chinese strategists are keeping a distance from popular suspicions about the US conspiracy to contain China, stressing instead the need to "lie low" in international affairs, conduct a moderate foreign policy, and refrain from directly challenging US policy goals. Beijing has issued a number of official statements emphasizing China's commitment to the "road to peaceful development" and to the goal of building up a "harmonious world" with other countries. The previously endorsed idea of China's "peaceful rise" has been replaced by "peaceful development" in the official media, partly due to fear that the word "rise" would be misinterpreted as boasting of China's newly gained power.[10]

Wang Jisi emphasized that China is wary of American political penetration into China. The Chinese perceive that their problems are all caused by America. He stated:

> No one should pretend that the Chinese are no longer worried about US power, either "hard" or "soft," that might overshadow China's road ahead. Since the "color revolutions" and America's pronounced goal of "transformational diplomacy," Beijing has tightened its grip on the activities of non-governmental organizations inside China to prevent Western political penetration. Beijing is kept alert and defensive by America's giving asylum to virtually all "anti-China" elements, from the Dalai Lama's supporters to Uigur separatists, from human rights activists to the Falungong. The Chinese worry that further opening their financial sector, as many Americans are pressing them to do, might threaten their domestic order. Indeed, in the eyes of the Chinese, it is hard to find a single political or diplomatic problem faced by China that could not ultimately be traced to an American root. [11]

Wang Jisi emphasized that the Chinese government recognizes that China has "many shared important interests" with America:

> Given all these negative circumstances, why is China reacting so calmly? Why not appear "tough" to satisfy nationalistic pride at home? My answer to this question is three-fold. First, China's reaction is based on the aforementioned sober analysis of American power in the region and around the world, especially the power balance between the US and China. It would be foolhardy for China to try to lead an anti-American coalition, even informally, or to challenge US dominance on its own.
> Second, while many conflicting interests and ideas exist

between the US and China, the two countries also share important interests and ideas, a fact clearly recognized by the Chinese. Neither wants to see any other Asia-Pacific country develop nuclear weapons, which is why the two governments are working closely with each other in the six-party talks to de-nuclearize North Korea. Shared fears about a military showdown across the Taiwan Strait are sobering, and both Washington and Beijing have quietly coordinated efforts to shatter Taiwan's independence dreams. The two governments are cooperating inconspicuously to counter international terrorism. Despite widely reported trade frictions, substantive talks are being conducted between Chinese and American government agencies and think tanks to identify common interests and seek solutions on such issues as energy security, the international monetary system, climate change and public health.

These common interests are so significant that some influential Chinese policy analysts have pointed out that it would not be in China's best interest to see America lose ground in the Middle East or elsewhere or shake off its international responsibilities in maintaining global order. Indeed, in recent years Beijing has ceased to refer to US foreign policy goals as seeking "global hegemonism." Chinese criticism of US behavior, except its response to actions seen to be directly against China, has been reduced. To the Chinese leadership, being rhetorically assertive in foreign affairs without being able to deliver tangible results might be politically useful in the short term, but it would not add to its authority and credibility in the long run. In this regard, the absence of electoral, cyclical politics helps keep China's foreign policy more consistent and strategically-oriented than those of many other governments.

Third, compared to the mounting pressures on China at home, the current international environment seems benign. No international crises involving China's core national interests are on the horizon, provided Beijing and Washington can find a way to keep de jure Taiwan independence at bay and to rein in Pyongyang's nuclear weapons program. Neither is an easy task, but both are achievable.[12]

The core point in these views is that Deng Xiaoping's advice is being adhered to 30 years after its implementation. China still pays relatively little attention to foreign policy intrigues and with its disciplined economic focus is getting rich quickly and peacefully.

Power advantages are economic, not military, in the Age of Species Lethal Weapons and Science. That is particularly so in China's case as China is relatively uninterested in the foreign policy problems and that preoccupy Americans. That needs to be understood by American policymakers and scholars.

The Realism of the Foreign Policy Advice of America and China's Noblest Generals and Statesmen

George Washington gave Americans, of all generations, valuable advice on what America's success required. His set of recommendations was informed by his success in leading the creation of America, and the independence war, and by his subsequent role as the first President of the United States. Neither America nor its Constitution will be successful in the 21st century if Americans do not to follow his advice. We reiterate Washington's recommendations at various points in Books 1 and 2 because it summarizes the fundamental genius of American moral authority, and because of its relevance to the American Experiment and the Human Experiment:

> Observe good faith & justice towards all nations. Cultivate harmony with all. Religion and morality enjoin this conduct; and can it be that good policy does not equally enjoin it? It will be worthy of a free, enlightened, and, in no distant period a great nation, to give to mankind the magnanimous and too novel example of a people always guided by an exalted justice & benevolence.[13]

This is not the advice of a weak man, or an inexperienced one consumed by the difficulties of leading people in war and peace. It is an advice that comes from a man who was successful in dealing with the selfish realities of human nature. Washington mastered the operation of a "good society" in achieving that so much needed "social progress." This is not the vision of a naive, unrealistic dreamer. This is the advice of a general and statesman who was able to lead Americans in its defense in a war and did so successfully. This is not the advice of a tyrant, a despot, or a fool. It is advice that expresses what the Chinese call the "right spirit" that enabled America to exist and prosper. If this advice is not followed by Americans in the 21st century they will not be successful in preserving America.

Fortunately for both China and America, modern China has also produced a general and statesman who gave the same advice. What Washington referred to as "morality and religion," Deng Xiaoping called "idealism and discipline." Both leaders understood the necessity of being a good example of treating other nations with "good faith and justice". Both emphasized "cultivating harmony with all." As Washington put it "that it will be worthy of a free, enlightened, and, in no distant period a great nation, to give to mankind the magnanimous and too novel example of a people always guided by an exalted justice and benevolence."

Deng Xiaoping similarly stated:

> We must...encourage all our people to have lofty ideals and moral integrity, to become better educated and to cultivate a strong sense of discipline.[14] We adhere to an independent foreign policy of peace and do not join any bloc. We are prepared to maintain contacts and make friends with everyone. We are against any country that commits aggression against others. We are fair in our words and in our deeds. This adds to China's potential influence. This policy has produced good results, and we shall follow it forever.[15]

America has not been following Washington's advice, while China is in fact following Deng Xiaoping's vision. Eight years of authoritarian rule was sufficient to cause the change in American politics that resulted in the election of President Barack Obama.

But America's new president must implement a very different set of policies, as well as a partnership between America and China that has broad support among the American people.

China was able to find exceptional leaders in two regime changes after Deng Xiaoping. China, has been preparing for America to find its way to prosperity and peace as priorities over ideology and hegemony.

China's successful Socialist Market Economy Model and its "Scientific Management" of its policies in a stable one-party-government state makes China a vital partner for the "American two-party-state Model of Capitalism."

Chapter 2

The Challenge of Living Up to the Exalted Justice and Benevolence of a Harmonious Society

Overview

China is meeting the challenge of prioritizing peace over hegemony. Its engagements reflect the character of the Mainland Chinese people and foster China's priorities in other nations. In the 21st century, prosperity and peace must become the priorities of America. China's leadership seeking and setting an example of a harmonious society by basing its policies on the Principles of Peaceful Coexistence is what we refer to as "China's Exceptionalism."

What does China mean by a "Harmonious World" and "One World, One Dream?"

The Chinese government has chosen "a Harmonious World" and "One World One Dream" to lead its vision for a sustainable state project. Hopefully, these different manifestations of the Harmonious

World concept do not envisage a set of universal values other than peace and prosperity. The Chinese have a saying about the troubles of marriages when there is "one bed, but two dreams." Hopefully the "One World, One Dream" concept is not a mirror image of the type of demand for the universality of American ideals as being inherently superior to other civilizations. Hopefully China's "One Dream" for the world is the universality of prosperity and peace.

It may be that the meaning Chinese leaders ascribe to "One World" amplifies the use of the words by Gandhi, who said to over 20,000 visitors, delegates and observers: at the closing session of the Inter-Asian Relations Conference on April 2, 1947 in New Delhi:

> ...I want you to understand if you can, that the message of the East, the message of Asia, is not to be learnt through European spectacles, through the Western spectacles, not by imitating the tinsel of the West, the gun-powder of the West, the atom bomb of the West. If you want to give a message again to the West, it must be a message of 'Love', it must be a message of 'Truth'. There must be a conquest (clapping), please, please, please. That will interfere with my speech, and that will interfere with your understanding also. I want to capture your hearts and don't want to receive your claps. Let your hearts clap in unison with what I'm saying, and I think, I shall have finished my work. Therefore, I want you to go away with the thought that Asia has to conquer the West. Then, the question that a friend asked yesterday, "Did I believe in one world?" Of course, I believe in one world. And how can I possibly do otherwise, when I become an inheritor of the message of love that these great un-conquerable teachers left for us? You can redeliver that message now, in this age of democracy, in the age of awakening of the poorest of the poor, you can redeliver this message with the greatest emphasis. Then you will, you will complete the conquest of the whole of the West, not through vengeance because you have been exploited, and in the exploitation, of course, I want to include Africa, and I hope that when next you meet in India, you will all be, exploited nations of the Earth will meet if by that time there aren't any exploited nations of the Earth. I am so sanguine that

if all of you put your hearts together, not merely your heads, but hearts together and understand the secret of the messages of all these wise men of the East have left to us, and if we really become, deserve, are worthy of that great message, then you will easily understand that the conquest of the West will be completed and that conquest will be loved by the West itself. West is today pining for wisdom. West today is in despair of multiplication of atom bombs, because a multiplication of atom bombs means utter destruction, not merely of the West, but it will be a destruction of the world, as if the prophecy of the Bible is going to be fulfilled and there is to be a perfect deluge. Heaven forbid that there be that deluge, and through men's wrongs against himself. It is up to you to deliver the whole world, not merely Asia but deliver the whole world from that wickedness, from that sin. That is the precious heritage your teachers, my teachers, have left to us.[16]

Such wisdom from India can assist America in surviving in the Age of Species Lethal Weapons and Science. That enlightenment from the East, if the American people can accept the wisdom of peaceful coexistence, will enrich and flow together with the visions from the West.

China's 5,000-Year Search for Peace

China's Premier Wen Jiabao has said:

China tomorrow will continue to be a major country that loves peace and has a great deal to look forward to. Peace-loving has been a time-honored quality of the Chinese nation. The First Emperor of Qin Dynasty commanded the building of the Great Wall two thousand years ago for defensive purposes. The Tang Dynasty opened up the Silk Road one thousand years ago in order to sell silk, tea and porcelain to other parts of the world. Five hundred years ago Zheng He, the famous diplomat-navigator of the Ming Dynasty, led seven maritime expeditions to seek friendly ties with other countries, taking along China's exquisite products, advanced farming and handicraft skills. The great Russian writer Leo Tolstoy was right when he called the Chinese nation "the oldest and largest nation" and "the most peace-loving nation in the world."

As the modern times began, the ignorance, corruption and self-imposed seclusion of the feudal dynasties led China to prolonged social stagnation, declining national strength and repeated invasions by the foreign powers. Despite compounded disasters and humiliation, the Chinese nation never gave up and managed to emerge from each setback stronger than before. A nation learns a lot more in times of disaster and setback than in normal times.[17]

This example of China's desire for peaceful coexistence is real and sincere and it must be respected by Americans as being such.

China's aspirations for a harmonious society have the moral authority that comes with seeking peaceful coexistence rather than conflict, and of being historically demonstrated. We will later examine the history of China making the Principles of Peaceful Coexistence the basis of its policies for 30 years.

There is further evidence that American policymakers must recognize, so that they can have the peace and prosperity that China is seeking to share. China has and 5000 year-old peaceful traditions expressed in Taoism, Confucianism, and Buddhism.

Lau Tzu's *Tao Te Ching*, from 300 BC, is the first great classic in the Chinese school of philosophy called Taoism. It posits a view of the cosmos and how human beings should respond to it. Compare the following advice from *Tao Te Ching's* chapters 30 and 31 with the "realist" views of Lau Tzu's contemporary Thucydides and other "realists" such as Machiavelli and American Cold War oriented scholars today:

> He who by Tao proposes to help a ruler of men
> Will oppose all conquest by force of arms;
> For such things are wont to rebound.
> Where armies are, thorns and brambles grow.
> The raising of a great host

Is followed by a year of dearth.
Therefore a good general affects his purpose and then stops;
He does not take further advantage of his victory.
Fulfils his purpose and does not glory in what he has done;
Fulfils his purpose and does not boast of what he has done;
Fulfils his purpose, but takes no pride in that he has done;
Fulfils his purpose, but only as a step that could not be avoided.
Fulfils his purpose, but without violence;
For what has a time of vigor also has a time of decay.
This is against Tao,
And what is against Tao will soon perish.
Fine weapons are none the less ill-omened things. That is
Why, among people of good birth, in peace the left-hand
Side is the place of honor, but in war this is reversed and
The right-hand side is the place of honor. The quietist,
even when he conquers, does not regard weapons as lovely
things. For to think them lovely meant to delight in them,
and to delight in them means to delight in the slaughter of
men. And he who delights in the slaughter of men will
Never get what he looks for out of those that dwell under
heaven. A host that has slain men is received with grief and
mourning; he that has conquered in batter is received with
rites of mourning.

The Chinese government is now renewing Confucian traditions that which further the goals of a harmonious society. The *China Daily* stated on September 28, 2005:

> Confucianism advocates benevolence: "One who, destining to develop himself, develops others and in destining to sustain himself, sustains others", "Don't do to others what you don't want others to do to you", and one should get along well with all peace-loving people. Refraining from seeking hegemony is a fine tradition of Confucianism.
>
> The world today is not in peace, this is mainly because of hegemony and terrorism. World peace requires treatment and cure of such modern world maladies. "Harmony without uniformity" proposed by Confucius can be taken as a good medicine for treating the illness. Confucius said, "A gentleman

gets along with others, but does not necessarily agree with them; a base man agrees with others, but does not coexist with them harmoniously".

What is the difference between harmony and uniformity? Harmony is the rational composition of different things and the unity of varied things; uniformity is the simple duplication and coincidence of things of different natures and is monotonous identity; the "harmony without uniformity" idea consists of three principles.

First is that one should have his own independent thinking, and should not drift with the tide, still less associate himself with evil elements. Second is that one should allow others to have their initiative, should not force others to obey him, and should not practice despotism, known as "let those who complied with me survive and those who resisted me perish". Third is that one must be good at engaging in friendly cooperation with others, be good at coordinating relations, particularly that he should protect and help the weak, so that the widower, the widow, the orphan and the childless as well as the disabled who have lost work ability and have no one to rely on can enjoy happiness in the world. This principle is required for the formation of a concordant family, the building of a harmonious society and the establishment of a peaceful world. Among a crowd of people, one should neither act as a lackey, nor as an overlord, nor as an individual isolated from others, but rather one should live in an organized, harmonious entity. This entity enables everybody to enjoy a happy life of working and living in peace and contentment. This principle is applicable to the relations between nations, between religions and between countries.

Fifty years ago, the Chinese government, together with India and Burma (Myanmar), initiated the Five Principles of Peaceful Coexistence for handling international relations, and thus made major contribution to world peace. The "one country, two systems" principle advanced by Deng Xiaoping has successfully solved the problem of the return of Hong Kong and Macao to the embrace of the motherland and it embodies China's traditional spirit of "harmony without uniformity", thus providing the world with a typical example for solving similar problems. This also represents a contribution to world peace. "Harmony without uniformity" between humankind and all creatures on Earth has provided today's world with a kind of rational idea for environmental protection, a correct outlook on sustainable development.

Buddhism originated in India, and was adopted in China because it suited the character of the Chinese people. Siddhartha, the founder of Buddhism, taught that, "Peace comes from within" and that anger and other negative states of mind are the cause of wars. Buddhists believe we can live in peace and harmony only if we abandon the anger in our minds and practice altruism:

As early as the days of the great Indian King Asoka (269-232 BCE), Buddhist traditions began to migrate out of India and to spread into the regions of South and Southeast Asia. Hinayana, or less derogatorily, Theravadin Buddhism spread south to Sri Lanka, and north and east to Burma, Thailand, Laos and Cambodia. By the fourth to the eighth centuries CE, Mahayana Buddhism had reached as far as Tibet, China, Korea and Japan. According to recent world census data, there are about 305 million Buddhists worldwide, most of them living in Asia. However, one finds nearly 1 million (some recent sources make this number 4-5 million) Western-born Buddhists. Like all of the major world religions, at its core, Buddhism is a religion of peace. An early Buddhist collection of verses on practice in everyday life, the Pali (Theravadin) Dhammapada, makes this abundantly clear. Verse five of the text (of 423 verses) states:

Hatred is never appeased by hatred.
Hatred is only appeased by Love (or, non-enmity).
This is an eternal law.

Buddhist teachings tell us that hatred and aversion, like their opposites desire and greed, all spring from a fundamental ignorance. That ignorance is our mistaken notion of our own permanent, independent existence. In ignorance, we see ourselves as separate beings, unconnected with others. Blinded to our true state of interdependence and interconnectedness, it is this basic ignorance that keeps us divided.

The Chinese government is now sponsoring traditional Buddhist values and renewing Buddhism:

> The First World Buddhist Forum opened in China's Zhejiang Province. Sponsored by the Chinese government and China's Buddhist Association and Religious Culture Communication Association, the forum is the first major international Buddhist conference since the founding of the People's Republic of China in 1949. Buddhist disciples from the Chinese mainland, Hong Kong and Taiwan proposed in October 2004 to hold a World Buddhist Forum in China. Liu Yandong, vice-chairwoman of the National Committee of the Chinese People's Political Consultative Conference (CPPCC), said at the opening ceremony that governments and peoples should exert concerted efforts to make religions play an active role in building a harmonious world. "Buddhism has made important contribution to world peace and human civilization in the history. The forum will play a positive role in exploring how Buddhism can contribute to building a harmonious world," Liu said. Buddhist Master Shenghui, also vice-president of the Buddhist Association of China, said at the opening ceremony that the forum serves as an equal, diversified and open platform for talks among the people who love the world and the general public, respect and support Buddhism, and cherish a caring heart. More than 1,000 Buddhist monks, experts and politicians from 34 countries and regions have come to attend the event. The monks will pray for world peace. With the theme of "A harmonious world begins in the mind," the participants will focus on three topics: Buddhism's unity and cooperation, social responsibility and peaceful mission to make different nations and religions work for a peaceful, prosperous and harmonious world.[18]

The peace that China has been pursuing comes from Chinese perspectives.

The Scramble for China in the 19th, 20th and 21st Centuries

China has a 5,000-year history of wanting to be a world unto itself, rather than obtaining authority over other civilizations. But, China was invaded many times. Two thousand years ago, the Chinese built a wall to keep foreigners out.[19] Geoff Mulgan notes in *Good and Bad Power: The Ideals and Betrayals of Government:*

> Awareness of the potential risks involved in giving protectors unbounded power may explain why in the Chinese tradition there was such a profound disdain for warriors, who were left out of the traditional lists of the main classes, which included scholars, farmers, artisans and merchant. Wu or violence was inferior to, and anathema to, the wei of civilization, and had to be constantly kept in check (which helps explain why so many non-Chinese rulers founded dynasties, ruling as warriors over Chinese scholar bureaucracies.)[20]

In recent centuries there were not enough foreigners to conquer China. But they tried in the 19th and 20th centuries and are trying again in the 21st century. Ultimately what protected China from aggression were its population, size, and resilience.

But, China succumbed to hubris and failure in the 17th and 18th centuries; it endured humiliation and hunger from 1840, which has been lessening in recent decades. China has the wisdom of a great power that has failed to govern itself well in the past, then under exceptional leadership achieved stable government and economic growth.

In contrast, America and Europe have histories of expanding their authority to foreign civilizations. In the 21st century, Europeans and Americans are in "future shock." Globalization of national economies has had unexpected consequences that are suddenly becoming evident.

China wanted to be Chinese and a world to itself.[8] It did not want to conquer the world or explore other cultures after the death of Mao Zedong and the disastrous failure of his economic policies. Unfortunately for China, its desire to be left alone juxtaposed with

America's desire to conquer the world in the 17th to 20th centuries. But China managed to defend itself from domination since 1949.

Ironically, China did so by importing and converting the European ideology of Marxism and Communism. With the Chinese will for self-determination, the leadership of Mao Zedong, and the adaptation of foreign ideology, China isolated itself from 1949 to 1972. During this period, China experimented with Marxist and Communist economic theories that decried capitalism had failed as an ideology.

Recognizing that failure, the Chinese government "opened China up to the world." During the period from 1978 to 2008, "Socialist Market Economics," is often referred to as "capitalism with Chinese characteristics," changed China for the better. That change is freeing hundreds of millions of Chinese from hunger and poverty.

The challenges of trade imbalances with China, and use of military authority in response, is not unique to the 21st century. Sung Chul Yang, a former South Korean Ambassador to the United Nations, has suggested that the following quote from Travis Hanes and Frank Sanello's *The Opium Wars* is relevant to America's current policy challenges:

> During the Qianlong reign...in 1736, China had become the richest and most populous country in the world. During his reign, the empire doubled in size and area as its armies conquered huge swaths of Central Asia, Outer Mongolia, and parts of Russia....
>
> Between 1710 and 1759, the imbalance in trade was staggering, draining Britain of silver, the only form of payment China accepted for its coveted tea. During this period, Britain paid out 26 million pounds in silver to China, but sold it only 9 million in goods...
>
> In 1773, opium earned the [British East India] Company 39,000 pounds. Twenty years later, the annual revenue from opium sold in China alone had ballooned to 250,000 pounds. The popular drug was incrementally beginning to reverse the

imbalance of trade between Britain and China. Between 1806 and 1809, China paid out eleven million Spanish dollars for opium.[21]

Sung Chul Yang suggests that nearly 140 years after the Opium Wars, the modern American equivalents of British opium are blue jeans, Big Macs and Coca Cola. He asserts that whatever the new opium is, it should not result in a new arms race or Cold War.[22]

Lord Macartney went to China as an emissary from England in 1793 and attempted unsuccessfully to use diplomacy to establish relations between the two countries. But China was not interested. A win-win facade revealed the zero sum game ruthlessness of the foreign supplicants.[9] Laurence Brahm has noted that:

> In 1860, foreign allied forces united with a single purpose: to cripple China politically and force it open to the West on Western terms economically.... Unable to attack the political nerve center of China, the allied forces attacked the cultural. Discovering the vast wealth outside Beijing's city walls, enshrined in the Yuan Ming Yuan and the Summer Palace, they broke into the palaces stealing every item of conceivable value and destroying what they could not take with them.... The statement was clear: precious items of immediate commercial value to China were to be had by foreign interests; precious items of cultural importance and value were to be destroyed completely....The key elements of Western policy towards China at this critical period in history were: to obtain unlimited access to China's market, that is, to sell Western manufactured and finished goods to the vast Chinese population without restrictions or import duties; to have unlimited access to China's vast natural and crafted products at cheap labor costs; and to control trade. Foreign powers knew that a weak political system would have to tolerate their interests and commercial domination.
>
> In addition, Chinese law could not touch the rights of foreigners in China; foreign laws and administration were carried out within foreign enclaves and complete diplomatic immunity was accorded to all foreign interests. These elements of this diplomatic episode have remained part of the collective uncon-

scious underlying both Western diplomatic and commercial initiatives today in opening the China market and the Chinese government's approach to dealing with them.[23]

In the 20th century, America created and used nuclear weapons to make Japan surrender. In 1964, China, under Mao Zedong, developed nuclear weapons and was able to resist invasion. Applying pressure, the Soviet Union came very close to using nuclear weapons in an attack on China. That potential global disaster helped prompt President Nixon to initiate America's relationship with the People's Republic of China. China's conduct toward America *under Mao's successor*, Deng Xiaoping, and later with other Chinese leaders is defensive, not aggressive. Even Mao Zedong dreamed of a strategic alliance with America after the 1949 Revolution, but that was rejected by the American government.

Following Western protests and sanctions after the Tiananmen Square Demonstrations, Deng Xiaoping said:

> I am a Chinese, and I am familiar with the history of foreign aggression against China. When I heard that the seven Western countries, at their summit meeting, had decided to impose sanctions on China, my immediate association was to 1900, when the allied forces of the eight powers invaded China. Six of these same seven countries, excluding Canada, together with czarist Russia and Austria, constituted the eight powers that formed the allied forces in those days. Our people should study Chinese history; it will inspire us to develop the country.
>
> Some people abroad hate talking about the 'Asia-Pacific century.' Asia has a population of 3 billion people, and 1.1 billion of them live on the mainland of China. The so-called Asia-Pacific century will make no sense unless China develops. Of course, it will make no sense unless India develops too.....
>
> It will not be long before the People's Republic of China, which is already a political power, becomes an economic power as well.... We Chinese should bestir ourselves. The mainland has developed a solid economic foundation.[24]

What we will refer to as the second "Scramble for China" brought overseas financial and intellectual capital into China. Companies from Japan, America and Europe helped China to become "The Factory Floor of the World." However they did not do so out of altruism but out of greed. Such foreign investments in combination with the talents of the Chinese, resulted in these countries becoming unable to compete economically with China. That is extremely disturbing to Americans' identity, which is based on the perception that they are the best nation in the world.

China is the 100th poorest nation in the world and has the competitive advantages of necessity of economic development, talented and very hard working people, and government able to provide 1.5 billion people with unity, stability and economic development. The combined population of America, Europe and Japan is approximately 500 million less than China's. In order to measure and understand the achievements of the Chinese government imagine a government responsible for and successfully providing unity, stability and an average of GDP growth of 10% per year for the past 30 years to a single nation comprised of America, Europe and Japan. Although such a thing can be imagined, the only government that has achieved such an unlikely feat is China's.

The Management of China's Dream of a Harmonious World

One of the challenges to China's dream of a harmonious world can be traced to the challenges it is facing:

1. But, what are those "defects?"
2. Who defines what those defects are?
3. Who determines for the Chinese what the "nature of man" is, what a "good society" is, and what "social progress" is?

American policy toward China is based on America's criteria of what the nature of man, a good society and social progress are and America's Ideals. But, what gives Americans the right or the power to impose their criteria and ideals or seek to determine how the Chinese govern and organize China? Is it the Chinese who have the right and the power to determine China's fate or the Americans? Many Americans believe they have the right and duty to determine China's fate and dictate America's answers to those three questions about the nature of man, a good society and social progress to China. But who cares more about the well-being and future of China: the Americans or the Chinese? The answer should be self-evident, even if one assumes that America's definition of human rights and political correctness are divinely given or innately superior to Chinese ideals and ways of doing things and must have the opportunity to prove their charisma to the Chinese.

American Exceptionalism evangelizes ideals in its China policy for which America stands, but cannot always live up to itself, particularly so far in the 21st century. That dichotomy between the ideals that were the historical foundation of American Exceptionalism and the words and deeds of America's 43rd presidential administration are inconsistent with America's ideals. This should in fact disturb a large majority of Americans. Fortunately, for a complex mixture of reasons America's have chosen a very different 44th president. But, that is a good first step in restoring charismatic American Exceptionalism.

The nobility and necessity of governments of America and the American people living up to the Ideals of their nation is essential for America and mankind's survival in the Age of Species Lethal Weapons and Science. Therefore we emphasize that in the economic and national security circumstances of the 21st century:

1. To the degree that Americans do not live up to their ideals, Americans are either delusional or hypocritical.

2. If Americans and Americans do live up to the ideals they
    honor and evangelize the system of government by exempli-
    fying the Ideals that create American Exceptionalism.

But, even if the American government lived up to the requirements of charismatic American Exceptionalism it does not give
America the moral authority to say that China must copy America's
political system. Respecting the rights of others is reciprocal in
America's government of the people, by the people, for the people.
The American system of constitutionally limited majority-rule-
government has at its essence the respect of others' rights and the
tolerance of other people's opinions. But imposing these things has
been the central theme of American policy toward China.

With these fundamental points in mind, let's examine China's
controversial stances that most prominently disturb Americans. We
will apply the "Fairness Hypocrisy Test" and "Do as I Say, Not as I
Do Test" examined in chapter 3 of Book 1 to:

1. American Exceptionalism about the intrinsic superiority and
    universality of American values; and
2. Chinese Exceptionalism of harmoniousness.

In chapter 11 of Book 1 we examined Franklin Roosevelt's Four
Freedoms and noted that China had chosen to give Freedom from
Fear and Freedom from Want priority over Freedom of Speech and
Freedom of Religion. In reviewing China's Exceptionalism, we will
look into the freedom of speech and human rights from a China-
centric perspective. President Roosevelt noted that Freedom from
Fear and Want were necessary prerequisites for the other Freedoms.

Freedom of Speech in America and China

In 2000, China's president Jiang Zemin explained the different perceptions between the Western and Chinese media coverage of China in a 60 Minutes interview with Mike Wallace:

> Chinese news...must obey and serve the interest of protecting the state and the public. ...Chinese news, in particular the *People's Daily*, are followed closely by the people. If information is reported which is false, then the people will react. It is different from your press which can write a lot of things regardless of whether it is true or false, and nobody really cares. [25]

There is a different tone in China's *People's Daily* and America's *New York Times*. Each reflects the attitudes towards freedom in each country's. America's Rights Society has attained the highest GDP and per capita income in the world. China's annual GDP has increased since 1976 from US $ 64 billion to US $ 2.5 trillion in 2007, but China's per capita income is still only $1/12^{th}$ of America's.

Over one-and-a-half centuries of ineffective government and a decade of economic chaos during the Cultural Revolution created a consensus among the Chinese seeking hegemony: this goal must give way to the priorities of economic development and peace. At the same time, these are the First and Second theses of President Roosevelt's Four Freedoms: Freedom from Fear and Want.

The *People's Daily* focuses on covering topics that seek to create better social conditions and discourage misconduct. It notes China's progress and goals, and examples of responsible conduct as well as instances of errors in social conduct. Its tone seeks to inspire the Chinese people, and is useful in uniting and uplifting them.

To a significant degree, some of things Americans view as freedoms the Chinese people view as decadence. But if one judges the soundness of a society's system of government, structure and policies by whether it is socially stable, united and able to protect its sovereignty, then China has a sound system of government.

As we emphasize, the principle of self-determination is at the core of the Declaration of Independence, the American Constitution and the UN Charter. If Americans respect the principle of self-determination, then it follows that they must accept that China has the right to determine how it will conduct its own internal affairs. But there is a huge difference between theory and practice because in actuality Americans do not eagerly accept that.

Why must China be a copy of America? If America cannot tolerate the rights of the Chinese to maintain their sovereignty according to their own heritage and culture, what does that say about the nature of Americans' commitment to the ideals of free speech, human rights and self-determination?

There must be tolerance and respect of the rights of self-determination among nations. Peaceful Permission and Rights Societies that can tolerate each others' rights can coexist. To each nation according to their own indigenous needs, goals, heritage and culture.

Human Rights in America and China

For the reasons examined in *America and China's Emerging Partnership: A New Realistic Perspectives* if China were to adopt America's political system it, China would be less stable, and less capa ble to raise its living standards. That might benefit America but would not benefit China. Americans either:

1. Do not understand that reality; or
2. Understand that reality and intend the negative result for China.

Whether Americans view China as a laboratory for American-style democracy or as a threat, neither the Chinese government nor the people are going to surrender voluntarily or submit involuntarily to America's influence seeking to make China unstable. American policymakers do seem to expect such urgings to be acquiesced to by a nation as capable and large as China. At the same time, even Robert Zoellick, former US Undersecretary of State and current President of the World Bank stated that it is not possible to persuade the Chinese government to change a system that works for them. But that remains the conventional mindset among American policymakers, scholars and opinion leaders. For example, the 2008 American Council on Foreign Relations report allegedly compiled by an independent task force, titled *US China Relations: An Affirmative Agenda, A Responsible Course*, urges fundamental changes in China's political system, structure and policies. One of the members of the Task Force stated in his dissent:

> I have signed the report because as a total document, there are many sections that address issues between the United States and China that can lead to a better understanding, and hence a better relationship. A frank discussion of our objectives and those of China can only be helpful.
>
> Where I disagree with this report, however, is the persistent urging of democracy on China. I have been going to China since 1975 and have seen unbelievable change not just in the economy but in the lives of the people.
>
> Each country has its own culture and comes by its political system through its own history. In my opinion, democracy cannot be obtained by outside pressure on a nation but only adopted from within. In the case of China, I doubt that the incredible progress they have made since the end of the Cultural Revolution could have occurred if there were political turmoil in China.
>
> We should stop pressing China to adopt a democratic political system – that is up to the Chinese. If it is to occur, it has to be their own choice.
>
> A dialogue at senior levels is essential to better understand each other's intentions on important issues. Transparency is essential. Both nations must understand that there are likely always to be differences on a number of issues. That should not, however, deter a constructive relationship between the United States and China.

There were 21 members on the taskforce, all remarkably experienced Americans. Mr. Hank Greenberg and Mr. Herbert Levin who wrote the dissent, are correct. In large part their dissent is based on respect for the principle of self-determination, as well as pragmatism about what is required for American-style majority-rule-democracy to take root in China.

However, The Council of Foreign Relations Report reflects conventional American perspectives toward China. The features in it to which Mr. Greenberg and Mr. Levin dissented are not minor. Unfortunately for both nations, American policy toward China has been myopically self-interested and endangers both China and America. We refer to such policy as "Americentric."

China seems to be meeting Deng Xiaoping's criteria of a sound political system, structures and policies examined in chapter 7 of Book 1. Mr. Greenberg and Mr. Levin's dissent echo the words of Deng Xiaoping who stated in a speech in 1984 to the Third Plenary Session of the Central Advisory Commission of China's governing party:

> We should make it clear to the rest of the world that nobody can alter the principles, policies and strategies we have worked out. Why? Because experience has shown that they are sound and effective. The people's standard of living is rising, the country is thriving and China's international prestige is growing. These are the most essential facts. If the current policies were to change, the country and the people would suffer. So the people, primarily the 800 million peasants, would never agree to there being changed. If the rural policies were changed, their living standards would immediately decline. There are still tens of millions of people in the countryside who do not yet have enough food and clothing, although things are much better than before. Now that most parts of the country have become better off, the state can spare more resources to help the few poor areas develop. The central authorities have drawn up a plan in this regard. The problem will not be too difficult to solve, because both the state and the prosperous areas can lend a helping hand. We know from our own experience that our generation will not

change these policies; nor will the next generation or the next few after that.[26]

But having made these observations about human rights in China as viewed from an Americentric perspective, it is appropriate to examine human rights in China from a Chinacentric perspective and ask:

1. How good is China at operating a harmonious society?
2. How good is China at living up to its own ideals of a harmonious society?

The concept of a harmonious society is emphasized by the Chinese government. But Americans would say: "How can a one-party-state dictatorship without majority-rule-style elections be harmonious development when in fact it is Marxist-Leninism?

There is a difference between "freedom" and "harmony." Harmony requires the restriction of freedom. For example, US. Supreme Court Justice Oliver Wendell Holmes argued that taxes are the price of civilization. Sigmund Freud said: sexual repression is the price of civilization.

Recently, Jared Diamond in *Collapse: How Societies Choose to Fail or Succeed* examined the failure of civilizations, presumably as a wakeup call for mankind. Jared Diamond's work is vital background for better understanding of the failure of the American and Chinese civilizations if they remain zero sum game competitors rather than becoming win-win harmonious partners.

Is social stability wrong? If social stability can be achieved with out justice and cannot be achieved with justice, which is to be preferred: justice or social stability? As Socrates, pointed out, who can really tell what justice is?

But how is jailing meritorious dissidents consistent with human rights or a harmonious society? First, perhaps we should ask a different question: who decides whether the behavior of dissidents in China is meritorious or not? The dissident who got an official White House pass from the American government and interrupted China's President Hu Jintao's speech on April 20, 2007 was not prosecuted by American authorities. Two points are important:

1. America insists on administering its laws in America and China insists on administering its laws in China.
2. In the context of a genuine, committed partnership, America's influence on China and China's influence on America would be enhanced. China's political evolution might be more inclined to liberalize if America's foreign policy was not constantly pressing China to adopt America's vision of human rights. As we emphasize, this pressure impedes rather than facilitates changes within China.

Premier Wen Jiabao presented a summary of China's approach to human rights in a speech at Harvard University in 2003. It is an approach that seeks to bring China's traditional economy into a mixed urban and rural economy while ameliorating income differences that could potentially endanger China's sovereignty. The Chinese agree that escaping hunger and protecting China's sovereignty are two of the most vital attributes that the Chinese state should defend. Wen Jiabao said:

> China's reform and opening-up have spread from rural areas to the cities, from the economic field to the political, cultural and social arenas. Each and every step forward is designed, in the final analysis, to release the gushing vitality of labor, knowledge, technology, managerial expertise and capital, and allow all sources of social wealth to flow to the fullest extent. For quite some time in the past, China had a structure of highly-centralized planned economy. With the deepening restructuring toward the socialist market economy and progress in the devel-

opment of democratic politics, there was gradual lifting of the former improper restrictions, visible and invisible, on people's freedom in choice of occupation, mobility, enterprise, investment, information, travel, faith and life style. This has brought extensive and profound changes never seen before in China's history.

On the one hand, the enthusiasm of the work force in both city and countryside has been set free. In particular, hundreds of millions of farmers are now able to leave their old villages and move into towns and cities, especially in the coastal areas, and tens of millions of intellectuals are now able to bring their talent and creativity into full play. On the other hand, the massive assets owned by the state can now be revitalized, the private capital pool in the amount of trillions of Yuan can take shape, and more than 500 billion US dollars worth of overseas capital can flow in. This combination of capital and labor results in a drama of industrialization and urbanization of a size unprecedented in human history being staged on the 9.6 million square kilometers of land called China. Here lies the secret of the 9.4% annual growth rate that China's economy has been able to attain in the past 25 years.

The tremendous wealth created by China in the past quarter of a century has not only enabled our 1.3 billion countrymen to meet their basic needs for food, clothing and shelter, and basically realize a well-off standard of living, but also contributed to world development. China owes all this progress to the policy of reform and opening-up and, in the final analysis, to the freedom-inspired creativity of the Chinese people.

This is a sincere statement. Respecting its sincerity, which is proven by China's social progress since 1979, is an essential tolerance needed in a partnership of America and China. Wen Jiabao spoke in very personal terms during his 2003 speech at Harvard:

As China's Premier, I am often torn with anxiety and unable to eat or sleep with ease when I think of the fact that there are still 30 million farmers lacking food and clothing, 23 million city-dwellers living on subsistence allowances, and 60 million disabled and handicapped people in need of social security aid.

For China to reach the level of the developed countries, it will still take the sustained hard work of several generations, a dozen generations or even dozens of generations.

President Hu Jintao presented the following summary of China's approach to human rights development in a speech at Yale University in 2006:

... I would like to speak to you about China's development strategy and future against the backdrop of the evolution of Chinese civilization and China's current development. I hope this will help you gain an understanding of China.

...Between 1978 and 2005, China's GDP grew from US $147.3 to US $2.2 trillion. Its import and export volume went up from US $20 billion to US $1, 4221 trillion, and its foreign exchange reserves soared from US $167 million to US $818.9 billion. On the other hand, I need to point out that despite the success in its development China remains the world's largest developing country with a per capita GDP ranking behind the 100th place. The Chinese people are yet to live a well-off-life, and China still faces daunting challenges in its development endeavor...We aim to rise China's GDP to US $ 4 trillion by 2030...By then, China's economy will be better developed, and its democracy will be further enhanced.

We are pursuing today a people-orientated approach toward development because we believe that development must be for the people and by the people and its benefit should be shared among the people. We care about people's value, rights and interests, freedom, the quality of their life, and their development potential and happiness index because our goal is to realize that all-round development of the people.

Some of China's leaders as well as many older people have been shaped by the shared hunger and chaos of the ten years of the Cultural Revolution. Although China's per capita income of is still only one-twelfth of America's, 400 or 500 million Chinese have been lifted out of poverty since the end of the Cultural Revolution. There is a consensus among the Mainland Chinese that economic development and prosperity are a much higher priority than adopting American-style political changes. Americans, like President Roosevelt did, must recognize and accept that Freedom from Fear and Want are required as a base supporting Freedom of Speech and Religion.

Tibet and the Confederate States of America Hypocrisy

Americans who seek greater human rights in China should consider how secession movements could actually lead to fewer rather than more, human rights.

For example, the American history contains examples of governmental use of military force against eleven of its states to prevent American citizens from exercising their rights to end the authority of the Constitution over them. Alabama, Florida, Georgia, Louisiana, Mississippi, South Carolina, Texas, Virginia, North Carolina and Texas wanted to secede. When those states declared their independence as the Confederate States of America, the other states fought in a successful civil war and prevented them from seceding.

American government officials who complain about the China's policies in Tibet would be outraged if China sought to intervene in American domestic political affairs. America has "Do as I Say, Not as I Do" and "Fairness Hypocrisy" problems when American leaders involve themselves in secessionist tensions concerning China's policy in Tibet. At the core of these moral authority problems is the assumption that American Ideals are universal truths.

Americans either accept the principle of self-determination of states in the United Nations Charter or they do not. However, many Americans selectively accept the principle of self-determination in asserting it when convenient in some circumstances but ignoring it in others when inconvenient. The Confederates States of America and Tibet are cases in point.

The American Taiwan and Cuba Hypocrisy

Cuba has never been part of the United States. But, pursuant to the Monroe Doctrine and America's national security concerns, America has had a trade embargo on Cuba for almost 50 years. America would react very negatively if China were selling missiles to Cuba. Taiwan is a part of China and the subject of an ongoing dispute. America supported the losing side of the Chinese Revolution, which in 1949 fled to Taiwan. Before China adopted capitalism with Chinese characteristics there was a potential threat for a counter revolution.

America sells Patriot missiles and armaments to Taiwan. American policy is to support Taiwan militarily while having a one-China policy acceding to China's territorial rights regarding Taiwan. That has "Do as I Say, Not as I Do" characteristics and reflects Fairness Hypocrisy. Again, at the core of these moral authority problems are the assumptions that American Ideals are universal truths.

A significant degree of Chinese sensitivity to the American government's approach to issues involving Tibet and Taiwan comes from America's history in the 19th and 20th century of "gunboat diplomacy" that used military authority to directly usurp China's sovereignty.

Deng Xiaoping stated in 1987 in discussions with the Prime Minister of the Netherlands:

> We are well aware that the United States policy is to hang onto Taiwan. Over the past two or three years we have repeatedly criticized the hegemonism of the United States, which regards Taiwan as its unsinkable aircraft carrier. There are some people in the U.S. who are in favor of the reunification of Taiwan with the mainland, but their view does not prevail. The Carter Administration [1977-1981] committed itself to the withdrawal of American troops from Taiwan, but at the same time it adopted the Taiwan Relations Act, which constituted interference in China's internal affairs. We therefore need time to work on both

the Taiwan authorities and the U.S. government.

Both of them should be able to accept the 'one country, two systems' formula as a solution to the Taiwan question...Isn't the 'one country, two systems'– a formula under which neither side will swallow up the other – a better solution? [27]

Deng Xiaoping also conceived an innovative "joint development" solution to other disputes:

...I have also told foreign guests that to settle international disputes new solutions should be put forward in the light of new situations and new problems. The 'one country, two systems' solution was proposed in the light of realities in China, but it could also be applied to certain international problems. Many international disputes may reach the flash point if they are not handled properly. I asked our guests whether the 'one country, two systems' solution could not be applied in some cases and the 'joint development' solution in others. The notion of 'joint development' was also proposed first in light of our own realities. We have the question of Diaoyu Island and the question of the Nansha Islands. The question of Diaoyu Island was raised at a press conference during my visit to Japan. I replied that there was a controversy over this issue between China and Japan. There are different names for the same island – in Japan it is known as Senkako Shoto. This question, I said, could be set aside for the moment; probably the next generation would be cleverer than we and would find a practical solution.

At the time, I was wondering whether it would be possible for the two countries to develop the area jointly, without getting involved in the controversy over sovereignty. This would only mean joint exploitation of the offshore oil resources. We could have a joint venture that would profit both sides. It wouldn't be necessary to fight a war or to hold many rounds of talks. World maps have always shown the Nansha Islands as part of China. Now one of the islands is occupied by Taiwan, while others are occupied by the Philippines, Vietnam or Malaysia. What is to be done? One alternative is to take all these islands back by force; another is to set aside the question of sovereignty and develop them jointly. By so doing we can make the problems that have piled up over the years disappear. This question will be settled sooner or later. There are many international disputes of this kind. We Chinese stand for peace and wish to settle all disputes by peaceful means. What kind of peaceful means? 'One country, two systems' and 'joint development.' The foreign guests who talked with me all agreed that this was a new and interesting idea.[28]

American policymakers can be sure that China is sincere in seeking peace. China's governments under three generations of speak for themselves. Americans might assert "Yes, but China is just laying low until it can dominate us." But what does "dominate us" mean? More importantly, will America be better off in an international system operating on the Principles of Conflict or on Peaceful Coexistence?

The vision behind China's Exceptionalism was formulated because it was deeply entrenched in the heritage and culture of the Chinese people. But there is a risk that, as Huang Yanpei, a famous democratic campaigner and educator in China, said in 1945 to Mao Zedong:

> During my sixty years of life, I have seen much thriving out of diligence and destruction out of negligence. In every dynasty or every period of history, people were concentrated and devoted to what they did at the beginning, probably because of a hard situation and the need for change. However, when the situation took a better turn, people slackened their efforts and negligence set in, first seen on some people, then on a majority, until no force, no matter how big it was, was able to change the situation. Our history is a cycle of diligence and negligence, thriving and destruction, honor and disgrace. No one has ever been able to break this cycle.[29]

There is a risk that China will forget the wisdom of Deng Xiaoping as America has forgotten the wisdom of President Washington.. That is a risk innate in human nature. That cycle is why nations rise and fall. Preventing it is the responsibility of China's leaders and people. It is one of the reasons why human nature must be remade in the Manhattan II Project. If they fail, that cycle will reoccur because future generations are incapable of preserving the success of previous. But this time, in the Age of Species Lethal Weapons and Science, they will destroy China.

However, in the Age of Species Lethal Weapons and Science, China is mankind's only example of such an enormous nation guided by the exalted justice and benevolence of the Principles of Peaceful Coexistence as implemented in their foreign policy and defense strategies.

American Exceptionalism: The Dream of the Universality of Human Rights and Exalted Justice

Chapter 3

The Challenge of Living Up To the American Ideals of Exalted Justice and Benevolence

Overview

There are two very different phenomena exemplified in America's earliest and most recent history that can be termed as charismatic and uncharismatic "American Exceptionalism." Historically, American Exceptionalism grew out of the European Enlightenment which inspired American innovations in government, when America escaped colonial domination and developed its Constitutional Majority-rule-democracy. That "American Exceptionalism," was a charismatic innovation three centuries ago. Under the administration of America's 43rd president, George W. Bush, an arrogant "American Exceptionalism" manifested itself, which is authoritarian and does not respect the rights of other nations. It is inconsistent with America's historic charismatic Exceptionalism. American Exceptionalism must live up to its historic ideals in the 21st century for America to remain charismatic and successful.

The Evolution of Freedom and Control in Societies

Americans have fostered the concept of "government of the people, by the people, for the people" that seeks to successfully combine "freedom" and "order." However, it also becomes critical to ask: What makes either "freedom" or "order" sustainable or successful in human societies? History suggests that achieving a sustainable and successful human society is always temporary. Mankind has seen many brief examples of unsustainable "freedom" and "order" in the past 10,000 years since the last Ice Age. The Chinese civilization has sustained itself for over 5,000 years relying on order more than freedom. The American civilization is not yet 500 years old. Will it be able to sustain itself 5000 years? America gave birth to the Age of Species Lethal Weapons and Science. Can America survive in it?

Western civilization's moral and political philosophy and political science trace their roots to a spontaneous, extraordinary radical democracy in Athens in which any adult male who was born in Athens citizen was thought to be qualified for any public office. in the Greek city state of Athens, which This helped pioneer a the concept of "freedom for its citizens." That radical democracy was able to defeat what we might call "totalitarian" Persia, which included today's Iran, but was in the end defeated and destroyed by what might be called "totalitarian" Sparta, which prized order over freedom.

The Athenian democracy was both more and less extensive than America's democracy. It exceeded American democracy by giving every adult male citizen a share in direct instead of representative rule and any citizen could address the Athenian assembly that met once every month and propose deciding policy. Direct rule was limited to 40,000 male citizens out of a population of approximately 300,000 people, residing in Athens. But, it was highly restrictive compared to current, but not earlier stages in the evolution of American democracy in denying political rights to women and slaves. Plato rejected the lack of professionalism in Athenian political affairs and policy making. Plato's concerns were similar to the results of the absence of what the Chinese government today term's calls the "scientific management" of the state.

The Roman Empire was built on the idea of "freedom" among its citizens, and added tremendous success at "order," at organized conduct, and was particularly noted for its prowess in military organization. It conquered many nations including England before it was no longer able to sustain itself. Edmond Gibbon's *The Decline and Fall of Rome* retrospectively traced the causes of its failure. A prescient analysis of America's fate was provided in Paul Kennedy's The Rise and Fall of Great Nations, published in 1987 in America and in 1989 in China. Kennedy's view was that America was like the empires of Rome, Spain and England over extending itself militarily and thus damaging itself economically and militarily. American policy makers have not yet taken Kennedy's advice, but Chinese policy makers have.

The Evolution of the Land of the Free From Sea to Sea

America began as the homeland of Indians who are believed to have come from Asia across an ice bridge. It became host to thirteen colonies of England that rebelled and pioneered a new system of national government. During the European Enlightenment it was asserted that reason made people capable of order, freedom, and self-government. Edmund Gibbon, who lived from 1737 to 1794, indicated in his autobiography that he held the minority view in the great debate of his time: he believed that the average European could be taught to read and write. A developing nation, America proved it was possible.

Are the American People a Safe Repository for the Ultimate Powers of Society in the Age of Species Lethal Weapons and Science?

America had few, if any, indigenous people, and was populated by waves of immigrants from every nation in the world and all races of mankind. America has been a beacon of hope. The United States of America has struggled throughout its history to improve its system of government of the people, by the people, for the people. America struggled and compromised to define itself and, then to redefine itself in a Civil War that was amongst other things a clash of slave owning and non-slave owing civilizations. The American people's experiment in building the Constitution, indigenous to America is one of mankind's greatest achievements, and inspirations encouraging tolerance for the opinions and respect for the rights of others.

Neither America, China nor mankind can survive if the American people are not "a safe repository of the ultimate powers of society" as Thomas Jefferson asserted. The Age of Species Lethal Weapons and Science is an unforgiving test of that fundamental proposition of Jefferson's in what we term the "American Experiment." The fates of America, China, and mankind depend upon:

1. The decisions the American people produce about their relationship with China.
2. The decisions America and China's leaders as partners make in collaborating to design and help manage a new international system that is able to solve the fundamental issue in the Age of Species Lethal Weapons and Science of preventing human extinction.

Now every generation in both the American and Chinese civilizations must produce leaders able to successfully guide their civilizations to take the road less traveled, on which they respect the opinions and respect of the rights of other civilizations. The American people now must consistently produce such leaders or fail as a nation and civilization. America must not start wars it will lose, as Athens did, nor become unable to defend itself, as the Rome did.

The conflicts and genius of our species have created the Age of Species Lethal Weapons and Science, invented by America in seeking to defeat Japanese aggression. After creating the Age of Species Lethal Weapons, America led the way in the creation of the United Nations and its Charter, which seek to create an epochal change in which the inspiring and noble instincts of mankind could proliferate globally. But, human nature is a complex dynamic in which conflict and collaboration compete. Before 1945, these complex dynamics in of conflict and collaboration human nature and civilizations vexed but could not destroy mankind. And now, the proliferation of Species Lethal Weapons and Science can destroy us.

The Right of Self-Determination and Creation of a Rights Society in America

The American Declaration of Independence is a classic expression of people's right of self-determination. It begins with the words:

> When in the Course of human events it becomes necessary for one people to dissolve the political bands which have connected them with another, and to assume among the powers of the earth, the spate and equal station to which the Laws of Nature and of Nature's Good entitle them, and decent respect to the opinions of mankind requires that they should declare the cause which impel them to the separation.
>
> We hold these truths to be self-evident, that all men are created equal, that they are endowed by their Creator with certain unalienable Rights, that among these are Life, Liberty and the pursuit of Happiness. That to secure these rights, Governments are instituted among Men, deriving their just powers from the consent of the governed. That whenever any Form of Govern-

ment becomes destructive of these ends, it is the Right of the People to alter or to abolish it, and to institute new Government, laying its foundation on such principles and organizing its powers in such for, as to them shall seem most likely to affect their Safety and Happiness. Prudence, indeed, will dictate that Governments long established should not be changed for light and transient cause; and accordingly all experience hath shown that mankind are more disposed to suffer, while evil are sufferable, than to right themselves by abolishing the forms to which they are accustomed. But when a long train of abuses and usurpations, pursing invariably the same Object evinces a design to reduce them under absolute Despotism, it is their right, it is their duty, to throw off such Government, and to provide new Guards for their future security....

These ideas which Americans assert are self-evident truths were, at the time they were asserted, an intellectual and social revolution. in mainland's evolution. The first draft of the American Declaration of Independence was written by Thomas Jefferson, 47 amendments were made by John Adams and Benjamin Franklin, and 39 amendments were made by the Continental Congress including removing a reproach directed at the British people and a condemnation of slavery. Fifty-six brave men signed it. They were resisting the hegemony of a nation which had the greatest military and economic authority in the world. Their cause and the military and economic authority they mustered had profound moral authority. They were militarily successful in triumphing over the most able professional army with relatively highly motivated and poorly equipped citizen soldiers. From the perspective of the English government of the time, the leaders of the American Revolution that we revere, were criminals. In modern terminology they would be termed "terrorists." Benjamin Franklin declared at the signing of the Declaration of Independence: "We must all hang together, gentlemen...else, we shall most assuredly hang separately."

The Constitution of the United States of America begins with the war tested words:

> We the People of the United States, in Order to form a more
> perfect Union, establish Justice, insure domestic Tranquility,
> provide for the common defense, promote the general Welfare,
> and secure the Blessings of Liberty to ourselves and our Posterity,
> do ordain and establish this Constitution for the United States
> of America....

Thomas Jefferson said that: "I know of no safe repository for the ultimate powers of society but the people themselves." That seems automatic and obvious to most Americans today, yet it was radical and had not been tested in previous centuries. It is natural for 20th and 21st century for Americans to celebrate that proposition's success, but it is one of the most revolutionary and controversial ideas in mankind's history:

> The United States is the first nation in the world created by the
> pen as well as the sword; the ideas expressed in these documents
> have shaped the lives of all Americans: indeed these ideas, per-
> haps more than the vast and rich continent and the American
> people themselves, have given America a unique identity among
> the nations of history.[30]

In 1826, Thomas Jefferson wrote in the final letter of his life of the hope of Americans:

> May it be to the world, what I believe it will be (to some parts
> sooner, to others later, but finally to all), the signal of arousing
> men to burst the chains under which monkish ignorance and
> superstition had persuaded them to bind themselves and to
> assume the blessings and security of self-government. That
> form, which we have substituted, restores the free right to the
> unbounded exercise of reason and freedom of opinion...[31]

Alexis de Tocqueville wrote in *Democracy in America*, published in 1835:

"It is evident to all alike that a great democratic revolution is going on amongst us; but there are two opinions as to its nature and consequences. To some it appears to be a novel accident, which as such may still be checked; to others it seems irreversible, because it is the most uniform, the most ancient, and permanent tendency which is to be found in history."[32]

Tocqueville observed:

The territory now occupied or possessed by the United States of America forms about one-twentieth part of the habitable earth. But extensive as these confines are, it must not be supposed that the Anglo-American race will always remain within them; indeed, it has already far overstepped them.[25] The time will therefore come when one hundred and fifty millions of men will be living in North America, equal in condition, the progeny of one race, owing their origin to the same cause, and preserving the same civilization, the same language, the same religion, the same habits, the same manners, and imbued with the same opinions, propagated under the same forms. The rest is uncertain, but this is certain; and it is a fact new to the world – a fact fraught with such pretentious consequences as to baffle the efforts even of the imagination.

In the 1830's Tocqueville foresaw that:

There are, at the present time, two great nations in the world which seem to tend towards the same end, although they started from different points: I allude to the Russians and the Americans. Both of them have grown up unnoticed; and whilst the attention of mankind was directed elsewhere, they have suddenly assumed a most prominent place amongst the nations; and the world learned their existence and their greatness at almost the same time.[33]

The great power contest of the 20th century was that of USA versus. USSR and capitalist versus. communist economics. In the 21st century the great question is whether one-party and multi-party government capitalist states can align their goals and success? Another way of expressing this is: can Rights Societies and Permission Societies work together and align their successes?

Tocqueville, while recognizing that a great democratic revolution had occurred in America was also able to foresee that:

> ...if a democratic republic similar to that of the United States were ever founded in a country where the power of a single individual had previously subsisted, and the effects of a centralized administration had sunk deeply into the habits and the laws of the people, I do not hesitate to assert, that in that country a more insufferable despotism would prevail than any which now exists in the monarchical States of Europe, or indeed than any which could be found on this side of the confines of Asia.[34]

Immigrants to America and their decedents and waves of other immigrants forced out of their way the indigenous people they found, skirmished with French colonies and bought one of them, made war on and annexed Spanish colonies. The new government's territory expanded with the Louisiana Purchase, the North West Ordinance, the Spanish American War, and the purchase of Alaska from Russia to establish the land of the free from sea to sea. Generation after generation of Americans had the courage and other requirements to sustain the American Experiment for over 200 years. All this was proclaimed to be America's "Manifest Destiny."

President James Monroe promulgated "The Monroe Doctrine" in 1823 It stipulated that any interference by a European state in the affairs of Spanish-American republics would be regarded as a hostile act unfriendly towards America and that the American continents were no longer open to European colonial settlement.

President Theodore Roosevelt created and sent a significant American naval force around the world in 1908.[35] Wars of aggression expressing each civilization's sense of its manifest destiny have been carried out with fists, clubs, swords, bows, arrows and, on foot and horseback and with, guns, ships and cannons. Now airplanes, missiles, and Species Lethal Weapons and Science enable aggressors to widen the reach and destructive power of their ambition, anger, and military authority. Has the creation of Species Lethal Weapons and Science made human survival impossible? Has it made America's survival impossible?

In the 20th century, America's Rights Society Model was victorious in World War I, World War II with the exhaustion of European and Japanese military authority in 1945. It also proved successful in the Cold War, with the implosion of communist economic authority. In this century, America is a world leader because of its economic, military, and moral authority. Generations of Americans, flushed with the adrenalin of struggle and the confidence of economic and military victory, fee America could liberate the world from un-American ideals and political systems. What could possibly be wrong with that noble goal?

Where Did America Go Wrong? How Can America Succeed in the 21st Century?

Many nations, including China, do not want to be liberated from their own traditions. They cling to their values and political systems, even when they admire America's success, culture, and wealth; and even if they accept America's stabilization of the international system. That stubbornness, which is innate in human nature, is ironically hard for Americans to understand. As a result, many Americans do not accept other nations' resistance to American ideals, just as Americans resist foreign values and political systems.

Early in the 21st century, America's era of being the innovative and economic leader of the world in the past two centuries is dissipating. Americans understandably do not like this change! The new realities and trends of the 21st century are terrifying, confusing challenges to their values and their identity. Americans successfully led mankind on an road to a "shining city on a hill." But, America will play a less dominant role. To make matters worse, under its 43rd president, America did not play an inspiring, uplifting role. The limits of American economic, military and moral authority are shockingly evident to mankind now. The American people will decide what their values will be in the 21st century. Will they pursue the Ideals of their Constitution or succumb to authoritarian and uninspiring values? Fortunately, Americans have made a very different and fundamental choice in selecting their 44th president.

Americans must correct the reality that America also produced a staggeringly unsuccessful government under its 43rd president from among its 300 million people and experienced the rule of an indigenous authoritarian government early in the 21st century.

Living up to the charismatic Ideals of majority-rule-democracy, human rights, and rule of law, is a profound challenge for the Americans character. Ironically for Americans maintain their charismatic ideals they must become capable of tolerating and protecting other civilizations' rights of self-determination. Other civilizations are becoming too successful to be dominated.

How can Americans accept that other civilizations may never evolve and proliferate America's values and concepts of the Four Freedoms? How can they accept that some nations will seek Freedom from Fear and Want as priorities rather than Freedom of Religion and Speech? Or that some nations may even reject Freedom of Religion or Freedom of Speech as goals? How can Americans accept that they must restrain their pride in order to protect their moral authority? What if America's values and behavior are different from America's ideals?

America created the Age of Species Lethal Weapons and Science to preserve its freedoms by defeating authoritarian aggressors. Now, for any of the Four Freedoms to survive, must renew its ideals by respecting, for example, China's right of self-determination. That is a profound challenge to Americans' identity.

During the first decade of the 21st century, America has given the world the far too familiar example of economic and military authority without moral authority. As is examined next, that example does not live up to the need for moral authority emphasized in President Washington's Farewell Advice, President Lincoln's speeches, President Roosevelt's Four Freedoms speech, or President Kennedy's June 10,1963 address to America. At the same time, the limitations of American military and economic authority have been revealed to the world. Fortunately, Americans understand that they have faltered and must to do better. This requires a genuine, successful partnership that aligns China's and America's successes. That constitutes a profound change from the zero sum mindset of Americans toward China. Now America's policies towards China cannot be only determined by what America wants.

America's Economic Authority

In contrast to the zenith of its 20th century strength as the world's superpower, America now finds itself in the early stages of being economically dwarfed by China, which embraced capitalism within a one-party system. At the same time, America has succumbed to the use of military and economic authority without moral authority.

For the reasons examined in *America and China's Emerging Partnership: A New Realistic Perspective,* China has achieved unprecedented economic development, social stability and enormous reforms. China's population, which is five times America's, with effective government such as it has produced in the past 30 years, is likely to produce an economy of commensurate proportions. China's growth rate has been accelerating and will compound. It averaged 9.5% GDP growth annually between 1978 and 2005, and then 10.5% in 2006, 11.7% in 2007, 8.2% in 2008, 8.7% in 2009, and at 11.9% early in 2010. China's GDP growth has been fueled by very successful government policies, frugality, restrained consumer spending, and the hard work of 1.5 billion Chinese. After 2008, the global economy has been unstable. American GDP growth from 1978 to 2008 oscillated between 2% and 4% per year America was a primary cause of most serious financial crises in a century.

America's decline reflects what the *Financial Times* called "the long standing global consensus that fiscal retrenchment in the US and Japan is needed to help reduce huge trade imbalances." [36] It is increasingly evident that the mismanagement of America's fiscal and foreign policies can bankrupt America and that the world economic order is changing. While it has been the case in the past, it is not likely that America will be the world's major engine for economic growth in the future. Over time, it will likely be China, India and other developing nations that experience the enormous economic growth America achieved when it was a developing nation. As the world is seen in this new light, the influence of America's economic policies and military authority are being reduced by being overextended without the moral authority it had prior to the sole superpower's reckless mismanagement. However, America's economic mismanagement may seriously damage China's and the global economies. The global economic crisis will be lengthy, and we are in its early stages. To restore America's charismatic moral authority American policy makers must stop thinking only about America's own problems and embrace a larger perspective and new economic and military policies that are sustainable and successful. That also is a major challenge to American's identity and political system.

America's excessive consumer spending, used as its engine of economic growth, has led it to the brink of bankruptcy. The solution to America's problems is not for China to emulate America, but for America to respond to China's priorities and its consumer consumption restraint. China's and America's partnership is essential to reducing the aggressive and catastrophic use of military authority in the Age of Species Lethal Weapons and Science.

American economic trends beginning in 2001 and culminated in 2008 in the subprime, credit, liquidity, and bank solvency and related crises. They revealed the unstable underpinnings of America's economy, the insolvency of many of America's global banks and insurers, and triggered what is recognized by America's former Federal Reserve Chairman, Alan Greenspan, as "the most serious financial crisis in 100 years." These faults in America's economic authority, and others, such as the federal government's deficit levels and level of foreign borrowing, the costs of two wars, have been growing for many years. America's financial crises in effect end the 20th century's economy and begin the 21st century's.

For all these reasons presented above, we believe that America is currently at an economic, military, and diplomatic crossroads. Chaos will eventually replace stability if America's trajectory and conventional economic, military and ideological policies towards China continue. The United States cannot afford to choose leaders and polices that are unable to lead the world with economic and most importantly moral authority.

America's Use of Military Authority

On September 11th, 2001 America was attacked in military and symbolic ways. At that moment, the United States had a presidential administration that had less compunction than is wise in using military power. An authoritarian faction, which called itself "neoconservative," was highly adroit at organized political campaigns, and was able to respond to the "9/11" attacks with military power without moral authority. In response the administration, the United States began acting like a bully instead of a respected policeman who follows the letter of the law. The Bush administration ways of dealing with the 9/11 attacks mark the dramatic shift in how the United States was seen and perceived by people all over the world.

A "bully" is a person who uses strength and power to coerce

others by intimidation.[37] Human beings instinctively resent bullies. Bullies have "immoral authority," the exact opposite of "moral authority." Whether they are children in the school yard or powerful nations, bullies use fear and force as motivators. This degrades into weakness, because the more a bully uses strength to coerce others, the more opposition a bully generates, eclipsing his own power.

> Colin Powell, America's Secretary of State at the time of the 9/11 attacks, wanted to characterize the 9/11 attacks as "crimes." But President George W. Bush sought instead to go to war. The choices America's President made in responding to the 9/11 attacks were increasingly perceived and then revealed to be reliance on military authority without moral authority or the use of military authority with what neoconservatives leading a Presidential Administration viewed as moral authority. That Administration's doctrine of preemptive and sometimes unilateral use of force, often based on known-to-be-false or shown-to-be-false information and assumptions, followed by the reliance on military authority alone, has alienated many friends and other observers of American economic and military power, and degraded American moral authority.[38]

Many Americans and much of the world disapproves of the unilateral use of American military authority. They were revolted by the profound disregard of the American government with respect to human rights and the Geneva Conventions proscription of torture. Having elected an authoritarian government, America ceased being the admired policeman of the world and became the disrespected bully. An authoritarian American government set out with ideological certainty on a declared mission to democratize the Arab world, without paying sufficient attention to Arab public opinion.[39] It became difficult to portray America's War on Iraq as an example of a people motivated by an exalted justice and benevolence. By 2008, it was easy to compare what the American government succeeded in doing in the invasion of Iraq to what Saddam Hussein attempted and failed to do in invading Kuwait. The *New York Times* reported on June 19, 2008:

> Four Western oil companies are in the final stages of negotiations this month on contracts that will return them to Iraq, 36 years after losing their oil concession to nationalization as Saddam Hussein rose to power.
>
> Exxon Mobil, Shell, Total and BP – the original partners in the Iraq Petroleum Company – along with Chevron and a number of smaller oil companies, are in talks with Iraq's Oil Ministry for no-bid contracts to service Iraq's larges fields according to ministry officials, oil company officials and an American diplomat. The deals expected to be announced on June 30, will lay the foundation for the first commercial work for the major companies in Iraq since the American invasion, and open a new and potentially lucrative country for their operations.
>
> The no-bid contracts are unusual for the industry, and the offers prevailed over others by more than 40 companies, including companies in Russia, China and India. The contracts would run for one to two years and are relatively small by industry standards, would none-the-less give the companies an advantage in bidding on future contracts in a country that many experts consider to be the best hope for a large-scale increase in oil production.
>
> There was suspicion among many in the Arab world and among parts of the American public that the United States had gone to war in Iraq precisely to secure the oil wealth these contracts seek to extract. The Bush administration has said that the war was necessary to combat terrorism. It is not clear what role the United States played in awarding the contracts; there are still American advisors to Iraqi's Oil Ministry.
>
> Sensitive to the appearance that they were profiting from the war and already under pressure because of record high oil prices senior officials of two of the companies, speaking only on condition they not be identified, said they were helping Iraq rebuild its decrepit oil industry.
>
> For an industry being frozen out of new ventures in the world's dominant oil-producing countries, from Russia to Venezuela, Iraq offers a rare and prized opportunity. While

enriched by $ 140 per barrel oil, the oil majors are also struggling to replace their reserves as ever more of the world's oil patch becomes off limits. Governments in countries like Bolivia and Venezuela are nationalizing their oil industries or seeking a larger share of the record profits for their national budgets. Russia and Kazakhstan have forced the major companies to renegotiate contracts.[40]

Since America is the only military superpower and has over 50% of mankind's military assets and expenditures, most other nations, in their external affairs are not emulating America's use of military authority without moral authority. But, the strategies of the George W. Bush administration have undermine America's national security and are a degrading and destabilizing example that assert the precedent that might is right. America was not obeying rules it helped create, but chose to exempt itself from, while imposing its rule where it saw fit on others. There is no moral authority in America asserting by word and deed that for a more powerful nation dealing with less powerful nations there is no international law, only rules the strong nation chooses to assert.

Fairness Hypocrisy whether of a militarily aggressive American government in a War on Iraq or of Muslim fundamentalists in jihad feels subjectively like moral authority, but it is perceived as immoral authority. Both seek to change other people's minds, or obtain their compliance by intimidation. or to eliminate the opinions and rights of people by killing them.

The use of military or economic authority without moral authority is a shortsighted and ultimately self-defeating strategy for America. It strengthens countervailing forces while American human and financial resources that the use of military authority consumes decline. Prosperity and peace cannot be sustained using Fairness Hypocrisy and the other Principles of Conflict in the Age of Species Lethal Weapons and Science. That is examined in chapter 3 of Book 1.

Chapter 4

Will People Perish from the Earth?

Overview

The fundamental foreign policy, defense strategy and scientific issue confronting all nations in the Age of Species Lethal Weapons and Science is the survival of mankind. Government as it has evolved in America must accommodate this issue and the right for self-determination of other nations. and civilizations in the Age of Species Lethal Weapons and Science or America, China and mankind will perish from the earth.

How Can Mankind Govern Itself in the Age of Species Lethal Weapons and Science?

We must successfully answer the following questions:

1. How can *mankind* govern itself effectively enough to survive in the Age of Species Lethal Weapons and Science?
2. How can *America's government* of the people, by the people,

for the people not perish from the earth in the Age of Species Lethal Weapons and Science?

Armed conflict, and war, the ultimate zero sum games, which have governed much of human history, are becoming increasingly destructive and potentially lethal to our species. The proliferation of Species Lethal Weapons and Science and of accidents, natural disasters, attacks and war threatens to make the world ungovernable and us a failed species. Extinction is an objective criterion. It ends all human differences of opinion, prejudices and conflicts..

President Lincoln defined America's experiment with democracy as "government of the people, for the people, by the people." in the midst of a civil war determining whether the American Constitution's Ideals could continue to become realities or vanish from the earth at that defining moment in our human odyssey. Today, amid growing the horrors of intolerance, growing more dangerous, and obvious with 21st century media, only with the audacity of hope, made compelling among our species *by the genius of moral authority*, can enable the world to remain governable. Moral authority will rule or no one and nothing will successfully rule our dying future as a species, which will be "brutish, nasty and short"[41].

The humane rather than the animal in us must triumph in us or we will fail. Our weapons and science will no longer be able to coexist with our species' violent and intolerant nature. The challenge is absolute because any individual, small group, or nation among us can commit species suicide.

Will America's Government of the People, by the People, for the People Perish from the Earth?

China has been waiting for decades to enter into a harmonious relationship with America. We do so because the 21st century partnership of America and China must be deployed successfully by

America's future presidents for America and China to be successful.

Mankind is divided into 192 nations in the United Nations, which never have agreed to be American. That "house" of 192 states nations can *only* stand divided. World War II was an attempt to unite it under one world government envisaged by Hitler. The only hope Americans can realistically have is that their choice of Ideals and system of government, because they are "right" will have the "might" to someday become universal.

George Washington's and Deng Xiaoping's Advice to their Nations

George Washington and Deng Xiaoping were both leading generals in successful revolutionary wars founding their nations, and revered and inspiring heads of state who exemplified the very best of their civilizations. They both successfully led fragile, impoverished, agrarian and developing countries. Deng Xiaoping initiated China's strategy, as a developing nation, of focusing on economic development rather than on world hegemony. Deng Xiaoping's advice in the 1980s and 1990s to China is strikingly similar to the advice that George Washington gave in his Farewell Address in 1796, in which he said:

> Observe good faith & justice towards all nations. Cultivate harmony with all.... It will be worthy of a free, enlightened, and, in no distant period a great nation, to give to mankind the magnanimous and too novel example of a people always guided by an exalted justice & benevolence.[42]

Deng Xiaoping's advice was:

> We must...encourage all our people to have lofty ideals and moral integrity, to become better educated and to cultivate a strong sense of discipline. Of these, lofty ideal and a strong sense

of discipline are most important. We must constantly urge our
people, young people in particular, to have lofty ideals.[43]

We adhere to an independent foreign policy of peace and
do not join any bloc. We are prepared to maintain contacts and
make friends with everyone. We are against any country that
commits aggression against others. We are against any country
that commits aggression against others. We are fair in our words
and in our deeds. This adds to China's potential influence. This
policy has produced good results, and we shall follow it forever.[44]

China is following Deng Xiaoping's advice. As we emphasize,
it is important for Americans to understand that Deng Xiaoping's
approach is a sincere win-win strategy and reflects China's 5,000-
year-old culture. China remains the world's 100th wealthiest nation
with a per capita income is 1/12th that of Americas. Unfortunately
Americans are not following George Washington's advice. President
Washington warned in his Farewell Address of the danger of factions
and "the costs of unavoidable wars." The War on Iraq, which at least
54% of Americans think was a mistake, was projected to cost US
$50 to 60 billion. It has cost $3 trillion to date and may exceed US
$4 trillion[45] or an average of US $16,900 per American family, and
has cost more than 4000 American lives and between 50,000 and
1,000,000 Iraqi lives. The indirect costs are horrendous. For example,
oil cost $30 a barrel at the start of the war and was over $147 a barrel
in July 2008[46]. Such fluctuations can wreck the global economy as
we live in an interdependent international system.

China is becoming increasingly prosperous and is at peace with
all nations. American hegemony may seek prosperity and peace, but
has not produced them. America's way of doing things, even with a
Constitution which successfully answered in the 17th to 20th centuries problems of human ignorance and governance that all civilizations struggle with, has been challenged by the 9/11 attacks on
the World Trade Center, Pentagon, and Congress or White House.
The United State's role as a global power has been undermined by

America's response.

Washington's "Example" vs. Jefferson's "Signal" of American Ideals to All Mankind

The use of military force without moral authority is not prudent foreign policy and military strategy because it does not: "give to mankind the magnanimous and too novel example of a people always guided by an exalted justice and benevolence."

America's authority is insufficient for the to imposition of its ideals on the world's population. It is possible, under an ideal scenario for America's ideals to become universally accepted. But such a scenario is tenuous and perhaps decades away. If Americans can accept that, it will mark a massive change for America's future.

General Washington's contemporaries recognized his merit as the nation's first leader because of George Washington's personal character and example, which stood out above all others'. General Washington's personal character and example gave special significance to the way, as President Washington, he presented the ambition of an American Exceptionalism in his Farewell Address:

> Observe good faith & justice towards all nations. Cultivate harmony with all... It will be worthy of a free, enlightened, and, in no distant period a great nation, to give to mankind the magnanimous and too novel *example* of a people always guided by an exalted justice & benevolence. (emphasis added)[47]

Compare that to the belief Thomas Jefferson expressed in the eventual universality of American ideals and political system:

> May it be to the world, what I believe it will be (to some parts sooner, to others later, but finally to all) the *signal* of arousing men to burst the chains under which monkish ignorance and superstition had persuaded them to bind themselves and to assume

the blessings and security of self-government. That form, which we have substituted, restores the free right to the unbounded exercise of reason and freedom of opinion. (emphasis added)

Only the moral authority of America's *living up* of its exceptional ideals of America's indigenous political system, not merely the *intrinsic merit* that Americans perceive in America's exceptional ideals and system of government can have charisma of an "example" that might be capable of being the "signal" that Jefferson hoped for America's ideals to become universally accepted. There is a difference between the genius of an "example" and inadequacy of a mere "signal." That difference is fundamental to the fate of America's Ideals.

Washington envisaged America being an "example" to mankind. Jefferson envisaged America being,: "to the world, what I believe it will be (to some parts sooner, to others later, but finally to all) the signal of arousing men to burst the chains under which monkish ignorance and superstition had persuaded them to bind themselves and to assume the blessings and security of self-government." This is a goal worth pursuing.

Washington's advice, that America be an "example" of America's Ideals and system of government in order for such ideals to be accepted by other nations, better expresses the real nature and power of American Ideals than the "signal" envisaged in the hopes expressed in the words quoted in Jefferson's final letter. It is not merely the "blessings and security of self-government" as defined and enshrined among mankind by the American Constitution that are capable of having such universal influence. But it may be that the "magnanimous and too novel example of a people always guided by an exalted justice & benevolence" might at some time in appeal to people all over the world.

There is a fundamental distinction between America actually being "an example of a people always guided by an exalted justice and benevolence" and America seeking to be "the signal of arousing men to burst the chains of monkish ignorance and superstition...

and to assume the blessings and security of self government." That distinction makes a profound difference. Washington's "example" and Jefferson's "signal" offer different roads for Americans to follow. If America seeks to be a "signal" rather than an "example" in other civilizations, America will fail to be either. But if America returns to being the example that Washington envisioned, then America will make its best case for its ideals and political system.

An example has far more moral authority than a signal. General Washington put himself in harm's way for what he believed in. Recall the example he provided at Trenton, New Jersey, in 1777, when he moved ahead of his men, on a white horse. The British front line fired their first volley. Not a single ball hit General Washington or his horse but ripped into his men. Washington then advanced to 50 yards from the British soldiers. They fired their second volley. But again, not a single ball hit Washington or his horse. After this example, Washington turned to his men and said: "It's a fox hunt boys...get them." His men inspired beyond the fear and carnage of battle, attacked and eventually defeated the British. We believe that General Washington was not missed because the British soldiers were incompetent marksmen, but that his example of courage was so brave that not a single British soldier tried to hit him.

In any event, President Washington's farewell address expresses the essence of American Exceptionalism while Jefferson's view of America as a "signal" expresses the arrogance of American Exceptionalism. Thomas Jefferson was a lawyer, scholar, political philosopher, farm owner, diplomat and politician. He never fought in the Revolutionary War, but said "Every citizen should be a soldier. This was the case with the Greeks and Romans, and must be that of every Free State." Jefferson's roles in creating American Exceptionalism was different than Washington's. Washington, although the universal choice as America's first leader, declined to be its new king, and chose instead to be its first President. He also insisted on establishing the precedent of voluntary resignation after two terms. Washington led by example.

Alexis de Tocqueville believed that American government would not fit all societies, which conflicts with Jefferson's ideas, but is compatible with Washington's advice to the American people. Tocqueville believed:

> ...if a democratic republic similar to that of the United States were ever founded in a country where the power of a single individual had previously subsisted, and the effects of a centralized administration had sunk deeply into the habits and the laws of the people, I do not hesitate to assert, that in that country a more insufferable despotism would prevail than any which now exists in the monarchical States of Europe, or indeed than any which could be found on this side of the confines of Asia.[48]

Washington's advice that America be an example "in no distant period a great nation, to give to mankind the magnanimous and too novel example of a people always guided by an exalted justice and benevolence" is a more realistic guide for Americans than Jefferson's hope that America be a signal: "to the world, what I believe it will be to some parts sooner, to others later, but finally to all."

Lincoln's 19th Century Model: A House Divided Cannot Stand

Abraham Lincoln's election as President in 1860 precipitated America's inevitable civil war over the meaning of its Constitution and its future character. America's Ideals and system of government required a civil war to determine which of two visions of America would prevail. But that conflict about the definition of American Ideals, was a class of civilizations or civil war *among Americans* whose forefathers had accepted the American Constitution.

Abraham Lincoln was committed to preserving the Union. In 1858, he warned that:

A house divided against itself cannot stand. I believe that this government cannot endure, permanently half slave and half free. I do not expect the Union to be dissolved. I do not expect the house to fall, but I do expect it will cease to be divided. It will become all one thing or all the other. [49]

That American "house" is far smaller than the global village of 192 nations today. That "house" could not stand divided. But it is not wise for Americans to ask for, support or impose a foreign policy based on Christian principles that should be obeyed by *all nations in the global village.*

Lincoln's goal was always to unite America. As President, Abraham Lincoln's empathetic nature and his extraordinary insight enabled him to embrace even those he was leading a war against. In 1863, Lincoln in dedicating a cemetery in which the dead of both persuasions had fought and been buried together addressed mankind in the Gettysburg Address:

Four score and seven years ago our fathers brought forth on this continent, a new nation, conceived in Liberty, and dedicated to the proposition that all men are created equal.

Now we are engaged in a great civil war, testing whether that nation, or any nation so conceived and so dedicated, can long endure. We are met on a great battle-field of that war. We have come to dedicate a portion of that field, as a final resting place for those who here gave their lives that that nation might live. It is altogether fitting and proper that we should do this. And that government of the people, by the people, for the people, shall not perish from the earth.

But, in a larger sense, we cannot dedicate – we cannot consecrate – we cannot hallow – this ground. The brave men, living and dead, who struggled here, have consecrated it, far above our poor power to add or detract. The world will little not, nor long remember what we say here, but it can never forget what they did here. It is for us the living, rather, to be dedicated here to the unfinished work they who fought here have thus far so nobly advanced. It is rather for us to be here dedicated to the great task remaining before us – that from these honored dead we take increased devotion to that cause for which they gave the last full measure of devotion – that we here highly resolve that these dead shall not have died in vain – that this nation, under God, shall have a new birth of freedom – and that government of the people, by the people, for the people, shall not perish from the earth.

President Lincoln defined America in the powerfully arranged words of his Gettysburg Address. The exceptional experiment in which his country led mankind was a "government by the people, of the people, for the people shall perish from the earth." In the Gettysburg Address, Americans found a much needed definition of their purpose and direction.

America needs a new "Gettysburg Address" to redefine America and its misguided "War on Terror." President Lincoln's definition of American Ideals was an example, not merely a signal. Lincoln fought to preserve the example of America's Ideals but he only did so within America. President George W. Bush's government sought to impose American Ideals and extend them to foreign nations. An authoritarian America cannot protect nor present American Constitutional Ideals of human rights, rule of law, and majority-rule government with moral authority.

Lincoln's extraordinary insight prevailed in that struggle among the different definitions of America. In the celebration of their victory, a crowd outside the White House called for President Lincoln to address them. He appeared and asked them to sing one of his favorite tunes that he hadn't heard in several years. It was *Way Down South in the Land of Dixie,* a favorite song in the Confederate states.

On April 11, 1865, shortly after the surrender of Confederate General Robert E. Lee's army, a jubilant crowd gathered outside the White House calling for President Lincoln, who gave what became his farewell address. A reporter Noah Brooks wrote:

Outside was a vast sea of faces, illuminated by the lights that burned in the festal array of the White House, and stretching far out into the misty darkness. It was silent, intent, and perhaps surprised, multitude.

Within stood the tall, gaunt figure of the President, deeply thoughtful, intent upon the elucidation of the generous policy which should be pursed toward the South. That this was not the sort of speech which the multitude expected is tolerably certain.

Lincoln stood at the window over the building's main door, a place where presidents customarily gave speeches. Brooks held a light so Lincoln could read his speech, while young Tad Lincoln grasped the pages as they fluttered to his feet. The speech addressed the complex topic of reconstruction, especially as it related to the state of Louisiana. For the first time in a public setting, Lincoln expressed his support for black suffrage. This statement incensed John Wilkes Booth, a member of the audience, who vowed, 'That is the last speech he will make.' A white supremacist and Confederate activist, Booth made good on his threat three days later.[50]

Tempered by the terrible knowledge of the challenges of human nature Lincoln's last speech was about the work of building a lasting peace among Americans. He said:

We meet this evening not in sorrow, but in gladness of heart. The evacuation of Petersburg and Richmond, and the surrender of the principle insurgent army, give hope of a righteous and speedy peace whose joyous expression cannot be restrained....By these recent successes the re-inauguration of the national authority – reconstruction – which has had a large share of thought from the first, is pressed much more closely upon our attention. It is fraught with great difficulty. Unlike a case of a war between independent nations, there is no authorized organ for us to treat with. No one man has authority to give up the rebellion for any other man. We simply must begin with, and mold from, disorganized and discordant element. Nor is it a small additional embarrassment that we, the loyal people, differ among ourselves as to the mode, manner, and means of reconstruction.[51]

Lincoln's focus on unifying America is exemplified in his Gettysburg Address and final advice to Americans in defining America. Lincoln, like Washington, is an example of the genius and power of moral authority and of the tolerance of the opinions of others. This is the case even when military authority has been decisive, as it was in America's Revolutionary War and Civil War.

Without Lincoln's success in the Civil War the world may have gone in a very different direction in the two World Wars in the 20th century fought to define the future of mankind. But, mankind would have continued to exist. Civilization would have had other chances for the "better angels of our nature," in the words Lincoln used in the last sentence in his first Inaugural Address in 1861, to assert themselves and make mankind more humane. The last sentence in Lincoln's Second Inaugural Address in 1865 was:

> With malice toward none, with charity for all, with firmness in the right as God gives us to see the right, let us strive on to finish the work we are in, to bind up the nation's wounds, to care for him who shall have borne the battle and for his widow and his orphan, to do all which may achieve and cherish a just and lasting peace among ourselves and with all nations.[52]

The 1961 Kennedy Model: Pax Americana

John F. Kennedy defined the meaning of America's Constitution's ideals, foreign policy and defense strategies and agenda after the first 15 years of the Age of Species Lethal Weapons and Science. His Inaugural Address had many contained, but not all, of the essential principles that must be part of America's redefinition.

President Kennedy's Inaugural Address built upon and modernized Lincoln's Gettysburg Address, and in insightful and inspiring terms defined America's exceptional goals It focused on was what we term "a civil war among mankind." It was about whether an American definition of the words "government by the people, of the people, for the people" would perish from the earth.

The difference that a hundred years had made included what we term two "civil wars among mankind" that are known as World Wars I and II, which culminated with in the creation of the Age of Species Lethal Weapons and Science. Kennedy like Lincoln spoke to issues of government, values, and the search for meaning that all people in all places at all times face. He did so in setting out a foreign policy and defense strategies and goals for the contest between communist and American values. It is useful to compare these two speeches in context of the world of today rather than the 19th and 20th centuries worlds of 150 and 50 years ago. Both speeches are among the defining expressions of the American Experiment. In President Lincoln's speech, none of the words defining America for Americans need be modified. It is instructive, in reading President Kennedy's speech, nearly 50 years after he gave it to update it by replacing the words "communist" with the words "one-party-state" and "communism" with the words "capitalism with Chinese characteristics." On entering office in 1961 President Kennedy said:

> We observe today not a victory of party, but a celebration of freedom – symbolizing an end, as well as a beginning – signifying renewal, as well as change. For I have sworn before you and Almighty God the same solemn oath our forbears prescribed nearly a century and three-quarters ago.
>
> The world is very different now. For man holds in his mortal hands the power to abolish all forms of human poverty and all forms of human life. And yet the same revolutionary beliefs for which our forebears fought are still at issue around the globe – the belief that the rights of man come not from the generosity of the state, but from the hand of God.
>
> We dare not forget today that we are the heirs of that first revolution. Let the word go forth from this time and place, to friend and foe alike, that the torch has been passed to a new

generation of Americans born in this century, tempered by war, disciplined by a hard and bitter peace, proud of our ancient heritage, and unwilling to witness or permit the slow undoing of those human rights to which this nation has always been committed, and to which wars are committed today at home and around the world.

Let every nation know, whether it wishes us well or ill, that we shall pay any price, bear any burden, meet any hardship, support any friend, oppose any foe, to assure the survival and the success of liberty. This much we pledge – and more.

To those old allies whose cultural and spiritual origins we share, we pledge the loyalty of faithful friends. United there is little we cannot do in a host of cooperative ventures. Divided there is little we can do – if we dare not meet a powerful challenge at odds and split asunder.

To those new states whom we welcome to the ranks of the free, we pledge our world that one form of colonial control shall not have passed away merely to be replaced by a far more iron tyranny. We shall not always expect to find them supporting our view. But we shall always hope to find that strongly supporting their own freedom – and to remember that, in the past, those who foolishly sought power by riding the back of the tiger ended up inside.

To those people in the huts and villages of half the globe struggling to break the bonds of mass misery, we pledge our best efforts to help them help themselves, for whatever period is required – not because the Communists may be doing it, not because we seek their votes, but because it is right. If a free society cannot help the many who are poor, it cannot save the few who are rich.

To our sister republics south of our border, we offer a special pledge: to convert our good words into good deeds, in a new alliance for progress, to assist free men and free governments in casting off the chains of poverty. But this peaceful revolution of hope cannot become the prey of hostile powers. Let all our neighbors know that we shall join with them to oppose aggression or subversion anywhere in the Americas. And let every other power know that this hemisphere intends to remain the master of its own house.

To that world assembly of sovereign states, the United

Nations, our last best hope in an age where the instruments of war have far outpaced the instruments of peace, we renew our pledge of support – to prevent it from becoming merely a forum for invective, to strengthen its shield of the new and the weak, and to enlarge the area in which its writ may run.

Finally, to those nations who would make themselves our adversary, we offer not a pledge but a request; that both sides begin anew the quest for peace, before the dark powers of destruction unleashed by science engulf all humanity in planned or accidental self-destruction.

We dare not tempt them with weakness. For only when our arms are sufficient beyond doubt can we be certain beyond doubt that they will never be employed. But neither can two great and powerful groups of nations take comfort from our present course – both sides overburdened by the cost of modern weapons, both rightly alarmed by the steady spread of the deadly atom, yet both racing to alter that uncertain balance of terror that stays the hand of mankind's final war.

So let us begin anew – remembering on both sides that civility is not a sign of weakness, and sincerity is always subject to proof. Let us never negotiate out of fear, but let us never fear to negotiate. Let both sides explore what problems unite us instead of belaboring those problems which divide us. Let both sides, for the first time, formulate serious and precise proposals for the inspection and control of arms, and bring those absolute powers to destroy other nations under the absolute control of all nations. Let both sides seek to invoke the wonders of science instead of its terrors. Together let us explore the stars, conquer the deserts, eradicate disease, tap the ocean depths, and encourage the arts and commerce. Let both sides unite to heed, in all corners of the earth, the command of Isaiah – to "undo the heavy burdens, and to let the oppressed go free."

And if a beach head of cooperation may push back the jungle of suspicion, let both sides join in creating a new endeavor – not a new balance of power, but a new rule of law - where the strong are just, and the weak secure, and the peace preserved.

All this will not be finished in the first one hundred days. Nor will it be finished in the first one thousand days; nor in the life of this Administration; nor even perhaps in our lifetime on this planet. But let us begin.

In your hands, my fellow citizens, more than mine, will rest the final success or failure of our course. Since this country was founded, each generation of Americans has been summoned to give testimony to its national loyalty. The graves of young Americans who answered the call to service surround the globe.

Now the trumpet summons us again – not as a call to bear arms, though arms we need – not as a call to battle, though embattled we are – but a call to bear the burden of a long twilight struggle, year in and year out, 'rejoicing in hope; patient in tribulation, a struggle against the common enemies of man: tyranny, poverty, disease, and war itself.

Can we forge against these enemies a grand and global alliance, North and South, East and West, that can assure a more fruitful life for all mankind? Will you join in that historic effort? In the long history of the world, only a few generations have been granted the role of defending freedom in its hour of maximum danger. I do not shrink from this responsibility – I welcome it, I do not believe that any of us would exchange places with only other people or any other generation. The energy, the faith, the devotion which we bring to this endeavor will light our country and all who serve it, and the glow from that fire can truly light the world.

And so my fellow Americans, ask not what your country can do for you; ask what you can do for your country. My fellow citizens of the world ask not what America will do for you, but what together we can do for the freedom of man. Finally, whether you are citizens of America or citizens of the world ask of us here the same high standards of striving and sacrifice which we ask of you. With a good conscience our only sure reward, with history the final judge of our deeds, let us go forth to lead the land we love, asking His blessing and His help, but knowing that here on earth God's work must truly be our own.[53]

The world in which we live is far more dangerous than the world in which Lincoln was president. People who today are in their fifties or older experienced being at the brink personally of one of mankind's defining moments. The thirteen days in October 1962 during which nuclear war was very nearly inevitable are among our lasting memories, as is the assassination of President Kennedy. Those few days culminated in "the most dangerous moment in human history." Things went well in that crisis in the Age of Species Lethal Weapons and Science. But as President Kennedy realized, what we have is not peace, but merely a hiatus between our extinction and evolution.

Arthur Schlesinger revealed in *War and the American Presidency* that:

> ...President Kennedy after the Cuban Missile Crisis in 1962 privately expressed his fear that people would conclude from his victory that all we would have to do thereafter in dealing with the Communists was to be rough and they would collapse. The missile crisis, he pointed out, had three distinctive features: it occurred in a place where we enjoyed local conventional superiority, where Soviet national security was not directly engaged, and where the Russians lacked a case which they could convincingly sustain before the world. Things would be different, he said, if the situation were one where the communists had local superiority, where their national security was directly engaged, and where they could persuade themselves and others that they were in the right.[54]

Schlesinger also recalled Winston Churchill's "principles of morals and action which may be a guide in the future" in *The Gathering Storm*, Churchill's history of the lead-up to World War II Churchill said:

> It may be well here to set down some principles of morals and action which many be a guide in the future. No case of this kind can be judged apart from its circumstances...
>
> Those who are prone by temperament and character to seek sharp and clear-cut solutions of difficult and obscure problems, who are ready to fight whenever some challenge comes from a foreign power, have not always been right. On the other hand, those whose inclination is to bow their heads, to seek patiently and faithfully for peaceful compromise, are not always wrong. On the contrary, in the majority of instances, they may be right, not only morally but from a practical standpoint...
>
> How many wars have been precipitated by firebrands! How

> many misunderstandings which led to war could have been
> removed by temporizing! How often have countries fought cruel
> wars and then after a few years of peace found themselves not
> only friends but allies![55]

From horror of leadership, the American people were able to find a wise leader in those 13 days. Ultimately, the fate of the world depended on two men, John Kennedy and Nikita Khrushchev who, with very different backgrounds, led two nations, in the ultimate zero sum game. Fortunately, both realized that nuclear war was only winnable if human competition did not play out to the conclusion of species suicide. The two men, took the road less traveled because the other option was lethal to all they represented. They managed to find a solution that had more moral than military authority, when many of their advisors urged a military solution. Two men, separated by thousands of miles, were nonetheless eyeball to eyeball with all of mankind and the ultimate responsibility of starting a war that no one could survive. Fortunately *bothas* they rejected a solution using military authority, because it could not have worked, since it was unsustainable.

Khrushchev was removed from office not long after "backing down" and successfully solving the Cuban Missile Crisis. Nuclear war was avoided, America was not attacked, and Cuba was never invaded. Kennedy's resistance of to his advisors' conventional advice cerecommendations, which was echoed forcefully in the conventional views in of the Congress, might, had the crisis not been successfully resolved in days rather than months, have lead to his impeachment. Later, the USSR collapsed without armed conflict because it was not working economically viable.

John F. Kennedy's empathetic nature and extraordinary insight, prevented the defining moment in history that was the Cuban Missile Crisis bombing mankind into extinction. President Kennedy, speaking in the much faster and dangerous Age of Species Lethal

Weapons and Science, President Kennedy defined what we refer to as the "Human Extinction Challenge" as whether "problems created by mankind could be solved by mankind." The problems on the road leading to extinction we face each day are whether human nature and intelligence are adequate to solve the problems human nature and intelligence create. The eon's-old struggle to survive, of which our species is either a finite or infinite part, confronts us all. It is what we term the "Mankind's New School of the Human Extinction Challenge."

The 1963 Kennedy Model: "Not Pax Americana – The Search for Genuine Peace"

What triggered the Cuban Missile Crisis? Not long after President Kennedy's Inaugural Address, an ill conceived and botched invasion of Cuba was followed by the Soviet Union's deployment of nuclear missiles in Cuba targeting America with 5 minutes between launch and impact. What we term a "civil war among mankind" was being conducted in a Cold War. But, for the first time, the responsibility for the extinction of mankind by the fouling of the earth in a massive, catastrophic, irreversible and unrecoverable exchange of anger, intolerance and weapons nightmarishly came in October 1962 to be in the hands and minds of the two leaders of competing civilizations' value systems and visions for mankind's future.

After that experience of the honor of leadership, in June 1963, almost at the end of the thousand days of in his Presidency, John F. Kennedy presented what we will term his "Not Pax Americana – The Search for Genuine Peace Speech" in which he advised:

> I have... chosen this time and this place to discuss a topic on which ignorance too often abounds and the truth is too rarely perceived--yet it is the most important topic on earth: world peace.

What kind of peace do I mean? What kind of peace do we seek? Not a Pax Americana enforced on the world by American weapons of war. Not the peace of the grave or the security of the slave. I am talking about genuine peace, the kind of peace that makes life on earth worth living, the kind that enables men and nations to grow and to hope and to build a better life for their children – not merely peace for Americans but peace for all men and women – not merely peace in our time but peace for all time.

I speak of peace because of the new face of war. Total war makes no sense in an age when great powers can maintain large and relatively invulnerable nuclear forces and refuse to surrender without resort to those forces. It makes no sense in an age when a single nuclear weapon contains almost ten times the explosive force delivered by all the allied air forces in the Second World War. It makes no sense in an age when the deadly poisons produced by a nuclear exchange would be carried by wind and water and soil and seed to the far corners of the globe and to generations yet unborn....

First: Let us examine our attitude toward peace itself. Too many of us think it is impossible. Too many think it unreal. But that is a dangerous, defeatist belief. It leads to the conclusion that war is inevitable – that mankind is doomed – that we are gripped by forces we cannot control.

We need not accept that view. Our problems are manmade, therefore, they can be solved by man. And man can be as big as he wants. No problem of human destiny is beyond human beings. Man's reason and spirit have often solved the seemingly unsolvable – and we believe they can do it again.

I am not referring to the absolute, infinite concept of peace and good will of which some fantasists and fanatics dream. I do not deny the value of hopes and dreams but we merely invite discouragement and incredulity by making that our only and immediate goal.

Let us focus instead on a more practical, more attainable peace – based not on a sudden revolution in human nature but on a gradual evolution in human institutions – on a series of concrete actions and effective agreements which are in the interest of all concerned. There is no single, simple key to this peace – no grand or magic formula to be adopted by one or two powers.

Genuine peace must be the product of many nations, the sum of many acts. It must be dynamic, not static, changing to meet the challenge of each new generation. For peace is a process – a way of solving problems.

With such a peace, there will still be quarrels and conflicting interests as there are within families and nations. World peace, like community peace, does not require that each man love his neighbor -- it requires only that they live together in mutual tolerance, submitting their disputes to a just and peaceful settlement. And history teaches us that enmities between nations, as between individuals, do not last forever. However fixed our likes and dislikes may seem, the tide of time and events will often bring surprising changes in the relations between nations and neighbors.

So let us persevere. Peace need not be impracticable, and war need not be inevitable. By defining our goal more clearly, by making it seem more manageable and less remote, we can help all peoples to see it, to draw hope from it, and to move irresistibly toward it.

Second: Let us re-examine our attitude toward the Soviet Union. It is discouraging to think that their leaders may actually believe what their propagandists write. It is discouraging to read a recent authoritative Soviet text on Military Strategy and find, on page after page, wholly baseless and incredible claims – such as the allegation that "American imperialist circles are preparing to unleash different types of wars . . . that there is a very real threat of a preventive war being unleashed by American imperialists against the Soviet Union . . . [and that] the political aims of the American imperialists are to enslave economically and politically the European and other capitalist countries . . . [and] to achieve world domination . . . by means of aggressive wars."

Truly, as it was written long ago: "The wicked flee when no man pursueth." Yet it is sad to read these Soviet statements – to realize the extent of the gulf between us. But it is also a warning -- a warning to the American people not to fall into the same trap as the Soviets, not to see only a distorted and desperate view of the other side, not to see conflict as inevitable, accommodation as impossible, and communication as nothing more than an exchange of threats.

No government or social system is so evil that its people

must be considered as lacking in virtue. As Americans, we find communism profoundly repugnant as a negation of personal freedom and dignity. But we can still hail the Russian people for their many achievements – n science and space, in economic and industrial growth, in culture and in acts of courage....

Today, should total war ever break out again – no matter how – our two countries would become the primary targets. It is an ironic but accurate fact that the two strongest powers are the two in the most danger of devastation. All we have built, all we have worked for, would be destroyed in the first 24 hours. And even in the cold war, which brings burdens and dangers to so many nations, including this Nation's closest allies – our two countries bear the heaviest burdens. For we are both devoting massive sums of money to weapons that could be better devoted to combating ignorance, poverty, and disease. We are both caught up in a vicious and dangerous cycle in which suspicion on one side breeds suspicion on the other, and new weapons beget counter weapons.

In short, both the United States and its allies, and the Soviet Union and its allies, have a mutually deep interest in a just and genuine peace and in halting the arms race. Agreements to this end are in the interests of the Soviet Union as well as ours – and even the most hostile nations can be relied upon to accept and keep those treaty obligations, and only those treaty obligations, which are in their own interest.

So, let us not be blind to our differences – but let us also direct attention to our common interests and to the means by which those differences can be resolved. And if we cannot end now our differences, at least we can help make the world safe for diversity. For, in the final analysis, our most basic common link is that we all inhabit this small planet. We all breathe the same air. We all cherish our children's future. And we are all mortal.

Third: Let us reexamine our attitude toward the cold war, remembering that we are not engaged in a debate, seeking to pile up debating points. We are not here distributing blame or pointing the finger of judgment. We must deal with the world as it is, and not as it might have been had the history of the last 18 years been different.

We must, therefore, persevere in the search for peace in the hope that constructive changes within the Communist bloc might bring within reach solutions which now seem beyond us. We must conduct our affairs in such a way that it becomes in the Communists' interest to agree on a genuine peace. Above all, while defending our own vital interests, nuclear powers must avert those confrontations which bring an adversary to a choice of either a humiliating retreat or a nuclear war. To adopt that kind of course in the nuclear age would be evidence only of the bankruptcy of our policy – or of a collective death-wish for the world.

To secure these ends, America's weapons are non-provocative, carefully controlled, designed to deter, and capable of selective use. Our military forces are committed to peace and disciplined in self-restraint. Our diplomats are instructed to avoid unnecessary irritants and purely rhetorical hostility.

For we can seek a relaxation of tension without relaxing our guard. And, for our part, we do not need to use threats to prove that we are resolute. We do not need to jam foreign broadcasts out of fear our faith will be eroded. We are unwilling to impose our system on any unwilling people – but we are willing and able to engage in peaceful competition with any people on earth.

Meanwhile, we seek to strengthen the United Nations, to help solve its financial problems, to make it a more effective instrument for peace, to develop it into a genuine world security system – a system capable of resolving disputes on the basis of law, of insuring the security of the large and the small, and of creating conditions under which arms can finally be abolished.

At the same time we seek to keep peace inside the non-Communist world, where many nations, all of them our friends, are divided over issues which weaken Western unity, which invite Communist intervention or which threaten to erupt into war. Our efforts in West New Guinea, in the Congo, in the Middle East, and in the Indian subcontinent, have been persistent and patient despite criticism from both sides. We have also tried to set an example for others – by seeking to adjust small but significant differences with our own closest neighbors in Mexico and in Canada.

Speaking of other nations, I wish to make one point clear. We are bound to many nations by alliances. Those alliances exist because our concerns and theirs substantially overlap. Our commitment to defend Western Europe and West Berlin, for example, stands undiminished because of the identity of our vital interests. The United States will make no deal with the Soviet Union at the expense of other nations and other peoples, not merely because they are our partners, but also because their interests and ours converge.

Our interests converge, however, not only in defending the frontiers of freedom, but in pursuing the paths of peace. It is our hope – and the purpose of allied policies – to convince the Soviet Union that she, too, should let each nation choose its own future, so long as that choice does not interfere with the choices of others. The Communist drive to impose their political and economic system on others is the primary cause of world tension today. For there can be no doubt that, if all nations could refrain from interfering in the self-determination of others, the peace would be much more assured.

This will require a new effort to achieve world law – a new context for world discussions. It will require increased understanding between the Soviets and ourselves. And increased understanding will require increased contact and communication. One step in this direction is the proposed arrangement for a direct line between Moscow and Washington, to avoid on each side the dangerous delays, misunderstandings, and misreadings of the other's actions which might occur at a time of crisis....

Finally, my fellow Americans, let us examine our attitude toward peace and freedom here at home. The quality and spirit of our own society must justify and support our efforts abroad. We must show it in the dedication of our own lives – as many of you who are graduating today will have a unique opportunity to do, by serving without pay in the Peace Corps abroad or in the proposed National Service Corps here at home.

But wherever we are, we must all, in our daily lives, live up to the age-old faith that peace and freedom walk together. In too many of our cities today, the peace is not secure because the freedom is incomplete.

It is the responsibility of the executive branch at all levels of government – local, State, and National – to provide and protect that freedom for all of our citizens by all means within their authority. It is the responsibility of the legislative branch at all levels, wherever that authority is not now adequate, to make it adequate. And it is the responsibility of all citizens in all sections of this country to respect the rights of all others and to respect the law of the land.

All this is not unrelated to world peace. "When a man's ways please the Lord," the Scriptures tell us, "he maketh even his enemies to be at peace with him." And is not peace, in the last analysis, basically a matter of human rights – the right to live out our lives without fear of devastation – the right to breathe air as nature provided it – the right of future generations to a healthy existence?

...The United States, as the world knows, will never start a war. We do not want a war. We do not now expect a war. This generation of Americans has already had enough – more than enough – of war and hate and oppression. We shall be prepared if others wish it. We shall be alert to try to stop it. But we shall also do our part to build a world of peace where the weak are safe and the strong are just. We are not helpless before that task or hopeless of its success. Confident and unafraid, we labor on -- not toward a strategy of annihilation but toward a strategy of peace.[56]

American policymakers must examine the fundamental issue at a most important level of the choice between the Principles of Conflict and Principles of Peaceful Coexistence and at the conventional level of traditional policy debates. These conventional debates discuss the strategies of achieving exploitation and defending domination. They do not address how we can survive in the Age of Species Lethal Weapons and Science. President Kennedy's experience of responsibility for the imminent destruction of mankind caused him to realized that a conventional analysis about an enemy's responses ignored the reality that America, the Soviet Union, and mankind would be obliterated, if he did not somehow find a way to avoid armed conflict.

Kennedy's and Deng's Goal of Genuine Peace in the Age of Species Lethal Weapons and Science

That road to genuine, lasting peace was envisaged in June 1963 by President Kennedy because he recognized the conventional road more traveled did lead to no future for America or mankind.

He outlined a new concept of peace that was not the "Pax Americana," that he envisaged before the experience of the Cuban Missile Crisis. We reiterate his words:

> What kind of peace do I mean? What kind of peace do we seek? Not a Pax Americana enforced on the world by American weapons of war. Not the peace of the grave or the security of the slave. I am talking about genuine peace, the kind of peace that makes the earth worth living, the kind that enables men and nations to grow and to hope and to build a better life for their children, not just peace for Americans but peace for all men and women – not merely peace in our time but peace for all time.
>
> I speak of peace because of t3he new face of war. Total war makes no sense in an age when great powers can maintain relatively invulnerable nuclear forces and refuse to surrender without resort to those forces. It makes nonsense in an age when a single nuclear weapon contains almost ten times the explosive force delivered by all the allied air forces in the Second World War. It makes no sense in an age when the deadly poisons produced by a nuclear exchange would be carried by the wind and water and soon reach the far corners of the globe and to generations yet unborn.

President Kennedy was assassinated five months later. This speech represents a farewell address of a head of state who narrowly prevented the obliteration of America.

Deng Xiaoping also chose the alternative of peaceful coexistence for the same reasons that President Kennedy gave Americans in June 1963. Between the 1970's and 1990's, Deng Xiaoping was allowed to take the road less traveled. *Without realizing it, Americans and mankind have been traveling with China on the peaceful coexistence road less traveled since 1978.*

Deng Xiaoping expressed China's strategy in implementing the Principles of Peaceful Coexistence in what we will refer to as China's "peaceful coexistence commitment." He emphasized it within the Chinese government, to the Chinese military, throughout China, and to American presidents throughout his leadership and until his death in 1997.

The strategy that Deng Xiaoping implemented was based on the Five Principles of Peaceful Coexistence as set forth by Premier Zhou Enlai.

The Principles of Peaceful Coexistence that China implemented are[57]:

1. Mutual respect for sovereignty and territorial integrity
2. Mutual non-aggression
3. Non-interference in each other's internal affairs
4. Equality and mutual benefit
5. Peaceful coexistence.

The Five Principles of Peaceful Coexistence were included in the joint communiqué issued by Premier Zhou Enlai and Prime Minister Jawaharlal Nehru. The five principles were first formally written into the preface to the Agreement between the People's Republic of China and the Republic of India on Trade and Intercourse Between the Tibet Region of China and India. India and China went to war before Deng Xiaoping's leadershp because Mao Zedong viewed the world from the Principles of Conflict perspective.

However, the Principles of Peaceful Coexistence have been "adopted in many other international documents and have become widely accepted as norms for relations between countries." [47] It is important to recognize that these Principles were pioneered by the Peoples Republic of China's Premier Zhou Enlai and the Republic of India's Prime Minister Nehru. Eastern civilizations embraced the concept of a harmonious world more readily than the Western civilizations that had lead in the creation of the United Nations. It is also important to recognize that the Principles of Coexistence were proposed by a Permission Society a Rights Society. The difference between majority-rule and a non-majority-rule systems of government and the ancient rivalry between China and India did not matter to peaceful coexistence. Instead, what made a difference was the common interests in trade, prosperity and peace did.

Deng Xiaoping frequently commented that foreigners did not believe him when he said that China remained committed to peaceful coexistence. We have observed that Americans are not currently inclined to believe this either. The concept of a peaceful rise to power is not part of Western tradition.

At the time of Premier Zhou Enlai's pioneering of the Principles of Peaceful Coexistence, the American Secretary of State Dulles' mindset was such that he refused even to shake hands with the Premier Zhou Enlai. Following the Korean and Vietnam Wars' testing conflicts, President Nixon's initiative in 1972 enabled China's leader to open diplomatic and trade relations with America.

Over the past 30 years, America has maintained barriers to trade with China while demanding that China be open to American companies and allow them to operate without restrictions.

To date, the past 30 years the publications of Chinese policymakers focus on China's reliance on the Principles of Peaceful Coexistence. But the publications of American policymakers do not typically focus on the Principles of Peaceful Coexistence or on China's consistent implementation of them. These ongoing differences in focus reflect the varied mindsets, strategies, and goals of America's and China's policies.

A key word search of the *Foreign Affairs* database, of "Principles of Peaceful Coexistence" suggests that China's implementation of those principles has received little attention. A similar Google search showed that Chinese scholars were writing about these Principles while the American scholars showed no interest in comment on them.

These fundamental differences in focus are better dealt with by

American policymakers and scholars by obtaining similar advantages for America by also implementing the Principles of Peaceful Coexistence.

The Chinese have not expressed themselves in ways Americans are able to accept as sincere. Americans, with their yearning for ideological and geopolitical hegemony cannot accept that the Chinese do indeed want peaceful coexistence.

America's conventional foreign policy goal towards China is flawed because it is based on the Principals of Conflict. Americans, not the Chinese, are the most pressing danger to a genuine lasting peace, which President Kennedy realized could not be a Pax Americana but on solving disputes with solutions that are reciprocally beneficial. The Principles of Conflict are not a safe basis for American foreign policymaking, in the Age of Species Lethal Weapons and Science or for any nation's foreign policy. The Principles of Conflict are not an example of justice and benevolence, but the Principles of Peaceful Coexistence are such an example. The impact of America operating on the Principles of Conflict is that the world is now a more dangerous place where Freedom from Fear and Want has been greatly diminished. The fundamental question of whether mankind has a future is not contingent upon whether mankind will adopt America's Ideals. The fundamental question is: will America adopt and implement the Principles of Peaceful Coexistence? American policymakers have a responsibility to the themselves and to mankind to implement the Principles of Peaceful Coexistence. The Principles of Conflict are not consistent with America's survival Ideals.

The Chinese will stand their ground against aggression and are proudly nationalistic but they also sincerely want peace.

America's and China's partnership can function successfully if Americans can accept the Principles of Peaceful Coexistence. The New School of America-China Relations articulates these Principles in terms that Americans can relate to.

Americans must embrace the opportunity China provides them

to achieve genuine peace. The reality is that Chinese implementation of peaceful coexistence is demonstrated by *thirty years of history*. China has shown that lasting peace based on accepting the diversity of nations and resolving differences in reciprocally beneficial ways *is possible. The responsibility of implementing, respecting and policing the Principles of Peaceful Coexistence must be accepted by American policymakers and people.*

Deng Xiaoping expressed this commitment from 1978 onward. For American's who may not be familiar with this, here are nineteen of countless examples. Note the range of audiences to whom Deng Xiaoping reiterated the peaceful coexistence commitment.

The shift of the basis of China's foreign policy and defense strategies from what we term the Principles of Conflict to the Principles of Peaceful Coexistence can be seen in remarks made on September 14, 1978, Deng Xiaoping, stated:

> Comrade Mao Zedong's strategic idea of differentiating the three worlds open up a road for us. We have gone on opposing imperialism, hegemonism, colonialism and racism, working to safeguard world peace, and actively developing relations, including economic and cultural exchanges, with other countries on the basis of Five Principles of Peaceful Coexistence. After several years of effort, we have secured international conditions that are far better than before; they enable us to make use of capital from foreign countries and of their advanced technologies and experience in business management. These conditions did not exist during Comrade Mao Zedong's life.[58]

In January 1981 in a talk with Senator Theodore Fulton Stevens, a Republican and assistant leader of the U.S Senate and Anna Chennault, Vice-Chairman for the Presidential Export Committee, Deng Xiaoping said:

> We hope that after assuming the presidency, Mr. Ronald Reagan will make new contributions to the development of

Sino-U.S. relations. It was the Republican Party that turned a new page in Sino-U.S. relations during the administration of Mr. Richard Nixon and Henry Kissinger. We will always remember it was Mr. Nixon who was determined to improve Sino-U.S. relations during his presidency. When Jimmy Carter served as president, Sino-U.S. relations witnessed new development. However, in the latter period of President Carter's term, there was the Taiwan Relations Act. On our part, we hope that Sino-U.S. relations will continue to develop. Frankly speaking, however, we were really disturbed by certain statements Mr. Reagan made in his election platform. When George Bush1 visited China, we said to him that we understood that statements made in election campaigns in his country might not necessarily be put into practice and that we would pay close attention to what actions Mr. Reagan takes after assuming office. When China and the United States established diplomatic relations in 1979, they settled the main question, the Taiwan question, and the United States recognized Taiwan as part of China. Only by settling this question could the two countries establish new relations and continue to develop them. The Taiwan question should be considered an issue of the past, but now it has been brought up again. We asked Mr. Bush to pass on to Mr. Reagan our clear-cut position on this question.

We have noticed that the American media and the statements of some people convey four viewpoints concerning this question. These viewpoints, if not clarified, are likely to cause regression in Sino-U.S. relations.

According to the first view point, China is a very weak and poor country and has backward equipment, so it is a country that is of little importance and not worth a great deal of attention. This is by no means a minor issue, but a matter of judgment about the world's balance of power. We have always admitted that we are a weak and poor country. Nevertheless, China has its own advantages, that is, a vast territory and a large population. However, it is true that China is poor and has backward equipment. But we do have a sober estimate of our strength. We enjoy the advantages of being a vast country with a large population and we refuse to be misled by fallacies. The Chinese people have always acted in accordance with their own views. It is clear to all that the People's Republic of China was built through self-reliance. Even in times of great difficulty, we dared to face reality and confronted powerful forces with our limited strength. Poor and weak as it may be, China dares to face reality to handle its own affairs. Therefore, those who misjudge China's position in world politics will not have a correct international strategy.

According to the second viewpoint, China now looks to the United States for help, but not vice versa. Such a view has been expressed in the U.S. media on more than one occasion. Over the past two years, we did something undesirable, thereby causing some people's misconception. Due to a lack of proper control, quite a few Chinese delegations went to the United States. Worse still, some members of the delegations were imprudent in their words and deeds. Visits are a good rather than a bad thing, but they have created a false impression among some people that China must look to others for help. This is true not only in the United States but probably in European countries as well. From now on, we shall control the number of delegations sent abroad. Of course, this does not mean that there will be no more normal exchanges. Recently, we have been conducting economic readjustment. The fact that we published the amount of our deficits demonstrates that we still have some sort of self-confidence. Through readjustment, we can balance revenue with expenditure this year. Our Japanese friends say they do not believe balance between revenue and expenditure can be achieved by means of control. We, however, shall manage to do so. Furthermore, we affirm that in its drive for modernization China must adhere to the principle of self-reliance. It is true that China is poor, but it, has a strong point: it is relatively highly capable of surviving without outside help. Moreover, the Chinese are accustomed to being poor. The most typical example is that of the days of Yan'an when we did not have adequate food or clothing. We survived under extremely difficult circumstances in the anti-Japanese base areas at that time. Today, even if all connections with other countries were severed, China would continue to exist. Even if major turmoil and unexpected changes occurred in the world, China would endure. Therefore, the judgment that China has to look to others for help will lead to erroneous policy decisions.

According to the third viewpoint, if the U.S. government

adopts a hard-line policy towards the Soviet Union, China must in turn set aside questions such as the one concerning Taiwan. However, we simply cannot and will not do that. Should this really be the case, that is, should the Taiwan question force a regression in Sino-U.S. relations, China will definitely not give way. Instead, China will certainly make an appropriate response. We maintain that stagnation in Sino-U.S. relations are undesirable and that regression is even more undesirable. However, if something forces a regression in relations, we cannot but face reality squarely: As to what degree relations may regress, that depends on the cause of the regression. While it is improper to dwell too much upon this matter, we must be clear that if the Taiwan question causes a regression in Sino-U.S. relations, China cannot but face reality and take an approach quite contrary to what some Americans have declared. China will not simply set aside the Taiwan question out of consideration of its strategy against the Soviet Union.

Recently, an event occurred in the Netherlands, reportedly concerning a Dutch company which was prepared to sign a contract with Taiwan to manufacture two submarines. The Dutch government intervened in order to stop this. However, some members of the Dutch government were in favor of this business deal and had support from Dutch citizens. We are currently focusing seriously on this matter. If the Netherlands refuses to alter its decision, Sino-Dutch relations will definitely suffer a setback. Of course, we shall make some effort in the hope that the Netherlands will change its position, because we are aware that the Dutch parliament adopted the decision by only a narrow majority. Therefore, it is not completely impossible to reverse it. If our efforts fail, we shall then adopt further measures. We hope similar events will not occur between China and the United States. Since Sino-U.S. and Sino-Japanese relations were normalized after settling the issue of recognizing Taiwan as part of China's territory, this remains the key issue determining whether or not Sino-U.S. relations, Sino-Japanese relations and China's ties with other countries will continue to develop.

We have noted that some people say that Mr. Reagan will send a private representative to Taiwan. Today I shall put it frankly that if this does take place, we shall not interpret this as a matter of sending a private representative, but rather as the establishment of a formal intergovernmental relationship. If this or similar events occur, we shall definitely consider it a policy decision of the U.S. government, that it has deviated from the principles as defined in the Communiqué on the Establishment of Sino-U.S. Diplomatic Relations and the Shanghai Communiqué. The nature of such events will mean not only stagnation but also a regression in Sino-U.S. relations.

According to the fourth viewpoint, the ideology the Chinese government follows is designed to destroy governments such as that of the United States. This concept is neither of the 1970s nor of the 1980s, but rather a viewpoint prevalent prior to the 1960s.

I reiterate that we sincerely hope Sino-U.S. relations will not stagnate, but will continue to develop. We pay close attention to the speeches given by a President both during the election campaign and prior to his assumption of office, and we formulate a certain understanding according to these speeches. However, we shall attach great importance to the actions taken by a new administration after it assumes office. What I have just said represents the official position of the Chinese government. I deem it highly important and necessary to let our American friends clearly understand the position of the Chinese government.[59]

Deng Xiaoping expressed China's commitment to peaceful coexistence in the following terms in August 1982 in a talk with the Secretary General of the United Nations:

> China is aware of its responsibilities as a permanent member of the Security Council of the United Nations. First China adheres to principles. Second, China means what it says. ... China's foreign policy can be summed up in three sentences. First, we oppose hegenonism. Second, we safeguard world peace. Third, we are eager to strengthen unity and cooperation, or what might be termed 'union and cooperation' with other Third World countries. The reason I lay special emphasis on the Third World is that opposition to hegemonism and safeguarding world peace are of special significance to the Third World. Who are the victims of hegemonism? Is it the United States or the Soviet Union? No, it is the United States and the Soviet Union

that practice hegemonism, so they are not the victims. Neither are developed countries such as Japan, Canada, and countries in Europe and Oceania the victims. Eastern Europe suffers a little. If world peace is disrupted, who will be the first to become victims? Actually, there has been no peace since the end of World War II. Although no major wars have been fought, minor ones have continued. Where are the minor wars fought? In the Third World. It is the superpowers that practice hegemonism and sow discord. They are the ones with their hands in that arena. For many years, the superpowers have cashed in on conflicts between the Third World countries, in order to achieve their objectives. Although the Third World itself faces various problems, it is the Third World countries and their peoples that become the real victims. For this reason it must be the Third World that is the genuine and primary force for safeguarding world peace...[60]

To a delegation from the Center for Strategic and International Studies of Georgetown University, Deng Xiaoping said:

> There are many disputes in the world, and we must find ways to solve them. Over the years I have been considering how those disputes could be solved by peaceful means, rather than by war. The plan we have proposed for reunifying the mainland with Taiwan is fair and reasonable. After reunification, Taiwan can go on practicing capitalism while the mainland maintains socialism, all within the same unified China. One China, two systems. The same approach will be applied to the Hong Kong question – one China – two systems. But Hong Kong is different from Taiwan in that there is a free port.
>
> I think this is a sensible solution to many similar disputes in the world. If opposing sides are locked in stalemate, sooner or later they will come to conflict, even armed conflict. If war is to be averted, the only alternative is an approach like the one I have just mentioned, an approach the people will accept. It can help stabilize the situation, and for a long time too, and is harmful to neither side. Since you specialize in international issues, I hope you will have a better understanding of our proposal for the solution of the Hong Kong and Taiwan questions and make

a study of it. Anyhow, we must find a way out of this impasse.

I have also considered the possibility of resolving certain territorial disputes by having the countries concerned jointly develop the disputed areas before discussing the question of sovereignty. New approaches should be sought to solve such problems according to realities.[61]

Deng Xiaoping expressed China's peaceful coexistence commitment in the following termssaid in October 1984 to the President of Myanmar:

> There are two outstanding issues in the world today. One is the question of peace, the other the relationship between North and South. We find many other problems too, but none of them has the same overall, global, strategic significance as these two. In the present-day world the North is developed and rich while the South is underdeveloped and poor. And relatively speaking, the rich are getting richer and the poor poorer. The South wants to shake off its poverty and backwardness, and the North needs a developed South. For where can the North find a market for its products if the South remains underdeveloped? The biggest problems facing the developed capitalist countries are the pace of their progress and continued development. In this connection, there is another side to South-South cooperation.
>
> The Five Principles of Peaceful Coexistence provide the best way to handle the relations between nations. Other ways – thinking in term of 'the socialist community,' 'bloc politics' or 'spheres of influence,' for example – lead to conflict, heightening international tension. Looking at the history of international relations, we find that the Five Principles of Peaceful Coexistence have a potentially wide application.
>
> We could take the idea a step further. These principles could probably help solve some of a country's internal problems as well. The 'one country, two systems' model, which we have proposed, in accordance with Chinese realities, to reunify the nation, is likewise an embodiment of peaceful coexistence. To settle the Hong Kong question, we are allowing Hong Kong to keep its capitalist system unchanged for 50 years. The same principle holds true for Taiwan. And since Taiwan is different

from Hong Kong, it may also retain its army....

The question of Taiwan is the main obstacle to better relations between China and the United States, and it might even develop into a crisis between the two nations. If the 'one country, two systems' approach is adopted, not only would China be reunified, but the interests of the United States would remain unimpaired. There is a group of people in the United States today who, carrying on the 'Dulles doctrine,' regard Taiwan as a US. aircraft carrier or a territory within the U.S. sphere of influence. Once the Taiwan question was solved through peaceful coexistence, the issue would be defused and these people would shed their illusions accordingly. That would be a very good thing for the peace and stability of the Pacific region and of the rest of the world.[62]

Deng Xiaoping expressed China's peaceful coexistence commitment in the following terms in December 1984 to the Prime Minister of England, Margaret Thatcher:

> In reaching an agreement on the question of Hong Kong, the leaders of our two countries have done something highly significant for our countries and peoples. This problem has lasted for a century and a half. As long as it remained unsolved, it casts a shadow over the relations between us. Now that the shadow has been lifted, a bright prospect has opened up for cooperation between our two countries and friendly contact between our two peoples.
>
> If the concept of "one country, two systems" has international significance, that should be attributed to Marxist dialectical materialism and historical materialism or, in the words of Chairman Mao Zedong, to the principle of seeking truth from facts. This concept was formulated on the basis of China's realities. The practical problem confronting China was how to settle the questions of Hong Kong and Taiwan. There were only two possible ways: one was peaceful, the other non-peaceful. To settle the Hong Kong question peacefully, we had to take into consideration the actual conditions in Hong Kong, in China and in Great Britain. In other words, the way in which we settled the question had to be acceptable to all three parties.

If we had wanted to achieve reunification by imposing socialism on Hong Kong, not all three parties would have accepted it. And reluctant acquiescence by some parties would only have led to turmoil. Even if there had been no armed conflict, Hong Kong would have become a bleak city with a host of problems, and that is not something we would have wanted. So the only solution to the Hong Kong question that would be acceptable to all three parties was the "one country, two systems" arrangement, under which Hong Kong would be allowed to retain its capitalist system and its status as a free port and a financial centre. There was no alternative. The idea of "one country, two systems" had first been suggested not in connection with Hong Kong but in connection with Taiwan. The nine principles concerning the Taiwan question, as proposed by Ye Jianying, Chairman of the Standing Committee of the National People's Congress, on the eve of National Day in 1981, were not summed up in the formula "one country, two systems", but that is in fact what they meant.19 And when the Hong Kong question was put on the table two years ago, we presented the idea in those terms.

When this idea was put forward, it was considered a new formulation, one that had never been offered by our predecessors. Some people doubted that it would work. They will have to be convinced by the facts. It seems to have worked so far. The Chinese, at least, think it works, because the negotiations of the past two years have proved that it does. This concept of "one country, two systems" has played a very important, if not decisive, role in the settlement of the Hong Kong question. It has been accepted by all three parties. Its viability will have been further demonstrated 13 years from now and 50 years after that. Some people are worried whether China will abide by the agreement once it has been signed. Your Excellency and the other British friends present here and people all over the world may be sure that China will always keep its promises.

A Japanese friend once asked me: Why do you specify a further period of 50 years? Why do you need to keep Hong Kong's current capitalist system unchanged for 50 years after 1997? What is the basis for this proposal? Do you have any particular reason in mind? I answered that we had, that this proposal too was based on China's realities. China has set itself the ambitious goal of quadrupling its GNP in two decades—that is, by the end of this century—and of reaching a level of comparative prosperity. But even then, China will still not be a wealthy or developed country. So that is only our first ambitious goal. It will take another 30 to 50 years after that for China to become a truly developed country, to approach—not surpass—the developed countries. If we need to follow the policy of opening China to the rest of the world until the end of this century, then 50 years later, when we are approaching the level of the developed countries, we shall have even more reason to follow it. If we departed from it, we could not accomplish anything. It is in China's vital interest to keep Hong Kong prosperous and stable. When we gave the figure of 50 years, we were not speaking casually or on impulse but in consideration of the realities in China and of our need for development. Similarly, we need a stable Taiwan for the rest of this century and the first half of the next. Taiwan is a part of China. China can have two systems within one and the same country. That is what we had in mind when we formulated our state policy. If people understand our fundamental viewpoint and the basis on which we have put forward this concept and established this policy, they will be convinced that we are not going to change it. I also explained to the Japanese friend that if the open policy remains unchanged in the first half of the next century, it will be even less likely to change in the 50 years after that, because then China will have more economic exchanges with other countries, and all countries will be more interdependent and inseparable.

I should also like to ask the Prime Minister to make it clear to the people of Hong Kong and of the rest of the world that the concept of "one country, two systems" includes not only capitalism but also socialism, which will be firmly maintained on the mainland of China, where one billion people live. There are one billion people on the mainland, approximately 20 million on Taiwan and 5.5 million in Hong Kong. The problem arises of how to handle relations between such widely divergent numbers. The fact that one billion people, the overwhelming majority in a vast area, live under socialism is the indispensable precondition that enables us to allow capitalism in these small, limited areas at our side. We believe the existence of capitalism in limited areas will actually be conducive to the development of socialism. We have opened some 20 cities to the outside world, on condition that the socialist economy remains predominant there. These cities will not change their socialist nature. On the contrary, the policy of opening to the outside world will favor the growth of the socialist economy there.[63]

Deng Xiaoping expressed China's peaceful coexistence commitment in the following terms in March 1985 in a speech to a delegation for the Japanese Chamber of Commerce and Industry:

> Different people may have different attitudes towards the development of China. They analyze this question from different standpoints, depending on whether they think China's development will or will not be in their own interest. I should like to examine this question from two points of view, one political, the other economic.
>
> From the political point of view, there is one thing that I can state clearly and positively, and that is that China seeks to preserve world peace and stability, not to destroy them. The stronger China grows, the better the chances are for preserving world peace. Some people used to regard China as a war-like country. In reply to that view, not only I but also other Chinese leaders, including the late Chairman Mao Zedong and Premier Zhou Enlai, have stated on many occasions that China desires peace more than anything else. In the days when Chairman Mao and Premier Zhou were leading the country, China was already strongly opposed to superpower hegemony, regarding it as the source of war, by which we meant not local war but potential world war. Only the two superpowers have the capacity to launch world war, while the other countries, such as China, Japan and the European countries, are not in a position to do so. It follows that opposing superpower hegemony means preserving world peace. Since the downfall of the Gang of Four, we too have made it a state policy to oppose superpower hegemony and keep world peace.
>
> Generally speaking, the forces for world peace are growing, but the danger of war still exists. Not much progress has been made in the talks on control of nuclear arms and of weapons in outer space. That's why for many years we emphasized the dan-

ger of war. Recently, however, there have been some changes in our views. We now think that although there is still the danger of war, the forces that can deter it are growing, and we find that encouraging. The Japanese people do not want war, nor do the people of Europe. The Third World countries, including China, hope for national development, and war will bring them nothing good. The growing strength of the Third World—and of the most populous country, China, in particular is an important factor for world peace. So from the point of view a stronger China will help promote peace and stability in the Asia- Pacific region and in the rest of the world as well.

Some people are talking about the international situation in terms of a big triangle. Frankly, the China angle is not strong enough. China is both a major country and a minor one. When we say it is a major country, we mean it has a huge population and a vast territory, although it has more mountains than arable land. But at the same time, China is a minor country, an underdeveloped or developing country. It is a minor one in terms of its ability to safeguard peace and deter war. When China is fully developed, that ability will be greatly enhanced. I can say with certainty that, as I once told Mr. Masayoshi Ohira, by the end of the century China will have quadrupled its gross national product and reached a level of comparative prosperity. When that time comes, China will surely play a bigger role in maintaining world peace and stability.

From the economic point of view, the two real issues confronting the world today, issues of global strategic significance, are first, peace, and second, economic development. The first involves East-West relations, while the second involves North-South relations. In short, countries in the East, West, North and South are all involved, but the North-South relations are the key question. What problems will the developed countries, such as Japan and the countries in Europe and North America, be faced within their continued development? You will have to seek outlets for your capital and expand your trade and markets. Unless these problems are solved, the growth of the developed countries can only be very limited in the long run. I have discussed this question with many Japanese friends and also with friends from Europe and the United States. They have been preoccupied with it too. There are more than 4 billion people in the world today, about three quarters of whom live in the Third World. The other quarter—about 1.1 or 1.2 billion —live in the developed countries, including the Soviet Union, countries in Eastern Europe (which cannot be regarded as fully developed), in Western Europe and in North America, and Japan, Australia and New Zealand. It is not likely these developed nations, with a combined population of only 1.1 -or 1.2 billion, can continue to grow while the developing countries, with a combined population of more than 3 billion, remain in poverty. Of course, some Third World countries are becoming more prosperous, but they cannot yet be considered developed. And many others are still extremely poor. Unless their economic problems are solved, it will be hard for all the Third World countries to develop and for the developed countries to advance the total volume of even so large a country as China was only US$50 billion last year. If China could double that figure, making it $100 billion, the world market would be expanded, wouldn't it? If China could quadruple that figure, making it $200 billion, it would have even more exchanges with other countries. Foreign trade involves both import and export. With a quadrupled volume of foreign trade China would be able to absorb more foreign capital and products. Some developed countries are worried that if China were fully developed and expanded its exports that would adversely affect their own exports. I agree that it would create competition. But with all their advanced technology and first-rate products, what do the developed countries have to fear? In short, if the countries in the South are not duly developed, the countries in the North will find only very limited outlets for their capital and products; indeed, if the South remains poor, the North will find no outlets at all. So, I think the decision of Japanese entrepreneurs to take a positive attitude towards economic and technological cooperation with China is of strategic importance.[64]

Deng Xiaoping expressed China's peaceful coexistence commitment in the following terms in June 1985 in a speech to an enlarged meeting of the Military Commission of the Central Committee of the CPC:

At this important meeting I should like to say a few words first about troop reduction. We are determined to reduce the People's Liberation Army by one million men. This bears witness to the strength and confidence of the Chinese Communist Party, the Chinese government and the Chinese people. It shows that the People's Republic of China, with a population of one billion, is willing to take concrete actions to help maintain world peace. In fact, reducing the army by one million men will not weaken but enhance its combat effectiveness. Even if the world situation deteriorates, this reduction will still have been necessary – indeed, all the more necessary. As we said before, if we don't cut back the overstaffed army units, in wartime it will be difficult for us to disperse them, let alone to command the troops. But if we do cut back, it will be hard to find jobs for several hundred thousand demobilized army cadres. At the group discussion Comrade Yang Shagkun raised this problem, and we have to find a solution to it. This meeting has been going on successfully, and we have reached a consensus. I think there are no differing opinions on this subject. That shows that our comrades from the army approach problems by taking into consideration the overall interests and the situation both at home and abroad.

Today I should like to speak mainly about the international situation. China's international status and our foreign policy... since the Third Plenary Session of the Party's Eleventh Central Committee, we have made two important changes in our assessment of the international situation and in our foreign policy.

The first change is in our understanding of the question of war and peace. We use to believe that war was inevitable and imminent. Many of our policy decisions were based on this belief, including the decision to disperse production projects in three lines, locating some of them in the mountains and concealing others in caves. In recent years, after careful analysis of the situation, we have come to believe that only the two superpowers, the Soviet Union and the United States, are in a position to launch world war. But neither dares do so yet. First, these two countries have atomic bombs and many conventional weapons and the military strength to destroy each other. They cannot exterminate mankind, but I am afraid they can cause untold destruction. So neither one dares to be the first to launch a war. Second, these two countries are striving for global strategic deployment but have suffered setbacks and met with failures, so neither dares to start a war. At the same time, they are engaging in an arms race, so there is still a danger of world war.

However, the world forces for peace are growing faster than the forces for war. The forces for peace are first of all, the Third World, to which China belongs. The people of the Third World, which account for three fourths of the world population, do not want war. The forces for peace also include developed countries other than the United States and the Soviet Union. If a world war breaks out, they will not let themselves be dragged into it. In fact, the American and Soviet peoples themselves do not support war. The world is vast and complex, but if you analyze the situation you will find there are only a few people who support war; most people want peace.

We should also recognize that the new revolution in science and technology all over the world is developing vigorously and that economic strength, science and technology play an outstanding role in worldwide competition. Neither the United States and the Soviet Union, nor the other developed countries, nor the developing countries can afford to ignore this. Thus we can conclude that it is possible that there will be no large-scale war for a fairly long time to come and that there is hope of maintaining world peace. In short, after analyzing the general trend in the world and the environment around us, we have changed our view that the danger of war is imminent.

The second change is in our foreign policy. In view of the threat of Soviet hegemonism, over the years we formed a strategic line of defense – a line stretching from Japan to Europe to the United States. Now we have altered our strategy, and this represents a major change. People around the world are talking about the big triangle composed of the Soviet Union, the United States and China. We don't put it that way, because we have a sober estimate of our own strength, but we do believe that China has considerable influence in international affairs. We pursue a correct, independent diplomatic line and foreign policy, opposing hegemonism and safeguarding world peace. We side firmly with the forces that stand for peace and oppose those that stand for hegemonism and war. So China's development represents the development of the forces for peace and against war. It is important for us to be seen as part of those forces, and indeed, that is the role we want to play. In accordance with our independent foreign policy of peace, we have improved our relations with the United States and with the Soviet Union. China will not play the card of another country and will not allow another country to play the China card, and we mean what we say. This will enhance China's international status and enable us to have more influence in international affairs.

In short, we have made two major changes: in our assessment of the international situation and in our foreign policy. Now we can see that we were correct to make these changes and that they are beneficial to us. So long as we persist in the new assessment and the new policy, we can concentrate without fear on the drive for modernization. We shall continue to rely on ourselves, but we shall also follow the policy of opening up and taking advantage of the peaceful international environment to absorb as many useful things as possible from other countries. That will help accelerate our development.

Finally, I want to add one more point. We are all concerned about building the army and modernizing its equipment, and this also has an important bearing on the overall situation. The four modernizations include the modernization of defense. Without that modernization there would be only three agriculture, industry, and science and technology. But the four modernizations should be achieved in order of priority. Only when we have a good economic foundation will it be possible for us to modernize the army's equipment. So we must wait patiently for a few years. I am certain that by the end of the century we can surpass the goal of quadrupling the GNP. At that time, when we are strong economically, we shall be able to spend more money on updating equipment. We can also buy some from abroad, but we should rely on ourselves to conduct research and design superior planes for the air force and equipment for the navy and army. If the economy develops, we can accomplish anything. What we have to do now is to put all our efforts into developing the economy. That is the most important thing, and everything else must be subordinate to it.[65]

Deng Xiaoping expressed China's peaceful coexistence commitment in the following terms in May 1987 to the Prime Minister of the Netherlands:

> With regard to the international situation, it seems to me that relatively long-lasting peace is possible and that war can be avoided. Our two countries share this view. It was on the basis of this appraisal of the international situation that in 1978 we decided to devote all our energies to economic development. Without a peaceful environment, economic development would be out of the question. At the same time that we determined the policies for domestic development, we also made some adjustments in our foreign policy. We pursue an independent foreign policy of peace, a policy that helps to preserve world peace. We do not 'play the card' of any other country; in other worlds we do not play the 'Soviet card' or the 'U.S. card.' Nor do we allow others to play the 'China card.'

> In analyzing the world situation, we pay particular attention to Europe, because Europe is the key area determining whether there will be peace or war. For a very long time our relations with the East European countries were not normal. Having made an objective analysis of the world situation, we believe that the East and West European countries represent forces safeguarding peace. Those countries need to develop, and the more they develop the greater force they will become for peace. Why do we say Europe is a force for peace? Because Europe has gone through two catastrophic world wars. If there were to be a third world war, only the two superpowers would have the capacity to unleash it. And once the war began, Europe would be the first to bear the brunt of its. We are hoping for a united, strong and developed Europe. As long as the countries of Europe – I mean both Eastern and Western Europe – do not harness themselves to another country's war chariot, war will not break out.

> So we think that a relatively long period of peace is possible. If, in the first 50 years of the next century, all Europe and the countries of the Third World, including China, can make gratifying progress in developing their economies, the danger of war can truly be eliminated. We have the impression that Europe is comparatively liberal, especially about the transfer of technology; we are pleased on that score, although we are not completely satisfied. We have established the policy of developing friendly and cooperative relations with Europe including both Eastern Europe and Western Europe. That's not just for the

purpose of developing our economy but also for the purpose of safeguarding world peace.[66]

Deng Xiaoping expressed China's peaceful coexistence commitment in the following terms in July 1987 to the President of Bangladesh:

> Both our countries belong to the Third World, and we both hope for world peace. At present it looks unlikely that a third world war will break out soon. Of course, the danger of war still exists, but we can world for quite a long period of peace. If the forces for world peace grow and the Third World countries develop, world war will be avoided. The countries of the Third World should make good use of this time to develop their economies, gradually shaking off poverty and backwardness. In the past we were too sure that world war was imminent, and we neglected the development of our productive forces and our economy. Now, however, in accordance with our new observations and our new analysis of the situation, we are totally committed to economic development. Having been engaged in development for eight years now, we have achieved some preliminary results, but the road ahead is still long and we must keep to it unswervingly. I am sure China can shake off poverty and attain a comfortable standard of living by the end of the century. But it will take us another 50 years or so to reach the level of the moderately developed countries. We are therefore hoping for at least 70 years of peace. We do not want to miss this opportunity for development.[67]

Deng Xiaoping expressed China's peaceful coexistence commitment in the following terms in December 1988 with the Prime Minister of India:

> Under the present favorable and peaceful international circumstances, China and India have a common responsibility to mankind—to develop. Why so? Because together our two countries have a population of 1.8 billion, or more than one-third of the world's total.

There are two major issues in the world today: one is peace and the other is development. There is hope of peace, but the problem of development has not yet been solved. People are saying that the North-South question is very serious. I think it is only a question of development. In talking with foreign friends I have said on many occasions that we should look at this problem in terms of the development of mankind as a whole. As things stand, only one-quarter of the present world population lives in developed countries, while the other three-quarters are in the developing or so-called underdeveloped countries. Although the international community has talked for years about the need to settle the North-South question, the gap between countries in the two hemispheres is not narrowing but constantly widening. Most of the three quarters of the world population live in China and India.

In recent years people have been saying that the next century will be the century of Asia and the Pacific, as if that were sure to be the case. I disagree with this view. If we exclude the United States, the only countries in the Asia-Pacific region that are relatively developed are Japan, the "four little dragons", 101 Australia and New Zealand, with a total population of at most 200 million. Even if we include in the region the far eastern part of the Soviet Union and the West of the United States and Canada, the population is still only about 300 million. But the population of China and India adds up to a billion. Unless those two countries are developed, there will be no Asian century. No genuine Asia-Pacific century or Asian century can come until China, India and other neighboring countries are developed. By the same token, there could be no Latin-American century without a developed Brazil. We should therefore regard the problem of development as one that concerns all mankind and study and solve it on that level. Only thus will we recognize that it is the responsibility not just of the developing countries but also of the developed countries.

History has shown that it is precisely the richer countries that are the less generous. In the final analysis, we have to depend on ourselves to develop and lift ourselves out of poverty. However, while relying on our own efforts, we should not close our doors but seek friends everywhere. China welcomes cooperation with developed countries, and we should also be happy to see cooperation between developing countries. This last is very important. In particular, the developing countries with large populations should have good policies in this respect. China is now carrying out the policies of reform and opening to the outside world and will strive to become developed in 50 to 70 years. If China and India are developed, we can say that we have made our contributions to mankind. It is precisely for this great goal that the Chinese government has suggested that all developing countries should improve relations and increase cooperation with each other. China and India in particular should do so. That is the view of our government.

The general world situation is changing, and every country is thinking about appropriate new policies to establish a new international order. Hegemonism, bloc politics and treaty organizations no longer work. Then what principle should we apply to guide the new international relations? I have talked about this matter recently with some foreign leaders and friends. Two things have to be done at the same time. One is to establish a new international political order; the other is to establish a new international economic order. With regard to the latter, I spent a long time on the subject when I spoke at the United Nations General Assembly in 1974. We have been talking about it all along, and we shall go on talking about it.

As for a new international political order, I think the "Five Principles of Peaceful Coexistence," initiated by China and India, can withstand all tests. These principles, established by Premier Zhou Enlai and Prime Minister Nehru, are very clear and simple. We should take them as norms for international relations. If we want to recommend these principles as a guide to the international community, first of all, we should follow them in our relations with each other and with our other neighbors. So far as we ourselves are concerned, our two countries should make some readjustments in relations with our neighbors. I am suggesting we do this; please consider it, Your Excellency. It would be an extraordinary thing, which many people would disapprove of. But if we act wisely and adopt a bold strategy, we can surely accomplish it. First of all, let us see to it that the Five Principles of Peaceful Coexistence are reflected in the press communiqué about the visit of Your Excellency.

The world is changing, so people's minds have to change

with it. Because of mistakes made in the past, especially during the "cultural revolution," we have wasted about twenty years when we could have been building our country. After the downfall of the Gang of Four, everything has been changing here in China too. For example, we have changed from taking class struggle as the central task to concentrating on modernization, we have changed from stagnation and a closed-door policy to reform and a policy of opening to the outside world, and we are carrying out all sorts of reforms. I think your country will also encounter this problem of change. Development means change; without change, there can be no development.[68]

Deng Xiaoping expressed China's peaceful coexistence commitment in the following terms in May 1989 in a talk with the leader of the Soviet Union Mikhail Gorbachev:

The Chinese people sincerely hope that Sino-Soviet relations will improve. I suggest that we take this opportunity to declare that henceforth our relations will return to normal.... The purpose of our meeting is to put the past behind us and open up a new era. By putting the past behind us, I mean ceasing to talk about it and focusing on the future. However, I am afraid it is no good for us just to keep silent about the past. We have to make our views clear. I should like to tell you what the Chinese people and the Chinese Party think about the past. You don't have to respond to these views or debate them. Let each of us talk about our own. That will help us advance on a more solid basis. I shall only mention two things in brief. First, how China suffered from the oppression of the big powers before liberation; second, where, as the Chinese see it, the threats have come from in recent decades – specifically, during the last 30 years.

About the first question. Starting from the Opium War, because of the corruption of the Qing Dynasty, China was subjected to aggression and enslavement by foreign powers and reduced to a semi-colonial, semi-feudal status. Altogether, about a dozen powers bullied China, chief among them being Britain. And before Britain, Portugal had compelled China to lease its territory of Macao. The countries that took greatest advantage of China were Japan and czarist Russia—and at certain times and concerning certain questions, the Soviet Union.

At various times Japan occupied many parts of our country; for 50 years it occupied Taiwan. It carved spheres of influence out of China. In the North in particular, there were Japanese concessions in many big cities. In 1931, Japan started a war of aggression against China; and in 1932, it set up the Manchukuo regime in the Northeast. 102 In 1937, it launched a full-scale war that lasted for eight years. Thanks to China's resistance, to the joint struggle waged by the antifascist Allies and to the dispatch of Soviet troops to the Northeast, in the end Japan was totally defeated. Japan had inflicted untold damage upon China. Tens of millions of Chinese had died in the war, not to mention other losses. If we were to settle historical accounts, it would be Japan that would owe China the most. Since Japan was defeated, China recovered all the places that had been occupied. The only outstanding issue is Senkaku Shoto [Diaoyu Island], a small and uninhabited island. When I visited Japan, reporters asked me about it. I replied that the problem could be shelved and that if our generation could not solve it, the next generation would be wiser and would eventually find a way to do so. To settle similar disputes, we proposed later that such places be exploited jointly.

The other country that took greatest advantage of China was czarist Russia and later the Soviet Union. Through unequal treaties, Russia seized more than 1.5 million square kilometers of Chinese territory. China was also encroached upon after the October Revolution. For instance, in 1929, the Soviet Union seized the Heixiazi Islands. When victory in the Second World War was in sight the United States, Britain and the Soviet Union signed in Yalta a secret agreement dividing up spheres of influence among them, greatly to the detriment of China's interests. That was the period under Stalin. At that time, the Kuomintang government signed a pact with the Soviet Union recognizing the arrangements of the Yalta agreement.

After the People's Republic of China was founded, it signed a new treaty with the Soviet Union. It established diplomatic relations with the People's Republic of Mongolia and reached an agreement on the boundaries between the two countries. Later, China held negotiations on borders with the Soviet Union, asking the Soviet Union to recognize the historical fact that the treaties between czarist Russia and the Ong Dynasty rulers were unequal and had permitted Russia to encroach upon Chinese territory. Nevertheless, since more than 1.5 million square kilometers were seized under the treaties, and in view of past and present realities, we are still willing to settle border disputes on the basis of those treaties. That was the first question. Spelling out our views may help solve problems left over by history and clarify what I mean by opening up a new era. So it was worth mentioning.

Now about the second question. Where have the threats come from in recent decades? Shortly after the end of the Second World War, the Chinese revolution triumphed, and the People's Republic was founded. China did not invade other countries and posed no threat to them, but other countries threatened China. Our country was poor and weak but independent. Where did the major threats come from? As soon as it was founded, the PRC was confronted with this question. At that time, the threat came from the United States. Glaring examples were the Korean War and then the Vietnam War. In the first, China sent volunteers to fight the United States. The Soviet Union supplied us with arms but asked us to pay for them, albeit at half price. In the following years Sino-Soviet relations deteriorated, and China was beset with economic difficulties. But no matter how serious our difficulties were, we were determined to pay that bill, and we paid it two years ahead of time.

In the 1960's the Soviet Union strengthened its military presence all along the borders between China and the Soviet Union and Mongolia. The number of missiles was increased to one-third of the Soviet Union's total, and troops were increased to one million, including those sent to Mongolia. Where was the threat coming from? Naturally, China drew its conclusions. In 1963, I led a delegation to Moscow. The negotiations broke down. I should say that starting from the mid-1960's, our relations deteriorated to the point where they were practically broken off. I don't mean it was because of the ideological disputes; we no longer think that everything we said at that time was right. The basic problem was that the Chinese were not treated as equals and felt humiliated. However, we have never forgotten that in the period of our First Five-Year Plan the Soviet Union helped us lay an industrial foundation.

If I have talked about these questions at length, it is in order

CHAPTER 4 WILL PEOPLE PERISH FROM THE EARTH? | 161

to put the past behind us. We want the Soviet comrades to understand our view of the past and to know what was on our minds then. Now that we have reviewed the history, we should forget about it. That is one thing that has already been achieved by our meeting. Now that I have said what I had to say, that's the end of it. The past is past. More contacts are being made between our two countries. After bilateral relations are normalized, our exchanges will increase in depth and scope. I have an important suggestion to make in this regard: we should do more practical things and indulge in less empty talk.

There is only one thing I shall have left undone in my lifetime: the resolution of the Taiwan question. I'm afraid I shall not live to see it. In foreign affairs, I have participated in accomplishing the following: we have readjusted our relations with Japan, the United States and the Soviet Union; and we have decided to recover Hong Kong and have reached an agreement with Britain in that regard. In domestic affairs, I have participated in defining the Party's basic line, deciding to concentrate on modernization, adopting the policies of reform and opening China to the rest of the world and upholding the Four Cardinal Principles. 27 What I have not accomplished is to abolish the system of life tenure in office; that is an important problem concerning the system of leadership.[69]

Deng Xiaoping expressed China's peaceful coexistence commitment in the following terms in September 1989 in a talk regarding his retirement with leading members of the CPC Central Committee:

So far as the international situation is concerned, there is a question of war. If the United States and the Soviet Union don't fight each other, there will be no world war, but small wars will be unavoidable. The current wars between underdeveloped countries are actually what the developed countries need. Their policy of bullying backward countries has not changed. China should hold its ground, or others will plot against us. There are many people in the world who hope we will develop, but there are also many who are out to get us. We ourselves should maintain vigilance. We should safeguard our reputation for acting independently, for keeping the initiative in our own hands and for refusing to be to be taken in by fallacies or to tremble in the face of danger. And under no circumstances should we show any weakness. The more afraid you are and the more weakness you show, the more aggressive other nations will be. They will not be kind to you because see you are weak. On the contrary, if you are weak, they will look down upon you. What are we afraid of? We are not afraid of war. We don't think there will be a world war. And even if there were, we would not be afraid. Anyone who dared invade China could never get out again. China has a wealth of experience in resisting foreign aggression. We would first defeat the invaders and then start reconstruction.

Another aspect of the international situation is the upheaval in some socialist countries. I think the upheavals in Eastern Europe and the Soviet Union were inevitable. It is hard to predict how far they will go; we still have to observe developments calmly. If, while these countries are in turmoil, China doubles it's GNP in real terms for the second time, according to plan, that will be a success for socialism. If we have basically realized modernization by the middle of the next century, we shall have further reason to say that socialism has succeeded. Of course, we should not boast.

There is no doubt that we are more modest than the imperialists who want socialist countries to change their nature. The problem now is not whether the banner of the Soviet Union will fall—there is bound to be unrest there—but whether the banner of China will fall. Therefore the most important thing is that there should be no unrest in China and that we should continue to carry on genuine reform and to open wider to the outside. Without those policies, China would have no future. How did we achieve what we did over the past ten years? Through reform and opening to the outside. As long as we pursue those policies, as long as our socialist banner stands firmly planted, China will have tremendous influence.

Of course, that will put the developed national all the more on guard against us. Notwithstanding, we should maintain friendly exchanges with them. We should keep them as friends but also have a clear understanding of what they are doing. We should not criticize or condemn other countries without good reason or go to extremes in our words and deeds.

That is what I think of the situation as a whole. The crucial thing for us is to avoid unrest. We have a solid foundation, a foundation laid during decades of fighting. We should pass this fighting spirit on to future generations for them to maintain, because it is our capital. What's gone on in other countries is not our business, but we should make one thing clear: in China socialism will not change. China will surely follow to the end the socialist road it has chosen. No one will be able to overwhelm us. As long as China doesn't collapse, one-fifth of the world's population will be upholding socialism. We are full of confidence that socialism has a bright future.

In short, my views about the international situation can be summed up in three sentences. First, we should observe the situation coolly. Second, we should hold our ground. Third, we should act calmly. Don't be impatient; it is not good to be impatient. We should be calm, calm and again calm, and quietly immerse ourselves in practical work to accomplish something—something for China.

Will we be able to quadruple the GNP by the end of the century? I hope I shall be around at that time to see that it has been done. The second stage in our three-stage strategy is essential, because what is achieved then will serve as the foundation for the third stage. We should build some large projects to demonstrate our confidence. With stable policies of reform and opening to the outside world, China can have great hopes for the future.[70]

Deng Xiaoping expressed China's peaceful coexistence commitment in the following terms in October 1989 in a talk with the Prime Minister of Thailand:

The relations between our two countries are a model of friendship between countries with different social systems. Recently I have said to foreign friends on many occasions that a new international economic order should be establish, so as to settle the North-South question. A new international political order should also be established that would be in conformity with the new international economic order. I have especially recommended that the Five Principles of Peaceful Coexistence, which we Asians put forward in the 1950s, be made norms governing the future international political order. It can be said that ever since our two countries established diplomatic relations in the 1970s, we have followed those principles to the letter.

There are no problems between our two countries. Or if there are, they are only the need to increase our cooperation and contacts, especially in economic development. Politically, we are working together for world peace and, first of all, for peace in Asia. No one can shake China's determination to build socialism. The socialism we are building is a socialism that is adapted to our own conditions, a socialism that helps to constantly develop the productive forces and that favors peace. Only by constantly developing the productive forces can a country gradually become strong and prosperous, with a rising standard of living. Only in a peaceful environment can we develop smoothly. China will safeguard its own interests, sovereignty and territorial integrity. It also maintains that a socialist country should not infringe upon other countries' interests, sovereignty or territory.

The world used to be dominated by two superpowers. Now things have changed. Nevertheless, power politics is escalating, and a few Western developed countries wish to monopolize the world. This is something of which we are very aware. It can be seen from the Paris summit of leaders of the Group of Seven. It was at that meeting that they decided to impose both economic and political sanctions on China, such as the ban on contacts between high-ranking officials. Will the sanctions have any effect? The decision-makers of both the United States and France have failed to understand at least two aspects of China. First, the People's Republic was established after 22 years of war. After its founding, it fought for three more years in the War to Resist U.S. Aggression and Aid Korea. Without popular support, we would not have won those wars. Is it possible that a country like this will be brought down so easily? No, it is not. Neither people in China nor those in other countries, such as the superpowers and the rich countries, have the ability to bring China down. Second, the last country in the world to be afraid of isolation, blockade or sanctions is China. For several decades after the founding of the People's Republic, we were isolated and subjected to blockades and sanctions. But in the final analysis, that did not do us much damage. Why? Because China is so huge and so populous, and the Communist Party and the people have such high aspirations. In addition, foreign aggression and threats arouse the Chinese people's sense of unity, their patriotism and their love for socialism and the Communist Party and only make us clearer in our thinking.

So we think it is not wise for foreigners to resort to aggression and threats; that only works to our advantage. Facts show that those who have imposed sanctions on us have begun to rethink what they have done. In short, the Chinese people are not afraid of isolation and will not be bullied. No matter what changes take place in the international situation, China will be able to hold its ground. I think this is the true way to understand China.[71]

Deng Xiaoping expressed China's peaceful coexistence commitment in the following terms in October 1989 in a talk regarding his retirement with former President Richard Nixon:

You are visiting China at a time when relations between China and the United States are strained. The relations between our two countries were hostile for 23 years, from the founding of the People's Republic of China in 1949 to 1972. It was not until you served as President of the United States that this situation began to change. I appreciate very much your view that, in determining relations between two countries, each party should proceed from his country's own strategic interests. I too think that each country should proceed from its own long-term strategic interests, and at the same time respect the interests of the other. Each country, whether it is big or small, strong or weak, should respect others as equals, giving no thought to old scores or to differences in social systems and ideologies. In this way all problems can be properly solved. But it takes courage to use this approach. So you were not only wise but courageous to visit China in 1972. I know that you are an anti-Communist, while I am a Communist. Nevertheless, in studying and handling problems, both of us place the highest importance on the national interest. In dealing with a major question like this, both of us are realistic, broad-minded and respectful of each other.

When trying to improve relations with the Soviet Union and

the East European countries, which had been strained for several decades, we always said the most important thing was to put the past behind us and open up a new era. Now perhaps we can say that, by the same token, China and the United States should put behind them the strained relations of the last few months and open up a new era. Frankly, the recent disturbances and the counter-revolutionary rebellion that took place in Beijing were fanned by international anti-communism and anti-socialism. It's a pity that the United States was so deeply involved in this matter and that it keeps denouncing China; actually China is the victim. China has done nothing to harm the United States. Each country can have its own views of this event, but you cannot ask us to accept incorrect criticism from others. The American public got its information from the Voice of America and from American newspapers and periodicals, which reported that blood was flowing like a river in Tiananmen Square and that tens of thousands of people had died. They even gave the exact number of casualties. The Voice of America has gone too far. The people working for it tell lies; they are completely dishonest. If the American leaders determine their state policies on the basis of information provided by the Voice of America, they will be in trouble.

We have forgiven the students, including the ones overseas, who participated in demonstrations and signed petitions. No action will be taken against them. As for the handful of people with unbridled ambitions who tried to overturn the Government of the People's Republic of China, we shall punish them to varying degrees as necessary. We cannot tolerate turmoil, and whenever it arises in future we shall impose martial law. This will do no harm to anyone or to any country. It is our internal affair. The purpose of imposing martial law is to maintain stability; only with stability can we carry on economic development. The reason is very simple. In China, which has a huge population and a poor economic foundation, nothing can be accomplished without good public order, political stability and unity. Stability is of overriding importance.

I am not saying that governments of Western countries are trying to overthrow the socialist system in China. But at least some Westerners are trying to. This can only arouse the resentment of the Chinese people and make them work harder for the prosperity of their country. People who value human rights should not forget the rights of the state. When they talk about human dignity, they should not forget national dignity. In particular, if the developing countries of the Third World, like China, have no national self-respect and do not cherish their independence, they will not enjoy that independence for long.

I should like you to tell President Bush that the United States should take the initiative in putting the past behind us, because only your country can do that. The United States can take some initiative, but it's not possible for China to do so, because the U.S. is strong and China is weak, China is the victim. Don't ever expect China to beg the United States to lift the sanctions. If they lasted a hundred years, the Chinese would not do that. If China had no self-respect, it could not maintain its independence for long and would lose its national dignity. Too much is at stake. If any Chinese leader made a mistake in this regard, the Chinese people would never forgive him, and he would surely fall. I'm telling you the truth.

In handling relations between countries, we should follow the principle of noninterference in each other's internal affairs. The People's Republic of China will never allow any country to interfere in its internal affairs. Foreign interference could create difficulties and even turmoil in our country for a time, but it can never shake our People's Republic, because under the leadership of the Communist Party the life of the Chinese people has been improving day by day, especially in the last ten years. The improvement is genuine, not a sham. Our people support the reform and the open policy, and they see a bright future for China.

I can assure you that no one can stop China's reform and opening to the outside world. Why? For the simple reason that without those policies we could not continue to make progress and our economy would go downhill. If we returned to the ways of the past, living standards would decline. So no one can alter the trend of reform. Whether I'm alive and at my present post or not, the policies and principles formulated under my guidance over the last decade will not be changed. I am convinced that my colleagues will not change them.

Some people say that we are reforming only our economic structure and not our political structure. That is not true. But we can reform our political structure only on condition that we adhere to the Four Cardinal Principles. We can't build anything if the country is in disorder; for economic development we need stability. If people are busy staging demonstrations today and airing their views or writing big-character posters tomorrow, they cannot concentrate on economic construction.

Sino-U.S. relations have a good foundation; the two countries can help each other develop their economies and defend their economic interests. The Chinese market is by no means fully developed yet, and the United States can take advantage of it in many ways. We shall be happy to have American merchants continue doing business with China. That could be an important way of putting the past behind us.[72]

Deng Xiaoping expressed China's peaceful coexistence commitment in the following terms in December 1989 in a talk with a delegation from the Japanese Association for the Promotion of International Trade:

Just as international monopoly capitalists are imposing sanctions on China, you come to visit us with a large delegation. That is an expression of true friendship. In China we have an old saying: A friend in need is a friend indeed. Although we cannot say that we are really in need, we appreciate your showing your friendship by visiting us at this time. We do not feel isolated, since the number of people who offer us sympathy and support far exceeds the number of those who impose sanctions on us.

The national leadership of our country has been shifted to members of a new generation, and it is now they who are dealing with state affairs. Reviewing the past five months when they have been exercising overall leadership, we can see that my retirement has brought no change in China's strategy for development or in its principles and policies. The leaders of this Central Committee and of succeeding Central Committees will continue to uphold the line, principles and policies that have been formulated since the Third Plenary Session of the Eleventh Central Committee. Why is it that these principles and policies cannot be changed? Because the practice of the last ten years has proved them correct. If we gave up the policies of reform and opening to the outside world, that would be tantamount to abandoning our fundamental development strategy.

Although we had made some mistakes in our work, the international climate was also partly responsible for the recent incident.10' Western countries, particularly the United States, set all their propaganda machines in motion to fan the flames, to encourage and support the so-called democrats or opposition in China, who were in fact the scum of the Chinese nation. That is how the turmoil came about. In inciting unrest in many countries, they are actually playing power politics and seeking hegemony. They are trying to bring into their sphere of influence countries that heretofore they have not been able to control. Once this point is made clear, it will help us understand the nature of the problem and learn from experience.

This turmoil has been a lesson to us. We are more keenly aware that first priority should always be given to national; sovereignty and security. Some Eastern countries, on the pretext that China has an unsatisfactory human rights record and an irrational and illegitimate socialist system, attempt to jeopardize our national sovereignty. Countries that play power politics are qualified to talk about human rights. How many people's human rights have they violated throughout the world! Since the Opium War, when they began to invade China, how many Chinese people's human rights have they violated! The Group of Seven summit meeting held in Paris123 adopted resolution-imposing sanctions on China, which meant they thought they had supreme authority and could impose sanctions on any country and people not obedient to their wishes. They are not the United Nations. And even the resolutions of the United Nations have to be approved by a majority before they come into force. What grounds have they for interfering in the internal affairs of China? Who gave them power to do that? The Chinese people will never accept any action that violates the norms of international relations, and they will never yield to outside pressure.

This turmoil has also made us more aware of the importance of stability. When Nixon and Kissinger came to visit China not long ago, I told them that if China wanted to shake off and modernize, stability was crucial. Actually I had said the same thing to other Americans before this incident. We can accomplish nothing without a stable environment. So we had to quell the turmoil by imposing martial law. If factors cause unrest emerge in future, we shall take tough measures to eliminate them as quickly as possible, so as to protect our country from any external interference and to secure our national sovereignty.

We have also drawn another lesson: that we must quickly correct the mistakes we made in certain areas. Ideological education should be strengthened. We still have to work hard. But in recent years we haven't talked enough about the need to work hard, and we haven't even done it ourselves. We haven't said much either about the need to rely chiefly on ourselves. And we have to readjust the economic order to ensure more rapid development.

Although I have retired, I am still concerned about the development of Sino-Japanese relations. After all, our two countries are close neighbors, and I have always cherished a special feeling for the friendship between us. Even during the years when Japanese militarists were waging a war of aggression against China, many Japanese opposed the war. When we evaluate history. We should take all the elements into consideration. We should remember that Japan invaded China, but we should also remember that many Japanese people, including public figures, have worked hard to promote friendship between our two countries. Indeed, there have been a great many of them! Surely not everyone will be pleased that so large a delegation as yours has come to China. However, you have demonstrated by your courageous action that the Japanese people, like the Chinese people, hope that China and Japan will be friends from generation to generation. The only way to answer those few people who are unhappy to see China and Japan on good terms is to increasingly -strengthen our friendship and expand our cooperation.[73]

Deng Xiaoping expressed China's peaceful coexistence commitment in the following terms in December 1989 in a talk regarding his retirement with Brent Scowcroft, special envoy of President George H. W. Bush and assistant to the President for National Security Affairs:

Your visit to China at this time is very important. Although there are various disputes, problems and differences between China and the United States, relations between the two countries must eventually be improved. That is required for world peace and stability. It is our common wish to solve as quickly as possible the problems that have arisen between us since June, so that new progress can be made in our relations. I have retired, and this interview is no longer part of my duties. However, you are the special envoy of my friend President Bush, and it is only reasonable that I should meet you.

China is of special international importance; what happens here can affect world stability and security. If there were disturbances in China, that would be a big problem that could have repercussions elsewhere. It would be a misfortune not only for China but also for the United States.

China cannot be a threat to the United States, and the United States should not consider China as a threatening rival. We have never done anything to harm the United States. In the 17 years since 1972, the general situation in the world has been relatively stable. One important reason for this is that Sino-U.S. relations have developed. China and the United States should not fight each other—I'm not talking just about a real war but also about a war of words. We should not encourage that. As I have said on many occasions, China cannot copy the system of the United States. It is up to the Americans to say whether their system is good or bad, and we do not interfere.

In relations between two counties, each side should respect the other and consider the others interests as much as possible. That is the way to settle disputes. Nothing will be accomplished if each country considers only its own interests. But if both sides make concessions, they can reach a good settlement acceptable to both. It will require efforts by both China and the United States to restore good relations. This must not be put off too long, or it would be damaging for both sides.

I hope that as special envoy you will tell President Bush that there is a retired old man in China who, is concerned about the improvement of Sino-U.S. relations.[74]

Deng Xiaoping expressed China's peaceful coexistence commitment in the following terms in March 1990 in a talk regarding his retirement with leading members of the CPC Central Committee:

How are we to view the changes in the international situation? Has the old world pattern come to an end and a new one taken shape? There are various opinions on this question both at home and abroad. It seems to me that many of the views we have formed about international issues are still valid. Actually, the old pattern is changing but has not come to an end, and the new one is yet to take shape. As for the two great issues of peace and development, the first has not yet been resolved, and the second is even more pressing than before.

The situation in which the United States and the Soviet Union dominated all international affairs is changing. Nevertheless, in future when the world becomes three-polar, four-polar or five-polar, the Soviet Union, no matter how weakened it may be and even if some of its republics withdraw from it, will still be one pole. In the so-called multi-polar world, China too will be a pole. We should not belittle our own importance: one way or another, China will be counted as a pole.

Our foreign policies remain the same: first, opposing hegemonism and power politics and safeguarding world peace; and second, working to establish a new international political order and a new international economic order. These two policies should be emphasized repeatedly. Specifically, we should maintain our contacts with all other countries and increase our contacts with both the Soviet Union and the United States. Whatever changes take place in the Soviet Union, we should steadily expand relations with it, including political relations, on the basis of the Five Principles of Peaceful Coexistence and refrain from arguing over ideological differences. We should continue to observe the international situation. True, there are some questions that we do not fully understand right now, but that doesn't mean the whole picture is black. We should not think that the situation has deteriorated seriously or that we are in a very unfavorable position. Things are not so bad as they seem. In this world there are plenty of complicated contradictions, and some deep-seated ones have just come to light. There are contradictions that we can use, conditions that are favorable to us, opportunities that we can take advantage of—the problem is to seize them at the right moment.

Considering the overall situation, no matter what changes may take place over the next ten years, we should do solid work to develop the economy without delay. If we can quadruple the GNP in this decade, we shall have achieved an extraordinary success. We should pay particular attention to the question of the drop in the economic growth rate. I am worried about this. If our economy grows at the rate of only four or five per cent a year, it will be all right for a couple of years. But if that rate continues for a long time, it will represent a decline compared with the growth in the rest of the world, especially in the East Asian and Southeast Asian countries and regions. Some countries have problems basically because they have failed to push their economy forward. In those countries people don't have enough food and clothing, their wage increases are wiped out by inflation, their living standards keep dropping and for a long time they have had to tighten their belts. If our economy continues to grow at a slow rate, it will be hard to raise living standards. Why do the people support us? Because over the last ten years our economy has been developing and developing visibly. If the economy stagnated for five years or developed at only a slow rate—for example, at four or five per cent, or even two or three per cent a year—what effects would be produced? This is not only an economic problem but also a political one. When we work to improve the economic environment and rectify the economic order, we should therefore try to quickly attain an appropriate growth rate.

What rate is appropriate? An appropriate rate is one that will enable us to redouble the GNP in this decade. To calculate the target GNP for the year 2000, we have to use constant, unexaggerated 1980 prices as the base and take into consideration the anticipated population growth. That will tell us how much the economy has to grow every year. Is this method of calculation correct and sellable? We must calculate honestly whether we can quadruple the GNP with an annual growth rate of six per cent. After all, the actual increase in GNP will be reflected in the standard of living. The people can tell very well what their standard of living is. We leaders can never calculate it so well as they do; their judgment is most accurate.

What I mean is that the political stability we have already

achieved is not enough to rely on. And although we have to strengthen ideological and political work and stress the need for hard struggle, we cannot depend on those measures alone. The crucial factor is economic growth, which will be reflected in a gradual rise in living standards. Only when people have felt the tangible benefits that come with stability and with the current systems and policies will there be true stability. No matter how the international situation changes, so long as we can ensure appropriate economic growth, we shall stand firm as Mount Tai.

If we are to ensure such growth, we cannot confine ourselves to handling immediate routine affairs. We must analyze problems from an overall, strategic point of view and work out concrete measures. We should seize every opportunity and make timely policy decisions. We should do some research to determine which localities have the most favorable conditions and promise the best economic returns. For example, it is of prime importance to develop Shanghai; that city is a trump card. By developing Shanghai we shall be taking a short cut.

From a long-term point of view, the reform and development of agriculture in socialist China will proceed in two leaps. The first leap was to abolish the people's communes and institute the responsibility system, the main form of which is the household contract that links remuneration to output. This system marks a great step forward and should remain unchanged for a long time to come. The second leap will be to introduce large-scale operations and to expand the collective economy, so as to facilitate scientific farming and socialized production. This will be another great step forward. Of course, it will be a long process. The township and village enterprises play an important role in the rural economy and need to be expanded and improved. But at the same time we must always pay close attention to agriculture. It is easy for the countryside to become prosperous, but it is also easy for it to become poor. If farming is neglected, the rural economy will collapse.

In short, it is still a big question whether we can prevent the economy from going downhill and quadruple the GNP by the end of this century. I am afraid that for at least the next ten years this question will keep us awake at night. If China wants to withstand the pressure of hegemonism and power politics and to uphold the socialist system, it is crucial for us to achieve rapid economic growth and to carry out our development strategy.[75]

Deng Xiaoping expressed China's peaceful coexistence commitment in the following terms in December 1990 in a talk regarding his retirement with leading members of the CPC Central Committee:

There are many unpredictable factors affecting the international situation, and the contradictions are becoming increasingly evident. The current situation is more complex and chaotic than in the past, when the two hegemonist powers were contending for world domination. No one knows how to clear up the mess. Some developing countries would like China to become the leader of the Third World. But we absolutely cannot do that —this is one of our basic state policies. We can't afford to do it and besides, we aren't strong enough. There is nothing to be gained by playing that role; we would only lose most of our initiative. China will always side with the Third World countries, but we shall never seek hegemony over them or serve as their leader. Nevertheless, we cannot simply do nothing in international. affairs; we have to make our contribution. In what respect? I think we should help promote the establishment of a new international political and economic order. We do not fear anyone, but we should not give offence to anyone either. We should act in accordance with the Five Principles of Peaceful Coexistence and never deviate from them.

I am satisfied with the work of the Central Committee over the last year and a half. I am completely in favor of the effort made at the Seventh Plenary Session of the Thirteenth Central Committee to seek unity of thinking within the Party, and I fully agree with the new five-year plan and the ten-year programme. It seems to me that agriculture has great potential for development, and we should never relax our efforts in this regard. As for steel, to meet our needs we have to produce 100 to 120 million tons a year. That is a goal of strategic importance. We should build more nuclear power stations. It's also very important to develop oil and gas fields, to build railways and highways and to protect the natural environment. To reach the goal of quadrupling GNP by the end of the century we shall have to do solid work. But if we can reach it, in another 30 to

50 years our country will rank among the first in the world in overall strength. That will really demonstrate the superiority of socialism.

We must understand theoretically that the difference between capitalism and socialism is not a market economy as opposed to a planned economy. Socialism has regulation by market forces, and capitalism has control through planning Do you think capitalism has absolute freedom without any control? The most-favored-nation status is also a form of control. You must not think that if we have some market economy we shall be taking the capitalist road. That's simply not true. Both a planned economy and a market economy are necessary. If we did not have a market economy, we would have no access to information from other countries and would have to reconcile ourselves to lagging behind.

Don't be afraid of taking a few risks. By now we have developed the ability to take risks. Why were we able to control inflation so quickly without having much effect on the market and the currency? Because we have been carrying out the reform and opening for eleven or twelve years. As we go further with the reform and open wider to the outside world, we shall be better able to cope with problems if they arise. Don't be afraid of risks: we can't do anything without taking some risks.

It is a big problem to find ways for the coastal areas to assist the inland areas. We can have one coastal province help one or two inland provinces. Nevertheless, we should not lay too heavy a burden on the coastal areas all at once. During the initial period they can just transfer certain technologies to the interior. Since the very beginning of the reform we have been emphasizing the need for seeking common prosperity; that will surely be the central issue some day. Socialism does not mean allowing a few people to grow rich while the overwhelming majority live in poverty. No, that's not socialism. The greatest superiority of socialism is that it enables all the people to prosper, and common prosperity is the essence of socialism. If polarization occurred, things would be different. The contradictions between various ethnic groups, regions and classes would become sharper and, accordingly, the contradictions between the central and local authorities would also be intensified. That would lead to disturbances....[76]

China is leading on the road of peaceful coexistence that President Kennedy recognized was the only road worth traveling. Americans sensed that President Kennedy had their welfare as his goal in his June 1963 speech. They can instinctively understand that he was searching for a permanent solution to "the most dangerous moment in human history" that he experienced in the Cuban Missile Crisis. Like President Kennedy nearly 50 years ago, Americans today must accept that America must go in a peaceful direction in the Age of Species Lethal Weapons and Science.

What many Americans have great difficulty in understanding *because of the way they look at the world*, is that Deng Xiaoping and China were sincere in implementing of peaceful coexistence President Kennedy recognized was essential. The reality is that Deng Xiaoping and his successors were able to implement peaceful coexistence, for the past 30 years.

China's success that Deng Xiaoping's policies produced are well known. But China's greatest benefit to mankind is its implementation of policies that transcend the Principles of Conflict. That feature of Deng Xiaoping's and his successors' policies is why Deng is America's most insightful foreign policy strategist.

How did China's leaders escape the flaws in human nature that lead to use of the Principles of Conflict? Deng Xiaoping and his successors are products of 50 centuries of tumultuous Chinese history. Their and China's desire for peace is sincere because of that cultural heritage. China has been able to succeed in providing an example of peaceful coexistence of societies with different systems of belief and government.

China's population is waiting to move beyond the peaceful coexistence it has created, to the collaborative partnership with America.

Doing so is the "social progress that is essential in the Age of Species Lethal Weapons and Science." Fundamental shifts in perspective priorities are not the stock and trade of conventional policy tinkering. President Kennedy's successful resolution of the Cuban Missile Crisis did not implement the conventional strategies recommended by his advisors.

The challenges of the economic, military, and moral problems America faces in the Age of Species Lethal Weapons and Science are not solvable with conventional foreign policy. Solving those problems is what we term the "new frontier of social progress".

One might thing that it is not possible for a nation to both change and not change, China has changed economically without changing its political system or cultural values. Its economic changes preserved the viability of its political system and national pride. Under Deng Xiaoping's leadership China dropped its ideological hectoring and developed economically. All America has to do is what China has done and what Presidents Washington and Kennedy urged Americans to do. That advice is the proven road to property and peace.

By changing their strategy of evangelizing American Ideals and preserving military and economic hegemony, Americans will protect the charisma of their Ideals to achieve their goal of enhancing their leadership in global security. This is "social progress" towards the realization of America's Ideals.

In the 21st century, the outcomes of the "competition" between what might be contrasted as Chinese socialist capitalism and American liberal democratic capitalism, and America and China's two and one party systems of government, cultures, and two and fifty century old civilizations will be determined by how well America and China each deals with economic, military, and moral crises. A nation that cannot adjust to changing circumstances \and emerging problems and solve them is failing to be able to sustain its success., its ideals and itself.

China was able to make the hard choices and change to a Permission Society One of the defining issues for America is whether it is capable of making these profound Doing so is "social progress".

Having examined President Kennedy's and Deng Xiaoping's recognition of the necessity of peaceful coexistence, we will now compare their views in detail, in what we term the "war mindset" and the "peace mindset."

Search for Peace in the Hope that Constructive Changes within the Communist Bloc Might Bring Solutions

We must update President Kennedy's understanding of the need for peace in light of the new framework China has created. Two decades before communist economic theory imploded, President Kennedy said that:

> We must search for peace in the hope that constructive changes in the Communist bloc might bring within reach solutions which now seem beyond us.

The Soviet Union collapsed in spite of its military authority the 20th century because its communist centrally planned economy was not sustainable. It collapsed in spite of its military authority because its economic authority imploded. China's Socialist Market Economy and capitalism with Chinese characteristics is profoundly different from the communist economy of the former Soviet Union. The Chinese evolving capitalist and socialist economic model has been progressing and reforming China and economically and therefore politically and socially stable.

America's mismanaged economy is also evolving. But America is economically and politically unstable. It has reached a tipping point and polls found in 2008 that 91% of Americans sensed they were going in the "wrong direction."

In the 21st century, China is safeguarding peace with the hope that changes might bring within reach solutions that now seem beyond American perspectives. If American capitalism and two-party majority-rule-democracy system is not aligned with the size, speed, will not be able to progress as quickly as China's system. That could eliminate the prosperity and peace that China and America need.

The Drive to Impose a Political and Economic System on Others

President Kennedy recognized that it was the desire to impose political and economic systems on others that was the primary cause of world tension:

> The Communist drive to impose their political and economic system on others is the primary cause of world tension today. For there can be no doubt that if all nations could refrain from interfering with the self-determination of others, the peace would be more assured.

Deng Xiaoping stated:

> In my recent talks with foreign guests, I never failed to assure them that our current policies would not change, that they could rely on their continuity. Still they were not completely convinced....The policy of 'one country, two systems' has been adopted out of consideration of China's realities. China is faced with the problems of Hong Kong and Taiwan. There are only two ways to solve them. One is through negotiations and the other is by force. To solve a problem by peaceful negotiation requires that the terms be acceptable to all parties. The solution to the Hong Kong question should be acceptable to China, Britain and the inhabitants of Hong Kong. What formula would they accept? A socialist transformation of Hong Kong would not be acceptable to all parties. Therefore, the formula of 'one country, two systems' was proposed

China believes its system is better for developing nations but does not seek to impose it on other nations. But under both Republican and Democratic presidents America has sought to impose its political and economic systems on other. If all nations, could refrain from interfering with the self-determination of peaceful nations, as China does, America could become China's genuine partner.

Refraining from Interfering with the Self-determination of Others

President Kennedy said:

> It is our hope – and the purpose of allied powers – to convince the Soviet Union that she, too, should let each nation chose its own future, so long as that choice does not interfere with the choice of others.

Deng Xiaoping recognized that:

> China cannot be a threat to the United States, and the United States should not consider China as a threatening rival. We have never done anything to harm the United States. In the 17 years since 1972, the general situation in the world has been relatively stable. One important reason for this is that Sino-U.S. relations have developed. China and the United States should not fight each other—I'm not talking just about a real war but also about a war of words. We should not encourage that. As I have said on many occasions, China cannot copy the system of the United States. It is up to the Americans to say whether their system is good or bad, and we do not interfere.

As Deng Xiaoping said to the Prime Minister of Thailand:

> The relations between our two countries are a model of friend-ship between countries with different social systems. Recently I have said to foreign friends on many occasions that a new international economic order should be established, so as to settle the North-South question. A new international political

order should also be established that would be in conformity with the new international economic order. I have especially recommended that the Five Principles of Peaceful Coexistence, which we Asians put forward in the 1950s, be made norms governing the future international political order. It can be said that ever since our two countries established diplomatic relations in the 1970s, we have followed those principles to the letter.

There are no problems between our two countries. Or if there are, they are only the need to increase our cooperation and contacts, especially in economic development. Politically, we are working together for world peace and, first of all, for peace in Asia. No one can shake China's determination to build socialism. The socialism we are building is a socialism that is adapted to our own conditions, a socialism that helps to constantly develop the productive forces and that favors peace. Only by constantly developing the productive forces can a country gradually become strong and prosperous, with a rising standard of living. Only in a peaceful environment can we develop smoothly. China will safeguard its own interests, sovereignty and territorial integrity. It also maintains that a socialist country should not infringe upon other countries' interests, sovereignty or territory.

China is letting each nation choose its own future and respecting the principle of self-determination. America has not been doing so.

A New Effort to Achieve World Law – A New Context for World Discussions

President Kennedy recognized that:

> It will require a new effort to achieve world law – a new context for world discussions. It will require new understanding between the Soviets and ourselves. And increased understanding will require increased contact and communications.

Deng Xiaoping said to a delegation from the Center for Strategic and International Studies of Georgetown University:

There are many disputes in the world, and we must find ways to solve them. Over the years I have been considering how those disputes could be solved by peaceful means, rather than by war. The plan we have proposed for reunifying the mainland with Taiwan is fair and reasonable. After reunification, Taiwan can go on practicing capitalism while the mainland maintains socialism, all within the same unified China. One China, two systems. The same approach will be applied to the Hong Kong question – one China – two systems. But Hong Kong is different from Taiwan in that there is a free port.

I think this is a sensible solution to many similar disputes in the world. If opposing sides are locked in stalemate, sooner or later they will come to conflict, even armed conflict. If war is to be averted, the only alternative is an approach like the one I have just mention, an approach the people will accept. It can help stabilize the situation, and for a long time too, and is harmful to neither side. Since you specialize in international issues, I hope you will have a better understanding of our proposal for the solution of the Hong Kong and Taiwan questions and make a study of it. Anyhow, we must find a way out of this impasse.

I have also considered the possibility of resolving certain territorial disputes by having the countries concerned jointly develop the disputed areas before discussing the question of sovereignty. New approaches should be sought to solve such problems according to realities.[77]

Deng Xiaoping said to the President of Myanmar:

There are two outstanding issues in the world today. One is the question of peace, the other the relationship between North and South. We find many other problems too, but none of them has the same overall, global, strategic significance as these two. In the present-day world the North is developed and rich while the South is underdeveloped and poor. And relatively speaking, the rich are getting richer and the poor poorer. The South wants to shake off its poverty and backwardness, and the North needs a developed South. For where can the North find a market for its products if the South remains underdeveloped? The biggest problems facing the developed capitalist countries are the pace of their progress and continued development. In this connection, there is another side to South-South cooperation.

The Five Principles of Peaceful Coexistence provide the best way to handle the relations between nations. Other ways – thinking in terms of 'the socialist community,' 'bloc politics' or 'spheres of influence,' for example – lead to conflict, heightening international tension. Looking at the history of international relations, we find that the Five Principles of Peaceful Coexistence have a potentially wide application.

China's Principles of Peaceful Coexistence have a broad application as a new effort to achieve world law and as – a new context for world discussions. The "One-China" policy, Two Systems approach is a sensible solution to many similar disputes among nations.

Strengthen the United Nations

President Kennedy recognized that:

> Meanwhile, we seek to strengthen the United Nations, to help solve its financial problems, to make it a more effective instrument for peace, to develop it into a genuine world security system – a system capable of resolving disputes on the basis of law, of insuring the security of the large and the small and of creating conditions under which arms can finally be abolished.

But America has not strengthened the United Nations, as its "semi democratic procedures" currently thwart America's goals.

Deng Xiaoping said in a talk with the Secretary General of the United Nations:

> China is aware of its responsibilities as a permanent member of the Security Council of the United Nations. First China adheres to principles. Second, China means what it says. ...China's foreign policy can be summed up in three sentences. First, we oppose hegenonism. Second, we safeguard world peace. Third,

we are eager to strengthen unity and cooperation, or what might be termed 'union and cooperation' with other Third World countries. The reason I lay special emphasis on the Third World is that opposition to hegemonism and safeguarding world peace are of special significance to the Third World.

The reality is that China is a responsible major power. China fulfills its responsibilities as a member of the Security Council of the United Nations with its low key leadership. America's approach to the UN does not strengthen the existing international system.

Set an Example for Others by Seeking to Adjust Small but Significant Differences

President Kennedy recognized that:

> At the same time we seek to keep peace inside the non-Communist world, where many nations, all of them our friends, are divided over issues which weaken Western unity, which invite Communist intervention or which threaten to erupt into war. Our efforts in West New Guinea, in the Congo, in the Middle East, and in the Indian subcontinent have been persistent and patient despite criticism from both sides. We have also tried to set an example for others – by seeking to adjust small but significant differences with our own closest neighbors in Mexico and in Canada.

But under its first president of the 21st century America did not set such an example. Deng Xiaoping and China are finding ways to adjust to significant differences their China's neighbors:

> Over the years I have been considering how those disputes could be solved by peaceful means, rather than by war. The plan we have proposed for reunifying the mainland with Taiwan is fair and reasonable. After reunification, Taiwan can go on practicing capitalism while the mainland maintains socialism, all within

the same unified China. One China, Two systems. I think this is a sensible solution to many similar disputes in the world. If opposing sides are locked in stalemate, sooner or later they will come to conflict, even armed conflict. If war is to be averted, the only alternative is an approach like the one I have just mentioned, an approach the people will accept. It can stabilize the situation, and for a long time too, and is harmful to neither side.

The War Mindset

Americans have published many books envisioning war with China. In 2005, for example, Constantine Menges argued in *China: The Gathering Threat,* published in 2005 that Cold War strategies adopted against the former Soviet Union should be continued against China. In 2008 Peter Navarro, an American business professor, published an update of: *The Coming China Wars.* Jed Babbin and Edward Timperlake's book: *Showdown: Why China Wants War With The United States*, published in 2006, talks about preventing war between America and China through diplomacy, containment, and deterrence. Babbin and Timperlake state:

> Our adversary, China, is either an emerging capitalist colossus with peaceful intentions or the most powerful and dangerous enemy we have faced since the collapse of the Soviet Union. China exhibits two faces to the world. One can be seen in Major General Zhu Chenghu, a dean at China's National Defense University. In July 2005, General Chenghu, speaking in the context of a conflict over Taiwan, said that if America interfered militarily in any conflict between Beijing and Taiwan, China would make a nuclear first strike on America. He also declared that China would be prepared to absorb the destruction of most of its cities in a nuclear exchange that would wipe out hundreds of American cities. At the opposite pole are the endless professions of peaceful intent that come from China's leaders, including its president, Hu Jintao.
> With nations, as with people, actions are the best barometers

of future behavior, and China's actions demonstrate hostility toward the United States. The Pacific Cold War is being fought from the oil fields of the Middle East, Africa, South America, and the Far East – where China's presence is growing – to the seas around Taiwan, in diplomatic battles at the United Nations, and in a public propaganda war. China faces no military threats, yet is engaged in a military buildup that is larger and more intense than anything the world has seen since Nazi Germany's mad dash for arms in the 1930's. This implies a similar momentum toward war. China's cold war against America will almost certainly become a shooting war within the next ten years.

China pursues war without provocation. America has welcomed China as a trading partner, but we can't close our eyes to the military threat it poses. It is a threat we must deter if we can and defeat on the battlefield if we must.

What might a war with China look like? That's what this book is about. Using a series of scenarios...we hope to illustrate how wars with China might break out and be fought based on China's history, capabilities, and intentions. The crises we portray might happen singly or together, next year or five years from now. But they will, we believe, come to pass not because they are inevitable, but because China's chosen route to power leads inexorably to them. If we can explain in vivid terms how war is likely to occur, perhaps America and its allies can find ways to avoid it thorough diplomacy, containment, and deterrence.

If war does become reality, it will be because China has chosen, clearly and decisively, to make war on America, its allies, and its interests. It will not be an accident, the result of an economic clash or a misunderstanding – and our diplomatic efforts need to bear that in mind. We believe that China has already decided in favor of war. The challenge for American diplomacy is to reverse that choice, to convince China that a war against America, its allies, or its interests will not be won quickly or decisively by China.

Whatever the participating event that triggers war – be it China's aggression against Taiwan, North Korean proliferation of nuclear weapons, or any one of a host of other possibilities – this war will not wait until the global war against Islamic terrorism is over, until America's economy is protected from the use of oil as a weapon, or until we decide our own political future in a presidential election. This war will begin when China decides the time for it has come. And unless we are very lucky, very smart, and very resolute in our preparations, it will be as massive in loss of life, and economic damage to America and the world as either of the two world wars of the last century.

To win the Pacific Cold War, we must first understand that it has begun, and that its cause is China's regional ambitions and military buildup. We do not have the luxury of finishing the war on Terror before we rise to the challenge of China. We need to win both, and there is no time to waste.

America is failing badly at making the investments it needs to meet the military challenge from China. A possible future Democratic administration – with the anti-military mindset of that party – would make matters even worse. If we are to prevail in this Cold War as we did in the last, we need to invest constantly and significantly in the future capability of our military – and in our resolve to defend our interests and counter the rise of China.[78]

The Statements made by General Chenghu, Babbin and Timperlake statements are very different from Deng Xiaoping's" Principles of Peaceful Coexistence Model, General Chengu, Babbin and Timperlake exhibit what we term a "war mindset," while Deng Xiaoping and Presidents Washington and Kennedy exhibited a "peace mindset." We understand why Presidents Washington and Kennedy and Deng Xiaoping, recognize that war has changed in the Age of Species Lethal Weapons and Science. But we do not understand why General Chenghu, Babbin, and Timperlake see benefit in the war they envisage.

The Peace Mindset

President Kennedy in 1963 saw the need for a different future than that envisaged in the conventional War Mindset. He emphasized:

I have chosen this time and this place to discuss a topic on

which ignorance too often abounds, and the truth is too rarely
perceived – yet it is the most important topic on earth: world
peace. What kind of peace do I mean? What kind of peace do we
seek? Not a Pax Americana enforced on the world by American
weapons of war.

President Kennedy's use of the Latin term "Pax" conveys the
progress of a genuine lasting peace beyond the Roman peace
imposed by weapons of war. Some see America as the heir to the Roman Empire.[69] Given American Ideals is not a flattering comparison.
The Roman Empire collapsed in part because of the consequences of
its invasion of the Arab World.

China's implementation of Principles of Peaceful Coexistence is
"Chinese Exceptionalism." These Ideals are just as profound as the
ideals of the European Enlightenment enshrined in the American
Constitution.

If China and America can live up to their ideals it will be a
unique example of exalted justice and the cultivation of harmony
with all nations. That unprecedented achievement is essential in the
Age of Species Lethal Weapons and Science.

China has been an example of its ideals as expressed through the
Principles of Peaceful Coexistence. China has been able, as a better
Permission Society than India at implementing economic development. India's "Democratic Constraint" and the vulnerability of its
economic development are examined in chapter 12 of Book 1.

China has demonstrated that its goal of a harmonious world is
sustainable. But its benefits can become multilateral if Americans
can accept a new foreign policy based on the Principles of Peaceful
Coexistence. President Kennedy's hope for a "genuine peace," can
be realized through a "Harmonious World." The American people's
ability to accept Chinese ideals is the only hope for the peaceful
coexistence that is essential to survival.

The outcome of the American Experiment will determine the
outcome of the Human Experiment. The question facing us is: Can

we be sufficiently humane to not perish from the earth? The world is large enough for the existence of "One World with Two Systems" because neither Rights Societies nor Permission Societies will accept the imposition of the other system. The One World, Two Systems formula must be accepted by America because as President Kennedy realized:

> I speak of peace because of the new face of war. Total war makes no sense in an age when great powers can maintain large and relatively invulnerable nuclear forces and refuse to surrender without resort to those forces. It makes no sense in an age when a single nuclear weapon contains almost ten times the explosive force delivered by all the allied air forces in the Second World War. It makes no sense in an age when the deadly poisons produced by a nuclear exchange would be carried by wind and water and soil and seed to the far corners of the globe and to generations yet unborn....
>
> With such a peace, there will still be quarrels and conflicting interests, as there are within families and nations. World peace, like community peace, does not require that each man love his neighbor--it requires only that they live together in mutual tolerance, submitting their disputes to a just and peaceful settlement. And history teaches us that enmities between nations, as between individuals, do not last forever. However fixed our likes and dislikes may seem the tide of time and events will often bring surprising changes in the relations between nations and neighbors? So let us persevere. Peace need not be impracticable.

One of President Kennedy's statements has become incorrect due to the implementation of the Principles of Peaceful Coexistence. President Kennedy said:

> There is no single, simple key to this peace--no grand or magic formula to be adopted by one or two powers. Genuine peace must be the product of many nations, the sum of many acts. It must be dynamic, not static, changing to meet the challenge of each new generation. For peace is a process--a way of solving

problems.

There is a "simple key to this peace." There is a "grand and magic formula to be adopted by one or two powers" as the basis of "the product of many nations, the sum of many acts." This is the partnership between America and China based on the Principles of Peaceful Coexistence. This partnership is the "simple key" achieving "genuine and lasting peace". The grand formulae are the Principles of Peaceful Coexistence.

President Kennedy could envisage in 1963 what Deng Xiaoping only began implementing in 1978. President Nixon opened relations between America and China in 1972, which allowed Deng Xiaoping to open China to the world.

President Kennedy was not able to "define our goal more clearly." But ten years before China and India defined it, in formulating the Principles of Peaceful Coexistence Today, Americans can define President Kennedy's goal more clearly as:

1. Implementing the Principles of Peaceful Coexistence in;
2. A genuine global partnership of China and America
3. Providing leadership in a new international system with combined economic, military, and moral authority to police failing states; and
4. The collaboration of civilizations rather than the clash of civilizations.

As long ago as 1963, it was clear to America's President that genuine peace rather than a "Pax Americana" must be our goal. President Kennedy's assassination the equality of the strong and the weak given the power of the weak and the vulnerability of the strong Kennedy advised America:

So let us persevere. Peace need not be impracticable, and war need not be inevitable. By defining our goal more clearly, by making it seem more manageable and less remote, we can help all peoples to see it, to draw hope from it, and to move irresistibly toward it.

President Kennedy was correct:

> Genuine peace must be the product of many nations, the sum of many acts. It must be dynamic, not static, changing to meet the challenges of each new generation. For peace is a process – a way of solving problems.
>
> With such a peace, there will still be quarrels and conflicting interests, as there are within families and nations. World peace, like community peace, does not require that each man love his neighbor--it requires only that they live together in mutual tolerance, submitting their disputes to a just and peaceful settlement. And history teaches us that enmities between nations, as between individuals, do not last forever. However fixed our likes and dislikes may seem the tide of time and events will often bring surprising changes in the relations between nations and neighbors.

Deng Xiaoping's "way of solving problems," like the "One nation Two Systems" solution to China's sovereignty over Hong Kong is a model for conflicts between Rights and Permission Societies. Deng Xiaoping's "joint exploitation of resources" is another "way of solving problems.'" If mankind can adopt such a solution it is very likely, as President Kennedy stated and Deng Xiaoping recognized, that:

> World peace, like community peace, does not require that each man love his neighbor--it requires only that they live together in mutual tolerance, submitting their disputes to a just and peaceful settlement. And history teaches us that enmities between nations, as between individuals, do not last forever. However fixed our likes and dislikes may seem the tide of time and events will often bring surprising changes in the relations between nations

and neighbors.

People must learn to tolerate other people's diversity. As China's solution to the dangers of the Age of Species Lethal Weapons and Science demonstrates, diversity is essential to our survival and evolution.

Because solving the Human Extinction Challenge is essential, the collaboration of civilizations is essential. One of the key themes of *America & China's Emerging Partnership*: A New Realistic Perspective is that a few leaders can end the Human Experiment. Books 1 and 2 address the danger that a single individual can use Species Lethal Weapons and Science. The events of September 11, 2001 were the signal of the new scope of the Human Extinction Challenge. These attacks did not use species lethal weapons or science. But such attacks are imminent and must not be ignored. The importance of the change in the power of an individual is examined in chapter 4 of Book 1. That aspect of the Human Extinction Challenge is almost too much for human minds to accept.

President Kennedy was only partly correct when he said:

> Let us focus instead on a more practical, more attainable peace--based not on a sudden revolution in human nature but on a gradual evolution in human institutions--on a series of concrete actions and effective agreements which are in the interest of all concerned.

We must focus on achieving sustainable peace, but we must also focus on "a sudden revolution in human nature" The ability of nations and individuals to perpetrate species lethal attacks makes "a gradual evolution in human institutions" too slow to solve the Human Extinction Challenge.

New policy goals based on the Principles of Peaceful Coexistence are a necessary, but not sufficient means by which to solve the Human Extinction Challenge. A sudden evolution in human nature is also essential. That is why the Manhattan II Project is, examined in chapter 6 of Book 1.

The Challenge of Ensuring that America Can Sustain Itself Economically, Militarily and Morally

"Gradual evolutions in human institutions" are exemplified in the incremental social progress that has occurred among the Chinese as a result of Deng Xiaoping's leadership in a single-party state. In 1978 China faced the type of choices that America now faces. It was obvious to the Chinese that their economy was not working. They had to reform their economic system and put aside aspirations for hegemony. America also must ensure that its economy and political system are sustainable domestically rather than interfering in other nations' internal systems.

Hard choices are *hard choices*. Perhaps it is harder for America to make these choices than it was for China which had suffered financial collapse as a result of the Cultural Revolution. Certainly it is harder for America, with its Rights Society, to make hard choices than it is for China, with its Permission Society.

It would have been extremely difficult for Americans to make hard choices before the financial crises become catastrophic in 2008. It was easier for China because heir choices sought to reform an "economic dictatorship" that was discredited by its own failure. This is easier than it is to reform an "economic democracy" that struggles due to a combination of regulatory mismanagement and excessive spending. Without extraordinary policymaking skills it will not be possible for Americans to respond effectively to declining economic conditions.

In 1978, the Chinese people achieved a consensus as a result of their shared suffering in the failed Cultural Revolution which made it evident that their economic system had to change. Now, it is likely that a similar consensus among the American people can occur. America can reform itself as successfully as China was able to in 1978.

It might be easy for Americans to blame others, rather than reform their own expectations of economic hegemony which are no longer realistic. But the changes in mindset and policy that China made were not as easy as they appear. To start with virtually nothing, as China did in 1978, and succeed sustainably does not happen by accident. Other countries have not done nearly as well such as those in the former Soviet Union.

The Chinese people produced as their leader, someone with an empathetic nature and extraordinary insight. The hard choices Americans face cannot be dealt with if America cannot produce such an extraordinary leader. Fortunately, this has happened. In times of great national crisis, America has done so, as the examples of George Washington, Abraham Lincoln, Franklin Roosevelt, and John Kennedy demonstrate.

America must elect a series of presidents who are all capable of preserving America and its Ideals. One leadership failure is all it could take for America to fail. The Age of Species Lethal Weapons and Science is unforgiving. The new American presidents must guide American policymaking, and the American acceptance of China's offer of partnership in creating a new international system is the first step. The next chapter examines the government that the American people are capable of in the context of the fundamental issue. In America, as in China, public opinion polls reported that an 81% to 91% consensus of Americans believed that America has gone in the wrong direction. That consensus is reflected in the election of America's 44th president, whose potential equals that of the greatest of his predecessors. Anticipating a partnership between America and China, it can be said that Barack Obama could be the "Deng Xiaoping of America."

The Human Extinction Challenge can only be beaten if both President Jefferson's assertion that the American people are a safe repository for the ultimate powers of society and President Kennedy's assertion that "Our problems are manmade therefore, they can be solved by man" are correct. What we term "Jefferson's hypothesis" depends ultimately on the nature of the American people and the viability of the political system indigenous to them. What we term "Kennedy's hypothesis" depends on the successful partnership of America and China and the attainment of the objectives examined in Books 1 and 2.

Leading 2008 American Presidential Candidates' Foreign Policy Perspectives

Chapter 5

What Government are the American People Capable of in the 21st Century?

Overview

All of the 2008 presidential candidates who attracted with major followings among the American people expressed foreign policy and defense strategies within the mindset of the Principles of Conflict. All of their policies focused on conventional foreign policy and defense strategy issues and none addressed the fundamental issue. Mankind will not survive unless we address and solve the fundamental issue.

America must implement the Principles of Peaceful Coexistence in the each presidential administration for it to succeed in the Age of Species Lethal Weapons and Science. This requires the genuine partnership of China and America.

American policymakers, scholars and opinion leaders must adopt an agenda suited to the reality of the Human Extinction Challenge in the Age of Species Lethal Weapons and Science. Downward economic trends threaten and increasing authoritarian trends have threatened the viability and charisma of America's Constitutional Majority-rule-democracy.

A revitalized alliance of Western democracies to counter the "ineffectiveness" of the United Nations is just part of the solution. A new American foreign policy agenda must create a partnership between the economic and militarily challenged American Rights Society and the economically rising Chinese Permission Society.

The new agenda must renew commitment to liberal democracy and prevent the empowerment of authoritarians in government leadership. To do so, it must raise standards of living for the working poor and middle class.

Competing American Foreign Policy Models in the Age of Species Lethal Weapons and Science

Jared Diamond in *Collapse: How Societies Choose to Fail or Succeed* focuses on four ways mankind can become extinct:

1. Failing to anticipate a problem before it actually arrives.
2. Failing to perceive the problem when it does arrive.
3. Failing to even try to solve the problem.
4. Failing to succeed in solving the problem.

Mankind is currently failing in all four ways. Some people fail to anticipate or perceive the Human Extinction Challenge while some do and do not try to solve it. Some who are trying are not succeeding because they have not yet defined it. The plan for solving the Human Extinction Challenge anticipates and perceives it.

We are beginning the process with a plan to leave a primitive state of mind like the Allegory of the Cave in Plato's *The Republic* to illustrate "our nature in its education and want of education." Plato wrote a dialog between Socrates and Glaucon about people who live chained in a cave all of their lives, facing a blank wall. They watch shadows projected on the wall by things passing in front of the cave entrance, and begin to ascribe forms to these shadows which are as close as the prisoners get to reality. Socrates says that a philosopher is like a prisoner who is freed from the cave and understands that the shadows on the wall are not constitutive of reality at all. In considering the following description of the Allegory of the Cave, understand that each nation is a cave and that John F. Kennedy and Deng Xiaoping, because of their respective geniuses are "prisoners" and "philosophers" who escaped their caves:

The prisoners who have been chained and held immobile since childhood: not only are their arms and legs held in place, but their heads are also fixed, compelled to gaze at a wall in front of them. Behind the prisoners is an enormous fire, and between the fire and the prisoners is a raised walkway, along which puppets of various animals, plants, and other things are moved. The puppets cast shadows on the wall, and the prisoners watch these shadows. There are also echoes off the wall from the noise produced from the walkway. Socrates asks if it isn't reasonable that the prisoners would take the shadows to be real things and the echoes to be real sounds, not just reflections of reality, since they are all what they had ever seen? Wouldn't they praise as clever whoever could best guess which shadow would come next, as someone who understood the nature of the world? And wouldn't the whole of their society depend on the shadows on the wall?...Suppose that a prisoner is freed and permitted to stand up. If someone were to show him the things that had cast the shadows, he would not recognize them for what they were and could not name them; he would believe the shadows on the wall to be more real than what he sees. Suppose further, Socrates the man were compelled to look at the fire:

wouldn't says, that he be struck blind and try to turn his gaze back toward the shadows, as toward what he can see clearly and hold to be real? What if someone forcibly dragged such a man upward, out of the cave: wouldn't the man be angry at the one doing this to him? And if dragged all the way out into the sunlight, wouldn't he be distressed and unable to see "even one of the things now said to be true," the shadows on the wall?

After some time on the surface, however, Socrates suggests that the freed prisoner would acclimate. He would see more and more things around him, until he could look upon the sun. He would understand that the sun is the "source of the seasons and the years, and is the steward of all things in the visible place, and is in a certain way the cause of all those things he and his companions had been seeing" Socrates next asks Glaucon to consider the condition of this man. Wouldn't he remember his first home, what passed for wisdom there, and his fellow prisoners, and consider himself happy and they, pitiable? And wouldn't he disdain whatever honors, praises, and prizes were awarded there to the ones who guessed best which shadows followed which? Moreover, were he to return there, wouldn't he be rather bad at their game, no longer being accustomed to the darkness? "Wouldn't it be said of him that he went up and came back with his eyes corrupted, and that it's not even worth trying to go up? And if they were somehow able to get their hands on and kill the man who attempts to release and lead up, wouldn't they kill him?"

After "returning from divine contemplations to human evils", a man "is graceless and looks quite ridiculous when — with his sight still dim and before he has gotten sufficiently accustomed to the surrounding darkness — he is compelled in courtrooms or elsewhere to contend about the shadows of justice or the representations of which they are the shadows, and to dispute about the way these things are understood by men who have never seen justice itself?" [79]

President Kennedy did not live long enough to free Americans from their cave. But, recall the advice he gave at the graduation ceremony of American University in 1963. In his "Not Pax Americana Speech-The Search For Genuine Peace Speech he said: "I have... chosen this time and place to discuss a topic on which ignorance abounds and the truth is too rarely perceived – yet it is the most important topic on earth: world peace."

Deng Xiaoping did live long enough to free the Chinese from their cave. Americans, as Socrates anticipates in his Allegory of the Cave, do not yet understand the Chinese economic development and the Principles of Peaceful Coexistence. Deng Xiaoping became the "John F. Kennedy of China" and Barack Obama can become the "Deng Xiaoping of America". Mankind's survival requires that each of us learn from the John F. Kennedys, Deng Xiaopings and Barack Obamas who are able to perceive the truth that is the most important topic on earth: the Principles of Peaceful Coexistence.

Societies do not choose to fail yet history is replete with the failure of societies. The failure of civilizations like America and China is normal in the natural order. The failure of species is normal also. But the failure of mankind occurs only once and is irreversible. Although societies rarely choose to fail, they can only succeed if they choose to succeed. Among the species of life on this planet, only one is capable of destroying itself, and only recently in history. As Deng Xiaoping provides us with a proof of in beginning the process:

> Man can be as big as he wants. No problem in human destiny is beyond human beings. Man's reason and spirit often solved the seemingly unsolvable – and we believe they can again.[80]

As we emphasize, the agenda presented in Books 1 and 2 that can deal with the realities of the 21st century requires that America not demand that other nations' political system become like theirs. It requires that America adopt the Principles of Peaceful Coexistence and eschew the Principles of Conflict. Economic strategies implementing the Principles of Peaceful Coexistence have profound authority among mankind. Those based on the Principles of Conflict do not. Societies that use economic and military authority without moral authority fail. It is easy to implement the Principles of Conflict which is why nations fail. It is unusual and harder to be an example of justice to other nations. Americans in Washington's time chose to succeed as a society. Americans in our time must also choose to succeed.

America has used military authority without moral authority

in its War on Terror. America has been using terror to fight terror. That is not an adequate approach. The American government is focused on killing or capturing terrorists, but has instead spawned them. The American people have sensed that something is wrong with the choices America's 43rd president's administration made. Fortunately, the "better angels" or good character of the American people selected a 44th president seeking new approaches. America is redefining itself with a different leader. But Americans cannot succeed unless the mindset of their conventional policies cease to implement the Principles of Conflict. No amount of even brilliant "tinkering" with America's conventional policies will secure prosperity or peace in the Age of Species Lethal Weapons and Science.

The Freedom Agenda

In May 2008 James Taub commented on contrasting American foreign policy approaches in a *New York Times Magazine* article titled "The Unfreedom Agenda" :

> We don't hear much about the propagation of democracy these days, largely because President Bush's own democratic crusade has sown so much chaos, and so little liberty abroad, and above all in the target region of the Middle East. Both Barack Obama and Hillary Clinton shy away from Bush's clarion calls. But not McCain. In the 2000 Republican primaries, it was he, and not Bush, who was the candidate of the so-called national greatness conservatives and argued for an assertive, interventionist policy. Now McCain sounds the same resonant tones that come so naturally to Bush. "Since the dawn of our republic," he declared in a speech last year, "Americans have believed that our nation was created for a purpose — the universalization of our own democratic principles. The League of Democracies would be the body through which we would advance that great mission.
>
> McCain did not conjure this idea from thin air. A number of Democratic thinkers, including Anthony Lake, one of Obama's key advisers, have proposed a "Concert of Democracies," which,

despite the mild-mannered 19th century name, also foresees free societies as the global peacekeeper of last resort. The appeal of some kind of action-oriented democratic body has grown in recent years as Russia, China and other authoritarian states have used their positions in the United Nations Security Council to block almost all proposed forms of intervention, whether economic or military, in places like Sudan, Myanmar or Zimbabwe. The logic is straightforward: if it's only the world's democracies that accept the universality of fundamental human rights, then only an organization of such states will authorize action to protect victims of abusive dictators, such as Robert Mugabe.

There are, however, several large and possibly insuperable problems with this theory. For one, many democratic countries might well refuse to join an organization of global security that excludes China. For another, such an organization would be acting only in the countries of nonmembers, which would undermine its claims to legitimacy. (What happens when the league imposes sanctions on, say, Syria, and only Israel, of all the countries in the region, gets to vote?) And finally, most third-world democracies are profoundly reluctant to meddle in neighbors' affairs, as the tepid response of President Thabo Mbeki of South Africa to Mugabe's depredations has made all too plain.

McCain's democracy talk has a "soft-power" side as well as a hard-power one. His underlying premise is that the United States has a deep national-security interest in the growth of democracy abroad. Our strategy of relying on autocrats to protect our interests in the Middle East and elsewhere has backfired, he said in his March speech; we should promote democracy abroad because "it is the democracies of the world that will provide the pillars upon which we can and must build an enduring peace." In an effort to change the face of the Islamic world, he said, "scholarships will be far more important than-smart bombs."

Of course, George Bush and Condoleezza Rice have said the same thing for years, and we are more unpopular today, above all in the Middle East, than we have ever been before. McCain seems to understand that the United States needs to re-earn the right to talk about its principles. The league itself, he said, would be an exercise in multilateralism, founded on "mutual respect and trust." What's more, he added, "America must be a model citizen if we want others to look to us as a model. ... We can't torture or treat inhumanely suspected terrorists we have captured." McCain called for the detention facility of Guantanamo Bay to be closed.

But it isn't only our audience in the Middle East and elsewhere that has stopped paying attention after more than seven years of pious talk from the Bush administration. The American people themselves have lost faith in the language of adventurous idealism. We recognize that our heroic designs have come to grief in Iraq. We see how very little we have accomplished in the Middle East, for all our swelling rhetoric. And we have learned, to our pain, that most of the world does not look to us for guidance, does not accord us much moral authority, does not even believe that our wish to propagate democracy is sincere. The national mood is retrenchment — perhaps not cynicism or isolationism, but at least a wary and pragmatic realism. A big hangover, at home as well as abroad, awaits whoever inherits the presidency.

And yet McCain may very well be right that retrenchment is not in our national interest. If that's so, the challenge that either he or one of his Democratic adversaries will face is to persuade Americans, as well as people around the world, that it is not idealism and the democratic mission that have come to grief in the Middle East, but inattention, self-delusion and arrogance.[81]

An Agenda Suited to the 21st Century Waits to be Formulated

Americans must compare their new President's agenda with the highest ideals of the American Constitution. To facilitate this, we have presented examined speeches of Presidents Washington, Jefferson, Lincoln, Roosevelt, and Kennedy and compared them with Deng Xiaoping's. With that preparation, we now examine foreign policy statements of the leading presidential candidates in 2008 because they are expressions of the American people's character.

We will never know what course America might have followed if it had been led by Al Gore or John Kerry after September 11, 2001, which is the epochal dividing line between the 20th and 21st centu-

ries in America. But we do know what course America took under
an authoritarian President of the world's sole superpower. The result
is an overwhelmingly strong desire for a new approach. One poll in
2008 reported that 81% of Americans felt America was on the wrong
track, and another reported the percentage reached 91% before the
2008 presidential election. Those were the most negative responses
that pollsters had found in 25 years. Other polls asking similar
questions found levels of distress among Americans that were at 30-
to 40-year high. The fearful mood of the American people and their
lack of confidence in an authoritarian approach is an extremely
positive sign because of their character's defining role in mankind's
success or failure in the Age of Species Lethal Weapons and Science.

America's 2008 presidential candidates' visions and the level of
support they received people are important factors in the start of the
formulation of an agenda suited to the 21st century. What we refer
to as a "military authority" approach was espoused by many of the
leading candidates while a "moral authority approach" was verbal-
ized by some. The "moral authority" approach was formulated most
by the Democratic Party's Barack Obama, John Edwards, and Bill
Richardson, who asserted that moral and military authority should
be combined in American foreign policy. No candidate among the
Republican contenders could attract sufficient support for a staying
of America's neoconservative course.

That does not mean that authoritarianism is discredited in
America. It merely indicates that the polarization of American
opinion that enabled George W. Bush to become president was
supplanted by what the *Wall Street Journal* termed "America's Race
to the Middle."[82] Chapter 2 of Book 1 examined the instincts of
authoritarian intolerance in human nature. Chapters 7, 8 and 9of
Book 1 examine neoconservatism from the perspective of it as an
example of a well organized faction From that focus, the race to the
middle constitutes the counteracting of that faction's control.

Looked at from the perspective of Benjamin Franklin's warning that the American Constitution would not protect Americans from despotic government, the American people have experienced the consequences of eight years of a government with despotic propensities. In 2008 they seem to want no more of it and to recognize that those propensities are imprudent because they lead the country in the "wrong direction."

That is encouraging. It provides some support for President Jefferson's proposition that: "I know of no safe depository of the ultimate powers of society but the people themselves." Jefferson used the word "safe" not the word "proper". That is the test: are the American people a "safe repository" for the ultimate powers of mankind? The negative reaction of Americans to the disastrous results they experienced under the *particular neoconservative government* of George W. Bush, in the *particular circumstances existing in 2008*, is encouraging. The American people recognized that the leadership they generated was not "safe". All the leading presidential candidates offered new approaches. But they were all operating within the mindset of the Principles of Conflict, of which neo-conservatives are extreme examples.

Americans' reaction in 2008 does not guarantee that under different circumstances a despotic American government is not possible. It is, after the lessons of 2000 to 2008, a clear danger to. America's new president has a mandate to sow the seeds of the too novel example of a people guided by an exalted justice and benevolence. In this chapter we examine the statements of the eight major presidential candidates, and current Vice President Joe Biden, who received less support. Several of them have a vision of such a novel example as the requirement for national security. Some did not. Some recommended that right must be united with might in American foreign policy. But others emphasized might.

Only history reveals how well Americans choose their leaders and how well or inadequately they lead. The problem in the Age of Species Lethal Weapons and Science is that a poor choice by the leader of a nation can deprive Americans of the capability of correcting mistakes. The President America selects and the choices that person makes will determine whether there is a safe repository for the ultimate powers of America.

It is noteworthy that President Washington included a question in the assertions in the advice we have focused on. He asked:

> Observe good faith & justice toward all nations. Cultivate harmony with all. Religion and morality enjoin this conduct; *and can it be that good policy does not equally enjoin it?*

There are powerful factions in America, and realist policymakers not accept that observing good faith towards all nations is a realistic basis for foreign policy. The first American presidential administration in the 21st century did not observe "good faith & justice to all nations or cultivate harmony with all." An overwhelming majority of Americans believe that the result was not "good policy." That is encouraging. But what if observing good faith towards all nations does *not* result in "good policy"? And what if the taking of President Washington's advice is does not adequately protect America's economic and national security?

The New School's perspective is that "morality authority," as President Washington defined it, and good faith towards all nations must be the basis of American foreign policy. But what if:

1. America's values and self-interest make the moral authority of observing good faith and justice impossible for it?
2. America's aspirations in the 21st century are fundamentally inconsistent with cultivating harmony with all nations?
3. Either ideology or the desire for hegemony are or more powerful among Americans than the desire for peace and prosperity?
4. Americans' wisdom is insufficient to accept that it is impos-

sible to make ideology, hegemony, peace and prosperity all priorities?

Ultimately, the temptations of self-interest, and the difficulty of doing "the right thing" struggle in human nature, and in America. We believe there is a choice Americans must make between:

1. Making America's foreign policy priorities evangelizing its ideology and preserving its hegemony; or
2. Making peace and prosperity America's foreign policy priorities.

Before examining the leading 2008 presidential candidates' perspectives, in summary the New School's perspectives are that if:

1. Americans make peace and prosperity their priorities; and
2. America cultivates good faith (which the Chinese term "the right spirit") and justice, (i.e., seeking fair treatment and giving fair treatment, which is exalted justice and benevolence); and
3. America and China collaborate in seeking to cultivate harmony with all peaceful nations; then
4. American ideology will be more effectively evangelized by the example Americans provide in living up to their Ideals; and
5. American hegemony and America's security will be sustained in an alignment with China's priorities.

The New School's perspectives are that:

1. Americans, to make their Constitutional rule-of-law and majority-rule-election systems vibrant rather than moribund in the circumstances of the 21st century, must find it within

themselves the capability of remaining a free and enlightened people that give mankind the magnanimous and too novel example of a nation always guided by an exalted justice and benevolence.

2. The Soviet Union collapsed in the 20th century, in part, because it's economic system could not compete successfully with America's capitalism.

3. If America's capitalism is not aligned with China's capitalism-with-Chinese–characteristics, then America will not be able to compete successfully in the 21st century and its economy could collapse triggering the collapse of the global economy as it nearly did in 2008.

4. Failing to align America's economic success and national security with China's also will cause the collapse of America's Constitutional Majority Rule Government, Rule of Law and Human Rights.

5. The key to the continued international charisma of American Ideals is the degree to which they produce prosperity in America.

With these perspectives in mind, consider the foreign policy agendas produced from among the presidential candidates the American people supported most.

America needs presidents able to explain what we do not yet understand and inspire us to live by charismatic Ideals rather than the hubris of American Exceptionalism.

In the essays published in *Foreign Affairs* all of the leading candidates emphasized military authority, and one of the Republican candidates also emphasized economic authority, while three of the four leading Democratic candidates and one of the four leading Republican candidates emphasized moral authority.

Barack Obama: Renewing American Leadership

Here are excerpts from the Democratic Party's presidential nominee and America's 44th president Barack Obama's essay "Renewing American Leadership" in *Foreign Affairs:*[83]

Common Security For Our Common Humanity

At moments of great peril in the last century, American leaders such as Franklin Roosevelt, Harry Truman, and John F. Kennedy managed both to protect the American people and to expand opportunity for the next generation. What is more, they ensured that America, by deed and example, led and lifted the world – that we stood for and fought for the freedoms sought by billions of people beyond our borders.

As Roosevelt built the most formidable military the world had ever seen, his Four Freedoms gave purpose to our struggle against fascism. Truman championed a bold new architecture to respond to the Soviet threat – one that paired military strength with the Marshall Plan and helped secure the peace and well-being of nations around the world. As colonialism crumbled and the Soviet Union achieved effective nuclear parity, Kennedy modernized our military doctrine, strengthened our conventional forces, and created the Peace Corps and the Alliance for Progress. They used our strengths to show people everywhere America at its best.

Today, we are again called to provide visionary leadership. This century's threats are at least as dangerous as and in some ways more complex than those we have confronted in the past. They come from weapons that can kill on a mass scale and from global terrorists who respond to alienation or perceived injustice with murderous nihilism. They come from rogue states allied to terrorists and from rising powers that could challenge both America and the international foundation of liberal democracy. They come from weak states that cannot control their territory or provide for their people. And they come from a warming planet that will spur new diseases, spawn more devastating natural disasters, and catalyze deadly conflicts.

To recognize the number and complexity of these threats is

not to give way to pessimism. Rather, it is a call to action. These threats demand a new vision of leadership in the twenty-first century – a vision that draws from the past but is not bound by outdated thinking. The Bush administration responded to the unconventional attacks of 9/11 with conventional thinking of the past, largely viewing problems as state-based and principally amenable to military solutions. It was this tragically misguided view that lead us into a war in Iraq that never should have been authorized and never should have been waged. In the wake of Iraq and Abu Ghraib, the world has lost trust in our purposes and our principles.

After thousands of lives lost and billions of dollars spent, many Americans may be tempted to turn inward and cede our leadership in world affairs. But this is a mistake we must not make. America cannot meet the threats of this century alone, and the world cannot meet them without America. We can neither retreat from the world nor try to bully it into submission. We must lead the world, by deed and by example.

Such leadership demands that we retrieve a fundamental insight of Roosevelt, Truman, and Kennedy – one that is truer now than ever before: the security and well-being of each and every American depends on the security and well-being of those who live beyond our borders. The mission of the United States is to provide global leadership grounded in the understanding that the world shares a common security and a common humanity.

The American moment is not over, but it must be seized anew. To see American power in terminal decline is to ignore America's great promise and historic purpose in the world. If elected president I will start renewing that promise and purpose the day I take office.

Revitalizing The Military

To renew American leadership in the world, we must immediately work to revitalize our military. A strong military is, more than anything, necessary to sustain peace....

We must also consider using military force in circumstances beyond self-defense in order to provide for the common security that underpins global stability – to support friends, participate in stability and reconstruction operations, or confront mass atrocities. But when we do use force in situations other than self-defense, we should make every effort to garner the clear support and participation of others – as President George H. W. Bush did when we led the effort to oust Saddam Hussein from Kuwait in 1991. The consequences of forgetting that lesson in the context of the current conflict in Iraq have been grave.

To renew American leadership in the world, we must confront the most urgent threat to the security of America and the world – the spread of nuclear weapons, material, and technology and the risk that a nuclear device will fall into the hands of terrorists. The explosion of one such device would bring catastrophe, dwarfing the devastation of 9/11 and shaking every corner of the globe.

As George Shultz, William Perry, Henry Kissinger, and Sam Nunn have warned, our current measures are not sufficient to meet the nuclear threat. The nonproliferation regime is being challenged, and new civilian nuclear programs could spread the means to make nuclear weapons. Al Qaeda has made it a goal to bring a 'Hiroshima' to the United States. Terrorists need not build a nuclear weapon from scratch, they need only steal or buy a weapons or the material to assemble one. There is now highly enriched uranium – some of it poorly secured – sitting in civilian nuclear facilities involve 40 countries around the world. In the former Soviet Union, there are approximately 15,000 – 16,000 nuclear weapons and stockpiles of uranium and pluto-nium capable of making another 40,000 weapons – all scattered across 11 time zones. People have already been caught trying to smuggle nuclear material to sell on the black market.

As president, I will work with other nations to secure, destroy, and stop the spread of these weapons in order to dramatically reduce the nuclear dangers for our nation and the world. America must lead a global effort to secure all nuclear weapons and material at vulnerable sites within four years – the most effective way to prevent terrorists from acquiring a bomb.

This will require the active cooperation of Russia. Although we must not shy away for pressing for more democracy and accountability in Russia, we must work with the country in areas of common interests – above all, in making sure that nuclear weapons and material are secure. We must also work with Russia to update and scale back our dangerous outdated

Cold War nuclear posture and de-emphasize the role of nuclear weapons....

As we lock down existing nuclear stockpiles, I will work to negotiate a verifiable global ban on the production of new nuclear weapons and ensure that countries cannot build – or come to the brink of building – a weapons program under the auspices of developing peaceful nuclear power. That is why my administration will immediately provide $50 billion to jump-start the creation of an International Atomic Energy Agency – controlled nuclear fuel bank and work to update the Nuclear Nonproliferation Treaty. We must also fully implement the law Senator Richard Lugar and I passed to help the United States and our allies detect and stop smuggling of weapons of mass destruction throughout the world.

Finally, we must develop a strong international coalition to prevent Iran from acquiring nuclear weapons, and eliminate North Korea's nuclear weapons program. Iran and North Korea could trigger regional arms races, creating dangerous nuclear flashpoints in the Middle East and East Asia. In confronting these threats, I will not take the military option off the table. But our first measure must be sustained, direct and aggressive diplomacy – the kind that the Bush administration has been unable and unwilling to use.

Combating Global Terrorism

To renew American leadership in the world, we must forge a more effective global response to the terrorism that came to our shores on an unprecedented scale on 9/11. From Bali to London, Baghdad to Algiers, Mumbai to Mombasa to Madrid, terrorists who reject modernity, oppose America, and distort Islam have killed and mutilated tens of thousands of people just this decade. Because this enemy operates globally, it must be confronted globally.

We must refocus our efforts on Afghanistan and Pakistan – the central front in our war against al Qaeda – so that we are confronting terrorists where their roots run deepest. Success in Afghanistan is still possible, but only if we act quickly, judiciously and decisively....

Here at home, we must strengthen our homeland security

and protect the critical infrastructure on which the entire world depends. We can start by spending homeland security dollars on the basis of risk. This means investing more resources to defend mass transit, closing the gaps in our aviation security by screening all cargo on passenger airliners and checking all passengers against a comprehensive watch list, and upgrading port security by ensuring that cargo is checked/screened for radiation.

To succeed, our homeland security and counterterrorism actions must be linked to an intelligence community that deals effectively with the threats we face. Today, we rely largely on the same institutions and practices that were in place before 9/11. We need to revisit intelligence reform, going beyond rearranging boxes on an organizational chart. To keep pace with highly adaptable enemies, we need technologies and practices that enable us to efficiently collect and share information within and across our intelligence agencies. We must invest still more in human intelligence and deploy additional trained operatives and diplomats with specialized knowledge of local cultures and languages. And we should institutionalize the practice of developing competitive assessments of critical threat and strengthen our methodologies of analysis.

Finally, we need a comprehensive strategy to defeat global terrorists – one that draws on the full range of American power, not just our military might. As a senior U.S. military commander put it, when people have dignity and opportunity, 'the chance of extremism being welcomed greatly, if not completely, diminishes.' It is for this reason that we need to invest with our allies in strengthening weak states and helping to rebuild failed ones.

In the Islamic world and beyond, combating the terrorists' prophets of fear will require more than lectures on democracy. We need to deepen our knowledge of the circumstances and beliefs that underpin extremism. A crucial debate is occurring with Islam. Some believe in a future of peace, tolerance, development and democratization. Others embrace a rigid and violent intolerance of personal liberty and the world at large. To empower forces of moderation, America must make every effort to export opportunity – access to education and health care, trade and investment – and provide the kind of steady support for political reformer and civil society that enabled our victory in the Cold War. Our beliefs rest on hope; the extremists' rest on fear. That

is why we can and will win this struggle.
Rebuilding Our Partnerships

To renew American leadership in the world, I intend to
rebuild the alliances, partnerships, and institutions necessary
to confront common threats and enhance common security.
Needed reform of those alliances and institutions will not come
by bullying other countries to ratify changes we hatch in isolation. It will come when we convince other governments and
peoples that they, to, have a stake in effective partnerships.

Too often we have sent the opposite signal to our international partners. In the case of Europe, we dismissed European
reservations about the wisdom and necessity of the Iraq war.
In Asia, we belittled South Korean efforts to improve relations
with the North. In Latin America, from Mexico to Argentina,
we failed to adequately address concern about immigration
and equity and economic growth. In Africa, we have allowed
genocide to persist for over four years in Darfur and have not
done nearly enough to answer the African Union's call for more
support to stop the killing. I will rebuild our ties to our allies in
Europe and Asia and strengthen our partnerships throughout
the Americas and Africa.

Our Alliances require constant cooperation and revision if
they are to remain effective and relevant. NATO has made tremendous strides over the last 15 years, transforming itself from
a Cold War security structure into a partnership for peace. But
today, NATO's challenge in Afghanistan has exposed, as Senator
Lugar has put it, 'the growing discrepancy between NATO's
expanding missions and its lagging capabilities.' To close this
gap, I will rally our NATO allies to contribute more troops to collective security operation and to invest more in reconstruction
and stabilization capabilities.

As we strengthen NATO, we must build new alliances and
partnerships in other vital regions. As China rises and Japan
and South Korea assert themselves, I will work to forge a more
effective framework in Asia that goes beyond bilateral agreements, occasional summits, and ad hoc arrangements, such
as the six-party talks on North Korea. We need an inclusive
infrastructure with the countries in East Asia that can promote
stability and prosperity and help confront transnational threats,

from terrorist cells in the Philippines to avian flu in Indonesia. I will also encourage China to play a responsible role as a growing power – to help lead in addressing the common problems of the twenty-first century. We will compete with China in some areas and cooperate in others. Our essential challenge is to build a relationship that broadens cooperation while strengthening our ability to compete....

Strengthened institutions and invigorated alliances and partnerships are especially crucial if we are to defeat the epochal, man-made threat to the planet: Climate Change. Without dramatic changes, rising sea levels will flood coastal regions around the world, including much of the eastern seaboard. Warmer temperatures and declining rainfall will reduce crop yields, increasing conflict, famine, disease, and poverty. By 2050, famine could displace more than 250 million people worldwide. That means increased instability in some of the most volatile parts of the world.

As the world's largest producer of greenhouse gases, America has the responsibility to lead. While many of our industrial partners are working hard to reduce their emissions, we are increasing ours at a steady clip – by more than ten percent per decade. As president, I intend to enact a cap-and-trade system that will dramatically reduce our carbon emissions. And I will work to finally free America of its dependence on foreign oil – by using energy more efficiently in our cars, factories, and homes, relying more on renewable sources of electricity, and harnessing the potential of biofuels.

Getting our own house in order is only a first step. China will soon replace America as the world's large emitter of greenhouse gasses. Clean energy development must be a central focus in our relationships with major countries in Europe and Asia. I will invest in efficient and clean technologies at home while using our assistance policies and export promotions to help developing countries leapfrog the carbon–energy–intensive stage of development. We need a global response to climate change that includes binding and enforceable commitments to reducing emissions, especially for those that pollute the most: the United States, China, India, the European Union, and Russia. This challenge is massive, but rising to it will also bring new benefits to America. By 2050, global demand for low-carbon energy could create an annual market worth $500 billion. Meeting that demand would open new frontiers for American entrepreneurs and workers.

Finally, to renew American leadership in the world, I will strengthen our common security by investing in our common humanity. Our global engagement cannot be defined by what we are against; it must be guided by a clear sense of what we stand for. We have a significant stake in ensuring that those who live in fear and want today can live with dignity and opportunity tomorrow.

People around the world have heard a great deal of late about freedom on the march. Tragically, many have come to associate this with war, torture, and forcibly imposed regime change. To build a better, freer world, we must first behave in ways that reflect the decency and aspirations of the American people. This means ending the practices of shipping away prisoners in the dead of night to be tortured in far-off countries, of detaining thousands without charge or trial, of maintaining a network of secret prisons to jail people beyond the reach of the law.

Citizens everywhere should be able to choose their leaders in climates free of fear. America must commit to strengthen the pillars of a just society. We can help build accountable institutions that deliver home police force, free press, and vibrant civil societies. In countries wracked by poverty and conflict, citizens long to enjoy freedom from want. And since extremely poor societies and weak states provide optimal breeding grounds for disease, terrorism, and conflict, the United States has a direct national security interest in dramatically reducing global poverty and joining with our allies in sharing more of our riches to help those most in need. We need to invest in building capable, democratic states that can establish healthy and educated communities, develop markets, and generate wealth. Such states would also have greater institutional capacities to fight terrorism, halt the spread of deadly weapons, and build health-care infrastructures to prevent, detect, and treat deadly disease such as HIV/AIDS, malaria, and avian flu....

There are compelling moral reasons and compelling security reasons for renewed American leadership that recognizes the inherent equality and worth of all people. As President Kennedy said in his 1961 inaugural address "To those people In the huts and villages of half the globe struggling to break the bonds of mass misery, we pledge our best efforts to help them help themselves, for whatever period is required - not because the communists may be doing it, not because we seek their votes, but because it is right. If a free society cannot help the many who are poor, it cannot save the few who are rich.' I will show the world that America remains true to its founding values. We lead not only for ourselves by also for the common good.

Restoring America's Trust

Confronted by Hitler, Roosevelt said that our power would be 'directed toward ultimate good as well as against immediate evil. We Americans are not destroyers; we are builders.' It is time for a president who can build consensus here at home for an equally ambitious course.

Ultimately, no foreign policy can succeed unless the American people understand it and feel they have a stake in its success – unless they trust that their government hears their concerns as well. We will not be able to increase foreign aid if we fail to invest in security and opportunity for our own people. We cannot negotiate trade agreements to help spur development in poor countries so long as we provide no meaningful help to working Americans burdened by the dislocations of a global economy. We cannot reduce our dependence on foreign oil or defeat global warming unless Americans are willing to innovate and conserve. We cannot expect Americans to support placing our men and women in harm's way if we cannot show that we will use force wisely and judiciously. But if the next president can restore the American people's trust – if they know that he or she is acting with their best interests at heart, with prudence and wisdom and some measure of humility – then I believe the American people will be eager to see America lead again.

I believe they will also agree that it is time for a new generation to tell the next great American story. If we act with boldness and foresight, we will be able to tell our grandchildren that this was the time when we helped forge peace in the Middle East. This was the time we confronted climate change and secured the weapons that could destroy the human race. This was the time we defeated global terrorists and brought opportunity to forgotten corners of the world. And this was the time when we renewed the America that has led generations of weary travelers from all over the world to find opportunity and liberty on our doorstep.

It was not all that long ago that farmers in Venezuela and Indonesia welcomed American doctors to their villages and hung pictures of JFK on their living room walls, when millions, like my father, waited every day for a letter in the mail that would grant them the privilege to come to America to study, work, live or just be free.

We can be this America again. This is our moment to renew the trust and faith of our people – and all people – in an America that battles immediate evils, promotes an ultimate good, and leads the world once more.

Few people noticed in 2006, but the junior senator from Illinois was seeking to figure out how America's and China's collaboration could work. On January 3, 2006 Senators Norm Coleman, a Republican from Minnesota and Barack Obama, a Democrat from Illinois, announced they had formed a new Senate policy group to gain better understanding of the growing influence of China on the global stage. The Senate China Working Group was created within the U.S.-China Inter-Parliamentary Group co-chaired in the United States by Senators Stevens (R-AK) and Inouye (D-HI) as a mechanism for dialogue between the U.S. and Chinese legislatures. The press release announcing the new Senate Policy Group indicated:

"It is important that all Americans, including United States Senators, get a better understanding of China on all fronts, which is exactly what our working group is prepared to do," said Coleman. "China is a rising economic and political power, and it is in our national security interest for our nations to work together while confronting our differences in a constructive way. I'm pleased to be joined by Senator Obama in this effort to strengthen America's future in light of an increasingly powerful China."

"In this era where American children are no longer just competing with other students in Chicago and Boston but also with their counterparts in Shanghai and Beijing, it's crucial that we begin a dialogue about the future of China's growing political and economic influence on the global economy and the United States," said Obama. "I look forward to working with Senator Coleman to start a dialogue about how to best shape future U.S. policy towards China." [84]

John Edward: Reengaging with the World: A Return to Moral Leadership

John Edward's essay "Reengaging with the World: A Return to Moral Leadership" emphasized the importance of moral authority in America's foreign policy: [85]

At the dawn of a new century and on the brink of a new presidency, the United States today needs to reclaim the moral high ground that defined our foreign policy for much of the last century.

We must move beyond the wreckage created by one of the greatest failures in U.S. history: the war in Iraq. Rather than alienating the rest of the world through assertions of infallibility and demands of obedience, as the current administration has done, U.S. foreign policy must be driven by a strategy of reengagement. We must reengage with our history of courage, liberty, and generosity. We must reengage with our tradition of moral leadership on issues ranging from the killings in Darfur to global poverty and climate change. We must reengage with our allies on critical security issues, including terrorism, the Middle East, and nuclear proliferation. With confidence and resolve, we must reengage with those who pose a security threat to us, from Iran to North Korea. And our government must reengage with the American people to restore our nation's reputation as a moral beacon to the world, tapping into our fundamental hope and optimism and calling on our citizens' commitment and courage to make this possible. We must lead the world by demonstrating the power of our ideals, not by stoking fear about those who do not share them.

The last century saw tremendous advances in the human condition--from increased economic prosperity to the spread of human rights and the emergence of a truly global community. But the century also brought two devastating world wars, the death of millions, and a Cold War that lasted two generations and risked the end of humanity. The new century too, will bring both promise and peril. We can look forward to incredible technological advances in communications and medicine and an expanding world economy that will lift millions out of poverty while raising the standards of living for working people at home and abroad.

But we must also prepare for a world filled with new risks: the increasing reach of non-state actors who reject our very way of life, the consequences of global climate change, and the possibility that dangerous technology will fall into the wrong hands. We can lead the world through these challenges, just as the United States led the world through the challenges of the previous century. But we can only do so if we reclaim the trust and respect of those countries whose cooperation we need but whose will we cannot compel.

This century's first test of our leadership arrived with terrible force on September 11, 2001. When the United States was attacked, the entire world stood with us. We could have pursued a broad policy of reengagement with the world, yet instead we squandered this broad support through a series of policies that drove away our friends and allies. A recent Pew survey showed the United States' approval ratings plummeting throughout the world between 2000 and 2006. This decline was especially worrisome in Muslim countries of strategic importance to the United States, such as Indonesia, where approval dropped from 75 percent to 30 percent, and Turkey, where it fell from 52 percent to 12 percent. Perceptions of America's efforts to promote democracy have suffered as well. In 33 of the 47 countries surveyed by the Pew Research Centre; majorities or pluralities expressed dislike for American ideas of democracy.

We need a new path, one that will lead to reengagement with the world and restoration of the United States' moral authority in the community of nations. President Harry Truman once said, "No one nation alone can bring peace. Together, nations can build a strong defense against aggression and combine the energy of free men everywhere in building a better future for all." For 50 years, presidents from Truman and Dwight Eisenhower to Ronald Reagan and Bill Clinton built strong alliances and deepened the world's respect for us. We gained that respect by viewing our military strength not as an end in itself but as a means to protect a system of laws and institutions that gave hope to billions across globe. In avoiding the temptation to rule as an empire, we hastened the fall of a corrupt and evil one in the Soviet Union. The lesson is that we cannot only be warriors; we must be thinkers and leaders as well.

And so as we contemplate a national security policy for a new century, we must ask ourselves far-reaching questions: Are we truly denying our enemies what they seek? Are we doing all we can to win the war not only of weapons but also of ideas? Are we battling the fear our enemies sow by planting seeds of hope instead?

This is about much more than convincing people to like us. There was a time when a president did not speak just to Americans--he spoke to the world. People thousands of miles away would gather to listen to someone they called, without irony, "the leader of the free world." Men and women in Nazi-occupied Europe would huddle around shortwave radios to listen to President Franklin Roosevelt. Millions cheered in Berlin when President John F. Kennedy stood with them and said, "Ich bin ein Berliner." Millions of people imprisoned behind the Iron Curtain silently cheered the day President Reagan declared, "Mr. Gorbachev, tear down this wall." Even if these ordinary men and women did not always agree with our policies, they looked to our president and saw a person--and a nation they could trust. Today, under the current administration, this is no longer the case. At the dawn of a new century, it is vital that we win the war of ideas in the world. We need to reach out to ordinary men and women from Egypt to Indonesia and convince them, once again, that the United States is a force to be admired.

Hillary Rodham Clinton: Security and Opportunity

President Obama selected Senator Hillary Clinton as Secretary of

State. *Newsweek* commented:

> The global response to Team Obama's nomination of Hillary Clinton for secretary of state has been largely positive, thanks in part to fond memories of Bill and in part to an "anybody but Bush" mentality. But one nation may soon find itself longing for the Bush fils years: China, long a target of Clinton's because of its economic practices and human-right violations.
>
> Clinton's focused a significant portion of her campaign rhetoric on China's economic impact on the U.S., which she says is causing a 'slow erosion of our own economic sovereignty,'…Clinton cosponsored the Foreign Debt Ceiling Act of 2005, which the senator said would 'start breaking our reliance on China'; and in April of this year, she released a plan to crack down on China's 'unfair' trade practices. She's also said she would consider a tariff on Chinese goods. For Beijing the next four years look a whole lot chiller.[86]

Senator Clinton experimented throughout her campaign with policies designed to attract the most support. Here are excerpts from Senator Clinton's essay: "Security and Opportunity for the 21st Century:" [87]

> To lead, a great nation must command the respect of others. America has been respected in the past as a powerful nation, a purposeful nation, and a generous and warm-hearted nation. In my travels around the world as senator and as first lady, I have met people from all walks of life. I have seen firsthand how many of our past policies have earned us respect and gratitude.
>
> The tragedy of the last six years is that the Bush administration has squandered the respect, trust, and confidence of even our closest allies and friends. At the dawn of the twenty-first century, the United States enjoyed a unique position. Our world leadership was widely accepted and respected, as we strengthened old alliances and built new ones, worked for peace across the globe, advanced nonproliferation, and modernized our military. After 9.11, the world rallied behind the United States as never before, supporting our efforts to remove the Taliban in Afghanistan and

go after the al Qaeda leadership. We had a historic opportunity to build a broad global coalition to combat terror, increase the impact of our diplomacy, and create a world with more partners and fewer adversaries.

But we lost that opportunity by refusing to let the UN inspectors finish their work in Iraq and rushing to war instead. Moreover, we diverted vital military and financial resources from the struggle against al Qaeda and the daunting task of building a Muslim democracy in Afghanistan. At the same time, we embarked on an unprecedented course of unilateralism: refusing to pursue ratification of the Comprehensive Nuclear Test Ban Treaty, abandoning our commitment to nuclear nonproliferation, and turning our backs on the search for peace in the Middle East. Our withdrawal from the Kyoto Protocol and refusal to participate in any international effort to deal with the tremendous challenges of climate change further damaged our international standing.

Our nation has paid a heavy price for rejecting a long-standing bipartisan tradition of global leadership rooted in a preference for cooperating over acting unilaterally, for exhausting diplomacy before making war, and for converting old adversaries into allies rather than making new enemies. At a moment in history when the world's most pressing problems require unprecedented cooperation, this administration has unilaterally pursued policies that are widely disliked and distrusted.

Yet it does not have to be this way. Indeed, our allies do not want it to be this way. The world still looks to the United States for leadership. American leadership is wanting, but it is still wanted. Our friends around the world do not want the United States to retreat. They want once again to be allied with the nation whose values, leadership, and strength have inspired the world for the last century.

To reclaim our proper place in the world, the United States must be stronger, and our policies must be smarter. The next president will have a moment of opportunity to restore America's global standing and convince the world that America can lead once again. As president, I will seize that opportunity by reintroducing ourselves to the world. I will rebuild our power and ensure that the United States is committed to building a world we want, rather than simply defending against a world we fear.

We should aim to lead our friends and allies in building a world of security and opportunity. America has long been the land of opportunity. But as we know at home and as we see today in Iraq and Afghanistan, opportunity cannot flourish without basic security. We must build a world in which security and opportunity go hand in hand, a world that will be safer, more prosperous, and more just.

We need more than vision, however, to achieve the world we want. We must face up to an unprecedented array of challenges in the twenty-first century, threats from states, non-state actors, and nature itself. The next president will be the first to inherit two wars, a long-term campaign against global terrorist networks, and growing tension with Iran as it seeks to acquire nuclear weapons. The United States will face a resurgent Russia whose future orientation is uncertain and a rapidly growing China that must be integrated into the international system. Moreover, the next administration will have to confront an unpredictable and dangerous situation in the Middle East that threatens Israel and could potentially bring down the global economy by disrupting oil supplies. Finally, the next president will have to address the looming long-term threats of climate change and a new wave of global health epidemics.

To meet these challenges, we will have to replenish American power by getting out of Iraq, rebuilding our military, and developing a much broader arsenal of tools in the fight against terrorism. We must learn once again to draw on all aspects of American power, to inspire and attract as much as to coerce. We must return to a pragmatic willingness to look at the facts on the ground and make decisions based on evidence rather than ideology.

Leadership requires a blend of strategy, persuasion, inspiration, and motivation. It is based on respect more than fear. America's founders wrote the Declaration of Independence to explain our actions to the world out of a decent respect for the opinions of mankind. Gaining the respect of other nations today requires that we harness our might to a set of guiding principles.

Avoid false choices driven by ideology. The Bush administration has presented the American people with a series of false choices: force versus diplomacy, unilateralism versus multilateralism, hard power versus soft. Seeing these choices as mutually exclusive reflects an ideologically blinkered vision of the world that denies the United States the tools and the flexibility it needs to lead and succeed. There is a time for force and a time for diplomacy; when properly deployed, the two can reinforce each other. U.S. foreign policy must be guided by a preference for multilateralism, with unilateralism as an option when absolutely necessary to protect our security or avert an avoidable tragedy.

Use our military not as the solution to every problem but as one element in a comprehensive strategy. As president, I will never hesitate to use force to protect Americans or to defend our territory and our vital interests. We cannot negotiate with individual terrorists; they must be hunted down and captured or killed. Nor can diplomacy alone stop the perpetrators of genocide and crimes against humanity in places such as Darfur. But soldiers are not the answer to every problem. Using force in lieu of diplomacy compels our young men and women in uniform to carry out missions that they may not be trained or prepared for. And it ignores the value of simply carrying a big stick, rather than using it.

Make international institutions work, and work through them when possible. Contrary to what many in the current administration appear to believe, international institutions are tools rather than traps. The United States must be prepared to act on its own to defend its vital interests, but effective international institutions make it much less likely that we will have to do so. Both Republican and Democratic presidents have understood this for decades. When such institutions work well, they enhance our influence. When they do not work, their procedures serve as pretexts for endless delays, as in the case of Darfur, or descend into farce, as in the case of Sudan's election to the UN Commission on Human Rights. But instead of disparaging these institutions for their failures, we should bring them in line with the power realities of the twenty-first century and the basic values embodied in such documents as the Universal Declaration of Human Rights.

Ensure that democracy delivers on its promises. Gnawing hunger, poverty, and the absence of economic prospects are a recipe for despair. Globalization is widening the gap between the haves and the have-nots within societies and between them. Today, there are more than two billion people living on less than $2 a day. These people risk becoming a vast permanent underclass. Calls for expanding civil and political rights in countries plagued by mass poverty and ruled by tiny wealthy elites will fall on deaf ears unless democracy actually delivers enough material benefits to improve people's lives. The Bush administration's policy in Iraq has temporarily given democracy a bad name, but over the long term the value of democracy will continue to inspire the world.

Stand for and live up to our values. The values that our founders embraced as universal have shaped the aspirations of millions of people around the world and are the deepest source of our strength---but only as long as we live up to them ourselves. As we seek to promote the role of law in other nations, we must accept it ourselves. As we counsel liberty and justice for all, we cannot support torture and the indefinite detention of individuals we have declared to be beyond the law.

Ending the war in Iraq is the first step toward restoring the United States' global leadership. The war is sapping our military strength, absorbing our strategic assets, diverting attention and resources from Afghanistan, alienating our allies, and dividing our people. The war in Iraq has also stretched our military to the breaking point. We must rebuild our armed services and restore them body and soul.

We must withdraw from Iraq in a way that brings our troops home safely, begins to restore stability to the region, and replaces military force with a new diplomatic initiative to engage countries around the world in securing Iraq's future....

Finally, we need to engage the world in a global humanitarian effort to confront the human costs of this war. We must address the plight of the two million Iraqis who have fled their country and the two million more who have been displaced internally. This will require a multibillion-dollar international effort under the direction of the Office of the UN High Commissioner for Refugees. Meanwhile, the United States, along with governments in Europe and the Middle East, must agree to accept asylum seekers and help them return to Iraq when it is safe for them to do so.

As we redeploy our troops from Iraq, we must not let down our guard against terrorism. I will order specialized units to engage in targeted operations against al Qaeda in Iraq and other terrorist organizations in the region. These units will also provide security for U.S. troops and personnel in Iraq and train and equip Iraqi security services to keep order and promote stability in the country, but only to the extent that such training is actually working. I will also consider leaving some forces in the Kurdish area of northern Iraq in order to protect the fragile but real democracy and relative peace and security that have developed there, but with the clear understanding that the terrorist organization the PKK (Kurdistan Workers' Party) must be dealt with and the Turkish border must be respected....

We must be unrelenting in the prosecution of the war on al Qaeda and a growing number of like-minded extremist organizations. These terrorists are as determined as ever to strike the United States. If they think they can carry out another 9.11, I have no doubt that they will try. To stop them, we must use every tool we have.

In the cities of Europe and Asia--such as Hamburg and Kuala Lumpur, which were the springboards for 9.11--terrorist cells are preparing for future attacks. We must understand not only their methods but their motives: a rejection of modernity, women's rights, and democracy, as well as a dangerous nostalgia for a mythical past. We must develop a comprehensive strategy focusing on education, intelligence, and law enforcement to counter not only the terrorists themselves but also the larger forces fueling support for their extremism....

To maximize our effectiveness, we have to rebuild our alliances. The problem we face is global; we must therefore be attentive to the values, concerns, and interests of our allies and partners. That means doing a better job of building counterterrorist capacity around the world. We must help strengthen police, prosecutorial, and judicial systems abroad; improve intelligence; and implement more stringent border controls, especially in developing countries.

We must also keep our guard up at home. As a senator from New York, I have long advocated full investment in our first responders and in protecting our critical infrastructure. I have pushed for new strategies and new technologies, such as a new federal interoperable communications and safety system. After years of Bush administration neglect, 80 percent of the 9/11

Commission's recommendations on homeland security have now been enacted, principally as a result of the Democratic Congress' work. But there is more to do. We must match the resources to the stakes and help the most vulnerable and at-risk cities prepare for an attack. We must improve health-care delivery systems in order to manage the consequences of attacks. Finally, we must improve the security of chemical plants and safeguard the transportation of hazardous materials so that terrorists do not have easy targets....

The Bush administration has opposed talks with our adversaries, seeming to believe that we are not strong enough to defend our interests through negotiations. This is a misleading and counterproductive strategy. True statesmanship requires that we engage with our adversaries, not for the sake of talking but because robust diplomacy is a prerequisite to achieving our aims....

To reassert our nonproliferation leadership, I will seek to negotiate an accord that substantially and verifiably reduces the U.S. and Russian nuclear arsenals. This dramatic initiative would send a strong message of nuclear restraint to the world, while we retain enough strength to deter others from trying to match our arsenal. I will also seek Senate approval of the Comprehensive Test Ban Treaty by 2009, the tenth anniversary of the Senate's initial rejection of the agreement. This would enhance the United States' credibility when demanding that other nations refrain from testing. As president, I will support efforts to supplement the Nuclear Nonproliferation Treaty. Establishing an international fuel bank that guaranteed secure access to nuclear fuel at reasonable prices would help limit the number of countries that pose proliferation risks.

In the Senate, I have introduced legislation to accelerate and reinvigorate U.S. efforts to prevent nuclear terrorism. As president, I will do everything in my power to ensure that nuclear, biological, and chemical weapons and the materials needed to make them are kept out of terrorists' hands. My first goal would be to remove all nuclear material from the world's most vulnerable nuclear sites and effectively secure the remainder during my first term in office.

Statesmanship is also necessary to engage countries that are not adversaries but that are challenging the United States on many fronts. Russian President Vladimir Putin has thwarted a carefully crafted UN plan that would have put Kosovo on a belated path to independence, attempted to use energy as a political weapon against Russia's neighbors and beyond, and tested the United States and Europe on a range of nonproliferation and arms reduction issues. Putin has also suppressed many of the freedoms won after the fall of communism, created a new class of oligarchs, and interfered deeply in the internal affairs of former Soviet republics.

It is a mistake, however, to see Russia only as a threat. Putin has used Russia's energy wealth to expand the Russian economy, so that more ordinary Russians are enjoying a rising standard of living. We need to engage Russia selectively on issues of high national importance, such as thwarting Iran's nuclear ambitions, securing loose nuclear weapons in Russia and the former Soviet republics, and reaching a diplomatic solution in Kosovo. At the same time, we must make clear that our ability to view Russia as a genuine partner depends on whether Russia chooses to strengthen democracy or return to authoritarianism and regional interference.

Our relationship with China will be the most important bilateral relationship in the world in this century. The United States and China have vastly different values and political systems, yet even though we disagree profoundly on issues ranging from trade to human rights, religious freedom, labor practices, and Tibet, there is much that the United States and China can and must accomplish together. China's support was important in reaching a deal to disable North Korea's nuclear facilities. We should build on this framework to establish a Northeast Asian security regime.

But China's rise is also creating new challenges. The Chinese have finally begun to realize that their rapid economic growth is coming at a tremendous environmental price. The United States should undertake a joint program with China and Japan to develop new clean-energy sources, promote greater energy efficiency, and combat climate change. This program would be part of an overall energy policy that would require a dramatic reduction in U.S. dependence on foreign oil.

We must persuade China to join global institutions and support international rules by building on areas where our interests converge and working to narrow our differences. Although the United States must stand ready to challenge China when its conduct is at odds with U.S. vital interests, we should work for a cooperative future....

We must also take threats and turn them into opportunities. The seemingly overwhelming challenge of climate change is a prime example. Far from being a drag on global growth, climate control represents a powerful economic opportunity that can be a driver of growth, jobs, and competitive advantage in the twenty-first century. As president, I will make the fight against global warming a priority. We cannot solve the climate crisis alone, and the rest of the world cannot solve it without us. The United States must reengage in international climate change negotiations and provide the leadership needed to reach a binding global climate agreement. But we must first restore our own credibility on the issue. Rapidly emerging countries, such as China, will not curb their own carbon emissions until the United States has demonstrated a serious commitment to reducing its own through a market-based cap-and-trade approach.

We must draw on all the dimensions of American power and reject false choices driven by ideology rather than facts. An America that rebuilds its strength and recovers its principles will be an America that can spread the blessings of security and opportunity around the world.

In 1825, 50 years after the Battle of Bunker Hill, the great secretary of state Daniel Webster laid the cornerstone of the Bunker Hill Monument that stands today in Boston. He exulted in the simple fact that America had survived and flourished, and he celebrated "the benefit which the example of our country has produced, and is likely to produce, on human freedom and human happiness." He gloried not in American power but rather in the power of the American idea, the idea that "with wisdom and knowledge men may govern themselves." And he urged his audience, and all Americans, to maintain this example and "take care that nothing may weaken its authority with the world."

Two centuries later, our economic power and military might have grown beyond anything that our forefathers could have imagined. But that power and might can only be sustained and renewed if we can regain our authority with the world, the authority not simply of a large and wealthy nation but of the

American idea. If we can live up to that idea, if we can exercise our power wisely and well, we can make America great again.

John McCain: A New League of Democratic Nations

Senator John McCain became the Republican Party's presidential nominee in 2008. He was not able to obtain the nomination in 2000, when the American people produced a neoconservative president. John McCain served his country as a fighter pilot and showed enormous moral authority as a prisoner of war in Vietnam. His "Freedom Agenda" approach appleaied to deep emotions in the American people in both Parties. But what if Senator McCain's type of "Freedom Agenda" cannot protect America's economic and national security? Here are excerpts from his essay: "An Enduring Peace Built on Freedom: Securing America's Future [88] in *Foreign Affairs*:

> Since the dawn of our republic, Americans have believed that our nation was created for a purpose. We are, as Alexander Hamilton said, "a people of great destinies." From the American Revolution to the Cold War, Americans have understood their duty to serve a cause greater than self-interest and to keep faith with the eternal and universal principles of the Declaration of Independence. By overcoming threats to our nation's survival and to our way of life, and by seizing history's great opportunities, Americans have changed the world.
>
> Now it is this generation's turn to restore and replenish the world's faith in our nation and our principles. President Harry Truman once said of America, "God has created us and brought us to our present position of power and strength for some great purpose." In his time, that great purpose was to erect the structures of peace and prosperity that provided safe passage through the Cold War. In the face of new dangers and opportunities, our next president will have a mandate to build an enduring global peace on the foundations of freedom, security, opportunity, prosperity, and hope.
>
> America needs a president who can revitalize our country's purpose and standing in the world, defeat terrorist adversaries

who threaten liberty at home and abroad, and build enduring peace. There is an enormous amount to do. Our wars in Iraq and Afghanistan have been costly in blood and treasure and in other less tangible ways as well. Our next president will need to rally nations across the world around common causes as only America can. There will be no time for on-the-job training. Given the present dangers, our country cannot afford the kind of malaise, drift, and fecklessness that followed the Vietnam War. The next president must be prepared to lead America and the world to victory--and to seize the opportunities afforded by the unprecedented liberty and prosperity in the world today to build a peace that will last a century.

Defeating radical Islamist extremists is the national security challenge of our time. Iraq is this war's central front, according to our commander there, General David Petraeus, and according to our enemies, including al Qaeda's leadership....

Our counterterrorism efforts cannot be limited to stateless groups operating in safe havens. Iran, the world's chief state sponsor of terrorism, continues its deadly quest for nuclear weapons and the means to deliver them. Protected by a nuclear arsenal, Iran would be even more willing and able to sponsor terrorist attacks against any perceived enemy, including the United States and Israel, or even to pass nuclear materials to one of its allied terrorist networks. The next president must confront this threat directly, and that effort must begin with tougher political and economic sanctions. If the United Nations is unwilling to act, the United States must lead a group of like-minded countries to impose effective multilateral sanctions, such as restrictions on exports of refined gasoline, outside the UN framework. America and its partners should also privatize the sanctions effort by supporting a disinvestment campaign to isolate and delegitimize the regime in Tehran, whose policies are already opposed by many Iranian citizens. And military action, although not the preferred option, must remain on the table: Tehran must understand that it cannot win a showdown with the world....

We should go further by linking democratic nations in one common organization: a worldwide League of Democracies. This would be unlike Woodrow Wilson's doomed plan for the universal-membership League of Nations. Instead, it would be similar to what Theodore Roosevelt envisioned: like-minded nations working together for peace and liberty. The organization could act when the UN fails--to relieve human suffering in places such as Darfur, combat HIV/AIDS in sub-Saharan Africa, fashion better policies to confront environmental crises, provide unimpeded market access to those who endorse economic and political freedom, and take other measures unattainable by existing regional or universal-membership systems.

This League of Democracies would not supplant the UN or other international organizations but complement them by harnessing the political and moral advantages offered by united democratic action. By taking steps such as bringing concerted pressure to bear on tyrants in Burma (renamed Myanmar by its military government in 1989) or Zimbabwe, uniting to impose sanctions on Iran, and providing support to struggling democracies in Serbia and Ukraine, the League of Democracies would serve as a unique handmaiden of freedom. If I am elected president, during my first year in office I will call a summit of the world's democracies to seek the views of my counterparts and explore the steps necessary to realize this vision--just as America led in creating NATO six decades ago.

The United States did not single-handedly win the Cold War; the transatlantic alliance did, in concert with partners around the world. The bonds we share with Europe in terms of history, values, and interests are unique. Unfortunately, they have frayed. As president, one of my top foreign policy priorities will be to revitalize the transatlantic partnership....

More broadly, America needs to revive the democratic solidarity that united the West during the Cold War. We cannot build an enduring peace based on freedom by ourselves. We must be willing to listen to our democratic allies. Being a great power does not mean that we can do whatever we want whenever we want, nor should we assume that we have all the wisdom, knowledge, and resources necessary to succeed. When we believe international action - whether military, economic, or diplomatic - is necessary, we must work to persuade our friends and allies that we are right. And we must also be willing to be persuaded by them. To be a good leader, America must be a good ally.

Power in the world today is moving east; the Asia-Pacific region is on the rise. If we grasp the opportunities present in the unfolding world, this century can become safe and both American and Asian, both prosperous and free.

Asia has made enormous strides in recent decades. Its economic achievements are well known; less known is that more people live under democratic rule in Asia than in any other region of the world. Japan's former prime minister spoke of an "arc of freedom and prosperity" stretching across Asia. India's prime minister has called democracy "the natural order of social and political organization in today's world." Asian countries are drawing closer together, striking trade and security agreements with one another and with other states....

The United States should participate more actively in Asian regional organizations, including those led by members of the Association of Southeast Asian Nations. As president, I will seek to institutionalize the new quadrilateral security partnership among the major Asia-Pacific democracies: Australia, India, Japan, and the United States.

Dealing with a rising China will be a central challenge for the next American president. Recent prosperity in China has brought more people out of poverty faster than during any other time in human history. China's newfound power implies responsibilities. It raises legitimate expectations that internationally China will behave as a responsible economic partner by developing a transparent code of conduct for its corporations, assuring the safety of its exports, adopting a market approach to currency valuation, pursuing sustainable environmental policies, and abandoning its go-it-alone approach to world energy supplies.

China could also bolster its claim that it is "peacefully rising" by being more transparent about its significant military buildup. When China builds new submarines, adds hundreds of new jet fighters, modernizes its arsenal of strategic ballistic missiles, and tests anti-satellite weapons, the United States legitimately must question the intent of such provocative acts. When China threatens democratic Taiwan with a massive arsenal of missiles and warlike rhetoric, the United States must take note. When China enjoys close economic and diplomatic relations with pariah states such as Burma, Sudan, and Zimbabwe, tension will result. When China proposes regional forums and economic arrangements designed to exclude America from Asia, the United

States will react.

China and the United States are not destined to be adversaries. We have numerous overlapping interests. U.S.-Chinese relations can benefit both countries and, in turn, the Asia-Pacific region and the world. But until China moves toward political liberalization, our relationship will be based on periodically shared interests rather than the bedrock of shared values.

The United States should set the standard for trade liberalization in Asia. Completing free-trade agreements with Malaysia and Thailand, realizing the full potential of our new trade agreement with South Korea, and institutionalizing economic partnerships with India and Indonesia so that they build on existing agreements with Australia and Singapore should set the stage for an ambitious Pacific-wide effort to liberalize trade. Such trade liberalization would benefit Americans and Asians...

The nuclear nonproliferation regime is broken for one clear reason: the mistaken assumption behind the Nuclear Nonproliferation Treaty (NPT) that nuclear technology can spread without nuclear weapons eventually following. The next U.S. president must convene a summit of the world's leading powers--none of which have an interest in seeing a world full of nuclear-armed states with three agenda items. First, the notion that non-nuclear-weapons states have a right to nuclear technology must be revisited. Second, the burden of proof for suspected violators of the NPT must be reversed. Instead of requiring the International Atomic Energy Agency board to reach unanimous agreement in order to act, as is the case today, there should be an automatic suspension of nuclear assistance to states that the agency cannot guarantee are in full compliance with safeguard agreements. Finally, the IAEA'S annual budget of $130 million must be substantially increased so that the agency can meet its monitoring and safeguarding tasks....

I will make America's economic leadership in the globalized world of the twenty-first century a centerpiece of its engagement in foreign affairs. Today, from Singapore to South Africa, more people than ever before have embraced our liberal capitalist model of economic freedom and our culture of opportunity. Some Americans see globalization and the rise of economic giants such as China and India as a threat. We should reform our job training and education programs to more effectively help displaced American workers find new jobs that take advantage of trade and innovation. But we should continue to promote free trade, as it is vital to American prosperity. Americans will thrive in a world of economic freedom because our products and services remain the best and because our country draws strength from the forces shaping the new global economy, ranging from inflows of foreign investment to new businesses created by highly skilled immigrants. Americans can be confident that a world of economic and political freedom will sustain our global leadership by promoting our values and enhancing our prosperity. To unite us with friends and allies in a common prosperity, as president I will aggressively promote global trade liberalization at the World Trade Organization and expand America's free-trade agreements to friendly nations on every continent.

American leadership has helped build a world that is more secure, more prosperous, and freer than ever before. Our unique form of leadership--the antithesis of empire--gives us moral credibility, which is more powerful than any show of arms. We are rich in people and resources but richer still in ideals and vision-- and the means to realize them. Yet today much of the world has come to challenge our actions and doubt our intentions. Polls indicate that the United States is more unpopular now than at any time in history and increasingly viewed as pursuing its narrow self-interest. The people who hold these views are wrong. We are a special nation, the closest thing to a "shining city on a hill" ever to have existed. But it is incumbent on us to restore our mantle as a global leader, reestablish our moral credibility, and rebuild those damaged relationships that once brought so much good to so many places.

As president, I will seek the widest possible circle of allies through the League of Democracies, NATO, the UN, and the Organization of American States. During President Ronald Reagan's deployment of intermediate-range nuclear missiles and President George H. W. Bush's Gulf War, the United States was joined by vast coalitions despite considerable opposition to American policies among foreign publics. These alliances came about because America had carefully cultivated relationships and shared values with its friends abroad. Working multilaterally can be a frustrating experience, but approaching problems with allies works far better than facing problems alone.

Almost two centuries ago, James Madison declared that "the great struggle of the Epoch" was "between liberty and despotism." Many thought that this struggle ended with the Cold War, but it did not. It has taken on new guises, such as Islamist terrorists using our technological advances for their murderous designs and resurgent autocrats reminiscent of the nineteenth century. International terrorists capable of inflicting mass destruction are a new phenomenon. But what they seek and what they stand for are as old as time. They are part of a worldwide political, economic, and philosophical struggle between the future and the past, progress and reaction, liberty and despotism. Our security, our prosperity, and our democratic way of life depend on the outcome of that struggle.

Thomas Jefferson argued that America was the "solitary republic of the world, the only monument of human rights, and the sole depository of the sacred fire of freedom and self-government, from hence it is be lighted up in other regions of the earth, if other regions of the earth shall ever become susceptible of its benign influence." Since that time two centuries ago when the United States was the "solitary republic the world," more people than ever before have come under the "benign influence" of liberty. The protection and promotion of the democratic ideal, at home and abroad, will be the surest source of security and peace for the century that lies before us.

The Wall Street Journal offered the following analysis of John McCain's foreign policy perspectives in an article "Will McCain's Hawkish View Play on the National Stage:" [89]

In his victory speech…John McCain ticked off his muscular foreign-policy plans and then, with clenched jaw, urged the rowdy crowd to 'stand up and fight for America.'

The Republican presidential nominees resolve will now be tested on a national stage. His record in Congress suggests that a McCain White House could assume a tougher posture oversees than has the current administration, which has itself often been criticized as too bellicose. Sen. McCain has joked about bombing Iran, ruled out talks with North Korea and, earlier this week, and condemned the new leader of Russia.

His world view will likely pose a contrast to his opponent, be it Illinois Sen. Barack Obama or New York Sen. Hillary Clinton. Sen. McCain and his Republican allies are preparing a campaign built around the assertion that either Democrat would be too soft. The Democratic nominee will likely portray Sen. McCain as a reckless saber-rattler.

'He's more confrontational, he's more coercion, he's more sticks,' said retired Air Force Maj. Gen. Scott Gration, who advises Sen. Obama on foreign policy and national security. 'It's time to go back to carrots.'

Even some of Sen. McCain's closest allies say he may need a little polishing. 'He's a street fighter – and that's a good thing,' said Utah Gov. Jon Huntsman, a longtime McCain supporter who has traveled with the senator to Iraq. 'But you have to learn to be a street fighter on the world's stage.'

In a recent Pew Research Center survey, 47% of respondents said they thought Sen. McCain was 'tough enough' on foreign policy, compared with 39% for Sen. Obama and 44% for Sen. Clinton. One in four thought Sen. McCain was 'too tough' – compared with only 3% for Sen. Obama and 9% for Sen. Clinton.

Sen. McCain has a long record of urging the use of force during cries from North Korea to Iran. In 1994, he accused President Clinton of trying to appease North Korea over its nuclear program. 'To get a mule to move, you must show it the carrot and hit it with a stick at the same time"....

Five years later, when the Clinton administration led a North Atlantic Treaty Organization bombing campaign against then-Yugoslavia, Sen. McCain was one of the loudest voices in the Senate urging the White House to prepare for a potential ground invasion. 'The credibility of America as a superpower is at stake' he said.

A decade later, during the Iraq war, U.S. credibility has again emerged as a big issue. The top Democratic contenders frequently promise to restore America's image overseas. But Randy Scheunemann, Sen. McCain's chief foreign-policy adviser, said the McCain campaign sees no similar need. 'At the end of the day, people are happy to engage with Americans,' he said. 'They know we're the sole superpower.'

Several of Mr. McCain's original advisors, including Mr.

Scheunemann, fell firmly in the camp of neoconservatives, the hawkish group that encouraged President Bush to invade Iraq. But as the presumptive Republican nominee, Sen. McCain has since attracted support from nearly all of the party's foreign-policy luminaries, including staunch realists like former Secretary of State James Baker.

Sen. McCain and his aides have devised a foreign-policy strategy that recommends pushing for tougher economic sanctions on Iran – including a possible gasoline embargo outside the auspices of the United Nations, a policy the Bush administration has eschewed as impractical.

Sen. McCain has also been among the Senate's harshest critics of Russia under Vladimir Putin. In 2005, Sen. McCain urged President Bush to boycott a summit in Russia of the Group of Eight leading nations. He continues to say that a 'revisionist Russia' should be ejected from the G-8.

Sen. McCain, whose father, grandfather and sons served in the military, has also vowed to increase the size of the armed forces to 900,000 from 750,000 – an expensive endeavor he says can happen without raising taxes. Sen. McCain plans to increase the efficiency of current programs and use the savings to fund the increase. ...

Today, Mr. McCain is also championing causes that are more on the liberal side of the spectrum. He is a strong opponent of torture and an advocate of taking steps to combat global warming. If elected he promises to start a League of Democracies that would be nimbler and more focused than the U. N. He stresses the need to rebuild ties with Europe and to regain what he calls the 'solidarity that united the West during the Cold War.'

Accomplishing that will take serious schmoozing, according to Adm. Bobby Inman, the former director of the National Security Agency. Mr. Inman, an unaffiliated independent, knew Sen. McCain's father and has know the senator since he was a teenager. He said he felt confident Sen. McCain would be able to establish working relationships with U.S. adversaries. Rebuilding relationships with allies, however, gave him pause. 'It's going to need some warmth,' said Mr. Inman. 'He has the capacity to do it. Will he have the time and patience? Harder for me to judge.'

Skeptics wonder how readily Europe will sign on to a revived trans-Atlantic alliance built around increased belligerence toward Russia or Iran. 'I am not sure the message fits the times,' say James Lindsay, director of the Robert S. Strauss Center at the University of Texas...who isn't allied with any campaign. 'The criticism you see cross a large swath of countries is that the U.S. remains an arrogant superpower telling everyone else what to do. Sen. McCain risks falling into that trap.'

Historians point out that Ronald Reagan was pilloried as a gunslinger during the 1980 campaign but acted with relative restraint while in office. Some analysts say Sen. McCain's steely reputation could give him latitude in the end for compromise.

'A President McCain would come to office very prepared to use military force to delay Iran's nuclear program, says Flynt Leverett, an Iran expert who served in the Bush White House until 2003.' But it is also possible that a McCain administration might actually be better positioned for a comprehensive deal with Iran.

The *Financial Times* commented in an article by Anatol Lieven, "Why we should fear a McCain presidency: " [90]

It may seem incredible to say this, given past experience, but a few years from now Europe and the world could be looking back at the Bush administration with nostalgia. This possibility will arise if the US elects Senator John McCain as president in November. Over the years the US has inserted itself into potential flashpoints in different parts of the world. The Republican Party is now about to put forward a natural incendiary as the man to deal with those flashpoints. The problem that Mr. McCain poses stems from his ideology, his policies and above all his personality. His ideology, like that of his chief advisers, is neo-conservative. In the past, Mr. McCain was considered to be an old-style conservative realist. Today, the role of the realists on his team is merely decorative. Driven in part by his intense commitment to the Iraq war, Mr. McCain has relied more on neo-conservatives such as his close friend William Kristol, the *Weekly Standard* editor. His chief foreign policy advisor is Randy Scheunemann, another leading neo-conservative and a founder of the Committee for the Liberation of Iraq. Mr. McCain shares their belief in what Kristol has called "national greatness conservatism".

In 1999, Mr. McCain declared: "The US is the indispensable nation because we have proven to be the greatest force for good in human history... We have every intention of continuing to use our primacy in world affairs for humanity's benefit." Mr. McCain's promises, during last week's visit to London, to listen more to America's European allies, need to be taken with a giant pinch of salt. There is, in fact, no evidence that he would be prepared to alter any important US policy at Europe's request. Reflecting the neo-conservative programme of spreading democracy by force, Mr. McCain declared in 2000: "I'd institute a policy that I call 'rogue state rollback'. I would arm, train, equip both from without and from within, forces that would eventually overthrow the governments and install free and democratically elected governments." Mr. McCain advocates attacking Iran if necessary in order to prevent it developing nuclear weapons, and last year was filmed singing "Bomb, bomb Iran" to the tune of the Beach Boys' "Barbara Ann". Mr. McCain suffers from more than the usual degree of US establishment hatred of Russia, coupled with a particular degree of sympathy for Georgia and the restoration of Georgian rule over Abkhazia and South Ossetia.

He advocates the expulsion of Russia from the Group of Eight leading industrialized nations and, like Scheunemann, is a strong supporter of early NATO membership for Georgia and Ukraine. Mr. Scheunemann has accused even Condoleezza Rice, secretary of state, of "appeasement" of Russia. NATO expansion exemplifies the potential of a McCain presidency. Apart from the threat of Russian reprisals, if the Georgians thought that in a war they could rely on US support, they might be tempted to start one. A McCain presidency would give them good reason to have faith in US support.

Mr. McCain's policies would not be so worrying were it not for his notorious quickness to fury in the face of perceived insults to himself or his country. Even Thad Cochran, a fellow Republican senator, has said: "I certainly know no other president since I've been here who's had a temperament like that." For all his bellicosity, President George W.Bush has known how to deal cautiously and diplomatically with China and even Russia. Could we rely on Mr. McCain to do the same? Mr. McCain exemplifies "Jacksonian nationalism" -- after Andrew Jackson, the 19th-century Indian-fighter and president -- and the Scots-Irish military tradition from which both men sprung. As Mr. McCain's superb courage in North Vietnamese captivity and his honorable opposition to torture by US forces demonstrate, he also possesses the virtues of that tradition. Then again, some of the greatest catastrophes of the 20th century were caused by brave, honorable men with a passionate sense of national mission. Not just US voters, but European governments, should use the next nine months to ponder the consequences if Mr. McCain is elected and how they could either prevent a McCain administration from pursuing pyromaniac policies or, if necessary, protect Europe from the ensuing conflagrations.

Mitt Romney: Rising to a New Generation of Global Challenges

Former Massachusetts Governor and Bain Capital Chairman Mitt Romney's essay in *Foreign Affairs "Rising to New Global Challenges"*[91] did not emphasize the power of America's use of moral authority but was not as bellicose as some other Republican candidates' essays:

> Less than six years after 9/11, Washington is as divided and conflicted over foreign policy as it has been at any point in the last 50 years. Senator Arthur Vandenberg once famously declared that "politics stops at the water's edge"; today, the chair of the House Foreign Affairs Committee declares that our major political parties should carry out two separate foreign policies. The Senate unanimously confirmed General David Petraeus, who pledged to implement a new strategy, as the commander of U.S. forces in Iraq. Yet just weeks later, the Senate began crafting legislation specifically designed to stop that new strategy. More broadly, lines have been drawn between those labeled "realists" and those labeled "neoconservatives." Yet these terms mean little when even the most committed neoconservative recognizes that any successful policy must be grounded in reality and even the most hardened realist admits that much of the United States'

power and influence stems from its values and ideals.

In the midst of these divisions, the American people--and many others around the world--have increasing doubts about the United States' direction and role in the world. Indeed, it seems that concern about Washington's divisiveness and capability to meet today's challenges is the one thing that unites us all. We need new thinking on foreign policy and an overarching strategy that can unite the United States and its allies--not around a particular political camp or foreign policy school but around a shared understanding of how to meet a new generation of challenges....

The economic rise of China and other countries across Asia poses a different type of challenge. It is easy to understand why Americans--and many others around the world--feel so much unease and uncertainty. Yet although we face fundamentally different issues today, the United States has a history of rising to meet even greater challenges. Indeed, we need not look to ancient history, but only to the courage and determination of our parents and grandparents to see a stark contrast with the confusion and infighting of Washington today....

In the 1940's, Americans rationed and saved, and mothers and daughters enlisted to work in factories. Together with the GIs who returned home, they built this country's prosperity and fueled a sense of optimism. In the 1960's, 1970's, and 1980's, America pursued learning and innovation to lead the world in space, technology, and productivity—out-competing the Soviets and driving them to an economic bankruptcy that matched their moral bankruptcy.

In the aftermath of World War II and with the coming of the Cold War, members of "the greatest generation" united America and the free world around shared values and actions that changed history. They unified U.S. military and security efforts, creating the Department of Defense and the National Security Council. They rethought U.S. approaches to the world, building the U.S. Agency for International Development, the Office of the U.S. Trade Representative, and the Peace Corps. They forged alliances, such as NATO, that magnified the power of freedom and created a world trading system that helped launch the greatest expansion of economic and political freedom and development in history. Our times call for equally bold leadership and for a renewed sense of service and shared sacrifice among Americans and our allies around the world. ...

First, we need to increase our investment in national defense. ...

The United States' strength goes beyond its military capacity. Indeed, a nation cannot remain a military superpower if it has a second-tier economy. The weakness of the Soviet economy was a vulnerability that President Reagan exploited. Our ability to influence the world also vitally depends on our ability to maintain our economic lead through policies such as smaller government, lower taxes, better schools and health care, greater investment in technology, and the promotion of free trade, while maintaining the strength of America's families, values, and moral leadership.

Second, the United States must become energy independent. This does not mean no longer importing or using oil. It means making sure that our nation's future will always be in our hands. Our decisions and destiny cannot be bound to the whims of oil producing states.

We use about 25 percent of the world's oil supply to power our economy, but according to the Department of Energy, we possess only 1.7 percent of the world's crude oil reserves. Our military and economic strength depend on our becoming energy independent—moving past symbolic measures to actually produce as much energy as we use. This could take 20 years or more; and, of course, we would continue to purchase fuel after that time. Yet we would end of strategic vulnerability to oil shutoffs by nations such as Iran, Russia, and Venezuela and stop sending almost $1 billion a day to other oil-producing nations, some of which use the money against us. (At the same time, we may well be able to rein in our greenhouse gas emissions.)...

Finally, we need to strengthen old partnerships and alliances and inaugurate new ones to meet twenty-first-century challenges. The inaction, if not the breakdown, of many Cold War institutions has made many Americans skeptical of multilateralism. Nothing shows the failures of the current system more clearly than the UN Human Rights Council, an entity that has condemned the democratic government of Israel nine times while remaining virtually silent on the serial human rights abuses of the governments of Cuba, Iran, Myanmar,

North Korea, and Sudan. In the face of such hypocrisy, it is understandable that some Americans would be tempted to favor unilateralism. But such failures should not obscure the fact that the United States' strength is amplified when it is combined with the strength of other nations. Whether diplomatically, militarily, or economically, the United States is stronger when its friends stand alongside it.

In the changing world we face, our alliances and engagement must change, too. Clearly, the United Nations has not been able to fulfill its founding purpose of providing collective security against aggression and genocide. Thus, we need to continue to push for reform of the organization. Yet where institutions are fundamentally incapable of meeting a new generation of challenges, the United States does not have to go it alone. Instead, we must examine where existing alliances can be strengthened and reinvigorated and where new alliances need to be forged. I agree with former Spanish Prime Minister Jose Maria Aznar that we should build on the NATO alliance to defeat radical Islam. We need to work with our allies to pursue Aznar's call for greater coordination in military, homeland security, and nonproliferation efforts.

The challenges we now face--especially terrorism, genocide, and the spread of weapons of mass destruction--require global networks of intelligence and law enforcement. We should also look for new ways to strengthen regional cooperation and security partnerships with responsible actors in order to confront challenges such as the genocide in Darfur. And if the UN Human Rights Council continues to be inactive or behave hypocritically, we should unite with nations that share our commitment to defending human rights in order to promote change....

If elected, one of my first acts as president would be to call for a summit of nations to address these issues. In addition to the United States, the countries convened would include other leading developed nations and moderate Muslim states. The objective of the summit would be to create a worldwide strategy to support moderate Muslims in their effort to defeat radical and violent Islam. I envision that the summit would lead to the creation of a Partnership for Prosperity and Progress: a coalition of states that would assemble resources from developed nations and use them to support public schools (not Wah-habi madrasahs), micro credit and banking, the rule of law, human rights, basic health care, and free-market policies in modernizing Islamic states. These resources would be drawn from public and private institutions and from volunteers and nongovernmental organizations....

America is unique in the history of the world. During this last century, there was only one nation that laid down hundreds of thousands of lives of its own sons and daughters and asked for nothing for itself. He explained that in the history of the world, whenever there has been a war, winning nations have taken the land of losing ones. "America is unique," he added. "You took no land from the Germans, no land from the Japanese. All you asked for was enough land to bury your dead."

We are a unique nation, and there is no substitute for our leadership.

Bill Richardson: New Realism: A Realistic and Principled Foreign Policy

New Mexico's governor and former US Ambassador to the United Nations, Bill Richardson's essay "New Realism: A Realistic and Principled Foreign Policy" [92] focused on what we term "moral authority" as need to be part of America's agenda for success:

Sixty years ago, in the pages of this magazine, George Kennan presented a compelling case for U.S. global engagement and leadership to contain Soviet power. His strategic vision laid the foundation for a realistic and principled foreign policy that, despite mistakes and setbacks united the United States and its allies for the duration of the Cold War.

In the wake of the Bush administration's failed experiment with unilateralism, the United States needs once again to construct a foreign policy that is based on reality and loyal to American values. Such a policy must address the challenges of our time with effective actions rather than naive hopes. And it must unite us because it is inspired by the ideals of our nation rather than by the ideology of a president....

America is a great nation that knows how to defend itself.

But its greatness is built on foundations more solid than self-absorption. We defend ourselves best when we lead others, and the key to our history of effective leadership has been our willingness to seek and find common ground, to blend our interests with the interests of others. Truman and Eisenhower understood that defending Europe and America from the Soviets required a strong military, but they also understood that we could not lead our allies if they did not wish to follow.

These and subsequent American presidents knew the importance of moral leadership. While our remarkable military and prosperous economy gave us the power to lead, our commitment to human dignity--including our willingness to struggle against our own prejudices—inspired others to follow. If America is to lead again, we need to remember this history and to rebuild our overextended military, revive our alliances, and restore our reputation as a nation that respects international law, human rights, and civil liberties.

Today, we are at the beginning of a new era of unprecedented global opportunities and global threats. New challenges demand that we chart a new strategic course. To do so, we must reject easy ideological recipes and examine carefully the assumptions that guided us in the twentieth century. We must assess what it means to be America in the world of today--a world of rapid economic and technological change, grave and worsening energy and environmental risks, and the simultaneous emergence of new world powers and asymmetric security challenges.

In the twenty-first century, globalization in all its forms is eroding the significance of national boundaries. Many of the greatest challenges that we face--from jihadism to nuclear proliferation to global warming--are not faced only by us. Urgent problems that once were national are now global, and dangers that once came only from states now come also from societies--not from hostile governments but from individuals or impersonal social trends, such as the consumption of fossil fuels.

American foreign policy must be able to cope effectively with these realities. We must reject both isolationist fantasies of retreat from global engagement and neoconservative fantasies of transforming other countries through the unilateral application of American military power. Our policy also must go beyond the balance-of-power realism of the last century. In this new, independent world, we need a New Realism--one driven by an understanding that to defend our national interests, we must, more than ever, find common ground with others, so that we can lead them toward our common purposes.

Looking reality in the face also requires recognizing that because of the failures of the Bush administration, U.S. influence and prestige are at all-time lows. The damage is extensive: in an age of terrorism, when we need all the friends we can get, we find ourselves isolated. The Bush administration's policies have weakened our alliances, emboldened our enemies, depleted our treasury, exhausted our armed forces, and fueled global anger against us. From global warming to weapons of mass destruction (WMD) to the number of troops that would be needed to pacify Iraq, this president has preferred ideology to evidence. He has been unwilling to accept that leadership requires not just the power to destroy but also the power to persuade. Rather than doing the hard, patient, necessary work of strategic diplomacy, he has indulged the fantasy that he could reorder the world through unilateralism and bullying.

The Bush administration's foreign policy also has lacked sound principles. The president has regularly employed the rhetoric of the virtuous, but his actions have not matched his words. Moralizing has substituted for moral leadership, lecturing others about democracy has substituted for respecting democratic values. George W. Bush has claimed to be championing democracy, but the rest of the world sees a great nation diminished by secret prisons, torture, and warrantless wiretapping. And every day that we remain mired in Iraq, the world is reminded of the folly, the dishonesty, and the disregard for the opinions of others that got us there.

The next president needs to send a clear signal to the world that America has turned the corner and will once again be a leader rather than a unilateralist loner....

The rise of India and China and the reemergence of Russia call for U.S. strategic leadership to integrate these powerful nuclear-armed nations into a stable global order.

A fifth trend transforming our world is the increase in global economic interdependence and financial imbalances without the sufficient growth of institutional capacities to manage these realities. Globalization has made every country's economy more vulnerable to resource constraints and financial shocks that originate beyond its borders. A global energy crisis or a sudden collapse of the U.S. dollar could do great damage to the world economy....

To cope with this new world, we need a New Realism in our foreign policy—an ethical, principled realism that harbors no illusions about the importance of a strong military in a dangerous world but that also understands the importance of diplomacy and multilateral cooperation. We need a New Realism based on the understanding that what goes on inside of other countries profoundly impacts us—but that we can only influence, not control, what goes on inside of other countries. A New Realism for the twenty-first century must understand that to solve our own problems, we need to work with other governments that respect and trust us.

To be effective in the coming decades, America must set the following priorities. First and foremost, we must rebuild our alliances. We cannot lead other nations toward solutions to shared problems if they do not trust our leadership. We need to restore respect and appreciation, for our allies--and for the democratic values that unite us--if we are to work with them to solve global problems. We must restore our commitment to international law and to multilateral cooperation. This means respecting both the letter and the spirit of the Geneva Conventions and joining the International Criminal Court (ICC). It means expanding the United Nations Security Council to include Germany, India, Japan, a country from Latin America, and a country from Africa as permanent members.

We must be impeccable in our own respect for human rights. We should reward countries that live up to the Universal Declaration of Human Rights, as we negotiate, constructively but firmly, with those who do not. And when genocide or other grave human rights violations begin, the United States should lead the world to stop them. History teaches that if the United States does not take the lead on ending genocide, no one else will. The norm of absolute territorial sovereignty is moot when national governments partner with those who rape, torture, and kill masses of people. The

United States should lead the world toward acceptance of a greater norm of respect for basic human rights—and toward enforcing that norm through international institutions and multilateral measures....

The United States needs to stop considering diplomatic engagement with others to be a reward for good behavior. The Bush administration's long refusal to engage diplomatically regimes such as Pyongyang and Tehran only encouraged and strengthened their most paranoid and hard-line tendencies. Both governments, not surprisingly, responded to Washington's snubs and threats about "regime change" by intensifying their nuclear programs....

We should support democracies and democrats around the world, but we should give up on the failed policy of promoting democracy at gunpoint. We must recognize that democratization is a complicated, difficult, long-term project. It took decades or centuries for today's democracies to consolidate themselves. I believe that all nations would benefit from democracy, but we need to recognize that democratization does not happen over overnight, especially in nations with deep ethnic or religious divisions or weak civil societies.

The United States' reputation as a model of freedom and human dignity is one of our greatest resources. We tarnish it at our peril. In the wake of the Bush administration's violations of our values, a skillful public diplomacy effort will be needed to convince the world that the United States has rediscovered itself. Such public diplomacy should include radio and television broadcasts in local languages, as well as expanded educational and exchange programs.

For such efforts to be credible, however, we really need to live up to our own ideals every day. If we want others to value civil liberties, we need to stop spying on our own citizens. Prisoner abuse, torture, secret prisons, denials of habeas corpus, and evasions of the Geneva Conventions must never again have a place in our policy. We should start by closing our prison at Guantanamo Bay, Cuba, and explaining clearly to the world why we have done so....

Finally, the United States should lead the global fight against poverty, which is the basis of so much violence.

Michael Huckabee: Priorities in the War on Terror

Michael Hukabee is a pastor and former Governor of Arkansas. His essay "Priorities in the War on Terror" [94] included these insightful points:

> The United States, as the world's only superpower, is less vulnerable to military defeat. But it is more vulnerable to the animosity of other countries. Much like a top high school student, if it is modest about its abilities and achievements, if it is generous in helping others, it is loved. But if it attempts to dominate others, it is despised.
>
> American foreign policy needs to change its tone and attitude, open up, and reach out. The Bush administration's arrogant bunker mentality has been counterproductive at home and abroad. My administration will recognize that the United States' main fight today does not pit us against the world but pits the world against the terrorists. At the same time, my administration will never surrender any of our sovereignty, which is why I was the first presidential candidate to oppose ratification of the Law of the Sea Treaty, which would endanger both our national security and our economic interests.
>
> A more successful U. S. foreign policy needs to better explain Islamic jihadism to the American people. Given how Americans have thrived on diversity--religious, ethnic, racial--it takes an enormous leap of imagination to understand what Islamic terrorists are about, that they really do want to kill every last one of us and destroy civilization as we know it. If they are willing to kill their own children by letting them detonate suicide bombs, then they will also be willing to kill our children, for their misguided cause. The Bush administration has never adequately explained the theology and ideology behind Islamic terrorism or convinced us of its ruthless fanaticism. The first rule of war is "know your enemy," and most Americans do not know theirs. To grasp the magnitude of the threat, we first have to understand what makes Islamic terrorists tick. Very few Americans are familiar with the writings of Sayyid Qutb, the Egyptian radical executed in 1966, or the Muslim Brotherhood, whose call to active jihad influenced Osama bin Laden and the rise of al Qaeda.

Qutb raged against the decadence and sin he saw around him and sought to restore the "pure" Islam of the seventh century through a theocratic caliphate without national borders. He saw nothing decadent or sinful in murdering in order to achieve that end. America's culture of life stands in stark contrast to the jihadists' culture of death.

The United States' biggest challenge in the Arab and Muslim worlds is the lack of a viable moderate alternative to radicalism. On the one hand, there are radical Islamists willing to fight dictators with terrorist tactics that moderates are too humane to use. On the other, there are repressive regimes that stay in power by force and through the suppression of basic human rights-- many of which we support by buying oil, such as the Saudi government, or with foreign aid, such as the Egyptian government, our second-largest recipient of aid.

Although we cannot export democracy as if it were Coca-Cola or KFC, we can nurture moderate forces in places where al Qaeda is seeking to replace modern evil with medieval evil. Such moderation may not look or function like our system--it may be a benevolent oligarchy or more tribal than individualistic--but both for us and for the peoples of those countries, it will be better than the dictatorships they have now or the theocracy they would have under radical Islamists. The potential for such moderation to emerge is visible in the way that Sunni tribal leaders in Iraq have turned against al Qaeda to work with us; they could not stand the thought of living under such fundamentalism and brutality. The people of Afghanistan turned against the Taliban for the same reason. To know these extremists is not to love them.

As president, my goal in the Arab and Muslim worlds will be a course between maintaining stability and promoting democracy. It is self-defeating to attempt too much too soon: doing so could mean holding elections that the extremists would win. But it is also self-defeating to do nothing. We must first destroy existing terrorist groups and then attack the underlying conditions that breed them: the lack of basic sanitation, health care, education, jobs, a free press, fair courts--which all translates into a lack of opportunity and hope. The United States' strategic interests as the world's most powerful country coincide with its moral obligations as the richest. If we do not do the right thing to improve life in the Muslim world, the terrorists will step in and do the wrong thing.

The criterion of never surrendering America's sovereignty that Mr. Huckabee used as the basis of his position that America should not ratify the Law of the Sea Treaty should not be included in America's agenda. It lacks moral authority and degrades America. That criterion says to the The criterion of never surrendering that America is lawless and smacks of the mindset of a great power that is not acting as a responsible stakeholder in the international system.

Rudi Giuliani: "Towards a Realistic Peace Defending Civilization and Defeating Terrorists by Making the International System Work"

Rudi Giuliani fortunately did not garner much support among Americans for his vision of the way forward for America. Rudi Giuliani's essay *"Towards a Realistic Peace Defending Civilization* and *Defeating Terrorists by Making the International System Work"* [93] exclusively relied on strengthening and using American's military authority. It was an agenda for disaster:

> We are all members of the 9/11 generation. The defining challenges of the twentieth century ended with the fall of the Berlin Wall. Full recognition of the first great challenge of the twenty-first century came with the attacks of September 11, 2001, even though Islamist terrorists had begun their assault on world order decades before. Confronted with an act of war on American soil, our old assumptions about conflict between nation-states fell away. Civilization itself, and the international system, had come under attack by a ruthless and radical Islamist enemy.
> America and its allies have made progress since that terrible day. We have responded forcefully to the Terrorists' War on Us, abandoning a decade long--and counterproductive--strategy of

defensive reaction in favor of a vigorous offense. And we have set in motion changes to the international system that promise a safer and better world for generations to come.

But this war will be long, and we are still in its early stages. Much like at the beginning of the Cold War, we are at the dawn of a new era in global affairs, when old ideas have to be rethought and new ideas have to be devised to meet new challenges.

The next U. S. president will face three key foreign policy challenges. First and foremost will be to set a course for victory in the terrorists' war on global order. The second will be to strengthen the international system that the terrorists seek to destroy. The third will be to extend the benefits of the international system in an ever-widening arc of security and stability across the globe. The most effective means for achieving these goals are building a stronger defense, developing a determined diplomacy, and expanding our economic and cultural influence. Using all three, the next president can build the foundations of a lasting, realistic peace.

Achieving a realistic peace means balancing realism and idealism in our foreign policy. America is a nation that loves peace and hates war. At the core of all Americans is the belief that all human beings have certain inalienable rights that proceed from God but must be protected state. Americans believe that to the extent that nations recognize rights within their own laws and customs, peace with them is achievable. To the extent that they do not, violence and disorder are much more likely. Preserving and extending American ideals must remain the goal of all U.S. policy, foreign and domestic. But unless we pursue our idealistic goals through realistic means, peace will not be achieved.

Idealism should define our ultimate goals; realism must help us recognize the road we must travel to achieve them. The world is a dangerous place. We cannot afford to indulge any illusions about the enemies we face. The Terrorists' War on Us was encouraged by unrealistic and inconsistent actions taken in response to terrorist attacks in the past. A realistic peace can only be achieved through strength.

A realistic peace is not a peace to be achieved by embracing the "realist" school of foreign policy thought. That doctrine defines America's interests too narrowly and avoids attempts to reform the international system according to our values. To rely solely on this type of realism would be to cede the advantage to our enemies in the complex war of ideas and ideals. It would also place too great a hope in the potential for diplomatic accommodation with hostile states. And it would exaggerate America's weaknesses and downplay America's strengths. Our economy is the strongest in the developed world. Our political system is far more stable than those of the world's rising economic giants. And the United States is the world's premier magnet for global talent and capital.

Still, the realist school offers some valuable insights, in particular its insistence on seeing the world as it is and on tempering our expectations of what American foreign policy can achieve. We cannot achieve peace by promising too much or indulging false hopes. This next decade can be a positive era for our country and the world so long as the next president realistically mobilizes the 9/11 generation for the momentous tasks ahead.

Are Americans Rejecting "Do as I say, not as I do" Immoral Authority?

After the failure of its neoconservative experiment America's two-party system nominated Barack Obama and John McCain as presidential candidates. Both men's lives play a large role in the moral authority of their visions. Both their life stories compare favorably to those of the current President and Vice President, who supported the use of military authority in the Vietnam War without having put themselves in harm's way.

But in 2008, did Americans reject "Do as I say, Not as I Do" Immoral Authority? Are they rejecting the Principles of Conflict? Unfortunately, they are not. There has been little recognition among American's of the ramifications of deficiencies in human nature. Most Americans yearn for ideological and pragmatic hegemony, which can no longer be imposed using only economic and military authority. Continuing to do so without moral authority will not work. That is a central foreign policy problem for the goals the American people and its leaders. They cannot implement both the Principles of Conflict and Principles of Peaceful Coexistence. Which will America support? What seemed apparent before the election was that both candidates still believe in the Principles of Conflict.

Barack Obama or John McCain, as president, would move in a very different direction than the other. But both their agendas operate on the Principles of Conflict. America's president must restyle their policies according to the collaboration mindset. In the future, he must accept and implement the Principles of Peaceful Coexistence. If he does not, then America's policy and defense strategies will result in conflict and failure.

It is possible that the new president may change his mindset once in office. By selecting John McCain as the Republican candidate for president, Republicans moved to a candidate who is of great moral authority as compared to the 43rd president. Democrats by voting president Barack Obama, they found a president they believe to be capable of moral and pragmatic leadership.

That Americans selected two such giants of moral character is important evidence, of a first step in sustaining the character of the American people.

The *Economist* commented in June 2008:

> American history of reinventing and perfecting itself has acquired another page. Both candidates have their flaws and their admirable points, the doughty but sometimes cranky old warrior makes a fine contrast with the inspirational but sometimes vaporous young visionary. Voters will now have those five months to study them before making up their minds... But, on the face of it, this is the most impressive choice America has had for a very long time.[95]

Americans' choices of candidates reflect their desire for pragmatism as well as their readiness for their military authority to have moral authority. But, Americans may have elected President Obama rather than John McCain because Senator Obama appeared better able to deal with the economic crisis successfully.

Although both candidates' mindsets remained mired in the Principles Conflict during the campaign, the contrast in directions offered by the nominees is stark. Some pundits commented that John McCain was effectively running for a third term for George W. Bush, while Barack Obama for a second term for John F. Kennedy. The comparisons seem apt in regards to their approaches to America's foreign policy.

Throughout history, the presidency moves back and forth between the Republican and Democratic Parties. Hopefully, President Obama will choose to lead, rather than to follow the perspectives of authoritarian factions with in his party.

Richard Nixon that opened America's door to China, which then assisted Deng Xiaoping in opening China to the world. But future American presidents may not be able to understand policies capable of sustaining America's economic success or national security. Destabilizing challenges await America, China, and the rest of the world in the Age of Species Lethal Weapons and Science. If the leaders elected by the American are not able to cope with the needs of the world, then America will truly become the greatest danger to world peace.

The conflict between America and China endangers each nation's security. In order to avoid this, both countries must support a successful partnership between them. But that requires that the American people understand the need for such a partnership which in turn requires extraordinary leadership in supporting the partnership. If either Party does not support a successful partnership, it will become unstable. How might America's political leaders sustain a consensus among the American people capable of sustaining a partnership?

Consensus Democracy in the Selection of American Cabinets in the 21st Century

Majority-rule-democracies, as Germany's demonstrated in the 1930's, can deteriorate rapidly into states with economic and military authority bereft of moral authority.

As examined in chapters 9 and 15 of *China & America's Emerging Partnership: A New Realistic Perspective,* the impacts of China's increasing role in the global economy affects different states in different ways. That results in interest-group pressure that seeks to affect and cause myriad changes in America's policies towards China. In addition to this dynamic, there is a danger of authoritarian factions controlling American policies.

We recommend, in order to ameliorate such unstable dynamics that each President experts from both Parties to serve in their cabinet as we believe that policy formation cannot be a "winner takes all" majority-rule-system in the Age of Species Lethal Weapons and Science. American majority-rule-democracy must embrace non-partisan appointments of men and women with diverse perspectives but a shared understanding of the needs for a successful partnership of America and China.

Events that occur in the next eight years will determine the relationship between America and China. Elections seek to replace the armed conflict of civil wars. They are much like the "justice" enshrined in the Code of Justinian in Ancient Rome, which counted the number of supporters each side could produce in court to support their claim, rather than focusing on what actually was right.

America has to choose one candidate as president. In doing so, it loses the strengths of some of its most able political leaders and alienates their supporters. But America's new presidents can, as one of their first and most important decisions, reach out to Americans of different views and priorities, and invite those experts to hold positions in the new Administration.

Consider a new Presidential Administration in which America chooses a president who, chooses for their administration Hillary Clinton to serve as the Secretary of State, John McCain as Secretary of Defense, John Edwards as Secretary of Labor, Bill Richardson as Ambassador to the United Nations, Mike Huckabee as Secretary of Education, Mitt Romney as Secretary of the Secretary of Commerce, and Rudi Giuliani as Secretary of Homeland Security.

This type of bipartisan leadership must be implemented in America. This solution to partisan battles is a simple, means by which America's new president can achieve a more representative government. Putting the most able political leaders of one party in the presidential administration, with most able leaders of the other party locked out of deliberations a recipe for discord when America's choices must reflect the wisdom and support of both Parties.

How else can any new president unify America, and get the intimate private advice of leaders with strong factional communities of support in America, but from a cabinet made up of their peers in political experience and popular appeal? It is difficult to imagine how the president or America can escape the partisanship of a two-party system when one party is put in opposition, often by the tiniest of majorities.

This "Bipartisan Presidential Cabinet Model" is what America needs. It puts leaders in the Cabinet who are representative of large communities of thought, with the president with the power to make final decisions. It is a "marriage" of a Majority-rule-democracy with the consensus building processes of a Consensus Democracy. Leaders and experts of the highest caliber, selected from America's presidential candidates, might strengthen American moral authority.

The Chinese one-party-state model entails producing a small number of leaders, currently 9 in a consensus-driven process. In China's political system, factions struggle for influence and the resulting small number of leaders struggle among themselves to identify the policies that Chinese stability and well being require.

That system has worked successfully since 1978 and is examined in chapter 10 of Book 1 and chapters 4, 5 and 6 of *China & America's Emerging Partnership: A New Realistic Perspective.*

Including both Parties' leaders in the new president's cabinet combines the geniuses of the American and Chinese political systems and ameliorates a weaknesses of American majority-rule-democracy.

The relative ideological homogeneity of George W. Bush's cabinet stands in contrast to this more balanced Bipartisan Cabinet Model. The Presidential Bipartisan Cabinet Model is consistent with America's Constitution and enhances its operation, the selection of the cabinet advisors and department administrations needed to craft and policies that rise above partisan gridlock.

America needs the strengths of all the major candidates, with the president having all the decision-making power set out in the US Constitution. It builds bipartisan-ship into the American process by selecting its most popular leaders and its ultimate leader, each of whom have different, strengths.

America should not have to choose, for example, between a president who "understands the economy" and one who "understands foreign policy." America must successfully address not merely some of its problems. The America government must address them all in all future administrations.

George Washington used the Presidential Bipartisan Cabinet Model. He picked Thomas Jefferson as Secretary of State, Alexander Hamilton as Secretary of the Treasury, Henry Knox as Secretary of War and Edmund Randolph as Attorney General. These men had very different philosophies, views, and goals.

Abraham Lincoln had the ability to see deeply into events that others saw more superficially. Lincoln had very little formal education, and many of his rivals for the presidency saw him as intellectually inferior. However, Lincoln, became president at a critical time in the American Experiment. Part of his genius was including his former presidential rivals in his cabinet. When he had successfully solved the problem of winning the Civil War and was assassinated, one of his rivals, Secretary of War Stanton commented "Now he belongs to the ages...."

President Kennedy also selected a bipartisan cabinet. That is the caliber of leadership America requires in the Age of Species Lethal Weapons and Science.

The Essential Republican and Democratic Parties' Genuine Commitment to the Partnership of America and China

Nothing less will succeed, because the genuine partnership of America and China requires that both parties be committed to it. The Presidential Bipartisan Cabinet Model is a crucible for achieving the understanding of the importance of the partnership that America's and China's future successes require. How, else could either party resist the temptation to oppose this partnership?

The American People's Choice between Military and Moral & Military Authority Approaches to China and America's Future

The choice of a president is a profound test of the character of the American people and of the American electoral process's viability in the conditions of the 21st century. The real issue is not when an American style system of government is adopted. It is whether such a system is able to produce security in either America or China. The question is whether a government of the people, by the people, for the people can endure in America. Can it produce the solutions that America needs now and in the future? America can survive what has been termed "the Democratic Constraint," which is examined in chapter 8 of Book 1."

Part of the danger is that:

1. The 21ˢᵗ century vulnerability of America may undermine American Constitutional Majority Rule Democracy, human right
2. The character of the American people today may become despotic, or despots may come to power in America;; ;
3. The American electoral decision-making process may be too domestically focused, too polarized, or too dominated by potent authoritarian factions, to understand and adapt to the challenges facing America.

In other words: the danger is that the character of the American people, may not be sufficient in a world where developing countries surpass America's achievements.

As examined in chapters 8 and 9 in Book 1, this horrible reality, must be prevented by Americans. Our 43ʳᵈ president's administration demonstrates the danger of despotism in America.

Recognize the course America might have taken had persons such as Presidents Washington, Lincoln or Roosevelt either not been in office or not accomplished what they did when America's survival and freedom were so vulnerable. Recognize that America's fate must not rely merely on gifted leaders being in power during crises. America needs economic development, foreign policy and defense strategies that are based on principles that have "moral authority." No amount of economic or military authority used without moral authority can protect the political system indigenous to the American people. In other words it is implementing the advice of President Washington on which we focus in Books 1 and 2. Implementing this advice manifests America's Ideals and system of government and strengthens America's economic and military authority. Authoritarian "realist'" perspectives are naïve because they are self-defeating.

Chapters 6 and 7 of Book 2 examine "the zero sum game mindset" and Principles of Conflict" currently prevailing in American policy. Those conventional must be "deinstitutionalized." As long as they remain "institutionalized in the mindset of Americans," America is at grave risk of failing as a nation.

China's success in "deinstitionalizing its zero sum game mindset" under the leadership of Deng Xiaoping is a unique case involving almost a quarter of mankind.

Just as the world learned so much from America's charismatic Exceptionalism in the last two centuries, America must in this century learn from the charismatic success of China's Exceptionalism.

America must not rely on the possibility of finding presidents capable of understanding the 21st century's realities. Selecting such presidents is essential but not sufficient. America must rely on *a new grand strategy of implementing President Washington's Farewell Advice.* America's policies and defense strategies must meet the criteria in President Washington's advice.

Only the *combination* of;

1. Presidents that are each capable of understanding the new centuries' realities, dangers and opportunities; and
2. The grand strategy of implementing policies that are based on President Washington's advice, (which is consistent with the Principles of Peaceful Coexistence and inconsistent with the Principles of Conflict) can provide America economic and national security.

Because China's grand strategy, in effect, implements President Washington's advice America, in finding its way forward, must implement a new strategy aligned with China's. America's new grand strategy, as we suggest in chapter 1 of Book 1 is:

> Because economic development is considered the only way to tackle all the pressing challenges that America is facing and will face, America's grand strategy must serve the central purpose of development. Therefore, the central objective of America's grand

strategy – a strategy that may well last to 2050 – can be captured in just one phrase: to secure and shape a security, economic, and political environment that is conducive to America concentrating on its economic, social and political development.

The New School's perspective uses the terms "collaborative equilibrium" and "the partnership of America and China" to describe such a strategy for America. By "collaborative equilibrium" we mean China and America's strategies collaborative equilibrium and by partnership of America and China we mean:

> Because economic and peaceful development are considered the only way to tackle all the pressing challenges that China and America are facing and will face, America's and China's aligned collaborative equilibrium grand strategy must serve the central purpose of economic development and peaceful coexistence of mankind. Therefore, the central objective of America and China's collaborative equilibrium grand strategy can be captured in just one phrase: to secure and shape a security, economic, and political environment that is conducive to America, China, and the other 190 nations concentrating on their economic, social and political development based on the Principles of Peaceful Coexistence which has been the central objective of China's grand strategy since 1978.

This aligned grand strategy is a "New School of America-China Relations" that implements principle of "collaborative equilibrium" and Principles of Peaceful Coexistence. We term this "China and America's Partnership."

Chapters 6, 7 and 8 in Book 2 examine conventional American policymaking regarding America's relationship with China so that American policymakers, and scholars can compare:

1. America's conventional mindset and strategies and
2. The New School's mindset and strategies; and
3. America's conventional mindset and strategies and the New

School's mindset and strategic perspectives with the advice of Presidents Washington, Lincoln, Roosevelt and Kennedy and Deng Xiaoping.

Chapters 6, 7 and 8 of Book 2 should be examined with the New School's perspectives and key questions focused on in Books 1 and 2 in mind and particularly:

1. Is economic and military collaborative equilibrium required for America and China's economic and national security?
2. Can economic and military collaborative equilibrium with China be obtained for America with America's conventional economic and foreign policies and defense strategies?
3. Can what you believe is required for America's economic and national security be obtained by America's conventional economic and foreign policy and military mindset, policies and strategies?
4. Precisely how and why can what you believe is required for America's economic and national security be obtained by America's conventional economic and foreign policies and defense strategies?
5. Do American policymakers and scholars' conventional economic and foreign policies and defense strategies enable more or less economic and national security for America than the New School's perspectives and new America and China partnership might enable?

Conventional American Principles of Conflict Based Policy on China

Chapter 6
The Limits of American Military Authority

Overview

Using military authority without moral authority can be a huge disadvantage for the United States which requires popular support for sustained use of military authority. America needs to use both moral authority and military authority in its defense strategies.

The Decisive Role of Moral Authority in American Warfare

President Nixon was unable to win the Vietnam War despite the massive American military deployed. This was in part because of the draft, which created massive resistance to that war in America. The draft was accepted by Americans in the Second World War after America was attacked by Japan and because Hitler's vision of mankind's future lacked moral authority.

Resistance to the Vietnam War within the country and the failure of American military power affected liberal, conservative and other Americans, albeit in different ways. President George W. Bush,

Vice President Cheney and Defense Secretary Rumsfeld lost popular American and international support for the war in Iraq, in part, because they tried to take America to war without the draft that caused America to fail in the Vietnam War. But the United States may be unable to stabilize Iraq politically and militarily as the war in Iraq lost its vestige of moral authority. President George W. Bush reportedly wanted to use nuclear weapons against Iran nuclear sites, and fortunately was persuaded not to do so. Subsequently, the CIA, announced Iraq was not making nuclear weapons following the "failure of intelligence" regarding the non-existent nuclear weapons program that was used as a pretext for the war in Iraq.

The Democratic Peace Theory that majority-rule-democracies do not start wars with peaceful nations is used to assert that promoting American-style government and human rights in other nations is essential for America's economic and national security. This theory has a number of theoretical and empirical deficiencies as well as erroneous assumptions in the real world. These include, for example, the right of self-determination's relationship to regime-change seeking attacks, the challenges in successfully imposing American-style government by force in some nations and cultures, and the belief that such democratic reforms will make nations less hostile to America. In any case, majority-rule democracies, such as the US with respect to Iraq, for example, in fact go to war with other states without adequate moral authority.

It is true that majority-rule-democracies cannot always *win* what their own citizens or others feel are immoral wars even when they have an overwhelming superiority in military power. But majority-rule-democracies can sometimes win wars with moral authority and inferior military authority. For example, the Athenians were successful in resisting an invasive attack from a larger military force. By the same token, disaffected colonialists with citizen soldiers in the American Revolution of 1776-1781 were successful against the world's then leading superpower. Moral authority is a powerful element in the successful use of and resistance to military authority.

Moral authority used to preserve peace can also be a powerful force. Americans must understand that their country's ultimate strength is its moral authority. When American policy is bereft of it, its military effectives, although the greatest in the world, are limited and they risk being defeated by weaker enemies, such as the Vietnamese and the Iraqi resistance.

America must reassert itself as a Moral Authority

America's involvement in the Two World Wars, and the pragmatic Marshall and Dodge Plans, gave it the role of the "Policeman of the World with Moral Authority." Unfortunately, during the Cold War America moved away from its earlier strategy based on a combination of military and moral authority.

The choices President Bush made in response to the 9/11 attacks were increasingly perceived as relying exclusively on military authority without moral authority. In addition, the charisma of the American political system was damaged by a government that implemented a series of policies which were inconsistent with America's Ideals. In 2008, Americans had the opportunity to select a new world leader who would give the world a new definition of what the United States can be in the 21st century. Unfortunately, for the previous eight years, the American people had a president that acted against the moral criteria presented by President Washington more than two hundred years ago:

> "Observe good faith & justice towards all nations. Cultivate harmony with all. Religion and morality enjoin this conduct; and can it be that good policy does not equally enjoin it? It will be worthy of a free, enlightened, and, in no distant period a great nation, to give to mankind the magnanimous and too novel example of a people always guided by an exalted justice & benevolence."

In the past, the vision that governed the policies and politics of President Lincoln, Roosevelt and Kennedy were imbued with moral authority. That "right spirit" is also reflected in the speeches of Deng Xiaoping and Hu Jintao, at Yale in 2006, as well as Premier Wen Jiabao, at Harvard. We argue that the strategies of these American and Chinese leaders, despite the fact that they were based on different experiments with two-and one-party governed states. In the 21st century's complex international order, American policymakers and scholars must understand that neither China's success with a one-party-state government nor America's success with a two-party-state government will be sustainable if the economic and military policies of the two states lack sufficient moral authority. This is important for many reasons.

First, American foreign policy makers who have constantly tried to impose American ideals on the rest of the world, have attempted to convince the Chinese citizens that China's economic and military authority lacks moral authority. Furthermore, some policymakers have also argued adamantly that the Chinese political and legal systems should follow the same pattern as the United States, despite the fact that China has been successful and stable from an economic point of view, while undergoing crucial reforms in many different socio-economic areas, since 1978.

In addition, during the first 8 years of the 21st century, America has used its economic and military authority without sufficient moral Authority. This has proven to be a serious error of judgment on behalf of the American executive branch as their careless policies are, at least in part, to blame for the "most serious economic crises in 100 years".

Lastly, China's unilateral implementation of the Principles of Peaceful Coexistence in its economic development and foreign policies has brought noticeable benefits to both Chinese citizens and the rest of the world.

Many Americans realize that they the United State must restore its reputation and leadership at an international level. Yet as long as America's economic, military and moral authority operates on the Principles of Conflict instead of the Principles of Peaceful Coexistence, America will not be able to restore either its reputation or its leadership. To do so, America must change its economic, foreign policy and defense strategies goals and priorities which can only be achieved if there is a. change in the conventional mindset.

Instead, as reality shows us, America's economic and military authority are currently not designed to change the conventional mindset. The danger of operating on failed strategies is clear in the 21st century, and it is unfortunately occurring at extremely high speeds.

The current deficiencies in human nature and human reasoning, are responsible for the zero sum game mindset that is currently being employed despite the fact that a win-win mindset would be far more adequate.

The Chinese culture combined with the sustainable strategies implemented for the last thirty years by the Chinese government win-win strategies that have produced better results in an international setting than the policies adopted by the American counterparts. As a result, in some areas, China is more prosperous than America currently is. The reality is that America should change its ideological and hegemonic goals and align its priorities with China's quest for prosperity and peace that are in accordance with the Principles of Peaceful Coexistence. we belive this is the only way America can achieve collaborative equilibrium, and align its economic and national security with the ones fostered by the Chinese state. In this way, The United States will become a more respected and effective policeman with moral authority as it was in the 20th century.

The War on Terror's Attack on America's Moral Authority

The 9/11 attacks caused a massive surge of support for America among most other nations. Unfortunately, that support was mismanaged and squandered by the President Bush administration choice of responses to the attacks. America's moral authority was profoundly damaged by waging war unilaterally rather than collaboratively with Americas' traditional allies, using the false pretexts of Iraq's non-existent involvement with al Qaeda and nonexistent nuclear weapons program. Many of the domestic and foreign policies chosen were inconsistent with both American Ideals of human rights and the Rule of Law and international norms and rules of conduct.

The American government response to the 9/11 attacks changed the way many individuals and nations perceived America. The self-inflicted damage to America's moral authority caused far reaching consequences Within that context, Americans had every reason to be frightened after 9/11; but the American government erred in not taking into consideration what their allies or foes thought, and most importantly by departing from America's ideals.

At the same time, it is important that the course of action implemented by the Bush administration was successful in preventing further major al Qaeda attacks since 9/11. It is important to ask whether an effective course of action limit-ing major terrorist attacks within America would have been as effective as the courses of action that were used.

There are three basic types of answers to the question: "no", "yes" or "maybe, but it is not possible to know for sure". If the new president concludes the answer is "no" it will have long-term ramifications for American Ideals. Even in this case, the New School's perspective is that if America cannot defend itself without moral authority, it cannot defend either its economic or national security. In other words, if Constitutional Majority Rule Democracy, human rights and the rule of law cannot protect Americans' economic and national security, the New School's perspective is that America could become what we term a Permission Society or police state of which

President Washington and Benjamin Franklin warned. Therefore, America should defend itself while adhering to the moral authority of its Ideals. When dangers are inevitable America should use military and economic authority combined with moral authority to defend itself.

If the answer is "maybe, but it is not possible to know for sure", then America must follow President Washington's advice and rely on America's Ideals as the deciding criteria.

If the answer is "yes", then courses of action with more moral authority than those used by America's 43rd president must be employed. An important part of America's national security is safeguarded by the charisma and strength of America's moral authority in giving "mankind the magnanimous and too novel example of a people always guided by an exalted justice & benevolence" as President Washington advised.

We address the scenarios in which the new president must make critical decisions. we have argued that labeling the "War on Terror" in such terms contains a tragic connotation that reflects its strategic insolvency. Homeland Security does not evoke the same connotations as War on Terror. Terror is fought with terror. War can be stopped with war. A war on terror, that uses terror as a principle way to fight terror, is a deeply flawed concept. The Bush administration may have prevented further attacks in America but its unilateral use of force, based on known-to-be-false and shown-to-be-false principles combined with America's reliance on military authority alone, has alienated many friends while generating new enemies.

The Criteria of Moral or Military Authority

China is a much older civilization than America. As a result, China has discovered more effective ways to act as a nation than America has. Governments have failed and been replaced many times in China. Administrations come and go, but the American civilization has not collapsed. In China, administrations were dynasties established initially by force and sustained as long as their ability to govern allowed it. Dynasties run for generations, not merely a succession of four year terms determined by elections. But each time, so far, America has had government leaders who allowed it to survive. Americans have not yet had to learn the hard lessons that come with political failure as Chinese people and their leaders have learned in its 5,000 year history.

Military force is a form of persuasion. It is the way of "neutralizing" or destroying what you do not like or what might harm you. Most importantly, in the Age of Species Lethal Weapons and Science, moral authority is an essential part of both our survival. We, as a species, have reached the stage in our evolution when military authority can cause our destruction. Our vulnerability to extinction as a species is the criterion that we must choose to respond to and to resolve human conflict. If the only possibility is in our human nature, is trial by combat, then we have no future, except suffering and oblivion as our fate. Yet military authority is not the only possibility. Being humane is what the human Extinction Challenge's solution requires.

We encounter moral authority very powerfully in our daily routines. Sometimes it is obvious when we witness for example the achievements of an individual like Nelson Mandela or Mahatma Gandhi. But sometimes it is more subtle. When we buy gasoline or food or greet a friend or stranger, moral authority is at work. Human society ceases to function when the moral authority which is trust no longer operates when people don't trust each other anymore. This subtle reliance of America's economic and national security or trust and confidence becomes dramatically apparent in the current global financial crises, and moral authority is the lubricant of human civilization's successful functioning.

Military Diplomacy and Intimidation

The issue on which we must focus is how to combine military and moral authority in a way that makes mankind adequately governable to prevent species suicide in the Age of Species Lethal Weapons and Science. The problem with military diplomacy and intimidation is that it easily leads to war.

We do not address or understand the fundamental foreign policy, defense strategy, and scientific research issues of our time. For example, the power of military authority is too dangerous and uncontrollable to be the means by which we resolve our differences. Policymakers focus their countries' foreign policy and defense strategy debates on economics, military, and geopolitical issues. Those might be important but the solution to our problems lies elsewhere. Societies that rely on military authority alone cannot survive. That is part of why the moral authority of American Exceptionalism and Chinese Exceptionalism is so vital to America's, China's and mankind's survival.

The Folly of Subjective Joy and Objective Horror of Military Authority

Military force and military diplomacy, which we term "military authority," seem inevitable and suitable when we impose it other countries. Yet when jets are crashed into the World Trade Center and the Pentagon, military force strikes us as outrageous and immoral. That dichotomy is caused by Fairness Hypocrisy. Such acts should make us investigate not just our military weakness but the underlining problem that is Fairness Hypocrisy, which is not always recognized because Fairness Hypocrisy is so much a part of thoughts and behavior that it has become the norm rather than the exception.

Great military prowess is a source of pride that we inflict on "our enemies" or "the enemies of freedom" or the "axis of evil". But when our enemies destroy the World Trade Center, the immorality of military authority is a source of horror and outrage because we see the shattered lives and bodies of our families or other members of our society.

The horror of that reality does not make us eschew the use of military authority on others because we do not want to suffer it ourselves. For most of us, it makes us morally outraged and revenge-seeking that we perceive as "policing the world or confronting the "enemies of freedom" or "axis of evil."

The immorality of the Fairness Hypocrisy should make us avoid the use of military authority and what might be termed as: "Bully Diplomacy."

What we are thinking and talking about in conventional American foreign policy, defense strategy and geopolitical debates is not what needs to be discussed and understood. We often talk about how to rule the world, when the issues are how to run the world and whether mankind is ungovernable or viable in the Age of Human Species Lethal Weapons and Science. Another issue is whether we operate, as we have done so far, with a zero-sum game or with win-win mindset. The reality is that we manifest both approaches in our behavior. Most of us are not all zero-sum minded or all win-win minded. But some of us exhibit one of the mindsets more than the other.

Children in the playground learn that the best way to stop a fight is not to start one in the first place. We see that calming effect ameliorating the anger of children as they mediate and defuse disputes once they flare into confrontations that threaten the peace of the group. That is what we must see adults and nations do as well.

The Bush administration's foreign policy failures are better understood in 2008 by a significant number of Americans. Military authority used without moral authority and Bully Diplomacy used against others have become the rule. Americans have invaded countries that have oil and other things they want. It rarely bothered

Americans that others in those countries often did not welcome foreign interference.

With its zero sum game mindset approach, America's War on Terror turned the sympathy the world had for America into loathing. The War on Terror as currently conceived and implemented lacks moral authority. It no doubt prevented some major further attacks in the America since 2001, but it has made America far less secure at the same time.

But the zero sum mindset so powerfully present in America's first 21st century presidential administration are based on subjective selfish calculations of self interest, undisciplined by adequate respect for the rights of other nations or the rights of American citizens. It is reducible to a simple motto put into practice by a sole global super-power of "might is right." It may be dressed up in phrases like: "Surrender is not an option," [96] or "fighting for freedom" or "axis of evil," but power used without moral authority is misused since it destroys freedom and creates evil. It predictably generates resistance that grows, and simultaneously weakens America's military, economic and moral authority and diplomatic resources in an interrelated complex community of nations. Using military authority without moral authority is bad policy for America in the Age of Species Lethal Weapons and Science because it proves to be a destructive force more often than not.

If America does not care what other nations think or when it analyses problems from an overwhelming Ameracentric perspective then its approach creates a world defined by one simplistic vision: "surrender is not an option." When America is unable to prove that the reasons and evidence given for a war were true, then its state project and ideology is no longer respected by its own subjects or foreign observers. Others who hate America are given new allies by America's self-interested way of doing politics at home and abroad.

Unilateral American Presidential Diplomacy

America must respect its friends and enemies in order to be respected by them. In 2008, during the presidential elections, the issue on how America should deal with its enemies was on the table. The *Wall Street Journal* commented:

> Sen. Hillary Clinton is trying -- hard -- to draw distinctions between herself and Sen. Barack Obama. Sometimes, the strain shows, but yesterday, she hit upon a difference that matters: how the U.S. should deal with its enemies in the post-Bush world....The difference, which reflects both candidates' tactical thinking and general mind-sets, is over how and when a president should talk directly with America's enemies. Sen. Clinton focused on her credentials and experience in a speech about foreign policy at George Washington University, Monday. Sen. Obama outlined his vision to shape the nation's foreign policy, including his call for "direct diplomacy" and ending the war in Iraq, at a Dec. 18 forum on foreign policy in Des Moines, Iowa.
>
> The split showed up early in the campaign when Sen. Obama said he would be willing to meet personally with the leaders of Iran, North Korea and Syria, and Sen. Clinton said she wouldn't. It emerged again last week when Sen. Obama said he would meet "without preconditions" with the new Cuban president, Raúl Castro. Sen. Clinton said she wouldn't do so "until there was evidence that change was happening"..."If I am entrusted with the presidency, America will have the courage, once again, to meet with our adversaries. But I will not be penciling in the leaders of Iran or North Korea or Venezuela or Cuba on the presidential calendar without preconditions; until we have assessed, through lower-level diplomacy, the motivations and intentions of these dictators"... "We simply cannot legitimize rogue regimes or weaken American prestige by impulsively agreeing to presidential-level talks that have no preconditions."
>
> As a political matter, both the Clinton and Obama reflexes are open to attack. The Clinton stance is subject to assault from the left for being overly cautious in breaking with the tendencies of the Bush administration. The Obama stance is subject to attack from the right for being naively unmindful of the need to

judiciously use the power of the presidency.

As a more-practical matter, the recent history of presidential engagement in diplomacy is checkered. Jimmy Carter used personal intervention to forge the Camp David peace accords between Egypt and Israel, and Bill Clinton used it to finish the Wye River agreement between Israeli officials and Palestinian leader Yasser Arafat -- although that one soon hit the rocks. The first President Bush used personal diplomacy to help achieve the peaceful reunification of Germany, one of the landmark events of the past century. But presidents can walk into land mines as readily as Nobel Peace Prizes. At a summit in Reykjavik, Iceland, in 1986, Ronald Reagan engaged in an unscripted discussion with then-Soviet leader Mikhail Gorbachev about eliminating all nuclear weapons, an ill-advised flier that rattled American allies and caused both sides to pull back from further talks for a time. Thus, the question of what presidential diplomacy can accomplish, and how, is a very real and very open one.

The Obama approach is an outgrowth of many Democrats' views that the Bush administration has been so allergic to diplomatic engagement that, among other things, it let the North Korean nuclear threat grow and missed exploring the chance for engagement with Iran before hard-liner Mahmoud Ahmadinejad took power as president. "Not talking doesn't make us look tough, it makes us look arrogant," Sen. Obama has said. The question he raises is, in effect, one of lost opportunities: What good might have come, what crises avoided, if America weren't so afraid to come face to face with its foes?

But the most common critique of Bush foreign policy isn't that it failed to engage America's enemies, but that it failed to adequately engage its friends. Earlier and more-energetic outreach to allies might have generated more help in the occupation of Iraq and a more united front in dealing with Iran's nuclear program.

The Clinton view tends toward the more-traditional one: A president's prestige is a potent force, to be used sparingly because its power is diminished the more it is deployed. Moreover, presidential engagement, in and of itself, lends respectability to those engaged, and hence is as much a reward to be offered as a tool to be employed. In addition, some believe the downsides of diplomatic failure are greater when the president is involved.

Once engaged, a president may be tempted to make unwise concessions to get results, lest failure cause a loss of face.

The downside of the Clinton view lies in its cautionary overtone, which could translate into a reluctance to expand the frontiers of American diplomacy in a changing world. But Lee Feinstein, a Clinton foreign-policy adviser, says the senator's formulation shouldn't be seen "as opposition to diplomacy, which it's not," but merely as a desire to use presidential diplomacy judiciously.

Beyond all that, the debate is most interesting because of what it says about the deeper differences between the candidates themselves. Sen. Clinton sees herself as an experienced leader who understands the meaning and use of American power. Sen. Obama views himself as a citizen of the world, thanks to his background as the son of an African father and American mother, and as one who spent formative years living in Indonesia. He said as much when he described his vision of foreign policy in a speech in Iowa in December: "It's a vision informed by knowing what it's like to live in the wider world, beyond the halls of power.... "If campaigns are about defining choices for the country, this is one coming into clearer focus.[97]

It is wise to respect other people and nations. It is unrealistic to expect them to submit to your will as a precondition for negotiations. The notion that the privilege of a head-of-state meeting with an American president is a "reward" mechanism that should not be offered "until there was evidence that change is happening" a shortsighted strategy. The traditional perspective that Senator Clinton argued for requires that other nations surrender unilaterally and adopt America's agenda and policy objectives. It is unlikely, that such a traditional Ameracentric approach is going to make new friends or even influence other nations. Basically, how can lower-level diplomacy be truly effective if no working relationship exists between various heads-of-state that would guide the agenda of a meeting or set the foundation for further policy discussions?

An international system in which America has growing rather than degrading moral, economic and military authority must be based on America's renewing itself as a nation that is a citizen of the world not merely an American. America's conventional Ameracentric mindset and international strategies and tactics were taken to an extreme by the Bush administration. It is essential for American leaders to recognize that even in a less extreme form, the traditional "my way as a precondition or no reward of a meeting" approach to dialogue between nations' leaders is *sometimes* corrosive to America's economic and national security interests. Moral, economic and military authority is enhanced when used fairly, and rapidly degraded when used unfairly or dictatorially.

America must choose between being a bully or a policeman of the world. It cannot be both at once as we noted in Chapter 1 of Book 1. If America eschews being a bully, then it must also be less Ameracentric and be prepared to engage diplomatically with friends and foes. America is unlikely to make its foes into friends if it is a bully. Americans are only 5% of humanity. The American 5% must accept that the other 95% are different in some ways for historical, cultural and economic reasons and are likely to remain different during our lifetimes.

The Need For American Moral Authority Diplomacy

The "America citizen of the world" perspective and sensitivity to whether America appears "arrogant" is highly relevant to America's being able to lead in the reformulation of the international system that is occurring whether Americans like it or not. With a "citizen of the world" perspective rather than an Ameracentric perspective, American presidents, by being more tolerant and open to other nations' perspectives, agendas needs, goals and political systems, can advance America's perspective, agenda, political system's appeals and objectives. The traditional view that: "We simply cannot legitimize rogue regimes or weaken American prestige by impulsively agreeing to presidential-level talks that have no preconditions" is arrogant and leads to conflict rather than détente or peaceful coexistence. A key word is "impulsively." Its alternate meanings are complex but the fundamental points are simple. The major danger of "impulsively" meeting with other nations' leaders is the Fairness Hypocrisy as well as the need for well thought-out and prepared American leaders.

In the simplest terms, a key feature the emerging 21st century international system is a contest between one-party states and multi-party states. The outcome of that contest will be determined by the nations that are able to conduct themselves in the court of world opinion more peacefully and prosperously Nations that are warlike and not prosperous will not lead the evolving international system to peace and prosperity.

The Failure of Zero Sum Game Strategies: the Bully's Folly

When the American government thinks and acts like a bully, then from an Americacentric perspective, a "win-win" strategy is one that is a win for America both militarily and economically. Such a defective definition of "win-win" is a lose-lose value proposition for China because America has selected a course of action without a positive outcome for China. Such strategies will be resisted, just as they would be by America if the roles were reversed. Equally important, if America presents such flawed "win-win" value propositions to China (or other nations) such zero sum game approaches will be lose-lose for America. Case studies of that are found in chapters 7 of book 2 and chapters 7 and 9 of *China & America's Emerging Partnership: A realistic New Perspective.*

A bully feels others are wrong when they resist it. Consider the following incident:

> Eight thousand American sailors and airmen will spend a lonely
> Thanksgiving on the South China Sea today after the Chinese

government unexpectedly denied the USS Kitty Hawk access to Hong Kong port. The aircraft carrier and its strike group had been expected in Hong Kong yesterday morning ahead of the Thanksgiving holiday....China had denied the visit at the last minute with no explanation....Families of the sailors aboard... had flocked to Hong Kong only to be left high and dry....The unexpected move comes in spite of the recent warming of Sino-US military ties, which appeared firmly on track during a visit to Beijing by Robert Gates, US Secretary of Defense, this month.

But there are plenty of potential sources of friction between the two pacific powers. Beijing recently denounced US plans to sell a $940m upgrade to the Patriot II anti-missile shield to its rival, Taiwan, saying it was a 'rude interference' in Chinese affairs that would disturb ties. 'Beijing needs to know that these gratuitous tit-for-tat moves are going to come back to haunt them,' said Michael Green, former senior Asia advisor to President George W. Bush.[98]

The normal requests and permission for American vessels to enter the Chinese port of Hong Kong also had a hiatus after a US Navy EP3 spy plane collided with a Chinese jet fighter near Hainan China in April 2001.

US Secretary of Defense Gate's failure to mention the sale of new upgrades to the Patriot II missile shield was rude, and the sale was an interference with and threat to China's national security. What insights are unconsciously or consciously missing from Michael Green's analysis of China's "gratuitous" tit-for-tat moves? First, what is missing is the willingness or ability to recognize that China's "tit-for-tat" move is not "gratuitous." The phrase: "gratuitously tit-for-tat" is self-contradictory. By definition "tit-for-tat" is not gratuitous. Secondly, and more importantly, what Michael Green is saying in essence is that America can do whatever it wants, and China must not and should not react negatively. The underlying assumption of a bully is that the victim is acting inappropriately and improperly if the victim resists the bully's desires or aggressive initiatives. This attitude of bullies is delusional, out of touch with the real world,[89] and the real world importance of China to America in 2008 and in the 21st century. America made the move of upgrading the Patriot II missile system in Taiwan. That was "gratuitous." The Chinese reacted by expressing their feelings that upgrading the Patriot II missiles was a "rude interference in Chinese affairs."

It is lost on or unrecognized by or ignored by some Amera-centric observers that Defense Secretary Gates' "warming of Sino-US Military ties" and upgrading the Patriot II missile system of Taiwan are inconsistent. Remember how Americans reacted when the former Soviet Union interfered with the American hemisphere by putting offensive weapons, in that case nuclear weapons, in Cuba. America, in strengthening Taiwan's military, is sending a dangerous signal of military support and bellicose stimuli to Taiwan. Americans should know that better military relations with China and arming Taiwan are inconsistent. The Chinese, quite obviously, although not obviously to the American administration, found that combination "rude interference" in China's affairs that will disturb ties. The signal China chose was reciprocal but non-violent "rude interference" with an American nuclear air-craft carrier and its strike force seeking access to a Chinese port. The lack of explanation, as if any were needed, was deliberately and appropriately, tit-for-tat "rude interference" with the American military at a level and *in a way* that the American military could, would and did notice. Selling upgraded missile systems to Taiwan and Michael Green's analysis of it are classic examples of unenlightened Ameracentric thinking and arrogance. It is not "gratuitous tit-for-tat." It is "tit-for-tat." Implicit in the American reaction is the American assumption that China has no right to object to what America does in China or to China. Such arrogance is delusional.

A Chinese government that adopted the practice of tolerating such injury and insults (reminiscent of gunboat diplomacy that burned the Summer Palace in 1862), would not remain the government of China. Perhaps that is an intended goal of such "rude interference" by America in China's affairs. In any event, in the Age of Species Lethal Weapons and Science, being a bully is not responsible major-power behavior. Putting enhanced missile systems in Taiwan is an encroachment on China's sovereignty. If China sold missile systems to secessionists in America, Americans would react to such impositions on America's sovereignty. America either recognizes Taiwan as part of China or it does not. It cannot do both. But it does. That is the Fairness Hypocrisy and other Principles of Conflict at work in American policymakers and therefore in American policy.

Chapter 7

The Limits of Conventional America Principles of Conflict Based Policy

Overview

Conventional American foreign policy and the Ameracentric Principles of Conflict-flawed perspectives on China and Asia are extremely relevant background to the creation and sustaining of the America and China Partnership and the New School's perspectives that support it. It is important to compare and judge conventional American foreign policy perspectives from the New School's perspectives on the fundamental and conventional foreign policy issues in the 21st century.

The New School's win-win mindset and strategies and the partnership of America and China are essential for America's prosperity and peace. But, American foreign policymakers and scholars have not recognized and accepted the different international leadership styles and roles America and China perform in the 21st century. China's leadership style and role is based on the Principles of Peaceful Coexistence. America's leadership style and role is based on the

Principles of Conflict. The conventional American foreign policy mindset and strategies see and treat America's relationship with China as a zero sum game. They must be replaced by a win-win mindset and strategies, because the conventional zero sum and Ameracentric mindset will undermine America and China's economic and national security and will destabilize and then destroy America and China.

China's Harmonious World Dream: Can Anyone Run the World Peacefully?

The Chinese Peaceful Coexistence Model of a new international system is more stabilizing, more stable, and better in many other respects than the existing international system designed by America that is based upon the Principles of Conflict. This chapter examines examples of the different American zero sum game and Chinese win-win game models of a 21st century international system. It does so by examining the American government's approach to America's relationship with 22% of mankind so far in the 21st century.

The New School's perspective is that China's culture, traditions and behavior norms emphasize and are based on creating harmony. China's President Hu Jintao met with President George W. Bush on April 20, 2006 in Washington and that evening President Hu stated in a speech that:

1. Both China and America share a strong desire to further develop a bilateral relationship and recognize that their relationship is of global importance.
2. The will of all people in all countries should be respected.
3. Democracy and the rule of law should be advocated in international relations.
4. The current international system should be gradually reformed and improved to make it more just and equitable.

5. A new security concept featuring mutual trust, for mutual benefit, equality and cooperation, should be advanced.
6. Disputes should be settled through dialogue and negotiation, and countries should make concerted efforts to safeguard world peace and security.
7. The international community should make development a priority and support developing countries in speeding up their development.
8. The international trade and financial systems should be reformed and improved to ensure that economic globalization will lead to common prosperity.
9. The historical and cultural traditions of different countries and their particular national conditions at different stages of development should be respected.
10. Dialogue between different civilizations should be strengthened to maintain diversity of the world and advance human civilization.

This is a classic Chinese statement of China's "Principles Peaceful Coexistence" approach to China and America's 21st century relationship. China is applying the Principles of Peaceful Coexistence unilaterally to America as America is unilaterally applying the Principles of Conflict to China.

President Hu explained:

> China's decisions to pursue peaceful developments is deeply rooted in its historical and cultural traditions. The Chinese nation has always been a strong advocate of good neighborliness. Over several thousand years China has maintained friendly relations and business and cultural exchanges with all other countries. In a period of over 100 years, from the Opium War in 1840 to the founding of the People's Republic in 1949, China was long subjected to aggression, and economic and social de-

velopment was simply off its national agenda. We, the Chinese, are therefore most appreciative of the value of peace.

The path of peaceful development is the national trait fostered in China's culture over several thousand years, and of course with the lofty pursuit of the Chinese people who love and value peace. China's pursuit of peaceful development conforms to the trend of the times and is in keeping with human progress; in today's world, countries are increasingly interdependent, and the destiny of their people is more connected than ever before. A peaceful environment is the prerequisite for development. Only by strengthening exchanges and broadening cooperation can countries realize common development.

To safe-guard world peace and develop friendly relations with other countries is in the best interests of China's modernization drive and contributes to stability and prosperity of the Asian-Pacific region and the whole world. In pursing peaceful development, China strives to advance both the fundamental interests of its own people and the common interests of the people in the world, and it plays a responsible and constructive role in promoting world peace and development. China actively participates in efforts to ease tensions over regional hot-spot issues, and works to promote regional cooperation of mutual benefit. China is firm in upholding the authority and the role of the United Nations and the UN Security Council. It takes as active part in international peacekeeping and international disaster relief operations. [99]

However, we note that Samuel Huntington asserted in 1996 that:

While Muslim states resorted to violence in 53.5 percent of their crises, violence was used by the United Kingdom only 11.5 percent, by the United States in 17.9 percent, and by the Soviet Union in 28.5 percent of the crises in which they were involved. Among the major powers only China's violence propensity exceeded that of the Muslim states: it employed violence in 76.9 percent of its crises.[100]

How can that be explained? Huntington does not elaborate,

as his focus at that point was on the high propensity to violence among Islamic states. His statement that "Islam has bloody borders" had attracted the most critical comment about his 1993 *Foreign Affairs* article. Huntington states the following basis for his assertion about China's supposed "violent propensity:" "I made that judgment on the basis of a casual survey of inter-civilization conflicts. Quantitative evidence from every disinterested source conclusively demonstrates its validity." Huntington does not indicate the period and length of time he used as his frame of reference for his "casual survey of inter-civilizational conflict". He also did not specify the sources he used as the basis for his statement that: "quantitative evidence from every disinterested source conclusively demonstrates its validity."

Our hypothesis is that Huntington's reference to China's "violent propensity" relates to the 1949 to 1976 period. From 1949 to 1976, under Mao Zedong's leadership, China's priorities were evangelizing ideology and resisting Russian and American hegemony. Mao Zedong was operating with a Principles of Conflict based world view. After 1978, under Deng Xiaoping's and then Jiang Zemin's leadership prosperity and peace replaced ideology and resisting hegemony as China's priorities. After 2002, under Hu Jintao's leadership, rhetoric attacking American ideology and hegemony deliberately disappeared as a theme in Chinese government foreign policy statements.

We examined in chapter 4 of Book 2 the consistent international approach that Deng Xiaoping took, from reaching power in 1978 to his death in 1997, to achieving Freedom from Fear and making harmony with other nations China's goals. In chapters 7, 10 and 11 of Book 1 we examined the consistent domestic approach China took to achieving a harmonious society by emphasizing and achieving Freedom from Want. In chapter 10 of Book 1 we examined why and how China controls factional conflict in a single-party rather than two-party political system.

In the 21st century China's behavior pattern under Hu Jintao's leadership shows China's restraint in both implementing its foreign policy and defense strategies and not using rhetoric expressing the Principles of Conflict. China's foreign policy statements of the Principles of Peaceful Coexistence and reciprocally beneficial economic relations and in foreign policy in rejecting the resort to violence by China against other states or interference other states cultural affairs are self-evident but generally not recognized or not accepted by American policymakers and scholars.

Huntington's finding is most likely based on earlier behavior patterns. Huntington's book was published in 1996. We note, however, that if it is historically correct prior to 1996 that "Among the major powers only China's violence propensity exceeded that of the Muslim states: it employed violence in 76.9 percent of its crises" then:

1. China's use of belligerent rhetoric and propensity to violence in border disputes against other nations has already spontaneously and voluntarily been very effectively corrected by the government of China as a policy priority consistent with China's priorities of prosperity and peace and goal of a harmonious world; and
2. It would be tragic and grossly undermine America's national and economic security if belligerent American foreign policies or defense strategies, or rhetoric or conduct caused China to have to resort to violent responses when it is currently committed to peaceful development and a harmonious world.

The Chinese government and people want peace and a genuine permanent partnership and collaborative equilibrium with America. But, as they demonstrated in the 1950's in Korea and 1960's and 1970's in Vietnam, they will and can very capably defend themselves. Ed note: it might be helpful to explain to readers how "China was defending itself in Korea and Vietnam. Most Americans probably wouldn't have any perspective for that.

Will American Foreign Policy With China Remain Delusional?

The New School's perspectives focus on important questions American policymakers and scholars do not focus on or answer. These questions are neglected, because Ameracentic mindsets consciously chose or simply unconsciously cannot deal with questions such as:

1. How can 300 million Americans prudently base their foreign policy toward China on changing the human rights values, legal system, and political system of China's 1.5 billion people in a 5,000-year-old civilization?
2. Why would anyone among the 300 million Americans in 2008 believe that any of American foreign policies' three goals of changing the human rights values, legal system, and political system of China's 1.5 billion people in a 5,000-year-old civilization can be accomplished by the Principles of Conflict based policies America has been using?
3. What rational or empirical basis exists for such American policy goals succeeding by means of America forcing or hectoring China to acquiesce to American dictates?
4. What rational or empirical basis exists in the circumstances for American policy goals of making China accept a "responsible stakeholder" role rather than its "responsible major power role" or accepting rather than reforming the existing international system?
5. Is conventional America foreign policymaking and scholar-

ship based largely on delusional goals and analysis?

6. Is the explanation of American conventional policy making and scholarship regarding China that Americans are obsessed with ideology and hegemony to the point that American foreign policy and scholarship is largely based on unsuccessful attempts at evangelizing ideals and seeking to retain hegemony at any cost to America's national security interests?

7. Is American foreign policymaking and scholarship regarding China irrational and delusional in making ideology and hegemony America's foreign policy priorities at the cost of America's prosperity and peace if empirically it is not possible for American foreign policy to obtain either the universality of the American ideals, Rule of Law or political system or to preserve the 20th century international system or American hegemony in the 21st century?

8. Is America able to remain economically or militarily secure, or survive in the 21st century if the combination of American Constitutional majority-rule-democracy and the character of the American people in the circumstances of the 21st century cannot avoid a clash of civilizations and economic and military conflict with China?

9. Is conventional American foreign policymaking and scholarship consistent with the success or the failure of America as a viable civilization in the 21st century?

10. At what stage is America currently at in Jared Diamond's four stages of why civilizations collapse?

11. Exactly how is conventional American China-directed economic and foreign policymaking and defense strategy and scholarship preventing rather than causing America's failure as a civilization in the 21st century?

The New School's recognizes that asking these crucial questions will also invigorate and correctly focus debate about:

1. What America's goals and strategies should be for responding to the fundamental foreign policy, defense strategies and scientific research issue in the 21st century?

2. What America's goals and strategies should be for responding to the conventional foreign policy issues policymakers and scholars do focus on in the 21st century?

3. How can America's economic and national security be aligned with China's?

4. How can America best adapt to the profoundly changing global economy, American economy, and China's economic growth in the 21st century.

The Dilemma of Cause and Effect: The Danger of Hedging and the Principles of Conflict

On the one hand, neither America nor China can unilaterally or even bilaterally disarm. They have to help police as well as pacify mankind. On the other, if they "hedge" against each other's power, that inevitably will "shape" each other's behavior, one as a Permission Society and the other as a Majority Rule Democracy, about which each is passionately nationalistic. Such "hedging" and strong nationalistic passions can lead to war[101] and our extinction. The hedging itself can be the cause of conflict as each nation's "hedges" negatively "shapes" the behavior of the other. A committed genuine partnership is the essential solution because it reduces conflict, promotes collaborations on and thereby synchronization of policies, and reduces the need for and use of "hedges" because it succeeds at "shaping" each nation's behavior into consensus, mutual alignment and acceptance of permanent reciprocal benefits, rather than zero sum game competition.

The clash of civilizations can be managed, but not the hubris of nations, like China at the end of the Quig Dynasty or America today. Neither had sufficient moral authority. China also lacked military authority at the end of the Quig Dynasty. America today, in contrast, has military authority, but America's military authority is limited by America's current deficiencies of moral authority and economic authority and the strains caused in its military authority.

American Policymakers, Scholars, Media and Press's Traditional Perspectives on China

How should America policymakers, scholars, and opinion leaders respond to the changes President Hu initiated in 2002 of eschewing the aggressive rhetoric that was a legacy of the Cold War between communist and capitalist ideology and hegemony struggles, and Mao Zedong's Principles of Conflict based perspectives and policies? As China shifted under Deng Xiaoping and Jiang Zemin from a communist planned economy to a socialist market economy and capitalist approach to China's development such rhetoric hostile to America. became outdated, inappropriate and detrimental to China Although the change to a capitalist economic mindset and strategies and change in China's rhetoric of confrontation to one of harmony has occurred, that has not changed the American people or American policymakers, scholars, medias and press's perspectives on China.

We examined the profound mindset and strategy changes in China after Mao Zedong's death in 1976 and the "hostile observer phenomenon" effecting non-Chinese perspectives on China in *America & China's Emerging Partnership: A New Realistic Perspective.* We emphasized the danger of the hostile observer phenomenon in shaping American public opinion and therefore domestic and foreign policy that is hostile to China and harmful to both America and China's economic and national security.

Laurence Brahm, an American fluent in Mandarin living in China, writing before 2002, was able to look at the world with both Ameracentric and Chinacentric perspectives. Brahm had the following comments on traditional Chinese media coverage of the West before the heightened emphasis of the "Harmonious World" perspective that President Hu Jintao and Premier Wen Jiabao implemented to reduce hostile rhetoric as it was not consistent with China's foreign and domestic policy toward America:

China's official media often reacts to the excessive negativism in Western reporting on China, which in turn stimulates more negative reporting. In turn, as China enters a new century and era, probably the single greatest handicap to Western business decision-makers and politicians in making informed decisions concerning China, is the lack of balanced and clear information—reflecting in the Western press—the reality of developments in China. To a great extent, this is due to the fact that Western perceptions of China have been formed within a framework of self-perpetuating misperceptions and prejudices, which more often than not serve as convenient political ammunition for domestic voter consumption where the electorate itself remains ill-informed on the subject. Unfortunately, this framework is not easy to dismantle, as it stems from over a century of misleading reporting.

In the 1800's, dogmatic foreign missionaries reported China as a vast population of "heathens" to convert into a "harvest of souls;" Western politicians supported this premise as it coincided with the political objectives of the day, that being to colonize Asia economically. During the cold war period, nascent American policies of containing China were premised on the domino theory of John Foster Dulles, who hyped a "red threat" consuming Asia and threatening American security interests. Journalist reports from the field by the likes of Edgar Snow and Theodore White, attempting to explain what communism meant for "New China," were suppressed by editors who sought to adhere to the Washington, D.C. line. The framework for Western media coverage of China had by that time more or less been set.

The tendency of the Western media is to cover China through the framework of stereotype, focusing on the exotic oddity or extreme situation. Often the Western press relies on rumors generated among the diplomatic or foreign business communities in China, not on actual circumstances.

These rumors or examples of situations which can be re-packaged to fulfill preconceived ideas of China are the substance of news which is absorbed by the western public as fact. This situation is extremely dangerous when one thinks that key business and political decision-makers are relying on speculation and recycled stereotypes when making policy which concerns the most populous nation on earth and the fastest-growing developing economy in the world today.

In fact, there is nothing new about blinkered reporting on China, a tradition in the Western media which dates back to the old Treaty Port era. Author Sterling Seagrave, in his biography of the Empress Dowager Ci Xi, described the tenor of China report-ing at the end of the Qing Dynasty as follows:

> Little historical background was understood by westerners in China, who were dependent upon what they could learn from Treaty Port compradors or hired interpret-ers, who were themselves ill-informed and far from disin-terested. Such people filled in the gaps in their knowledge with colorful inventions, because it was important to seem to know what was going on. Over drinks at the Long Bar in Shanghai or gossiping at the new racetrack, they mingled misinformation and supposition and passed it on by letter, diary, memoir, travelogue, diplomatic report, and journal-ism to the far corners of the earth, where it was accepted as fact.

The above, in fact, serves as a good description of the reporting situation as it exists today. Much of what is reported in the Western press, and in turn accepted as fact about China, is derived in very much the same way. The Shanghai Treaty Port atmosphere of speculation and hype described by Seagrave could very well be applied to Beijing, Shanghai, or Hong Kong, where most journalists' China scoops originate. The analysis provided in the Western media is often flat, viewing China's political dynamics as a struggle between extreme factions (conservative-hard-liner vs. liberal-reformist). Such extreme factions do not really exist. Deeper analysis of China's complicated politics is hard to find in the Western media, which tends to reduce everything to Hollywood, bad guy—good guy simplicity. As William Overholt, who wrote *China: The Next Economic Superpower*, has commented:

For any historian of Chinese–American relations, the mystery is why the outside world has failed to appreciate the positive aspects of China's course. Whereas any East European leadership that recorded one or two of China's achievements in 1994-1995 would have been hailed for its genius, most of China's accomplishments attracted no attention in the Western press. As far as the average American could tell [from the media] China did little in this period except oppress its people and plan an invasion of Taiwan.

While there is nothing wrong with reporting negative events in China, to simply focus exclusively on them and to blow them up, painting them out of context, does not help westerners coming to China, or their governments, to usefully comprehend those events and to place the economic, social and political transitions occurring here today in their correct context or perspective.

There is little attempt to understand the workings of the Chinese government, or the reasons underlying certain policies, or the psychology of the Chinese populace and their subsequent reactions. More often than not, the Western media seems to be forced to find stories to match the requirements of editorial boards in New York City or Washington, D.C., which need to keep fulfilling what they believe or imagine to be the state of affairs in China. When reading China press reporting in the major American newspapers, it seems as if these reports could be coming straight from the desk of the U.S. State Department, not from the cities or countryside of China. Little wonder Chinese officials—together with many from other Asian countries as well— tend to see Western media coverage as part of a conspiracy to retard China's economic growth and coming-of-age as a superpower. Whether correct or not, when somebody living or traveling regularly to China reads the Western Press coverage of China, it is easy to come up with such rationale as a logical explanation. [102]

As the New School's perspectives emphasize, the Chinese leadership's adoption of the Harmonious Society and World Model follows both the peaceful coexistence policy insights of Deng Xiaoping and the cultural traditions of China, which Americans insufficiently understand and therefore often perceive as insincere propaganda. But, if the fundamental contrast of America's Rights Society, majority-rule-democracy and zero sum game mindset and China's Permission Society, Consensus Democracy and win-win mindset are recognized by American policymakers, scholars and the American people, then what seems like false propaganda to a zero game mindset may not and should not seem false to a win-win mindset's perspective.

One of our goals is to facilitate Americans' being able to see, feel and think about China from both Ameracentric and Chinacentric perspectives. If Americans can perceive the Chinese way of seeing and reaching out to the world in addition to how Americans perceive themselves and their particular world view, it will be that much easier to achieve a prosperous and peaceful alignment of China and America's success, and for Americans to understand why a genuine committed partnership of America and China is essential now to achieve what we term "collaborative equilibrium" rather than competitive and confrontational disequilibrium Chinese frequently comment that the insights in our books are "common sense" to Chinese, but it is amazing for Americans to understand and accept what seems to be common sense to the Chinese.

The Bush administration's Mindset and Perceptions of and Strategies toward China

Fortunately, President George W. Bush's policy toward China evolved as noted in *America & China's Emerging Partnership: A Realistic New Perspective:*

> During his 2000 election campaign, President George W. Bush described China as a 'strategic competitor' whose ambitions

for global influence must be contained. Like Presidents Reagan and Clinton, President Bush came to office convinced that if he set tougher rules about engaging China, the Chinese would change their behavior. Presidents Reagan and Clinton came to abandon that view, and President George W. Bush seems to be being moved along in a similar reappraisal. He promised in his second inaugural address to confront 'every ruler in very nation' that resists the tide of freedom. But the relationship with China is increasingly important to America. In 2006, President Bush characterized America's relationship with China as 'complicated' and said 'China and the United States share extensive common strategic interests.' Those common strategic interests and China's economic power requires a collaborative breakthrough, which has not yet occurred but must occur.

America and China's leaders must directly collaborate in real time to deal effectively with increasingly complex geopolitical dangers. Diplomacy carried out by press conference is not a prudent way for the world's current and emerging super powers to communicate effectively. The speed and seriousness of 'real time' daily events through the world require a committed and formalized partnership between America and China and therefore between their Presidents.[103]

Victor D. Cha was Director of Asian Affairs at America's National Security Council from 2004-2007 and Deputy Head of the U.S. Delegation to the six-party talks with North Korea in 2006-2007. He presented an explanation of "Washington's Untold Success Story in Winning Asia" in *Foreign Affairs* that seeks to rebut criticism of the Bush administration's China policy:

> ...it has become increasingly popular to lament the demise of U.S. influence in Asia. Power transitions, resurgent Asian nationalism, and poor policy choices in Washington have supposedly undermined U.S. leadership in Asia. According to critics, the Bush administration has been distracted by Iraq, has failed to deal adequately with China's economic and political rise, and has alienated many Asians with its singular focus on counterterrorism. The lack of U.S. leadership after the Cold War, detrac-

tors charge, has made Asia ripe for conflict.

But the conventional wisdom is wrong. The United States' position in Asia is now stronger than ever, and Asia remains at peace. The United States has achieved a pragmatic, results-oriented, cooperative relationship with China, and it has expanded and strengthened its alliance with Japan just as Tokyo and Beijing are improving their bilateral relations. This confluence of events has created an emerging U.S.-Chinese-Japanese partnership that greatly enhances regional stability. Washington has also improved its defense relationship with South Korea and successfully facilitated the shutdown of North Korea's bomb-making capabilities through the six-party talks. Finally, the United States has steadily improved its relations with Southeast Asian nations, largely by building on the goodwill it created by leading the humanitarian response to the tsunami in 2004.

Few commentators in Japan, South Korea, or the United States will give any credit to the Abe, Rohm, and Bush administrations for these accomplishments. Rather than conceding that the Bush administration has made progress, naysayers in Washington tend to attribute Asia's good fortune to benign neglect while the administration's neoconservatives were busy focusing on Iraq. But they are wrong. President George W. Bush's Asia policy has worked.

WHO'S ASIA'S DADDY

Contrary to the dire warnings issued by many Asia pessimists, China is not eating the United States' lunch in Asia. Beijing is indeed building its military capabilities, pressing for free-trade agreements, and increasingly occupying central positions in various regional organizations. But those who argue that these moves signal a power transition, whereby China is displacing the United States as the region's new benefactor, are mistaken. A power transition may come to Asia someday, but not anytime soon.

Critics who predict an American sunset in Asia are missing a fundamental point: in order to be a region's benefactor, a leading power must be willing and able to provide for the region's public good. After World War II, the United States became the world's undisputed leader, first by providing markets for the recovering European and Asian economies but also by offering international security. Today, China offers a vast market to other Asian countries, but it has not proved itself as a provider of public goods. Beijing's response to the 2004 tsunami, for example, which killed 280,000 people and displaced over 1.8 million, was slow, feeble, and parochial (China initially provided only $60 million and one medical team). Meanwhile, within 48 hours of the disaster, the United States had enlisted Australia, India, and Japan and organized the largest emergency relief mission in modern history. It sent over 16,000 U.S. military personnel, two dozen ships, and 100 aircraft as part of its immediate $346 million relief package, followed by an additional U.S. commitment of $600 million. This rapid response gave UN agencies both the time and the infrastructure they needed to mobilize and get on the ground. No other nation, and no international organization, could have coordinated such a response. Faced with a crisis of unprecedented magnitude, the world reflexively turned to the United States for leadership. Whether the United States covets this role or not, it is still the only true leader in Asia.

WASHINGTON'S NEW COMRADES

Far from being supplanted by China, the United States is enlisting Beijing's help. The Bush administration's China policy, which was once confrontational, has evolved into a hard-nosed but cooperative dialogue. Its goal is to turn China into a "responsible stakeholder" in the international system, as Robert Zoellick, president of the World Bank and former deputy secretary of state, has put it. The Chinese leadership has welcomed this effort because it demonstrates the United States' acceptance of China's rightful place in the world, implies that China's growth is not threatening, and leads to cooperation on numerous global issues. The respect accorded to China through the stakeholder concept has allowed Washington to raise difficult issues such as democratic values. Because the United States is not imposing its values, China seems more open to discussing the need for greater political liberties as it seeks its proper place in the world.

This effort has paid off. High-level diplomatic talks, led by Deputy Secretary of State John Negroponte and his Chinese counterpart, Dai Bingguo, have produced cooperation on counter proliferation efforts, such as those aimed at North Korea and Iran, and on devising a post-Kyoto climate policy that focuses on programs that are both energy efficient and pro-growth rather than on unrealistic reductions of emissions. The dialogue has been less successful on human rights and China's policy toward Africa, but U.S. persuasion and the spotlight of the Beijing Olympics are likely to compel changes over the coming year. The U.S.-China Strategic Economic Dialogue, led by U.S. Treasury Secretary Henry Paulson, which seeks to manage difficult issues such as currency valuation and intellectual property rights, has made some progress. The yuan has appreciated by 9.4 percent since mid-2005, and Beijing is beginning to clamp down on software piracy. Tensions with China over trade remain high: 27 percent of current U.S. antidumping orders apply to Chinese goods, the U.S. trade representative has authorized four cases against China in the World Trade Organization since last year, and Congress is threatening to slap tariffs on all goods made in China. Nevertheless, these talks signal a U.S. commitment to manage trade tensions through negotiations, rather than through trade wars.

Discussions between President Bush and Chinese President Hu Jintao constitute the least formal but most important aspect of U.S.-Chinese relations. From early on, the Bush White House understood that the most effective way to get things done in China was to go to the very top. When agreements are made at this level, both sides take their commitments very seriously. For this reason, the administration worked to cultivate relations with Hu and his predecessor, Jiang Zemin. This channel was particularly important in garnering support for a firm UN Security Council response to Pyongyang's October 2006 nuclear test and in setting the diplomatic course toward the agreement last February that shut down North Korea's only known operating nuclear reactor.

The strength of the U.S.-Chinese relationship pays dividends in quiet but critical ways. Taiwanese President Chen Shui-bian has been pushing the envelope on independence in the run-up to the March 2008 elections in Taiwan (for example, Taipei recently applied for UN membership), yet China has not responded militarily because it is confident that Washington considers such antics a risk to peace in the region.

Similarly, Beijing has remained conspicuously quiet about former Japanese Prime Minister Shinzo Abe's much-publicized steps to upgrade Japan's military capabilities. China's poise stems from the current healthy state of U.S.-Chinese relations and an overarching fear of Japanese rearmament without the United States' presence as Tokyo's security guarantor. When U.S.-Chinese ties are strained, Beijing sees U.S.-Japanese cooperation as an effort to contain China, but when U.S.-Chinese relations are good, Beijing tends to view the U.S.-Japanese alliance as a check on Japan's regional ambitions. Today's goodwill has resulted in unexpected U.S.-Chinese-Japanese cooperation, which stabilizes Asia. The United States still talks tough about China's arms buildup (which is intended to intimidate Taiwan), expanding defense budget, and drive for an anti-satellite capability. But today, these difficult discussions constitute only one part, rather than the entirety, of the relationship.

Victor Cha described the Bush administration's relationship with Japan:

JAPAN'S GLOBAL ALLIANCE

The U.S.-Japanese alliance has reached an unprecedented level of intimacy. Beginning in his first term, President Bush chose to reinvest in Japan as the United States' key ally in Asia and to overhaul its military posture there. This base realignment -- the most significant in 30 years -- includes moving 7,000-10,000 U.S. marines from Okinawa to Guam, transplanting dangerously congested facilities in Okinawa to less populated areas, and creating joint training facilities in Guam. The changes will enable greater interoperability between the two militaries, give the United States more mobility in the Pacific (thanks partly to a U.S. nuclear carrier based at Yokosuka), and reduce civil-military tensions with Japanese host communities, thereby ensuring long-term domestic support for the alliance.

Washington and Tokyo are also advocating a "global alliance" that would focus on common values such as liberal democracy, free-market economics, the rule of law, and respect for human rights. As a result, Japan has taken unprecedented steps into the international arena. It has deployed ground forces in Iraq for humanitarian operations, flown C-130 supply missions, and become the second-largest donor to Iraqi reconstruction, with an assistance package valued at nearly $5 billion. In support of coalition forces in Afghanistan, Japan has deployed two naval vessels in the Indian Ocean, which provide critical water and refueling services. At the Bush-Abe summit last April, Tokyo committed to continuing its operations in Iraq and Afghanistan as well as stepping up assistance to the Federally Administered Tribal Areas in eastern Pakistan, a suspected al Qaeda haven. Japan has also joined the United States in efforts to improve the business climate in Indonesia and supported France, Germany, and the United Kingdom in nuclear negotiations with Iran. These are hugely important and unprecedented steps by Japan, and they represent a new norm in Japanese foreign policy.

As Japan expands its security profile to become more of a global player, it is doing so wholly within the context of the U.S.-Japanese alliance, which acts as a constraint on more ambitious Japanese rearmament. This should be comforting to other states in the region. Moreover, both Abe's October 2006 visit to Beijing and Chinese Premier Wen Jiabao's wildly popular visit to Japan last April helped thaw Chinese-Japanese relations, which had turned chilly under Abe's predecessor, Junichiro Koizumi. Historically, Asian states have become concerned whenever the United States has grown close to Japan in order to contain China or close to China at the expense of traditional U.S. allies and smaller regional powers. The situation today -- a cooperative U.S.-Chinese relationship, a strong U.S.-Japanese alliance, and good relations between Japan and China -- is a viable equilibrium.[104]

Victor Cha states:

Beijing's hosting of the six-party talks has *forced* China to take ownership of the problem. Indeed, China's own reputation has come to *depend* on its ability to bring nuclear disarmament in North Korea. At each critical point in the crisis, U.S. –Chinese cooperation has been vital.[99] (Emphasis Added)

The use of the concept of American foreign policy forcing

China to do things America wants and the concept that China's own reputation then depends on its ability to achieve America's goals exhibits the rule the world concept in American foreign policy makers' mindset. China does not seek to rule the world. China is content to let the world run itself and to focus on running China's 22% of the world's populations affairs successfully and being a responsible major power and well liked neighbor to other nations. The concept in American foreign policymakers' mindset is that America can make China do what America wants it to because China's reputation depends on it doing so. Looked at through the eyes of a win-win major world power, such as China, those concepts are part of a bully diplomacy ruling the world mindset.

China's leaders look past that because their win-win goals and strategies are working extremely well for China as Deng Xiao Ping foresaw. In our opinion, both the concept that America can force China to do what America wants and the concept that China's reputation can be made to depend on China doing what America wants are unrealistic and delusional.

Those concepts are components in an American foreign policy approach to China that, in our view, currently does not understand China from a Chinese perspective and therefore is very naive. In our view, the Chinese government's responses and diplomacy is mature, nuanced and extremely successful.

As is examined in Chapter 8 of Book 2, many American policy makers and scholars emphasize that these are serious deficiencies in what they see as several American governments inadequate approaches in Asia. Thus both the conventional Ameracentric and the New School's perspectives seek changes in America's goals and strategies with China. But the perspectives on what the goals and strategies should be are fundamentally different. They are a choice between the collaboration or clash of the American and Chinese nations and civilizations.

Victor Cha, having declared the George W. Bush administration's strategies a success stated:

In a quiet and unassuming way, the Bush administration has left Asia in good shape. So much for those academics, such as Paul Bracken, Kent Calder, and Aaron Friedberg, who once predicted that Asia would be a cauldron of conflict after the Cold War. Those predicting regional rivalry in Asia never anticipated Washington's adaptability and the centrality of U.S. alliances in Asia's new architecture. In addition to strong U.S. engagement with ASEAN and APEC, the new regional architecture is a patchwork of overlapping and interconnecting bilateral, trilateral, and quadrilateral relationships and five- and six-party networks. Bush bashers do not give the administration enough credit, nor even acknowledge that it has followed a consistent strategy. But few would be willing to trade the current situation in Asia for that of any other period in recent history.

CAMPAIGNING AGAINST ASIA

Unfortunately, there is a real risk that the situation could deteriorate. The presidential primary season in the United States threatens to disrupt the delicate balance that Washington has created in Asia. The candidates' views are already gravitating to two extremes. Republicans are focusing on China's alleged attempt to displace the United States in Asia and the threat China poses to Taiwan. On the Republican side of the aisle, discussions of cooperation with Beijing will likely be overtaken by discussions of China's defense budget, missile buildup, growing submarine fleet, and anti-satellite capabilities. At the other extreme are the trade protectionists. They focus on China's $233 billion trade surplus with the United States, its $1 trillion-plus reserves of foreign exchange, its undervalued currency, the inadequate quality of its exports, and the perceived threat China poses to U.S. workers. Pending legislation proposes to designate China as a currency manipulator and slap a uniform tariff on all Chinese goods sold in the United States unless it dramatically revalues its currency. Democratic presidential candidates Hillary Clinton and John Edwards have already opposed the FTA with South Korea in an effort to play to campaign crowds in the Midwest, where people fear the loss of more manufacturing jobs.[100]

Victor Cha then states:

This electoral posturing could have unintended consequences: in Asia, a polarized debate in the United States could
be viewed as the new reality. Beijing's impression that President
Bush is a lame duck, coupled with the harsh tone on the
campaign trail, may prompt Chinese leaders to ignore the Bush
White House and focus on laying down some markers with
the next U.S. administration. They may, for example, abandon
their restrained position on Taiwan and revert to the aggressive
behavior of the past. Faced with an environment of disintegrat-
ing U.S.-Chinese relations, Beijing might also feel the need to
openly oppose any attempt by a future Japanese government to
expand Japan's military.

Before any lasting damage is done, debates on Asia need to
move back to a pragmatic political center instead of being driven
by alarmists on the left and the right. It will be incumbent on
the new administration, Democratic or Republican, to keep Asia
on an even keel by building on the accomplishments of the
Bush White House. Its guiding principle should be that U.S. and
Asian interests are best advanced when the parties invest in their
bilateral alliances based on common values, pursue free and fair
trade, and enlist regional partners for multilateral solutions to
difficult security problems.

For example, the United States must maintain the balance
between its pragmatic working relationship with China and its
deepening cooperation with Japan. With China, it will need to
forge a broad-based relationship in which it can have a tough
dialogue with Beijing on military issues but at the same time
push China to contribute to resolving global problems such as
nuclear proliferation, climate change, and ballooning energy
needs. Meanwhile, the United States should continue to encourage Japan to step up its international involvement, as Japan has
done in Afghanistan and Iraq, while quietly pressing for more
deregulation and economic reform, which has helped spur
Japan's economic recovery.[105]

Victor Cha's view that "in a quiet and unassuming way, the
Bush administration has left Asia in good shape" forcing China to
be a responsible stakeholder doing what America wants it to do
and thereby protecting China's own reputation is unrealistic and

delusional, and may appear harmless. But America's creating a more militarily capable and proactive Japan is destabilizing. China and Japan were peaceful. America's using Japan as a hedge against China disturbs a peaceful nation in a peaceful region. China has ten times the population and potential of Japan. America's using Japan to hedge China may unleash forces in Japanese politics that are destabilizing in Asia and difficult in the future for America, Japan or China to control.[102]

America armed Iraq to hedge against Iran and Afghanistan to hedge against the former Soviet Union. That dynamic became difficult for America to control and contributed, with poor presidential leadership, to America's being entangled in wars in Afghanistan and Iraq. It may have been better for America and the region if American hedging and errors in presidential decision making had not occurred. That is hard to anticipate from an American Principles of Conflict driven perspective but is anticipated and ameliorated from a Chinese Principles of Peaceful Coexistence implementing perspective. After the collapse of the Soviet Union, in the years leading up to 911, America, the world's sole superpower's greatest national security threat was its policymakers' Principles of Conflict driven mindset and strategies. It remains among America's greatest national security threats. Ironically, it is a danger that is within America's control, if America recognizes that. The ramifications of America's Principles of Conflict driven mindset and strategies after the 911 attacks and misconceived War on Terror and War on Iraq are examined in chapter 4 of Book 1 which is titled "The Equality of the Strong and the Weak in the Age of Species Lethal Weapons and Science.

The creation of the partnership of America and China and the collaborative equilibrium mechanism and Principles of Peaceful Coexistence based new international system it creates will help to defuse the danger of America's policymakers' conventional Principles of Conflict driven mindset and strategies and increase

America's economic and national security. America's conventional mindset and strategies towards China limit the amount of collaborative equilibrium China currently can create for America.

None of America's economic and national security problems can be solved without America administrations' enabling themselves and China's government to achieve not merely better collaboration but collaborative equilibrium between themselves and with 190 other nations. American policymakers recognize this, but do not yet recognize that improving their own mindset and strategies are the keys to solving America's conventionally recognized foreign policy and defense strategy issues and the 21st century's fundamental issue. America's 43rd president's "Responsible Stakeholder" approach to China is a classic 21st century example of American policymaking being unrealistic and unpersuasive. Fortunately, there is much potential for rapid improvement.

"Responsible Stakeholder" Insult or "Responsible Major Power" Diplomacy

The Bush administration entered office with a hostile mindset and confrontational strategies toward China, which it identified as a strategic competitor. It's intended approach, rejecting the Clinton administration's "strategic cooperation approach" at the start of his Presidency changed after the 911 attacks into a "hard-nosed cooperative dialogue" with its goal being to turn China into "a responsible stakeholder" in the American-dominated international system, as Robert Zoellick, then deputy secretary of state and later Vice Chairman of Goldman Sachs International and now President of the World Bank has stated.[106] The "responsible stakeholder" concept apparently emanated from Robert Zoellick, while Deputy Secretary of State in the Bush administration. Here are excerpts that raise important issues from a speech entitled "Whether China: From Membership to Responsibility," which Mr. Zoellick, in that capacity, gave to an American audience. In examining Mr. Zoellick's mindset consider what he said from a Chinese rather than merely an America perspective:

> Earlier this year, I had the pleasure of making the acquaintance of Mr. Zheng Bijian, Chair of the China Reform Forum, who over some decades has been a counselor to China's leaders. We have spent many hours in Beijing and Washington discussing China's course of development and Sino-American relations. It has been my good fortune to get to know such a thoughtful man who has helped influence, through the Central Party School, the outlook of many officials during a time of tremendous change for China.
>
> This month, in anticipation of President Hu's visit to the United States, Mr. Zheng published the lead article in *Foreign Affairs*, "China's 'Peaceful Rise' to Great Power Status." This evening, I would like to give you a sense of the current dialogue between the United States and China by sharing my perspective.
>
> Some 27 years ago, Chinese leaders took a hard look at their country and didn't like what they saw. China was just emerging from the Cultural Revolution. It was desperately poor, deliberately isolated from the world economy, and opposed to nearly every international institution. Under Deng Xiaoping, as Mr. Zheng explains, China's leaders reversed course and decided "to embrace globalization rather than detach themselves from it."
>
> Seven U.S. presidents of both parties recognized this strategic shift and worked to integrate China as a full member of the international system. Since 1978, the United States has also encouraged China's economic development through market reforms. Our policy has succeeded remarkably well: the dragon emerged and joined the world. Today, from the United Nations to the World Trade Organization, from agreements on ozone depletion to pacts on nuclear weapons, China is a player at the table.
>
> And China has experienced exceptional economic growth. Whether in commodities, clothing, computers, or capital markets, China's presence is felt every day. China is big, it is growing, and it will influence the world in the years ahead. For the United States and the world, the essential question is – how

will China use its influence? To answer that question, it is time to take our policy beyond opening doors to China's membership into the international system: We need to urge China to become a *responsible stakeholder* in that system.

China has a responsibility to strengthen the international system that has enabled its success. In doing so, China could achieve the objective identified by Mr. Zheng: "to transcend the traditional ways for great powers to emerge." As Secretary Rice has stated, the United States welcomes a confident, peaceful, and prosperous China, one that appreciates that its growth and development depends on constructive connections with the rest of the world. Indeed, we hope to intensify work with a China that not only adjusts to the international rules developed over the last century, but also joins us and others to address the challenges of the new century.

From China's perspective, it would seem that its national interest would be much better served by working with us to shape the future international system. If it isn't clear why the United States should suggest a cooperative relationship with China, consider the alternatives. Picture the wide range of global challenges we face in the years ahead – terrorism and extremists exploiting Islam, the proliferation of weapons of mass destruction, poverty, disease – and ask whether it would be easier or harder to handle those problems if the United States and China were cooperating or at odds.

For fifty years, our policy was to fence in the Soviet Union while its own internal contradictions undermined it. For thirty years, our policy has been to draw out the People's Republic of China. As a result, the China of today is simply not the Soviet Union of the late 1940s:

> It does not seek to spread radical, anti-American ideologies.
>
> While not yet democratic, it does not see itself in a twilight conflict against democracy around the globe.
>
> While at times mercantilist, it does not see itself in a death struggle with capitalism.
>
> And most importantly, China does not believe that its future depends on overturning the fundamental order of the international system. In fact, quite the reverse: Chinese

leaders have decided that their success depends on being networked with the modern world.

If the Cold War analogy does not apply, neither does the distant balance-of-power politics of 19th Century Europe. The global economy of the 21st Century is a tightly woven fabric. We are too interconnected to try to hold China at arm's length, hoping to promote other powers in Asia at its expense. Nor would the other powers hold China at bay, initiating and terminating ties based on an old model of drawing-room diplomacy. The United States seeks constructive relations with all countries that do not threaten peace and security. So if the templates of the past do not fit, how should we view China at the dawn of the 21st Century?

On both sides, there is a gulf in perceptions. The overwhelming priority of China's senior officials is to develop and modernize a China that still faces enormous internal challenges. While proud of their accomplishments, China's leaders recognize their country's perceived weaknesses, its rural poverty, and the challenges of political and social change. Two-thirds of China's population – nearly 900 million people – are in poor rural areas, living mostly as subsistence farmers, and 200 million Chinese live on less than a dollar a day. In China, economic growth is seen as an internal imperative, not as a challenge to the United States.

Therefore, China clearly needs a benign international environment for its work at home. Of course, the Chinese expect to be treated with respect and will want to have their views and interests recognized. But China does not want a conflict with the United States. Nevertheless, many Americans worry that the Chinese dragon will prove to be a fire-breather. There is a cauldron of anxiety about China. The U.S. business community, which in the 1990s saw China as a land of opportunity, now has a more mixed assessment. Smaller companies worry about Chinese competition, rampant piracy, counterfeiting, and currency manipulation. Even larger U.S. businesses – once the backbone of support for economic engagement – are concerned that mercantilist Chinese policies will try to direct controlled markets instead of opening competitive markets. American workers wonder if they can compete.

China needs to recognize how its actions are perceived by others. China's involvement with troublesome states indicates at best a blindness to consequences and at worst something more ominous. China's actions – combined with a lack of transparency – can create risks. Uncertainties about how China will use its power will lead the United States – and others as well – to hedge relations with China. Many countries hope China will pursue a "Peaceful Rise," but none will bet their future on it.

For example, China's rapid military modernization and increases in capabilities raise questions about the purposes of this buildup and China's lack of transparency. The recent report by the U.S. Department of Defense on China's military posture was not confrontational, although China's reaction to it was. The U.S. report described facts, including what we know about China's military, and discussed alternative scenarios. If China wants to lessen anxieties, it should openly explain its defense spending, intentions, doctrine, and military exercises.

Views about China are also shaped by its growing economic footprint. China has gained much from its membership in an open, rules-based international economic system, and the U.S. market is particularly important for China's development strategy. Many gain from this trade, including millions of U.S. farmers and workers who produce the commodities, components, and capital goods that China is so voraciously consuming.

But no other country – certainly not those of the European Union or Japan – would accept a $162 billion bilateral trade deficit, contributing to a $665 billion global current account deficit. China – and others that sell to China – cannot take its access to the U.S. market for granted. Protectionist pressures are growing.

China has been more open than many developing countries, but there are increasing signs of mercantilism, with policies that seek to direct markets rather than opening them. The United States will not be able to sustain an open international economic system – or domestic U.S. support for such a system – without greater cooperation from China, as a stakeholder that shares responsibility on international economic issues.

For example, a responsible major global player shouldn't tolerate rampant theft of intellectual property and counterfeiting, both of which strike at the heart of America's knowledge economy. China's pledges – including a statement just last week by President Hu in New York to crack down on the criminals who ply this trade – are welcome, but the results are not yet evident. China needs to fully live up to its commitments to markets where America has a strong competitive advantage, such as in services, agriculture, and certain manufactured goods. And while China's exchange rate policy offered stability in the past, times have changed. China may have a global current account surplus this year of nearly $150 billion, among the highest in the world. This suggests that China's recent policy adjustments are an initial step, but much more remains to be done to permit markets to adjust to imbalances. China also shares a strong interest with the United States in negotiating a successful WTO Doha agreement that opens markets and expands global growth.

China's economic growth is driving its thirst for energy. In response, China is acting as if it can somehow "lock up" energy supplies around the world. This is not a sensible path to achieving energy security. Moreover, a mercantilist strategy leads to partnerships with regimes that hurt China's reputation and lead others to question its intentions. In contrast, market strategies can lessen volatility, instability, and hoarding. China should work with the United States and others to develop diverse sources of energy, including through clean coal technology, nuclear, renewables, hydrogen, and biofuels. Our new Asia Pacific Partnership on Clean Development and Climate – as well as the bilateral dialogue conducted by the U.S. Department of Energy and China's National Development and Reform Commission – offer practical mechanisms for this cooperation. We should also encourage the opening of oil and gas production in more places around the world. We can work on energy conservation and efficiency, including through standards for the many appliances made in China. Through the IEA we can strengthen the building and management of strategic reserves. We also have a common interest in secure transport routes and security in producing countries.

All nations conduct diplomacy to promote their national interests. Responsible stakeholders go further: They recognize that the international system sustains their peaceful prosperity, so they work to sustain that system. In its foreign policy, China has many opportunities to be a responsible stakeholder. [107]

Mr. Zoellick then referred to America's need for China's help in dealing with North Korea, the proliferation of weapons of mass destruction, Iran's nuclear program, the global fight against terrorism, financial aid contributions in Afghanistan and Iraq, and solving Sudan's human rights crisis. He said:

> The most pressing opportunity is North Korea. Since hosting the Six-Party Talks at their inception in 2003, China has played a constructive role. This week we achieved a Joint Statement of Principles, with an agreement on the goal of "verifiable denuclearization of the Korean peninsula in a peaceful manner." But the hard work of implementation lies ahead, and China should share our interest in effective and comprehensive compliance.
>
> Moreover, the North Korea problem is about more than just the spread of dangerous weapons. Without broad economic and political reform, North Korea poses a threat to itself and others. It is time to move beyond the half century-old armistice on the Korean peninsula to a true peace, with regional security and development. A Korean peninsula without nuclear weapons opens the door to this future. Some 30 years ago America ended its war in Vietnam. Today Vietnam looks to the United States to help integrate it into the world market economic system so Vietnam can improve the lives of its people. By contrast, North Korea, with a 50 year-old cold armistice, just falls further behind.
>
> Beijing also has a strong interest in working with us to halt the proliferation of weapons of mass destruction and missiles that can deliver them. The proliferation of danger will undermine the benign security environment and healthy international economy that China needs for its development.
>
> China's actions on Iran's nuclear program will reveal the seriousness of China's commitment to non-proliferation. And while we welcome China's efforts to police its own behavior through new export controls on sensitive technology, we still need to see tough legal punishments for violators.
>
> China and the United States can do more together in the global fight against terrorism. Chinese citizens have been victims of terror attacks in Pakistan and Afghanistan. China can help destroy the supply lines of global terrorism. We have made a good start by working together at the UN and searching for ter-

rorist money in Chinese banks, but can expand our cooperation further.

China pledged $150 million in assistance to Afghanistan, and $25 million to Iraq. These pledges were welcome, and we look forward to their full implementation. China would build stronger ties with both through follow-on pledges. Other countries are assisting the new Iraqi government with major debt forgiveness, focusing attention on the $7 billion in Iraqi debt still held by Chinese state companies.

On my early morning runs in Khartoum, I saw Chinese doing tai chi exercises. I suspect they were in Sudan for the oil business. But China should take more than oil from Sudan – it should take some responsibility for resolving Sudan's human crisis. It could work with the United States, the UN, and others to support the African Union's peacekeeping mission, to provide humanitarian relief to Darfur, and to promote a solution to Sudan's conflicts.

In Asia, China is already playing a larger role. The United States respects China's interests in the region, and recognizes the useful role of multilateral diplomacy in Asia. But concerns will grow if China seeks to maneuver toward a predominance of power. Instead, we should work together with ASEAN, Japan, Australia, and others for regional security and prosperity through the ASEAN Regional Forum and the Asia Pacific Economic Cooperation forum.

China's choices about Taiwan will send an important message too. We have made clear that our "one China" policy remains based on the three communiqués and the Taiwan Relations Act. It is important for China to resolve its differences with Taiwan peacefully.

The United States, Japan, and China will need to cooperate effectively together on both regional and global challenges. Given China's terrible losses in World War II, I appreciate the sensitivity of historical issues with Japan. But as I have told my Chinese colleagues, I have observed some sizeable gaps in China's telling of history, too. When I visited the "918" museum at the site of the 1931 "Manchurian Incident," I noted that the chronological account jumped from 1941 to the Soviet offensive against Japan in August 1945, overlooking the United States involvement in the Pacific from 1941 to 1945! Perhaps we could start to ease some misapprehensions by opening a three-way dialogue among historians.

Clearly, there are many common interests and opportunities for cooperation. But some say America's commitment to democracy will preclude long-term cooperation with China. Let me suggest why this need not be so.

Freedom lies at the heart of what America is... as a nation, we stand for what President Bush calls the "non-negotiable demands of human dignity." As I have seen over the 25 years since I lived in Hong Kong, Asians have also pressed for more freedom and built many more democracies. Indeed, President Hu and Premier Wen are talking about the importance of China strengthening the rule of law and developing democratic institutions.

We do not urge the cause of freedom to weaken China. To the contrary, President Bush has stressed that the terrible experience of 9/11 has driven home that in the absence of freedom, unhealthy societies will breed deadly cancers. In his Second Inaugural, President Bush recognized that democratic institutions must reflect the values and culture of diverse societies. As he said, "Our goal... is to help others find their own voice, attain their own freedom, and make their own way."

Being born ethnically Chinese does not predispose people against democracy – just look at Taiwan's vibrant politics. Japan and South Korea have successfully blended a Confucian heritage with modern democratic principles.

Closed politics cannot be a permanent feature of Chinese society. It is simply not sustainable – as economic growth continues, better-off Chinese will want a greater say in their future, and pressure builds for political reform.

China has one umbrella labor union, but waves of strikes. A party that came to power as a movement of peasants now confronts violent rural protests, especially against corruption. A government with massive police powers cannot control spreading crime.

Some in China believe they can secure the Communist Party's monopoly on power through emphasizing economic growth and heightened nationalism. This is risky and mistaken.

China needs a peaceful political transition to make its government responsible and accountable to its people. Village and grassroots elections are a start. They might be expanded – perhaps to counties and provinces – as a next step. China needs to reform its judiciary. It should open government processes to the involvement of civil society and stop harassing journalists who point out problems. China should also expand religious freedom and make real the guarantees of rights that exist on paper – but not in practice.

How we deal with China's rising power is a central question in American foreign policy.

In China and the United States, Mr. Zheng's idea of a "peaceful rise" will spur vibrant debate. The world will look to the evidence of actions.

Tonight I have suggested that the U.S. response should be to help foster constructive action by transforming our thirty-year policy of integration: We now need to encourage China to become a responsible stakeholder in the international system. As a responsible stakeholder, China would be more than just a member – it would work with us to sustain the international system that has enabled its success.

Cooperation as stakeholders will not mean the absence of differences – we will have disputes that we need to manage. But that management can take place within a larger framework where the parties recognize a shared interest in sustaining political, economic, and security systems that provide common benefits.

To achieve this transformation of the Sino-American relationship, this Administration – and those that follow it – will need to build the foundation of support at home. That's particularly why I wanted to join you tonight. You hear the voices that perceive China solely through the lens of fear. But America succeeds when we look to the future as an opportunity, not when we fear what the future might bring. To succeed now, we will need all of you to press both the Chinese and your fellow citizens.

When President Nixon visited Beijing in 1972, our relationship with China was defined by what we were both against. Now we have the opportunity to define our relationship by what we are both for.

We have many common interests with China. But relationships built only on a coincidence of interests have shallow roots. Relationships built on shared interests and shared values are deep and lasting. We can cooperate with the emerging China of today, even as we work for the democratic China of tomorrow. [108]

From a Chinacentric perspective, what is the value proposition in Mr. Zoellick's offer of America's recognizing China as a "responsible stakeholder" rather than just a "member" in the international system? A Chinese audience would not be shocked by yet it would be unimpressed by the hypocrisy in the assertion that when China decided in 1978 to embrace globalization rather than detach itself from it: "Seven U.S. Presidents of both parties recognized this strategic shift and worked to integrate China as a full member of the international system." Or that: "For fifty years, our policy was to fence in the Soviet Union while its own internal contradictions undermined it. For thirty years, our policy has been to draw out the People's Republic of China." Mr. Zoellick did not focus on the "containment" policies America had traditionally used with China Americentric. His Americentric mindset has been, prior to the American financial crises, virtually invisible to Americans. From such an Americentric perspective, what America has been proposing to China is normal and appropriate, and China has not behaved properly to responding negatively to these proposals.

China became a major responsible power a long time ago. The "Responsible Stakeholder" policy completely misunderstood China's foreign policies. The Chinese state is remaking the international system by implementing the Principles of Peaceful Coexistence. It had no interest in becoming a "Responsible Stakeholder" in Principles of Conflict based international system.

Mr. Zoellick correctly notes that on both sides there is a gulf of perceptions. But during this particular speech he does not expend on or remedy this problem. Instead, while saying that "on both sides there is a gulf of perceptions," Mr. Zoellick focuses on the idea that China's peaceful rise causes "a cauldron of anxiety" for Americans' because of their belief that "the Chinese dragon will prove to be a fire-breather." He does not address the fact that there are many misconceptions with respect to what America can possibly persuade, threaten or coerce China into doing. One of the most critical arguments is that the "responsible stakeholder" concept can be damaging to US – China relations, as it can mean that China is weak and must become an obedient client of the American state. This is something that China cannot and should not do as China has never been economically or militarily stronger or had better economic and defense strategies. China cannot improve these sectors by becoming a "responsible stakeholder" in a Principles of Conflict based international system which in actuality is not sustainable. The Chinese state waits and hopes that America become a responsible major power (or stakeholder) in a newly built international system based on the Principles of Peaceful Coexistence.

The Center for America-China Partnership and the America-China Partnership Book Series examining the New School of US-China Relations perspectives goals include:

1. Removal of the gulf of perceptions American scholars have been unable to transcend because of their zero sum game mindset and strategies.

2. Elimination of the communications gap due to which China has been unable to speak freely and persuasively to American policymakers and people.

3. The creation of a win-win strategy that would provide a new framework and strategy needed to create a comprehensive and feasible answer for America and China's success in the 21st century.

4. The creation and successful operation of a "collaborative equilibrium" essential for America and China's economic and national security.

The most profound and fundamental reality Mr. Zoellick and policymakers in past presidential administrations have not accepted is that it is not in either America's or China's interests for China to.

1. seek to copy America's multiparty political system, economic regulatory system, capitalism with American characteristics, or human rights at this time in development. In addition, we do not believe that China would or should

2. yield its sovereignty to American or other foreign nations. Also, we argue that the Chinese state should manage its monetary policy in order to meet the needs of America and its other trading partners.; or

3. Become an American client state; or Lastly, we strongly believe that China should not

4. stop its mission of creating an international system based on the Principles of Peaceful Coexistence rather than the Principles of Conflict.

Instead of focusing on the "gulf of perception" and proposing ways to bridge that gulf, Mr. Zoellick focused on "Wither China: From Membership to Responsibility' on the premise of the "responsible stakeholder" concept, which unfortunately can be interpreted as being America's assertion that China is weak and its economic success is vulnerable to American protectionism: "The overwhelming priority of China's senior officials is to develop and modernize a China that still faces enormous internal challenges. While proud of their accomplishments, China's leaders recognize their country's perceived weaknesses." He then observes "Therefore, China clearly needs a benign international environment for its work at home." Does this mean that China must accept the current system based on the Principles of Conflict?

Let's further examine the elements of misperception when considering Mr. Zoellick's speech from both Americentric and

Chinacentric perspectives.

Mr. Zoellick then refers to what precipitates America's having "a cauldron of anxiety", referring to a list that includes concern by large American businesses that do not want China to control its domestic markets.

America also does not want China to help "troublesome states." Zoellick says that if this happens, then China is not to be perceived as pursuing a "peaceful rise." He also cites China's military spending which is in fact an underdog if compared to America. For example, the United States has 53% of the world's military assets and annual expenditures. China's military spending is estimated to be approximately 12% of America's although it has a similar geographic size and five times the population. Although China has been at peace since 1979 the United State also feels anxious about China's "growing economic footprint," and America's trade deficit, though America gains from China's "voracious consumption." He then lists what a "responsible stakeholder" does not do, i.e., theft of intellectual property and counterfeiting.

Mr. Zoellick also identifies the rather limited reward that American government offers in return for China doing what America tells it to: "Of course, the Chinese expect to be treated with respect and will want to have their views and interests recognized. But China does not want a conflict with the United States."

He says that China should collaborate with American climate and clean environment initiatives, which are notorious for being inadequate, and work on energy conservation and efficiency. Mr. Zoellick says China should not seek to "lock up" energy supplies around the world. He makes only quick and undeveloped reference to: "We encourage the opening of oil and gas production in more places around the world." But Mr. Zoellick does not offer a China-America partnership in the joint development of new energy resources.

That is the kind of proposal Deng Xiaoping made decades ago.

Joint development of new energy resources must be pursued in this partnership.

Mr. Zoellick states that as a responsible stakeholder China should not "maneuver towards a predominance of power" in its home region. Asia is half a world away from America, and China has vital economic and national security interests to protect there.

Then Mr. Zoellick asserts that America does not "urge the cause of freedom to weaken China" and says:

1. "Our goal is to help others find their own voice, attain their own freedom"
2. "Closed politics cannot be a permanent feature of Chinese society" and
3. "Some in China believe they can secure the Communist Party's monopoly on power by emphasizing economic growth and nationalism."
4. "China needs a peaceful political transition to make its government responsible and accountable to its people."

Mr. Zoellick should know that these changes are a matter of self-determination for China. He may not realize that these changes would weaken China's economic and national security. If he does not know that he does not understand China's situation. If he does know that, then he seeks to weaken China's economic and national security. Mr. Zoellick admitted in a 2008 speech that it is hard to persuade the Chinese government to change the system that is working so well.

The Chinese government of the 21st century cannot accept the lose-lose value propositions of such privileges offered by an American government in return for China's being a "responsible stakeholder" in the current international system. The value propositions Mr. Zoellick offered in the speech are persuasive from a non-Americentric perspective as to why China should not accept the

American designed international system, but should instead reshape the international system so that it "of course, recognizes their views and interests." Boiled down to its essence, Mr. Zoellick's logic was as follows: since the international system sustains China's peaceful prosperity, China should work to take over that system. But the "responsible stakeholder in the current system" policy's value proposition is that China's peaceful development requires it to do what America wants even if that is not in the Chinese government best interests. It is a faulty logic: do what we say because you're weak and if you do not we will negatively impact your developmental goals. America will treat China in the same way it treated the USSR. The value proposition is not designed to be a "win-win" approach. It is merely seeking a additional leverage for American economic interests and a "win" for America's ideological and superpower hegemony.

In addition, the threat that is the premise of the "responsible stakeholder" value proposition is not compelling. The requirements America makes in connection with its policymakers' definition of what China needs to do to conform to American interests are bluntly working against China's interests. The most significant thing about its negative value proposition and requirements is that the American government was unable or unwilling to see that its value proposition is innately doomed to fail and therefore is not an effective or wise approach. This limitation in American policy formulation towards China and its bully diplomacy indicates that American policymakers are only able to see, articulate and act on their own goals and anxieties. Furthermore, it seems that American strategists themselves are unable to perceive America's own objectives in a realistic manner. The speech is reminiscent of a delusional or hypocritical thinking. Or both.

Mr. Zoellick as Vice Chairman International of Goldman Sachs Group published an article in the *Financial Times* on January 23, 2007: "A global mission for China and America."[109] His perspective remained Americentric, and his agenda for China, while framed to suggest what is good for China, was simply an Americentric pitch for what America wants from China.

What is missing in Mr. Zoellick's "agenda that builds confidence and support in both countries and beyond" is the concept and title of "A global mission for America and China's partnership." The "responsible stakeholder" based foreign policy, however described, is part of America's failed "opening up and containment strategy" towards China. It should be obvious, that China's influence will soon be wider than America's because China is a prospering and responsible power which can mobilize other developing countries in following, at least in part, China's developmental strategies. But these trends are neither recognized nor accepted by many Americans.

The "responsible stakeholder" policy towards China does not seek to align America's interests, national with the world's emerging 21st century's "mega superpower." Conventional American policy seeks to lead, dominate and exploit China. It addresses the China that President Nixon visited almost 4 decades ago. China today is past the point where America can realistically hope to lead China's domestic or foreign policy. It was past that point 60 years ago. The requirements the American government set out in its "responsible stakeholder" lectures to China ignore the reality of America's objective self-interest with an economy that is currently in profound crisis.

By 2008, China had created the world's most dynamic economy, while still only 30 years into the nascent stage of its modern development. China's developing economy has been growing many times faster than America's developed economy for 30 years.

The Failure of the Best and Brightest Zero Sum Game Strategy of Treasury Secretary Paulson

Hank Paulson, both as the CEO of Goldman Sachs and as America's Secretary of the Treasury, tried to persuade the Chinese government that it is in its interest to let foreign companies get involved in China's financial system. The Bush-Paulson Strategy, in effect, defined "win-win" as American economic and national security interests winning at the same time with China's economic and national security lose. The Bush-Paulson Strategy was naïve and failed to get control of China's financial system and economy, but was implemented by perhaps the most able and experienced American for the that particular objective, Hank Paulson. The Bush-Paulson Strategy was fundamentally flawed. Its rationale could be characterized as: China will be so overwhelmingly powerful from an economic point of view that America must make an attempt to get control of China's financial system as soon as possible. The Bush-Paulson Strategy was doomed to fail because of its zero sum game mindset and strategies and because China is proving to be a good partner to many other nations. But an American zero sum game mindset was perceived as the best strategy that the America government could formulate. They were obviously wrong and the Chinese government was quick to realize it.

Newsweek, in December 2007, summed up Treasury Secretary Paulson's "China Offensive's" failure:

> Is Henry Paulson's Big China Offensive dead in the water? As the US Treasury Secretary preps for the next meeting of his widely hyped Strategic Economic Dialogue in Beijing this week, some China watchers are heralding its demise. Paulson left as CEO of Goldman Sachs and took the Treasury post on condition that he'd be America's point man on China, yet so far he's not even meeting the right people. Prime Minister Wen Jiabao declined to lead China's side, shunting the job off to Wu Yi, who will be a lame duck when she meets Paulson this week. Worse, her likely successor is thought to be Zhang Jiang, a provincial party chief who learned his economics at Kim IL Sung University in Pyongyang, hardly a bastion of free-market liberalism.
>
> Treasury officials hope Paulson will end up working with Li Keqiang, a highly regarded reformer and rising star in the

Communist Party. But it's unlikely anyone on the Chinese side will give much more anyway. The dialogue was supposed to work like this: Beijing would make concessions on hot issues like piracy and the value of the yuan, and Paulson would dampen China bashing from Washington. It hasn't happened, because China was never going to make real concessions to relieve protectionist pressure, which has been rising in Congress and from U.S. presidential candidates anyway. It's not easy to manage a relationship with China when both Democrats and Republicans in the United States are 'screaming' about alleged Chinese misdeeds, notes Charles Freeman, a former senior trade official in the Bush administration.

Both sides sold each other a phony premise for the talks. A senior U.S. official not cleared to speak by name insists the dialogue has produced major achievements, including a recent air-service agreement and U.S. support for China's membership in the Financial Activity Task Force, an anti-money-laundering agency. Thin gruel, most analysts agree, compared with the expectations for what Paulson, an old China hand, could get done.

The United States, burdened by its trade deficit, needs this dialogue more than China does. Paulson's vision that it would become a permanent framework for U.S.-China relations lies in ruins. China is in a strong position, not in a mood to grant favors to itinerant foreigners. (A delegation from the European Union, which went to Beijing last week also seeking a higher price for the yuan, left empty-handed.) It now looks likely that this effort to regulate Sino-American affairs will fade away when Bush leaves office in 2009 – just one more misguided effort to 'hustle' the East, as Kipling put it.[110]

Mr. Paulson's "Big China Offensive" or "Strategic Economic Dialogues" faltered because they were not "win-win" strategies. They were flawed by the American desire to take the edge over China by eroding its economic wellbeing and ultimately its economic sovereignty. It is thus "win-win" for America's economic and national security interests that made the proposal unpersuasive.

Mr. Paulson's argument that it is in China's best interest for it to open its banking system and emulate capitalism with American characteristics was discredited by America's economic crises.

Since the approach, which we labeled a "Glass Trojan Horse Strategy," has failed, what comes next? One of two basic new strategies may be used. They are military authority and moral authority. The moral authority approach that we recommend is America's new Administration's policy and further Strategic Economic Dialogues should implement a committed partnership with China. In that new framework, which we refer to as "collaborative equilibrium," "reciprocal globalization" and "America and China's partnership," new win-win strategies can be formulated among American political leaders. Until the goals and value propositions are win-win, America does not have a successful China policy.

The other strategy, using military authority against China, is a strategy for failure that America must avoid in the Age of Species Lethal Weapons and Science.

Treasury Secretary Paulson's "Win-Win" Glass Trojan Horse Diplomacy: Deception or Delusion?

In order to better understand the moral authority and win-win mindset and genuine, permanent partnership approach, it is necessary to examine further how and why the conventional approach failed. Was the Bush-Paulson Strategy cunning deception or blind delusion or both? Mr. Paulson either did not understand China's goals in 2006 from an Chinacentric perspective after over 71 visits he or was being somewhat disingenuous in his recommendations to the Chinese government as the head of Goldman Sachs and as Treasury Secretary about as to what was is in the China's best interest of China and its economy. Mr. Paulson's strategy might have worked a little better a decade ago with then-President Jiang Zemin, the former mayor of Shanghai, but we doubt that as well. China has stubbornly and then successfully resisted such foreign pressures since 1949. The selection of Hu Jintao, whose prior executive experiences were in the poor inland parts of China as China's leader signaled that China's focus is quite different than it was not long ago.

Treasury Secretary Paulson manifested a zero sum game approach because he argued that the Chinese should let foreign companies, like Goldman Sachs, penetrate the Chinese market and participate deeply in the Chinese financial system. It was an updated version of the zero sum game approach that Mr. Paulson presented when he was the head of Goldman Sachs. He advised, for example, in 2002, that China let foreigners take over its banks because the Chinese banks were all poorly run and insolvent. That is a threatening approach. By the time he became Treasury Secretary in August 2006, China's economy had become so strong and successful that the zero sum game approach was recast as in China's interest. That is less of a threat-based approach. But the result would be the same: foreign firms would gain control of China's financial system. Assertions that China, whether to prevent its economy's collapse or to achieve its own goals, must let Americans who know better than the Chinese tell them how to operate their banks and economy is unpersuasive. It is the business and economic threat-based corollary to Mr. Zoellick's threat-based responsible stakeholder foreign policy approach.

Mr. Paulson's "Big China Offensive" was ineffective as a Glass Trojan horse. It is important for Americans to examine whether the Bush-Paulson Strategy was deceptive, delusional, or both as a prerequisite for making America's China strategy, persuasive and successfully aligned with China's economic and national security. If Mr. Paulson believed that what he was seeking was a win for China, then it was not deceptive; but it was at the very least incorrect. China recapitalized its banks and its economy grew at 11% in 2007 before the American financial crisis. It was the American banks that were insolvent and ineptly run, and the American economy that almost collapsed three times, as Mr. Paulson admitted in 2008. If he did not think that what he was proposing was a winning strategy for China, then he was not delusional, but deceptive. If he did not care, it was both. In all these events, what the Bush-Paulson Strategy was suggesting did not have moral authority. That should have been obvious to Mr. Paulson and the American administration as early as 2005, when the American government blocked a partly Chinese state owned, NYSE listed company, CNOOC, from acquiring a publicly listed third tier American oil company, Unocal. Yet that did not stop Paulson's attempt to try the deceptive or delusional "win-win" approach which he subsequently pursued. Moral authority was not consistently the goal of American foreign policy in the first presidential administration of the 21st century, which is partly why American economic and foreign policy is so disastrously harmful to America's security interests.

From the New School's perspective, the Bush-Paulson Strategy's inherent flaws are a clear lesson that the American government must develop genuine win-win value propositions in their China strategies. This is essential for American policymakers who wish to achieve a sustainable strategy for America's economic interests, since American companies would register significant profits in the booming Chinese economy. It will be a win for America's national security interests because China would answer favorably to creating collaborative equilibrium with The United States and the American companies.

The lack of sustainable value propositions in the Bush-Paulson made it such that no win-win strategies were advanced for either America or China. Treasury Secretary Paulson in dealing with China, often uses the argument: "Do what I tell you to do, because it is in your self interest to do so." This is a variation on the ultimatum approach: "Do what I tell you or prepare to be bombed back into the Stone Age."[108] The Bush-Paulson Strategy was combined with such an economic threat. American legislators threatened their

Asian counterpart with a 27.5% tariff on Chinese imports if China did not take a big bang approach to revaluing its currency, which would have in effect destabilized China's economy. This threat was made repeatedly by American Congressmen in order to put pressure on the Chinese government. Although the dynamics of America's executive and legislative policies towards China is complex, there was a "bad cop" and "good cop" dichotomy used in the Strategic Economic Dialogues from 2006 to 2008.

Secretary Paulson was the "friend of China" and members of the Congress were the common danger faced by America and China. No doubt the good cop and bad cop features of the executive and legislative branches had features of genuineness.

For example, after the 1994 Congressional elections gave the Republican Party control of Congress for the first time in 44 years, the Republican leadership in the House of Representatives focused on the "single-minded commercial focus of the Clinton Administration's China policy" and the Taiwan issue. The House passed a resolution in June 1996 by a vote of 417 to 7 supporting legislative initiatives against China, eventually resulting in a Senate bill that defined a "policy of freedom" towards China. This bill attempted to bring freedom, human rights, rule of law, religious and political freedom, free trade, and free markets into China.

In 1997 the Rumsfeld Commission, headed by Donald Rumsfeld, the Secretary of Defense in the Nixon and George W. Bush administrations, reported to Congress that China was in the process of modernizing its long-range missiles and nuclear weapons in "ways that will make it a more threatening power in the event of a crisis" and that it "poses a threat to the U.S. as a significant proliferator of ballistic missiles, weapons of mass destruction, and enabling technologies." The CIA reported in 1998 that China had 13 long-range ICBM missiles targeting American cities. America reportedly had 3,000 missiles targeting China.

The attacks on September 11, 2001, changed the George W. Bush administration's China policy, and America was distracted from the its planned campaign to confront and contain China during the Bush administration's 2000-8 terms. China, left in peace, prospered and reached a critical mass in its transformation in which it is less vulnerable economically. China's economic progress became well established as weel as unprecedented in scale, speed and success.

Although the American government's policies towards China are complex, from the New School's perspective neither branch has yet been able to formulate a coherent set of reliable policies that align America's and China's economic successes and securities. However, by 2009, Americans reorganized the necessity of a successful relationship with China. Yet American politicians and policymakers, have not been able to formulate a set of policies toward China that can meet America's needs, because it requires that America adhere to its ideals as well as that Americans change their goals and priorities in relation to their partnership with China.

The difficulties of America's Majority Rule Democracy in formulating a successful China strategy can also be seen in the light of the threats of American economic authority, such as trade sanctions and military authority, such as arming Taiwan and hedging China with a more militarily oriented Japan. For example, in February 2008 Treasury Secretary Paulson, cautioned senators against passing legislation aimed at forcing China to raise the value of its currency. He said such an effort was "bordering on the silly." Mr. Paulson also testified that:

> I have engaged very actively with China. Engaged and I think with some results when you look at the currency. Don't be confused by the fact that I say I'd like them to move quicker, because I would like them to move quicker, but their rate of appreciation of the currency roughly doubled last year to 6.7 percent. [111]

The Chinese government as it has for 30 years, used the Principles of Peaceful Coexistence in dealing with initiatives like the Bush-Paulson Strategy and the Bush-Zoellick Responsible Stakeholder Strategy. It politely refused the opportunity to become a responsible stakeholder in the current international system, as it was already a responsible major power committed to the Principles of Peaceful Coexistence. It also refused the "Big Bang" approach, but incrementally allowed Chinese currency to appreciate in a stable and responsible manner pver the course of three years.

The key to America's finding of a successful China strategy is embracing the exceptionalism of China's strategy toward America.

Changing the Goals of American Policy Towards China Will Produce the Results America Needs

It is fortunate that the Chinese put up with the misguided policies of the American diplomats. But it is good policy for China to do so, as Deng Xiaoping advised leading members of the Chinese government in September 1989:

> There is no doubt that the imperialists want socialist countries to change their nature. The problem now is not the banner of the Soviet Union will fall – there is bound to be unrest there – but whether the banner of China will fall. Therefore, the most important thing is that there should be no unrest in China and that we should continue to carry on genuine reform and to open wider to the outside. Without those policies, China would have no future. How did we achieve what we did over the past ten years? Through reform and opening to the outside. As long as we pursue those policies, and as long as our socialist banner stands firmly planted, China will have tremendous influence. Of course, that will put the developed countries all the more on guard against us. Notwithstanding, we should remain friendly exchanges with them. We should keep them as friends but also have a clear understanding of what they are doing. We should not criticize or condemn other countries without good reason or go to extremes in our words or deeds.[112]

Similarly President Kennedy advised Americans in June 1963:

> Genuine peace must be the product of many nations, the sum of many acts. It must be dynamic, not static, changing to meet the challenge of each new generation. For peace is a process – a way of solving problems.
>
> With such a peace, there will still be quarrels and conflicting interests, as there are within families and nations. World peace, like community peace, does not require that each man love his neighbor--it requires only that they live together in mutual toler-ance, submitting their disputes to a just and peaceful settlement. And history teaches us that enmities between nations, as between individuals, do not last forever. However fixed our likes and dislikes may seem the tide of time and events will often bring sur-prising changes in the relations between nations and neighbors.
>
> So let us persevere. Peace need not be impracticable, and war need not be inevitable. By defining our goal more clearly, by making it seem more manageable and less remote, we can help all peoples to see it, to draw hope from it, and to move irresist-ibly toward it.[113]

As we noted, Deng Xiaoping said in February 1984 to a delega-tion from the Center for Strategic and International Studies of Georgetown University that:

> There are many disputes in the world, and we must find ways to solve them. Over the years I have been considering how those disputes could be solved by peaceful means, rather than by war. The plan we have proposed for reunifying the mainland with Taiwan is fair and reasonable. After reunification, Taiwan can go on practicing capitalism while the mainland maintains socialism, all within the same unified China. One China, two systems. The same approach will be applied to the Hong Kong question – one China – two systems. But Hong Kong is different from Taiwan in that there is a free port.
>
> I think this is a sensible solution to many similar disputes in the world. If opposing sides are locked in stalemate, sooner or later they will come to conflict, even armed conflict. If war is

> to be averted, the only alternative is an approach like the one
> I have just mention, an approach the people will accept. It can
> help stabilize the situation, and for a long time too, and is harm-
> ful to neither side. Since you specialize in international issues,
> I hope you will have a better understanding of our proposal for
> the solution of the Hong Kong and Taiwan questions and make
> a study of it.[114]

Perhaps, nowadays scholars and policymakers, like those at the Center for Strategic and International Studies, will have a better understanding of China's Principles of Peaceful Coexistence-based proposals for solving the Hong Kong and Taiwan conflicts.

From 1978 to 2008, American policymakers have ignored China's pioneering of the Principles of Peaceful Coexistence in its policies and strategies. This is understandable in 1978 and 1989, but unacceptable in 2009.

The failure of key aspects of the economic practices on which America relied resulting in the near implosion of the American economy in 2008 is similar to the implosion of the economy in the former Soviet Union in 1989. For reasons arising from its nature in the 21st century, America's economic regulation relied on unstable economic practices.

In 1990, America began building up increasing trade deficits with China. On its end, the Chinese state accumulated larger and larger foreign currency reserves in US dollars and it is currently the largest holder of American government and corporate debt obligation in the world. At the same time, an economic trend of excessive consumer borrowing was on the rise and it culminated in the subprime mortgage, bond insurance, credit, and liquidity, crisis that revealed the rickety underpinnings of America's economy.

Some Americans try to blame China's economic policies for America's economic disaster. That is a deceitful perspective, though the interrelated nature of America's and China's economies underlying such assertions is correct. This mindset is harmful to America and China because it fails to accept the reality that America did not properly manage itself economically.

Achieving America's Goals to Change America's Policies Toward China

At the second Strategic Economic Dialogues meeting during the Bush Presidency in June 2008, the *New York Times* reported:

> Not long ago, Chinese officials sat across conference tables from American officials and got an earful. The Americans scolded the Chinese on mismanaging their economy, from state subsidies to foreign investment regulation to the valuation of their currency. Your economic system, the American strongly implied, should look a lot more like ours. But in recent weeks, the fingers have been wagging in the other direction. Senor Chinese officials are publicly and loudly rebuking the Americans on their handling of the economy and defending their own more assertive style of regulation. The Chinese officials seem to be galled by the apparent hypocrisy of Americans telling them what to do while the American economy is at best stagnant. China, on the other hand, has maintained its feverish growth. Some Chinese officials are promoting a Chinese style of economic management that they suggest serves developing countries better than the American mode, in much the same way they argue that they are in no hurry to copy American-style multiparty democracy. In the last six weeks alone, a senior banking regulator blamed Washington's 'warped conception' of market regulation for the subprime mortgage crisis that is rattling the world economy; the Chinese envoy to the World Trade Organization called on the United States to halt the dollar's unchecked depreciation before the slide further worsens soaring oil and food prices; and Chinese agencies denounced a federal committee charge with vetting foreign investments in the United States, saying the Americans were showing 'hostility' and a 'discriminatory attitude,' not least towards the Chinese.[115]

The *Financial Times* reported:

Mr. Paulson defended the strategic dialogue – his own creation – against critics who argue that it has achieved little concrete. He said there had been 'reasonable progress' on a number of fronts. Moreover, 'one of the most important economic relationships in the world has been kept on an even keel in times of tension.' Mr. Paulson, former Chairman of Goldman Sachs, acknowledged the credit crisis had made it harder to sell financial sector liberalization in China. 'I don't puff my chest out quite so far when I am talking about best practices in capital markets,' he said. 'But I can tell you that I still believe it would benefit China greatly – much more than it would benefit the US – if they continue to do what they have been doing and open up to more competition.'[116]

Some policies can only change with new people with new perspectives get in office. To sum up, what is hopefully evident in 2010, is that one-sided value propositions are beneficial only to American interests and lack a perspective that would be beneficial to the Chinese counterparts as well. As a result, they are self-defeating for America as they do not offer reciprocally beneficial policies and cannot succeed in achieving American goals. Beyond "keeping things on an even keel," they fail to meet America's urgent need for align its future economic success with China's. What comes next?

The New Best and Brightest Win-Win Genuine Strategic Global Partnership

President Obama has launched "a new era of partnership" and is seeking the solutions to America's economically and military problems. America must adopt the Principles of Peaceful Coexistence and implement them with China. *The Wall Street Journal* reported on June 17, 2008 that the then Senator Obama was trying to put together tax and spending policies that were designed to deal with two challenges. One was the competition from rapidly developing countries like India and China. The other was the "winner-take-all economy where the gains from economic growth skew heavily toward the wealthy." Senator Obama said that: "Globalization and technology and automation all weaken the position of workers." He stated "I've got Bob Rubin on one hand (as an advisor) and [former Labor Secretary] Bob Reich on the other... I tend to be eclectic." Mr. Reich has long championed infrastructure spending to boost jobs and the economy, and is a favorite of laborers. He frequently fought with Mr. Rubin, who favored slashing the deficit as a means of boosting economic growth and spending.

As America's new President, Barack Obama can find unique collaborative solutions in a partnership with China.

President Obama can transform the Strategic Economic Dialogues into discussions that deploy a military and diplomatic partnership with China. He will find President Hu Jintao is able, in such a reciprocally beneficial partnership to assist America and China in solving the other's problems. Neither can solve their own challenges without ensuring that the other solves theirs. That new strategy of partnership is essential to creating win-win mindsets among American leaders.

As we emphasized:

1. All future American administrations, both Republican and Democrat, must make the genuine committed partnership and win-win strategies their permanent policies toward China.
2. In order to be able to do that, Americans must accept the reality that China is a successful Permission Society, not a copy of America's Rights Society to be bullied around and that
3. There is no fundamental conflict of economic and military interests between America and China,
4. There is just a useful diversity of approaches in two very

different nations to governing and operating economies that are meant to benefit their citizens.

5. Diversity is healthy for mankind, because the American way, majority rule democracy way that can work in a Rights Society may be more dangerous than the Chinese Permission Society and win-win strategic approach in China.

6. Such a partnership with China is America's smart move economically and militarily, in the Age of Species Lethal Weapons and Science.

Capitalism is capitalism, whether it has Chinese or American characteristics. The alignment of goals in Mr. Paulson's roles as CEO of Goldman Sachs and American Treasury Secretary were analogous to the alignment of China's government and business goals. This is even more obvious after the new roles in managing America's failing major business that the American government entered into in 2008. Prior to the September 2008 crises Americans saw China's sovereign funds as "unfair" and asserted that a nation can only allow government, to run government not business. But politics runs business, and business runs politics in societies that are not morbund. China is successfully doing things differently than America. That is frightening for many Americans but it is not "unfair." What is unfair is for Americans to assert their norms as universally applicable irrespective of the views of other peaceful societies.

The Obama Biden Model: China as a Major Responsible Power

Senator Joe Biden was not able to garner significant support in 2008 as a presidential candidate, but was chosen as Barack Obama's running mate and is highly experienced in foreign policy issues. His views on China are significant. In June 2008, he gave a speech that laid out his agenda. Vice President Biden's analysis is in some ways more realistic and informed than those of the other 2008 presidential candidates who attracted higher levels of support. He defined America's problems insightfully. Although focused on a strengthened American and European alliance, his views regarding China are realistic and could provide a sound basis for America's entering into a partnership that will enable it and China to deal with economic and military issues with more efficiency. Senator Biden stated:

> An inflection point is where the slope of a curve changes from being positive to negative, or vice versa. To think about it another way, it's the moment when you're turning a car from left to right that the steering wheel is pointing straight ahead.
>
> Inflection points are critical because at that moment, you can go either way. You can straighten out, or turn back to one side or the other. But once you pass that juncture, you've largely determined your ultimate trajectory.
>
> We in the United States— an probably in the West as a whole— are at an inflection point. What happens at this juncture will likely determine the trajectory of our country and the Euro Atlantic community.
>
> The stakes could not be higher. We are talking about the destiny of our civilization.
>
> First, we face real security challenges: the rise of extremist groups; hot wars in Iraq and Afghanistan; a cold war with Iran that could become hot; and the spread of lethal weapons.
>
> Second, we face a new wave of stiff economic competition. For the last half century, those of us living in Europe and the United States have had the luxury of competing primarily against each other, and Japan.
>
> Those days are over. Countries like China and India have learned from our experience, adopted our playbook, and are now working hard to beat us at our own game. In many cases, their citizens are willing to work longer, harder, and more cheaply than Americans and Europeans. As a result, what qualified as good enough when we were competing against each other is not good enough now that we're up against the whole world.
>
> Lastly, we have been crippled in our attempts to address these problems by our reliance on an old resource: fossil fuel.

And it undercuts the advance of freedom, because regressive regimes swimming in a sea of high-priced oil from the Middle East to Africa to Central Asia can resist the pressure to reform.

We've knowingly created a system in which our way of life cannot be sustained without paying massive tribute to governments that do not share the principles that define us. Together, countries in the Middle East have amassed $4 trillion as a result of surging oil prices. The Congress recently heard testimony about how, if oil hits $200 a barrel, OPEC could buy the Bank of America with one month worth of production and purchase General Motors with three days of revenue. If energy consuming countries in the West are going to remain the masters of their own fate, this situation is unsustainable.

So, how do we handle this inflection point? I'd like to suggest a few ideas.

First, we need to radically revise our definitions of security problems and security solutions. Yes, we need to defeat extremists group and deny their efforts to acquire weapons of mass destruction. But we must not ignore the other forces that are shaping this century:

The emergence of China, India and Russia.

The spread of dangerous weapons and lethal diseases.

The shortage of secure sources of energy, water and even food.

The impact of climate change.

Rising wealth and persistent poverty.

A technological revolution that sends people, ideas and money hurtling around the planet at ever faster speeds.

The struggle between modernity and extremism.

No one country can control these forces, but more than any other country, the U.S. and Europe together have an ability to affect them— if we use the totality of our strength.

To state the obvious, not one of these challenges has any respect for borders. And not one can be met solely, or even mostly, with military force. We need to abandon the myopic view that any security problem worth solving can be dealt with by putting lead on a target.

Conversely, too many Europeans continue to operate under the false assumption that development assistance and economic incentives are the only legitimate forms of suasion.

It's time to revise these paradigms. America should do a better job playing by the rules of the international system and leveraging our power through alliances and international organizations. But Europeans must commit to help us enforce the rules when they are systematically violated.

That understanding could have been the basis for dealing effectively with Iraq. It can still be the foundation for a common approach to Iran.

In short, together, Americans and Europeans have to start using the full array of diplomatic, economic, and military tools at their disposal to solve a very full array of security challenges. Our problems are so big and so complex that we don't have the luxury of using just one set of tricks. Instead of taking sides on the phony debate between American hard power and European soft power, we need to start relying on smart power.

Second, there is no question that the world's economic center of gravity is going to shift east in the next 50 years. That's inevitable, and — to the extent the countries of Asia are able to lift their people out of poverty — it is also desirable. We should welcome their new prosperity. Countries like China and India are using market principles we originated — inside an international trade system we created — in an attempt to reach levels of prosperity we already possess.

We also have to put the economic challenge from Asia into perspective. For all of its remarkable growth, China still ranks only about 100th in the world in per capita income, about the same as Mali. China still has about 400 million people living on about $2 per day. China must create 20 million new jobs every year just to hold unemployment rates steady.

That one fact means that China will continue to place domestic economic growth above almost every other priority. When we talk to them about energy, or about climate change, they talk to us about economic development.

Based on those dynamics, and the fact that Europe and the United States still account for 60 percent of global GDP, We're well positioned to succeed in the global economy — if we're smart. The key will be leveraging our huge head start in human capital, the true wealth of a nation in the 21st century, and innovating rapidly enough to ensure the world can support a massive new global consumer base — and more than one billion new workers competing for jobs.

We need to develop a new Euro-Atlantic policy for managing relations with energy exporters.

We need to get our priorities straight and attack the challenge of hydrocarbon dependence with the same grit and determination we used to win the Cold War.

These are all monumental challenges, and I don't believe we do ourselves any favors by minimizing them. But I am convinced that our nations are still — and can remain — the masters of their fates.

Some day soon, we could pass that inflection point where these issues overwhelm us.

As stated, one of three strategies will be used: military authority, moral authority, or a combination of the two. Threatening China with America's economic authority could harm America as much as it could harm China. The moral authority approach is America's best approach. It is essential that America's new President adopts the less Americentric concept, recognizing that China is already a "major responsible power" and implementing the partnership that aligns American and Chinese interests in a reformed international system. That should be even more compelling now that America's economy has been harmed by mismanagement.

America's economic, military, and moral authority have been squandered and mismanaged early in 21st century and are weakening rapidly with catastrophic consequences for Americans and others around the world. The military and economic threats that are the premise and coercive power of the "responsible stakeholder" policy approach to China increasingly can rely only on America's military authority. The way an American administration has chosen to use its military authority has revealed again, as in the Korean and Vietnam Wars, the limits of the American people's willingness to sustain its projections and misuse of military authority bereft of moral authority's legitimatization and enhanced effectiveness.

Since 2001, America has spent US $ 1 Trillion so far on a regime-change-based foreign policy in Afghanistan and Iraq and alienated much of the world in the process. America has political limits on the use of military authority in the wake of the Korean, Vietnam, Afghanistan, and Iraq wars. It can pursue terrorists, but not catch their leader, nor prevent his followers from multiplying. During America's 43rd presidency, America's military authority prevented other major terrorist attacks in America, but not in many other nations.

Currently America cannot credibly attack China if it does not attack Taiwan. China is not going to attack Taiwan unless it causes a crisis. China is patient, and knows that time will solve old sensitivities. If China did attack Taiwan, which America has armed and thus encourage to be more belligerent than it might otherwise be, how many Americans would want to die in a civil war half a world away? Not many, and not for long. How many American's would support a shock and awe based use of military authority against a country as important to America economically, diplomatically and militarily as China? Not many and not for long. American use of military authority without moral authority is unsustainable in the Age of Species Lethal Weapons and Science.

American foreign and domestic policymakers, scholars and the American people must accept the reality that China is not Iraq, Afghanistan, or North Korea. Yet these policymakers' formulation of the "responsible stakeholder" policy includes regime change demands of China. Mr. Zoellick asserted the core driver of America's policy towards China since 1949 in stating that America does not "urge the cause of freedom to weaken China" and saying "Our goal is to help others find their own voice, attain their own freedom." Mr. Zoellick, representing the American government, presumed to say "Closed politics cannot be a permanent feature of Chinese society" and "Some in China believe they can secure the Communist Party's monopoly on power by emphasizing economic growth and nationalism." Conventional American foreign policy asserts that: "China needs a peaceful political transition to make its government responsible and accountable to its people."

When there was an ideological struggle between communism and capitalism, Americans emphatically objected to communist nations presuming to criticize and seek to change America's political order. What gives 5.6% of mankind the authority to force their political system on 22% of mankind? Even if America had such economic, military, and moral authority, why would China tolerate its instruction on how it should govern itself?

American policy needs to be based on the realism of win-win value propositions for China and must come to grips with the reality of the mess of its economic, domestic, and foreign policy, military choices has created for America early in the 21st century. In 1997, America was the world's largest creditor nation. A fast decade later America it is the world's largest debtor nation. The reality is that China is no longer a weak nation that can be granted "responsible stakeholder" status in the international system if America wishes. China is now, because of the pragmatic, energetic, and frugal way of the Chinese America's biggest creditor.

Unlike America, which seeks to preserve its dominance over an outdated international system, China follows the wisdom of Deng Xiaoping's blueprint for China's policies. China does not aggressively seek to force its self-interest unilaterally on other nations, or to redesign the international order in a zero sum game mindset. Nor does China wish to dominate the international system. China has been busy minding its own business and preparing for the responsibilities as a leading developing nation. It has a "win-win" template for reforming the international system and better understands, identifies with, and responds to other developing nations than America.

The international system that America designed after World War II was accepted because it was win-win for many other nations. To continue to lead in the 21st century's emerging new international system, America must make domestic and foreign policy choices correctly. Will America choose to lead in a win-win international system or insist on exploiting its advantages using a zero sum game mindset until it has completely exhausted any possible advantage? By then, America will be too misaligned with developing and developed worlds to make a major contribution to the prosperity and peace of the world.

The American Constitution is one of three classic "win-win" models for government of the people, by the people and for the people. Another model, which is validated by its success in producing prosperity and peace, is China under the exceptionally able leadership of Deng Xiao Ping and his successors.

The challenge that American policymakers now face is how to keep the zero sum game processes from undermining the win-win features of the American Constitution. The answer for America, which is obviously compelling, is for America, to offer other nations win-win value propositions and to live up to its Constitution's template of tolerance for the opinions and rights of others. It will be difficult for American policymakers to do so if they and the American people do not succeed in creating a partnership with China that achieves collaboration between the needs of the leading Rights and Permission Societies. That partnership must operate based on mutual respect and reciprocal benefits and combine the moral, economic, and military authorities of the current superpower and emerging mega superpower.

China will continue to implement its leaders' win-win value proposition for America and the other nations.

American policymakers face the need not to make the America's and China's ways of doing things an either/or choice. Neither nation can produce peace and prosperity unless it tolerates the needs of the other nation and respects their rights of self-determination an.

Another fact that American policymakers face is that the United Nations Charter is the third potential win-win model. As examined in chapter 11 of Book 2, the American Constitution was the model for the United Nations Charter, which some in American feel is unworkable, in effect, because it is democratic. The United Nations Charter, like America and, China, is a work in progress.

Both America and China must make the United Nations' Charter a successful form of win-win government. China has respected the peaceful coexistence goals of the United Nations Charter under its past 3 generations of leaders. After leading in the creation of the United Nations, America has been less and less willing to make the United Nations Charter work effectively or respect these goals. Instead, America has been obsessed with ideologically, geopolitically, and economically ruling the world, when all that is realistically sustainable is working to keep the world running without its prosperity and peace breaking down.

The Competing Charisma of Liberal Democratic Capitalism or Authoritarian Capitalism

Both the American and Chinese Constitutional systems have enormous potential benefits for their respective civilizations. Neither is a one-size-fits-all solution to the problems of managing prosperity and peace. The example of a successful partnership between America and China is essential in the new international system. It is also essential to presume American Exceptionalist Charisma.

Azar Gat, a Professor of National Security in Tel Aviv, recognizes that the success of China what he terms as what he terms an "authoritarian capitalist state...may represent a viable alternative path for developing nations, which in turn suggests that there is nothing inevitable about liberal democracy's ultimate victory or future dominance." He focuses on the contest for the hearts and minds of mankind between "liberal democratic capitalism" and "authoritarian capitalism."[117] He recognizes that it is a crucial issue now that capitalism has won and communism has collapsed. He states:

THE END OF THE END OF HISTORY

Today's global liberal democratic order faces two challenges. The first is radical Islam -- and it is the lesser of the two challenges. Although the proponents of radical Islam find liberal democracy repugnant, and the movement is often described as the new fascist threat, the societies from which it arises are generally poor and stagnant. They represent no viable alternative to modernity and pose no significant military threat to the developed world. It is mainly the potential use of weapons of mass destruction -- particularly by nonstate actors -- that makes militant Islam a menace.

The second, and more significant, challenge emanates from the rise of non-democratic great powers: the West's old Cold War rivals China and Russia, now operating under authoritarian capitalist, rather than communist regimes. Authoritarian capitalist great powers played a leading role in the international system up until 1945. They have been absent since then. But today, they seem poised for a comeback.

Capitalism's ascendancy appears to be deeply entrenched, but the current predominance of democracy could be far less secure. Capitalism has expanded relentlessly since early modernity, its lower-priced goods and superior economic power eroding and transforming all other socioeconomic regimes, a process most memorably described by Karl Marx in The Communist Manifesto. Contrary to Marx's expectations, capitalism had the same effect on communism, eventually "burying" it without the proverbial shot being fired. The triumph of the market, precipitating and reinforced by the industrial-technological revolution, led to the rise of the middle class, intensive urbanization, the spread of education, the emergence of mass society, and ever greater affluence. In the post-Cold War era (just as in the nineteenth century and the 1950s and 1960s), it is widely believed that liberal democracy naturally emerged from these developments, a view famously espoused by Francis Fukuyama. Today, more than half of the world's states have elected governments, and close to half have sufficiently entrenched liberal rights to be considered fully free.

But the reasons for the triumph of democracy, especially over its nondemocratic capitalist rivals of the two world wars,

Germany and Japan, were more contingent than is usually assumed. Authoritarian capitalist states, today exemplified by China and Russia, may represent a viable alternative path to modernity, which in turn suggests that there is nothing inevitable about liberal democracy's ultimate victory -- or future dominance.

CHRONICLE OF A DEFEAT NOT FORETOLD

The liberal democratic camp defeated its authoritarian, fascist, and communist rivals alike in all of the three major great-power struggles of the twentieth century -- the two world wars and the Cold War. In trying to determine exactly what accounted for this decisive outcome, it is tempting to trace it to the special traits and intrinsic advantages of liberal democracy. [117]

That is the real issue for those who cherish the ideals of liberal democracy. Gat defines the issue as he sees it:

China and Russia represent a return of economically successful authoritarian capitalist powers, which have been absent since the defeat of Germany and Japan in 1945, but they are much larger than the latter two countries ever were. Although Germany was only a medium-sized country uncomfortably squeezed at the center of Europe, it twice nearly broke out of its confines to become a true world power on account of its economic and military might. In 1941, Japan was still behind the leading great powers in terms of economic development, but its growth rate since 1913 had been the highest in the world. Ultimately, however, both Germany and Japan were too small -- in terms of population, resources, and potential -- to take on the United States. Present-day China, on the other hand, is the largest player in the international system in terms of population and is experiencing spectacular economic growth. By shifting from communism to capitalism, China has switched to a far more efficient brand of authoritarianism. As China rapidly narrows the economic gap with the developed world, the possibility looms that it will become a true authoritarian superpower.

Even in its current bastions in the West, the liberal political and economic consensus is vulnerable to unforeseen developments, such as a crushing economic crisis that could disrupt the global trading system or a resurgence of ethnic strife in a Europe increasingly troubled by immigration and ethnic minorities. Were the West to be hit by such upheavals, support for liberal democracy in Asia, Latin America, and Africa -- where adherence to that model is more recent, incomplete, and insecure -- could be shaken. A successful non-democratic Second World could then be regarded by many as an attractive alternative to liberal democracy.

MAKING THE WORLD SAFE FOR DEMOCRACY

Although the rise of authoritarian capitalist great powers would not necessarily lead to a nondemocratic hegemony or a war, it might imply that the near-total dominance of liberal democracy since the Soviet Union's collapse will be short-lived and that a universal "democratic peace" is still far off. The new authoritarian capitalist powers could become as deeply integrated into the world economy as imperial Germany and imperial Japan were and not choose to pursue autarky, as Nazi Germany and the communist bloc did. A great-power China may also be less revisionist than the territorially confined Germany and Japan were (although Russia, which is still reeling from having lost an empire, is more likely to tend toward revisionism). Still, Beijing, Moscow, and their future followers might well be on antagonistic terms with the democratic countries, with all the potential for suspicion, insecurity, and conflict that this entails -- while holding considerably more power than any of the democracies' past rivals ever did.

So does the greater power potential of authoritarian capitalism mean that the transformation of the former communist great powers may ultimately prove to have been a negative development for global democracy? It is too early to tell. Economically, the liberalization of the former communist countries has given the global economy a tremendous boost, and there may be more in store. But the possibility of a move toward protectionism by them in the future also needs to be taken into account -- and assiduously avoided. It was, after all, the prospect of growing protectionism in the world economy at the turn of the twentieth century and the protectionist bent of the 1930s that helped radicalize the nondemocratic capitalist powers of the time and precipitate both world wars.

On the positive side for the democracies, the collapse of the Soviet Union and its empire stripped Moscow of about half the resources it commanded during the Cold War, with eastern Europe absorbed by a greatly expanded democratic Europe. This is perhaps the most significant change in the global balance of power since the forced postwar democratic reorientation of Germany and Japan under U.S. tutelage. Moreover, China may still eventually democratize, and Russia could reverse its drift away from democracy. If China and Russia do not become democratic, it will be critical that India remain so, both because of its vital role in balancing China and because of the model that it represents for other developing countries.

But the most important factor remains the United States. For all the criticism leveled against it, the United States -- - and its alliance with Europe -- - stands as the single most important hope for the future of liberal democracy. Despite its problems and weaknesses, the United States still commands a global position of strength and is likely to retain it even as the authoritarian capitalist powers grow. Not only are its GDP and productivity growth rate the highest in the developed world, but as an immigrant country with about one-fourth the population density of both the European Union and China and one-tenth of that of Japan and India, the United States still has considerable potential to grow -- both economically and in terms of population -- whereas those others are all experiencing aging and, ultimately, shrinking populations. China's economic growth rate is among the highest in the world, and given the country's huge population and still low levels of development, such growth harbors the most radical potential for change in global power relations. But even if China's superior growth rate persists and its GDP surpasses that of the United States by the 2020s, as is often forecast, China will still have just over one-third of the United States' wealth per capita and, hence, considerably less economic and military power. Closing that far more challenging gap with the developed world would take several more decades. Furthermore, GDP alone is known to be a poor measure of a country's power, and evoking it to celebrate China's ascendancy is highly misleading. As it was during the twentieth century, the U.S. factor remains the greatest guarantee that liberal democracy will not be thrown on the defensive and relegated to a vulnerable position on the periphery of the international system. [118]

However, Gat's analysis does not go far enough into the heart of the issue as to whether the liberal or authoritarian capitalist models will remain in contest or whether one will win the respect and favor of all mankind. First, he leaves out a hybrid, which we will term "Socialist Capitalism," which believes in "scientific management" of society and the economy rather than majority-rule electoral management. Socialist Capitalism in China is neither liberal nor authoritarian capitalism. Looking at China's government more perceptively as "Socialist Capitalism" allows for a better understanding of what is occurring in China. Misunderstanding it as "authoritarian Capitalism" misguides American policy toward China.

Second, those who favor liberal democracy must make their own conduct reflective of its respect for the rights, opinions, and priorities of those who have different views. If they are not able to do so, what they see as "liberal democracy" will be seen by others as a form of "authoritarian democracy." One might describe the neoconservative administration's approach as "authoritarian democracy," and point to it as an example of how authoritarian mindsets degrade the democratic features of "liberal democracy."

Third, it is critical for those who favor the expansion of a successful model of liberal democratic government not to use American foreign policy as weapon, or as Mr. Zoellick put it: "Our goal is to help others find their own voice, attain their own freedom."

Americans who wish to champion liberal democracy in China should not presume to say "Closed politics cannot be a permanent feature of Chinese society." Nor "Some in China believe they can secure the Communist Party's monopoly on power by emphasizing economic growth and nationalism." Nor "China needs a peaceful political transition to make its government responsible and accountable to its people." That manifests a zero sum mindset that could push the Chinese government away from political reform and. The Chinese are no different than the Americans in their desire for self-determination and sovereignty.

A "democracy" among nations cannot require that all nations be liberal democracies. Some nations may not be capable of stable majority-rule democracy for many reasons. A "democracy" among nations also does not mean that all nations become authoritarian capitalist states.

If one champions liberal democracy, the most effective way to propagate that belief is to perfect liberal democracy at home. As Gandhi put it: "You must be the change you want to see in the world." If "liberal democracies" can work as liberal democracies, they will be a beacon for many other nations. But if "liberal democracies" do not behave as liberal democracies they will not be able to retain the illusion that they are. They will not present a charismatic argument for the proliferation of liberal democratic processes in a world that has discovered that authoritarian capitalist nations and socialist capitalist nations can be economically successful and, in some cases, politically stable.

Indeed, America's experiment with its evolving Rights Society is in jeopardy of becoming a Permission Society. That would be a disaster for Americans, the Chinese, and all mankind in the Age of Species Lethal Weapons and Science.

China's Responsible Major Power Concept

In 2007 the *China Daily* discussed China's international role as "a responsible major power" and articulated China's concept and definition of a responsible major power:

"This year China has made significant achievements as a member of the United Nations (UN). Playing the role of a participant, a constructor and protector of the international system represented by the UN, the nation has held high the banner of the UN Charter, carried out its independent foreign policies based on the philosophy of a harmonious world, persisted in strategic talks with other major powers, enhancing friendly relations with neighboring countries and strengthening and expanding good relations with other developing nations. China has shown the world the attitude of a 'responsible major power.' [119] (Emphasis added)

China looks past the terms offered by America in the "responsible stakeholder" concept, and implements in a "low key way" the Responsible Major Power concept. Because American policymakers are trying to persuade China to fit into the existing Principles of Conflict based international system, they have been unable to recognize that China is already operates in the emerging international system it is creating based on the Principles of Peaceful Coexistence. American policy makers, scholars and opinion leaders are looking for progress in achieving their conventional goals, while China is building a better international system based on better goals and principles. For example, China does not support American unilateral action, and accepts the United Nations' Charter as the framework of the modern world. America under its 43rd president in effect rejected the Charter and the United Nations' role.

Under America's 43rd president, the American government demeaned its charismatic Exceptionalism and obligations under the United Nations' Charter. It is not in America's interest to reject two of the three win-win models for a peaceful and prosperous international system. What is required is that America accepts all three models. But American policymakers can only do that if they change America's conventional priorities. That takes presidential leadership and the support of a consensus among the American people.

The approach laid down by Deng Xiaoping, is for China to be a "Responsible Great Power". The Chinese quietly move ahead, keeping the peace. The Chinese governments' response to the "responsible stakeholder" approach is now the "Responsible Major Nation" approach. China does not accept the characterization that it is a "stakeholder" and carries out its role in creating a better international system. Note that what the two characterizations have in common is the "responsible" role for China. Is China a stakeholder? Yes. Is China a major nation? Obviously it is. The difference is a stakeholder has fewer rights than a major nation.

The responsible stakeholder approach is part of the classic containment approach towards China ·pursued by America and European nations since foreign nations' interaction with China became a problem in 1800 for China. China sought to ignore America and Europe, but could not, as they would not leave China alone and in peace and sought to weaken and destroy it by carving it into pieces and giving parts of it to each of them. For example, America and the European victors gave part of China to the Japanese after the First World War, although even though China had supported the winners.[120]

The simple and realistic solution is for America to acknowledge that China is a major power rather than a stakeholder in the world. But to an Americentric mindset, if China is a major power, or is admitted to be then America must inevitably be losing something valuable. To such a mindset, human affairs are about conflict. So those with zero sum mindsets must delude themselves and others. They must trumpet that China is a "stakeholder" rather than a major power, which is condescending and poor diplomacy.

China is using a win-win approach in spite of America's zero sum strategies. China peacefully goes about getting stronger economically. Unfortunately, America has been aggressive, has weakened its military and moral authority, made more enemies, and declined economically. The win-win approach wins, because it offers win-win value propositions and results. The zero sum game approach loses in the long term. That is also the result in game theory research, where no strategy in the Prisoners' Dilemma is as successful as the Generous Tit-for-Tat strategy. But game theory assumes people are rational and well informed, and we are neither. Foreign policy based on the Principles of Peaceful Coexistence ameliorate the irrationality of the Principles of Conflict in human nature.

The James Baker Model: China accepts America not being displaced in return for America not containing China

In 2007, an alternate formulation of the "responsible stakeholder" approach was put forward by the George H. W. Bush administration's former Treasury Secretary James Baker. Its value proposition was that if China accepts America not being displaced, America would in return not seek to contain China. This has the benefit of being a less delusional basis for America's policies toward China. It is perhaps disingenuous because America would likely go on trying to contain China. It acknowledges China as more than a "stakeholder," without explicitly acknowledging that China is a "major power." But it has more mutual respect than the responsible stakeholder approach to China.

The Baker Model, like the Responsible Stakeholder Model, has as its premise not only the assumption of permanent American world dominance, but of American power being protected in Asia, far from home, in China's backyard. It is a unipolar, sole global superpower preservation seeking model. It ignores China's own interests in both preserving and protecting itself from America's military authority, at a time when the American government was, as Undersecretary of State. Zoellick's words indicate, seeking regime change in China, and practicing regime change and unilateral wars both without United Nations sanction or United Nations sanction procured by incorrect or knowingly incorrect intelligence. An American government was seen by the world as not being trust-worthy in the first 8 years of this century. It did not provide accurate intelligence about Iraq's nuclear weapon development program or the presence of weapons of mass destruction in Iraq to the United Nations. It was an episode that is a low point in the history of American foreign policy. It is similar to the loss of moral authority the former Soviet Union suffered in being caught lying about its nuclear missiles in Cuba in 1962. Lying to the world is not sound military or moral diplomacy. It is an approach that has no chance of leading long term to a safer world and a safer America.

The Baker Model however does however put America in a weaker, more equal posture to China, than the previous approaches. America is asking China to accept America not being displaced in Asia, half a world away from the American homeland. China had arrived by 2007 as a major power that had to be approached like a major power and bargained with rather than a poor developing country that could be bullied, in James Baker's perspective. But, latent in the Baker Model is the threat that if China does not accept America not being displaced in China's part of the world, America will contain China. The Baker Model is still an insulting offer, but is not perhaps intended to be insulting. It is just a zero sum game mindset approach being what it is and being offered too late to be a compliment. America, having tried to contain China since 1949 and having failed to do so by 2007, was offering to purportedly give up an option it no longer has or may not be able to afford economically or militarily in the future. Like other past approaches, it insults the Chinese government's intelligence. The Baker Model is flawed, as are all other current American foreign policy models that are based on zero mindset and strategies in the Age of Species Lethal Weapons and Science.

The behavior of America and its destabilizing results in many regions of the world since September 11th, 2001 raise the questions:

1. Is it safe to allow America to set the agenda for the world?
2. Is it acceptable to other civilizations, nations and peoples?
3. Is there a better way to run the world?
4. Is there a better model of military and moral authority and diplomacy than America has used since September 11th, 2001?
5. Is China's Peaceful Coexistence model of the 21st century international system better than America's Principles of Conflict based 20th century model?

These questions and problems must be recognized, studied and debated in American and other nations' policymaking and scholarship.

A New American Perspective That Accepts China's Peaceful Development as a Major Power in an American Led and Dominated International Order

The Baker Model's offer of peaceful coexistence so long as the world's sole military superpower is not displaced in Asia is not difficult for China to accept, because it is consistent with China's highly successful peaceful coexistence foreign policy designed by Deng Xiaoping. Since China's model for its foreign policy and a new international system is based on win-win rather than zero mindset approaches, China can look beyond the Baker Model and the Responsible Stakeholder Model. They are not completely inconsistent with China's Responsible Major Nation and Harmonious World Model.

The end of the Cold War and the collapse of the Soviet Union improved China's security situation. However, the American-led Western reaction to the 1989 Tiananmen crackdown encouraged stronger emphasis on nationalistic themes within China. Tension between the Mainland China and Taiwan governments leads the

Mainland Chinese people to see America as a destabilizing hegemonic power, striving to pressure and intimidate China. But Deng Xiaoping advised Chinese leaders to avoid confrontation, to "bide time," "take a low key" approach and work to develop international opportunities to build up China's 'comprehensive national power' and secure a more advantageous leadership position. Chinese leaders continue to implement Deng Xiaoping's principles.

James Baker's model is presented often by Americentric foreign policy scholars. For example, Princeton University's Professor John Ikenberry's work examines questions such as:

1. What are the merits and demerits of China's leaders' model of a new world order?
2. Will China overthrow the existing America-led and dominated international order or become part of it?
3. What if anything can America do to maintain its leadership and dominance of the 21st century's international order?[121]

Ikenberry points out that:

> ...there are different types of power transitions. Some states have seen their economic and geopolitical power grow dramatically and have still accommodated themselves to the existing order. Others have risen up and sought to change it. Some power transitions have led to the breakdown of the old order and the establishment of a new international hierarchy. Others have brought about only limited adjustments in the regional and global system.
>
> A variety of factors determine the way in which power transitions unfold. The nature of the rising state's regime and the degree of its dissatisfaction with the old order are critical: at the end of the nineteenth century, the United States, a liberal country an ocean away from Europe, was better able to embrace the British-centered international order than Germany was. But even more decisive is the character of the inter-

national order itself -- for it is the nature of the international order that shapes a rising state's choice between challenging that order and integrating into it.[122]

He proposes that:

As it faces an ascendant China, the United States should remember that its leadership of the Western order allows it to shape the environment in which China will make critical strategic choices. If it wants to preserve this leadership, Washington must work to strengthen the rules and institutions that underpin that order -- making it even easier to join and harder to overturn. U.S. grand strategy should be built around the motto "The road to the East runs through the West." It must sink the roots of this order as deeply as possible, giving China greater incentives for integration than for opposition and increasing the chances that the system will survive even after U.S. relative power has declined.

The United States' "unipolar moment" will inevitably end. If the defining struggle of the twenty-first century is between China and the United States, China will have the advantage. If the defining struggle is between China and a revived Western system, the West will triumph.

Some observers believe that the American era is coming to an end, as the Western-oriented world order is replaced by one increasingly dominated by the East. The historian Niall Ferguson has written that the bloody twentieth century witnessed "the descent of the West" and "a reorientation of the world" toward the East. Realists go on to note that as China gets more powerful and the United States' position erodes, two things are likely to happen: China will try to use its growing influence to reshape the rules and institutions of the international system to better serve its interests, and other states in the system -- especially the declining hegemony -- will start to see China as a growing security threat. The result of these developments, they predict, will be tension, distrust, and conflict, the typical features of a power transition. In this view, the drama of China's rise will feature an increasingly powerful China and a declining United States locked in an epic battle over the rules and leadership of the international system. And as the world's largest country emerges not from within but outside the established post-World War II international order, it is a drama that will end with the grand ascendance of China and the onset of an Asian-centered world order.

That course, however, is not inevitable. The rise of China does not have to trigger a wrenching hegemonic transition. The U.S.-Chinese power transition can be very different from those of the past because China faces an international order that is fundamentally different from those that past rising states confronted. China does not just face the United States; it faces a Western-centered system that is open, integrated, and rule-based, with wide and deep political foundations. The nuclear revolution, meanwhile, has made war among great powers unlikely -- eliminating the major tool that rising powers have used to overturn international systems defended by declining hegemonic states. Today's Western order, in short, is hard to overturn and easy to join.

Third, the postwar Western order has an unusually dense, encompassing, and broadly endorsed system of rules and institutions. Whatever its shortcomings, it is more open and rule-based than any previous order. State sovereignty and the rule of law are not just norms enshrined in the United Nations Charter. They are part of the deep operating logic of the order. To be sure, these norms are evolving, and the United States itself has historically been ambivalent about binding itself to international law and institutions -- and at no time more so than today. But the overall system is dense with multilateral rules and institutions -- global and regional, economic, political, and security-related. These represent one of the great breakthroughs of the postwar era. They have laid the basis for unprecedented levels of cooperation and shared authority over the global system. [123]

The Bush administration's unilateralism is among the worst possible strategies America could have. New administrations must ensure that this administration's approach is ephemeral historical accident not to be repeated.

Ikenberry recognizes that the existing international system is being destroyed by America:

But that will only happen if the United States sets about strengthening the existing order. Today, with Washington preoccupied with terrorism and war in the Middle East, rebuilding Western rules and institutions might to some seem to be of only marginal relevance. Many Bush administration officials have been outright hostile to the multilateral, rule-based system that the United States has shaped and led. Such hostility is foolish and dangerous. China will become powerful: it is already on the rise, and the United States' most powerful strategic weapon is the ability to decide what sort of international order will be in place to receive it.

The United States must reinvest in the Western order, reinforcing the features of that order that encourage engagement, integration, and restraint. The more this order binds together capitalist democratic states in deeply rooted institutions; the more open, consensual, and rule-based it is; and the more widely spread its benefits, the more likely it will be that rising powers can and will secure their interests through integration and accommodation rather than through war. And if the Western system offers rules and institutions that benefit the full range of states -- rising and falling, weak and strong, emerging and mature -- its dominance as an international order is all but certain.

The first thing the United States must do is to reestablish itself as the foremost supporter of the global system of governance that underpins the Western order. Doing so will first of all facilitate the kind of collective problem solving that makes all countries better off. At the same time, when other countries see the United States using its power to strengthen existing rules and institutions, that power is rendered more legitimate -- and U.S. authority is strengthened. Countries within the West become more inclined to work with, rather than resist, U.S. power, which reinforces the centrality and dominance of the West itself.

Renewing Western rules and institutions will require, among other things, updating the old bargains that underpinned key postwar security pacts. The strategic understanding behind both NATO and Washington's East Asian alliances is that the United States will work with its allies to provide security and bring them in on decisions over the use of force, and U.S. allies, in return, will operate within the U.S.-led Western order. Security cooperation in the West remains extensive today, but with the main security threats less obvious than they were during the Cold War, the purposes and responsibilities of these alliances are under dispute. Accordingly, the United States needs to reaffirm the political value of these alliances -- recognizing that they are part of a wider Western institutional architecture that allows states to do business with one another.

The United States should also renew its support for wide-ranging multilateral institutions. On the economic front, this would include building on the agreements and architecture of the WTO, including pursuing efforts to conclude the current Doha Round of trade talks, which seeks to extend market opportunities and trade liberalization to developing countries. The WTO is at a critical stage. The basic standard of nondiscrimination is at risk thanks to the proliferation of bilateral and regional trade agreements. Meanwhile, there are growing doubts over whether the WTO can in fact carry out trade liberalization, particularly in agriculture, that benefits developing countries. These issues may seem narrow, but the fundamental character of the liberal international order -- its commitment to universal rules of openness that spread gains widely -- is at stake. Similar doubts haunt a host of other multilateral agreements -- on global warming and nuclear nonproliferation, among others -- and they thus also demand renewed U.S. leadership.

The strategy here is not simply to ensure that the Western order is open and rule-based. It is also to make sure that the order does not fragment into an array of bilateral and "mini-lateral" arrangements, causing the United States to find itself tied to only a few key states in various regions. Under such a scenario, China would have an opportunity to build its own set of bilateral and "minilateral" pacts. As a result, the world would be broken into competing U.S. and Chinese spheres. The more security and economic relations are multilateral and all-encompassing, the more the global system retains its coherence.

In addition to maintaining the openness and durability of the order, the United States must redouble its efforts to integrate rising developing countries into key global institutions. Bringing emerging countries into the governance of the international order will give it new life. The United States and Europe must find room at the table not only for China but also for countries such as Brazil, India, and South Africa. A Goldman Sachs report on the so-called BRICs (Brazil, Russia, India, and China) noted that by 2050 these countries' economies could together be larger than those of the original G-6 countries (Germany, France, Italy, Japan, the United Kingdom, and the United States) combined. Each international institution presents its own challenges. The UN Security Council is perhaps the hardest to deal with, but its reform would also bring the greatest returns. Less formal bodies -- the so-called G-20 and various other intergovernmental networks -- can provide alternative avenues for voice and representation.

THE TRIUMPH OF THE LIBERAL ORDER

The key thing for U.S. leaders to remember is that it may be possible for China to overtake the United States alone, but it is much less likely that China will ever manage to overtake the Western order. In terms of economic weight, for example, China will surpass the United States as the largest state in the global system sometime around 2020. (Because of its population, China needs a level of productivity only one-fifth that of the United States to become the world's biggest economy.) But when the economic capacity of the Western system as a whole is considered, China's economic advances look much less significant; the Chinese economy will be much smaller than the combined economies of the Organization for Economic Cooperation and Development far into the future. This is even truer of military might: China cannot hope to come anywhere close to total OECD military expenditures anytime soon. The capitalist democratic world is a powerful constituency for the preservation -- and, indeed, extension -- of the existing international order. If China intends to rise up and challenge the existing order, it has a much more daunting task than simply confronting the United States.

The "unipolar moment" will eventually pass. U.S. dominance will eventually end. U.S. grand strategy, accordingly, should be driven by one key question: What kind of international order

would the United States like to see in place when it is less powerful? [124]

Ikenberry, and many American scholars, assume that an
American led international order is best. But is that assumption
correct? And if it is, how universal is any agreement that America's
conventional foreign policy offers for peace and prosperity in the
Age of Species Lethal Weapons and Science? We present the often
unconscious assumption that an America dominated international
order system is the optimal one for very careful analysis.

The "America led and dominated international system"
assumption may be incorrect for many possible reasons. In addition, even if it is correct, is it achievable? Will other nations
be sufficiently impressed by America's authority that they will
endorse and support an American led international system?

Working within the assumptions of Professor Ikenberry, it is correct that it is easy for China to join the existing institutions in the
international system America designed. But it does not necessarily
follow that "The Western order can turn the coming power shift
into peaceful change favorable to the United States." Ikenberry is
correctly zeroing in on a key problem in America's own willingness
to take into consideration the needs of other nations if those needs
are, in the subjective view of the American administration at any
given time, not the optimal ones. He states:

> The Western order's strong framework of rules and institu-
> tions is already starting to facilitate Chinese integration. At first,
> China embraced certain rules and institutions for defensive
> purposes: protecting its sovereignty and economic interests
> while seeking to reassure other states of its peaceful intentions
> by getting involved in regional and global groupings. But as
> the scholar Marc Lanteigne argues, "What separates China from
> other states, and indeed previous global powers, is that not only
> is it 'growing up' within a milieu of international institutions far
> more developed than ever before, but more importantly, it is do-

ing so while making active use of these institutions to promote the country's development of global power status." China, in short, is increasingly working within, rather than outside of, the Western order.

China is already a permanent member of the UN Security Council, a legacy of Roosevelt's determination to build the universal body around diverse great-power leadership. This gives China the same authority and advantages of "great-power exceptionalism" as the other permanent members. The existing global trading system is also valuable to China, and increasingly so. Chinese economic interests are quite congruent with the current global economic system -- a system that is open and loosely institutionalized and that China has enthusiastically embraced and thrived in. State power today is ultimately based on sustained economic growth, and China is well aware that no major state can modernize without integrating into the globalized capitalist system; if a country wants to be a world power, it has no choice but to join the World Trade Organization (WTO). The road to global power, in effect, runs through the Western order and its multilateral economic institutions.

China not only needs continued access to the global capitalist system; it also wants the protections that the system's rules and institutions provide. The WTO's multilateral trade principles and dispute-settlement mechanisms, for example, offer China tools to defend against the threats of discrimination and protectionism that rising economic powers often confront. The evolution of China's policy suggests that Chinese leaders recognize these advantages: as Beijing's growing commitment to economic liberalization has increased the foreign investment and trade China has enjoyed, so has Beijing increasingly embraced global trade rules. It is possible that as China comes to champion the WTO, the support of the more mature Western economies for the WTO will wane. But it is more likely that both the rising and the declining countries will find value in the quasi-legal mechanisms that allow conflicts to be settled or at least diffused. The existing international economic institutions also offer opportunities for new powers to rise up through their hierarchies. In the International Monetary Fund and the World Bank, governance is based on economic shares, which countries can translate into greater institutional voice. To be sure, the process of adjustment has been slow. The United States and Europe still dominate the IMF. Washington has a 17 percent voting share (down from 30 percent) -- a controlling amount, because 85 percent approval is needed for action -- and the European Union has a major say in the appointment of ten of the 24 members of the board. But there are growing pressures, notably the need for resources and the need to maintain relevance that will likely persuade the Western states to admit China into the inner circle of these economic governance institutions. The IMF's existing shareholders, for example, see a bigger role for rising developing countries as necessary to renew the institution and get it through its current crisis of mission. At the IMF's meeting in Singapore in September 2006, they agreed on reforms that will give China, Mexico, South Korea, and Turkey a greater voice.

As China sheds its status as a developing country (and therefore as a client of these institutions), it will increasingly be able to act as a patron and stakeholder instead. Leadership in these organizations is not simply a reflection of economic size (the United States has retained its voting share in the IMF even as its economic weight has declined); nonetheless, incremental advancement within them will create important opportunities for China.[125]

Ikenberry asserts that since America cannot be the sole leader of the international system, it must strengthen the existing international system because it can be a check on China. He recommends that America, in the interest of preserving its leadership, use the existing international system's institutions rather than weaken existing international law that America will need as a counterbalance to China's growing geopolitical power. That is good advice. It is consistent with President Washington's Farewell Advice to Americans. In the 21st century, America must not isolate itself or weaken the United Nations. But such existing institutions are rightly perceived by developing nations as used by America to help manage and manipulate other nations.

China has been helping to reform the existing international system while the 20th century international system is being weakened by America's misuse of its authority. America cannot succeed in urging China to become a responsible stakeholder (i.e. a minor rather than major responsible power) while it undermines the existing international system by not being a responsible stakeholder or responsible major power.

The existing international system, even as China decides to participate in it will not remain American dominated or unreformed. That Americentric assumption fails to look at the realities of China's future economic and geopolitical needs. The existing international system would only persist if China were implementing the Principles of Conflict.

Now the Americentric perspective is learning to see China, America and the rest of the world from a Chinese perspective. As China's economy grows larger than America's, the nations of the world will look to it for leadership. That is why it is the smart choice for America to become a partner with China and align its security with China's. One of the benefits for America will be achieving sustainable economic growth and what we term "collaborative equilibrium" and "reciprocal globalization," examined in *China & America's New Economic Partnership*, the fifth in the America-China Partnership Book Series.

Are the American people Capable of Accepting the Genuine, Committed Partnership America Needs with China?

China's current President, Premier, and government see the need for a strategic partnership with America. One of the most important decisions for America's new presidents, is whether to create and sustain a genuine partnership with China. China's leaders are offering America the foundations of such a partnership.

China's concept of a harmonious world is the defining impetus of a newly reformed and peaceful international system. What is America going to choose to do? That is a defining test as to whether or not the American people and system of government are a safe repository for the ultimate power of mankind. China is ready, willing and able. What will Americans decide to do?

As Deputy Secretary of State in 2005, Mr. Zoellick recognized that:

> The China of today is simply not the Soviet Union of the late 1940s: It does not seek to spread radical, anti-American ideologies. While not yet democratic, it does not see itself in a twilight conflict against democracy around the globe. While at times mercantilist, it does not see itself in a death struggle with capitalism. And most importantly, China does not believe that its future depends on overturning the fundamental order of the international system. In fact, quite the reverse: Chinese leaders have decided that their success depends on being networked with the modern world.
>
> If the Cold War analogy does not apply, neither does the distant balance-of-power politics of 19th Century Europe. The global economy of the 21st Century is a tightly woven fabric. We are too interconnected to try to hold China at arm's length, hoping to promote other powers in Asia at its expense. Nor would the other powers hold China at bay, initiating and terminating ties based on an old model of drawing-room diplomacy. The United States seeks constructive relations with all countries that do not threaten peace and security. So if the templates of the past do not fit, how should we view China at the dawn of the 21st Century? On both sides, there is a gulf in perceptions.[126]

In his role as Vice Chairman of Goldman Sachs International Mr. Zoellick stated in 2007:

> In reviewing some of the principal issues for China and the U.S. as international stakeholders, it is striking how often the question of energy security arises. I appreciate that China's

assured access to energy is fundamental to its development, growth, and social stability. Energy security is important for the United States, too.

In my September 2005 speech, I identified energy as a subject that could become either a point of conflict or cooperation between the United States and China. Both the United States and China have wasted energy, with poor environmental consequences. As a developing country, China is understandably sensitive to limitations on its energy use, just as its impressive growth is improving the livelihood of China's people. Even though our two countries are at different stages of development, our mutual interests should lead us to work in concert.

We both have an interest in developing alternative sources of supply, whether nuclear, clean coal technology, biofuels, or other renewables. We both would benefit from more diverse sources of oil and gas. We both gain from improved efficiency and conservation, which also contribute to cooperation on the environment and reducing greenhouse gas emissions. We both are strengthened by building strategic reserves, which should be employed cooperatively with others through the guidance of the International Energy Administration. And we both have an interest in ensuring that the energy trade is not stopped at chokepoints or manipulated through monopoly providers. Sino-American cooperation on energy security may also improve the context for our cooperation on the other topics I discussed today. It can build our confidence in working together to counter energy blackmail that could threaten regional or global security.

I was pleased that last year China's National Development and Reform Commission took the initiative to convene India, Japan, South Korea, and the United States to discuss the energy topic. It should also be part of foreign and security policy strategic discussions. And I hope we can build the trust in both societies to enable our energy companies to find common business ventures as well.[127]

As we emphasize, this suggestion by Mr. Zoellick is similar to Deng Xiaoping's suggested joint development of disputed territories approach put forward three decades ago.

Chapter 8

The Limitations of Conventional American Principles of Conflict Based Asian Policy Analysis

Overview

Few American policymakers and scholars specializing in Asian affairs emphasize a moral authority-based analysis of American domestic and foreign policy. That lack of a moral authority focus reflects America's obsession with ruling rather than helping to run the world. However, two policemen are more effective and each safer and have more military, economic and moral authority than either alone.

Americentric policymakers and typically write with a zero sum mindset based on the Principles of Conflict. That is myopic and points America in dangerous directions for both national security issues in the Age of Species Lethal Weapons and Science and in the emerging reality that Asian nations' economies will reduce America, and European dominance.

The Americentric perspective currently obscures a realistic cross-cultural perspective and a "Chinacentric" perspective must be combined with the Americentric perspective to achieve a realistic cross cultural perspective. Many new solutions to conventional foreign policy problems become identifiable when less Americentric criteria are applied. One of the indicia of the Americentric perspectives is a "maybe but not anytime soon" which is applied to analysis of the development of nations other than America. Another indicia is the "it is extremely successful, but" type of assertions about China and other countries' development. Another indicia is "it is wrong, because it is not the way we do it" assertion which is misleading because the other nations of the world are naturally "localcentric" and less Americentric.

Such observers with an Americentric perspective push unrealistic assumptions to the forefront of their analyses when the daily empirical data does not support their conclusions.

The Strategic Choice of "Hedging" or Aligning America's Economic and National Security with China's

Recall Zhang Yunling and Tang Shiping's comments examined in chapter 1 of Book 2:

> With the United States taking active measures to hedge against or even contain China's rise, and China becoming less attentive to U.S. concerns when it believes it is acting together with regional states, both situations have potential to increase the mutual suspicion between the two countries, resulting in a classic security dilemma. This security dilemma will add yet another dimension of uncertainty to bilateral relations.[128]

It is evident from an Asian perspective, that China behaving in a win-win fashion. It is developing peacefully which is reassuring other Asian nations because it is has been getting stronger but is not engaged in wars. America is acting in a zero sum, must win fashion. As a result of its mindset it has been losing stature and weakening economically, diplomatically, militarily, and morally.

China is minding its own business while behaving as a responsible major power. America has been making its business toppling regimes, invading countries, and thinking and acting irresponsibly. It is criticizing China for not acting as a policeman while behaving like a bully.

The issues on which Americentric policymakers focus on are not the issues that Chinese policymakers such as Zhang Yunling, Tang Shiping and Wang Jisi focus on. That is an aspect of the "gulf of perceptions" that Mr. Zoellick recognizes. In the commentaries of American foreign policy scholars examined in this chapter:

1. The American policy-makers and scholars do not refer to the Principles of Peaceful Coexistence which have been the foundation of Chinese foreign policy and defense strategies since 1978.

2. The Principles of Conflict underlie the American policymakers and scholars' analyses.

3. The American policymakers and scholars are not focused on the need to create a new international system in the 21st century which we refer to as "the Peaceful Coexistence International System." They are focused on tinkering with and preserving the outdated 20th century international system because America designed, leads and dominates it.

4. Chinese policymakers from as early as 1953 have led in creating with India the Principles of Peaceful Coexistence which is the embryo of the Peaceful Coexistence International System required in the Age of Species Lethal Weapons and Science.

5. The issues scholars with Americentric views focus on what are "20th century Cold War issues" although America and China now both have capitalist economies, albeit with American and Chinese characteristics.

6. Chinese foreign policy scholars are focused on "21st century

issues" of Chinese domestic economic development and on foreign policy viewed from the perspective of the goal of creating a harmonious world.

7. American foreign policy makers and scholars do not focus on the fundamental foreign policy issue of human extinction which President Kennedy and Deng Xiaoping focused on in speeches after the Cuban Missile Crisis.

8. America and China becoming partners in a genuine lasting peace is not among conventional America policymakers' or scholars' current list of possible "hedging strategies."

The New School's perspective is that only the committed, genuine partnership of China and America can successfully respond to or "hedge" dangers and provide the framework able meet the new century's security needs. However, in an increasingly ungovernable world, the current economic and geopolitical superpowers must achieve collaborative equilibrium rather than hedge against each other and succumb to:

1. Terrorist attacks,
2. Economic chaos such as the current global financial crises and increasing oil, food, and other commodity costs that can wreck economies, destroy governments, and cause wars
3. Space and arms races caused by rivalry and instability.

America's safest "hedge" against China is for it to become partners with China in implementing the Principles of Peaceful Coexistence in their bilateral and multilateral relationships. America can only effectively "hedge" its perceived risks with China as its partner. Neither America nor China can ensure its economic or national security otherwise.

American Neglect of Asia and Asian Concerns

American policymakers and scholars recognize the long term trend towards lessening influence in Asia and must focus on what can be done to preserve America's political influence authority in Asia. Many recognize that the Bush administration focused the War on Terror and other "Hot War" issues, though they debate the extent of its neglect of Asia. Asian and some American scholars were alarmed by the Bush administration's neglect of Asia and a subgroup of them urged America to remedy its deteriorating role in Asia. Others see America's declining influence as inevitable, given China's economic success.

This chapter examines a sampling of the conventional approach to Asian and Chinese affairs as a useful and necessary background to the New School's For perspectives.

Clyde Prestowitz an American who accompanied President Nixon and Secretary of State Kissinger on their early visits to China asserts that:

> In the wake of World War II, the purpose of American power in the Asia-Pacific region was very clear. It was first to reestablish Japan as a viable, democratic country while also getting the rest of the Asia-Pacific countries and territories back on their economic feet and moving out from under various colonial yokes toward independence and democracy.[129]

Prestowitz quotes a former European Union Commissioner's summary the past situation:

> The United States in 1945-50 was all-powerful; it had a nuclear monopoly and 15 million men under arms and accounted for over half of the world's GDP. It could have done whatever it wanted and no one could have stopped it. The incredible thing is that Americans defined their own interests broadly in terms of the interests of the rest of the world. They

sheathed their power in the multilateral institutions they created such as the UN, the IMF, the World Bank and the GATT. They committed to alliances like NATO and the Security Treaty with Japan and to consultation and consensus. Of course, they usually got their way. But not always and not without consultation and often changes to their original program. They opened their markets and moved to establish a liberal international economic regime. This was all very attractive to the rest of us and it created a tremendous reservoir of good will and cemented support for the United States around the world. Indeed by thus sheathing its power, America actually enhanced it.

Prestowitz summarizes the 1950 to 1990's context:

With the outbreak of the Cold War, the takeover of mainland China by the Chinese Communist Party, and the North Korean invasion of South Korea, the American purpose became even clearer, more focused and more urgent. It was to use American power in the Pacific to contain the spread of communism by the Soviets, Chinese, and North Koreans and to buy time for the rest of Asia to develop economically and politically. It was further to open the American market and to promote free-trade policies that would accelerate the economic recovery and rapid growth of the Asia-Pacific economies.

The United States at this time also established extensive foreign aid programs and championed World Bank lending. In particular, during and after the Korean War, the US established a number of bilateral security agreements in the region and maintained large military deployments that provided for the continued security of South Korea, Japan, Taiwan and the rest of the countries in the region. The American strategy was based on two pillars. The first was that of maintaining superior US Military power so that no country in the region could challenge America or its allies by the use of force. The second was promotion of economic development that it was believed would lead to the growth of middle classes and the emergence of democratic governments that would remain allied with the United States.

Although the Vietnam War strained relations between America and a number of Asia-Pacific countries, this strategy remained largely intact until the collapse of the Soviet Union in 1992. Moreover, it proved enormously successful. The Asia-Pacific economies boomed, beginning with Japan and then continuing with the Asian Tigers and finally with the current rise of China. Many of these countries did evolve into democracies, and some that were not fully democratic nevertheless adopted liberal domestic and foreign policies. So, one could say that by 1992, American power in the Asia-Pacific region had largely achieved its original purpose. The Soviet Union was gone. In China, the communist party was still in charge, but it had decided to drive on the capitalist road and had dramatically increased the day-to-day freedoms of its citizens. Much of the rest of East and Southeast Asia and the Pacific were economically advancing and politically pro democratic and liberal.[130]

In 2007, Prestowitz asserted that "America is blithely unaware that in the near future there may no longer be any point in thinking about the purpose of its power [in Asia] because there will no longer be any power for which there might be a purpose."[131] In his view:

Since 1992, it is difficult to say that American power has had any particular purpose in the Asia-Pacific region. The collapse of the Soviet Union coupled with the adoption for all practical purposes of capitalism by China should have been an occasion for American reappraisal and reconsideration of its purposes and strategy. It should have been a good time to ask difficult questions such as: Why are we maintaining large military deployments in Asia and the western Pacific when there appears to be little or no threat to us and when our Asian allies like Japan and South Korea are rich and powerful and perfectly capable of bearing more of the security burden in the Pacific? Do we want to encourage Taiwan to declare independence or to cut a Hong Kong-like deal with mainland China? Should we try to turn the Asia Pacific Economic Cooperation (APEC) forum, whose creation we led, into a full-blown Asia-Pacific free trade area? How can we build on the Association of Southeast Asian Nations (ASEAN) to create better and more balanced US-Asian ties? Can we any longer accept currency market intervention and export-lead growth strategies by key Asian governments whose economies are now fully developed? How can we mutually adjust our economy to achieve better long-term balance? It would have been a good time to ask those questions. But no one did.

Instead, US Policy in the region continued as if on autopilot. Even as the Soviet Union collapsed, a major Pentagon study concluded that the US should commit to keeping at least 100,000 troops and the Seventh Fleet in Asia and the Pacific more or less indefinitely. No one stopped to ask if the Koreans and Japanese and their political leaders would not continue to welcome such deployments, nor did anyone ask if the Chinese would welcome continued reconnaissance along their coast line....

Economically too, the policy attitude was 'steady as she goes.' Despite its loss of key industries, growing trade deficits, growing international debt, and stagnating middle class incomes, America maintained a high degree of confidence that globalization would be the magic bullet that would automatically solve all problems. Indeed, it was President Bill Clinton who emphasized "globalization is America's strategy." The idea was that globalization would make all countries right. As they became richer, they would automatically buy more from the U.S., thus reducing the US current account deficit. More importantly, they would also become democratic because it was believed that modern economies can only operate properly under democratic governments. The final assumption was the best. Being democratic, it was thought, countries would no longer go to war because democracies don't fight each other or so everyone said.

In the wake of 9/11, Washington completely forgot about Asia...and turned its attention to the Middle East....Today, America is blithely unaware that in the near future there may no longer be any point in thinking about the purpose of its power because there will no longer be any power for which there might be a purpose. Of course the appearance of power is still there.

...China has already displaced the US as the world biggest market in a number of key industries. The US current account deficit is now 7 percent of GDP. America's net international debt increases each year by nearly $1 trillion, so that within less than a decade the total debt will be equal to the US annual GDP. Financing this growing debt already absorbs most of the available savings of the rest of the world. Indeed, America's economic heart is totally dependent on continued massive lending from

Asia and the rich oil producers of the Persian Gulf. For a long time US economists argued that loss of its manufacturing industries was nothing for the US to worry about because America's future would be in services and high tech, in advanced design, consulting and innovation.

Recently, however, it has become apparent that those activities can also be done as well or better and less expensively in Asia. So the US finds itself in a situation of rapidly declining competitiveness while remaining married to the view that somehow continuing with the same policies and proactive will make it all come out right in the end. To complicate matters, the US needs a weaker dollar to help reduce its trade deficit, but it needs a strong dollar to facilitate financing its large and growing debt and in order to keep inflation under control. So it is at war with itself in a very real way. Yet it does not recognize these contradictions, telling itself that it is the richest, most powerful and most technologically adept country the world has ever seen.[132]

Prestowitz is equally frank and realistic about the fundamental change America's economic standing, which began in 1992. Many Americentric commentators do not accept this key assumption because their approach is not to the reality that increasingly, Asian nations such as Japan, Korea, India and China are catching up, though America, remains relatively rich, powerful, and technologically adept. Prestowitz recognizes that:

> Whereas the US had been the world's biggest creditor nation at the beginning of the 1980s, by 1992 it was already the world's biggest debtor nation and the outsourcing phenomena was moving from manufacturing to some service industries that had hitherto been considered strictly domestic business. Thus, the accomplishment of the original purpose in Asia did not leave America in an entirely strong or desirable position. It was militarily preeminent, even unchallenged, but economically it was steadily losing competitiveness and freedom of action.[133]

That shocking transition from the world's largest creditor to its largest debtor nation has profound implications, which we examine in *China & America's New Economic Partnership*. The mismanagement of the American economy stands in contrast with the successful management of China's economic growth. It is vital to ameliorate assess the ramifications of America's declining economic and moral authority while having 53% of the world's military expenditures and assets. Military authority cannot protect America's economic and national security in the Age of Species Lethal Weapons and Science.

Contrary to traditional Western assumptions, capitalism with Chinese characteristics is enormously successful despite the fact that China is not a Rights Society, a Majority Rule Democracy, or a Rule of Law system. China's Permission Society Model works more effectively than America's Rights Society Model. America's changing role, from a successful to an unsuccessful economic power whose debt is largely funded by Asian countries, is a dangerous challenge to Americans' national identity.

Prestowitz's diagnosis and proscription for American hubris and myopia in Asia is :

> Ironically, it may well be wise for the key Asian countries to attempt to give some purpose to this currently purposeless American power. The reason is that on current trends, a major financial and economic crisis is very likely as the economic imbalances become completely unmanageable. This would be bad for America, but it would also be bad for Asia. Since Americans don't realize the seriousness of their problem, they are unlikely to do anything about it until it is far too late to save the situation. Asian leaders would do well to ask the initiative to bring America to its senses. Perhaps Korea and/or Japan, along with Singapore, could call for consultations with key US leaders and explain the facts of international life to them. These leaders could propose to change some of their own economic policies on the condition that Washington will make major efforts to become competitive and get its fiscal and monetary house in order. These leaders could also suggest that it might be well for the world to start thinking in terms of 50 to 70% dollar devaluation and perhaps even moving away from the dollar as

the international currency in favor of a basket of currencies or a completely new global currency. In short, perhaps it is time to explain to America the purpose of American power.[134]

Prestowitz writing in 2007, was much more realistic than some Americentic observers. The combination of America's declining economic competitiveness and China's successful alternate model of capitalism was producing an economy growing in 2007 almost 600% faster than the American economy. Why China is stable and progresses as a Permission Society, Consensus Democracy, One Party State and Rule by Law Society, is not adequately addressed or understood by Americentric policymakers, scholars.

What is missing from Prestowitz's diagnosis and proscription, and what is at the core to the solution to America's challenges is that it is not "Korea, Japan and perhaps Singapore" that can effectively "call for consultations with key American leaders and explain the facts of international life to them." None of those nations individually can effectively do so. Prestowitz's failure to include China at the head of that list is a flaw in his otherwise realistic analytic framework. Also, none of those nations can assist America's economic recovery and ensure its stability in Asia. China is the only nation that can. Therefore the partnership between China and America must be the new cornerstone of America's Asia strategy.

An Asian Expert's Perspective on American Power in Asia

Kishore Mahbubani is a former Singaporean Ambassador to the United Nations and is the Dean of the Lee Kuan Yew School of Public Policy at the National University of Singapore. He also urges the American government to wake up to the fact that it has neglected and mismanaged its relationship with Asia. He is the author of one of the best books on the necessity and power of America and revitalization of its moral authority: *Beyond the Age of Innocence: Rebuilding Trust Between America and the World,*[135] published in America in 2005.

As an Asian scholar, with rich cross-cultural experience and as an experienced diplomat at the United Nations, Mahbubani understands the importance to America's military and economic security to its historic moral authority. Unfortunately, *Beyond the Age of Innocence: Rebuilding Trust Between America and the World* has been relatively ignored in America. That is indicative of the "mindset change" that is urgently needed.

Mahbubani states:

> President George W. Bush's decision to postpone his participation in the 30th anniversary celebrations of the US-ASEAN partnerships's an unmitigated disaster that was further aggravated by the decision of Secretary of State Condoleezza Rice once again to skip the latest ASEAN Ministerial meeting.
>
> Perhaps most pundits in Washington – if they even noticed – would dismiss these slights as inconsequential. In so doing, they would reveal that the mental map of America's strategic planners remains mired in the past, while the world's moving in a sharply different direction in the 21st century.
>
> The most important geopolitical theater in the current century will be the Asia-Pacific region. By 2050, three of the world's four largest economies will be Asian-Pacific powers – in this order: China, the United States, India and Japan. Not a single European economy will be on the list. The most important new geopolitical relationship will be between the world's greatest existing power, the United States, and the world greatest emerging power, China.
>
> Washington, it seems, continues to assume that the cards are stacked in its favor, but it ignores a crucial emerging reality: the best geopolitical card players are in Beijing, not in Washington.
>
> Beijing's recognition of the importance of ASEAN demonstrates how cut-off Washington is from the changing reality. Hence, while Beijing is busy in preparing for the future,

> Washington's stuck in the past. Diaries reflect priorities. The US
> President's schedulers wouldn't dream of canceling his participa-
> tion in either a G-8 meeting or a summit with the European
> Union (EU). Yet, the G-8 represents a sunset group and the EU
> represents a new peak of geopolitical incompetence, actively
> generating insecurity around its boarders while wasting time dis-
> cussing internal arrangements. The EU provides the best possible
> example of a contemporary international alliance rearranging
> the deck chairs on the Titanic.[136]

Mahbubani recognizes that America's Cold War containment
strategies that were successful in encouraging the collapse of the
Soviet Union will not work against 21st century China because the
"win-win" policies created by Deng Xiaoping have reassured China's
Asian neighbors. China has consistently aligned its win-win rhetoric
and action and shared its prosperity with its neighbors and taken a
low key, but stabilizing role, while becoming a global powerhouse of
economic growth.

Those who ignore *Beyond the Age of Innocence: Rebuilding Trust
Between America and the World* or dismiss it as "anti-American" are
tragically wrong. The following advice is typical of Mahbubani's
message which is insightful and encouraging:

> Many Asians may not admit this out of a sense of national
> pride, but the reality is that the American dream has become
> the Asian dream. The three most important societies in Asia are
> China, India and Japan. America has had a profound impact
> on the development of all three, but each in different ways. It
> was the Japanese who were the first beneficiaries of American
> largesse. Whatever they may say publicly, they know in their
> hearts that their long process of engagement with America has
> resulted in enormous benefits for Japanese society.
>
> Japan was perhaps the first nation in East Asia to appreci-
> ate the virtues of America. One of the last to appreciate those
> virtues was China. When Deng Xiaoping wanted to catapult his
> billion people into the modern world, he found the roadmap
> in America. Deng visited the United States in January 1979, and

he used the American dream to smash the "iron rice bowl." He allowed Chinese TV to show scenes of ordinary American homes filled with items that were then far beyond Chinese dreams: refrigerators, washing machines, and cars. In doing so, Deng shattered the Communist Party myth that ordinary American people toiled in poverty and misery. He also made the Chinese acutely aware of how backward their conditions were. The sharing of the American dream provided the Chinese people with critical ingredients for success: hope and motivation.[137]

Mahbubani urges America to adopt better strategies:

As a result of persistent surveys done by organizations like Pew and Zogby, most thoughtful Americans are now aware that world public opinion has turned against America. The latest Pew Global Attitudes survey in July 2007 confirmed how negatively America is viewed in many corners of the world. The survey findings revealed that favorable ratings of America were lower in 26 of 33 countries for which trends are available.

While many Americans may comprehend that anti-Americanism is rising, few understand the real roots of the phenomenon. Their failure to understand is a result of a simple category mistake. Americans judge America on the basis of America's domestic policies, since these are the policies that impact them. Since many, if not most, of these domestic policies are essentially benign, they continue to believe that America is inherently a benign power. Since many people from overseas continue to dream of migrating to America with the goal of sharing in the American dream, many Americans continue to assume that there are no fundamental or structural problems in America's relationship with the rest of the world.

Most people overseas do not experience America's domestic policies. Instead, they experience America's international policies. More importantly, they absorb the impact of America's power. While the intentions of American policymakers may largely be benign, there is no doubt that the impact of American policies has been less than benign. Take the case of US domestic cotton subsidies. The intent of the subsidies was to help American farmers, not hurt African farmers, but that is what happened. American farmers, thanks to massive subsidies, are assured of 70 cents per pound regardless of the world price of cotton, according to *The Wall Street Journal* (June 26, 2002). They are then able to dump the excess cotton they produce on the world market and depress world cotton prices. This in turn further impoverishes African farmers. People in East Asia are also aware of how decisions made in Washington by a few key players can rescue millions from poverty or throw them back into misery. One consequence of the Asian financial crisis on Indonesia was that over 50 million people returned to the ranks of the poor. Even now, more than a decade after the crisis began, the full story of the misery that the Indonesian people experienced has not been fully documented, nor have there been any proper studies of how crucial decisions made in Washington may have aggravated, rather than ameliorated, the crisis.

The latest example of the gap between the intentions of policymakers and the consequences of a policy is the case of Iraq. It is reasonably clear that neither President Bush nor the American Congress that authorized the intervention had any intention of conquering or colonizing Iraq. Apart from the ostensible goal of destroying weapons of mass destruction (WMDs), most American policymakers assumed that the removal of Saddam Hussein would mean the liberation of the people of Iraq. Hence, Iraq would no doubt be better off after the invasion.

It is amazing how few American policymakers can see beyond their intentions. In the lead up to the Iraq war, there was hardly any critical American debate on the war. Indeed, before the war began, most policymakers could not even conceive of the possibility that their invasion would produce such a multidimensional disaster. The world will have to live with the disastrous consequences for a long time.

One strange aspect of the times we live in is how few Americans, including thoughtful members of the intelligentsia, are aware that most of the international community believes that the Iraq war was illegal. Most Americans seem to find this notion inconceivable because President Bush went to war in Iraq with the approval of the US Congress. Hence, the Iraq war was legal in terms of US law. Since many Americans believe that the US Congress is the ultimate legal authority and trumps all other bodies, a decision by the US Congress is inherently legal. Yet by the principles of international law, which were established by America itself after World War II, the war is inherently illegal. Something has to give here. Both notions cannot coexist at the same time. Hence, the legal consequences of the Iraq war will also reverberate for generations.

The illegal dimensions of the Iraq war have created massive political problems all across the globe. But these problems have in turn been enormously aggravated by the remarkably poor execution of the war. Indeed, Iraq provides a textbook example of how not to invade or occupy a country. Any "competent" invasion of Iraq should have taken care of several obvious things before the invasion took place. First, the history of Iraq should have been studied with a view to understanding how to (and how not to) govern Iraq. A simple study would have exposed the difficulties in managing the joint interests of Sunnis, Shiites and Kurds. Second, the prevailing administration and methods of governance should have been studied. Decisions on what to retain of Saddam's order and what to remove should have been made before the invasion. Third, an attempt should have been made to study the artistic and cultural treasures of Iraq that had to be protected with a view to demonstrating that America was undertaking its occupation with grave responsibility.

Amazingly, none of this was done. Instead, disastrous decisions were made. America pushed for democracy without even thinking about how to protect the minority rights of the Kurds and the Sunnis, who would obviously be disadvantaged by the transfer of power to the majority Iraqi Shiites.

The other disastrous consequence is that Iraq has sucked away all the political attention of policymakers in Washington. Now the Democrats and the Republicans are engaged in a vicious political battle to turn the Iraq war to their advantage. As a result, the real losers are both the people of Iraq and the people of America. Policymakers are so bogged down with Iraq that they have left the field clear for China to take advantage of numerous geopolitical opportunities. Indeed, while Washington has been distracted and incompetent, Beijing has been focused and competent. America could learn a lesson or two from China on how to manage and use ASEAN to enhance its long-term interests in the region.

The historical irony of Beijing understanding the geostrategic value of ASEAN better than Washington is that ASEAN was an American-inspired creation. During the Cold War, when the US was bogged down in Vietnam and dealing with the challenges posed by both the Soviet Union and China (before the Sino-Soviet split in 1969), Washington encouraged the creation of ASEAN, and the alliance successfully fulfilled its key initial strategic assignment: to prevent the non-communist societies of Southeast Asia from becoming dominoes. It then did an equally brilliant job of working together with the US and China in foiling the Vietnamese occupation of Cambodia.

This period of cooperation made Chinese policymakers aware of the strategic potential of ASEAN. Hence, even after reversing the Vietnamese occupation of Cambodia, China continued to develop and strengthen its relations with ASEAN. By contrast, after having nurtured close relations with ASEAN for two decades, Washington effectively dropped ASEAN from its strategic radar screen when the Cold War ended. Overcome by post-Cold War hubris, the US decided that ASEAN was no longer useful or relevant. Hence, while maintaining nominal ties with ASEAN, Washington gave little attention to strengthening relations with ASEAN. I know this from personal experience. I used to attend US-ASEAN meetings in the 1990s. The Americans saw these as a chore and an inconvenience, not as a significant opportunity to enhance American influence vis-à-vis a significant diplomatic actor.

What does Beijing see in ASEAN that Washington does not? China, as it emerges as a great power, is acutely aware that the huge shifts of power in the Asia-Pacific region will have to be managed in order to avoid a negative outcome. New patterns of cooperation will have to be established. In most Western theories of international relations, it is generally assumed that the big jobs of geostrategic management can only be done by major powers. China recognized early that the major Asian powers could not do the job of engaging one another in new patterns of cooperation, because of longstanding distrust, either between China and Japan or China and India.

This is precisely where ASEAN's relative weakness was turned into an advantage. It gradually expanded its annual Foreign Ministers' meetings to include representatives from other major powers and raised these ministerial-level meetings to summit meetings. This is why US Secretary of State Rice is making a huge mistake in refusing to attend these meetings. The 10 Southeast Asian countries which form ASEAN have far smaller economies and national strength than the three Northeast Asian economic giants — China, Japan and South Korea — yet even as ASEAN is about to celebrate the 40th anniversary of its establishment, we have yet to see an Association of Northeast Asian Nations. Instead, whenever awkward moments develop between the three Northeast Asian countries and their leaders are unable to meet in a bilateral setting because of domestic political complications, they can talk on the fringes of an ASEAN meeting or a meeting spawned by an ASEAN initiative.

Some day, future historians will record the enormous contribution ASEAN has made to regional stability through both the annual ASEAN Ministerial Meetings and the other processes ASEAN has developed, such as the ASEAN+3 (China, Japan and South Korea), the ASEAN Regional Forum (ARF) and even the Asia-Europe Meeting. One key reason why the Asia-Pacific region remains stable is because of the diplomatic contributions of ASEAN.

Sadly, few strategic thinkers in the US have either understood or explained the enormous contributions of ASEAN. I find that the best way to shake Western commentators out of their intellectual complacency is to compare the diplomatic record of ASEAN with that of the European Union. In economic terms, the EU is an economic superpower (total GNP: US$13.386 trillion) while ASEAN is a relative economic mini-power (combined GNP: US$857 billion). Yet, in terms of diplomatic contributions, almost the reverse is true. One key fact about the EU that is under-reported in Western commentaries is how the EU has essentially failed in most of its initiatives to improve the geo-strategic environment in its own neighborhood. Just look at what the EU has done in North Africa, the Middle East, the Balkans, the Caucasus region and even vis-à-vis Russia. There appears to be a structural flaw in the EU's strategic behavior that has not been fully understood. Meanwhile EU leaders and ministers spend their time discussing the internal arrangements of the EU, somewhat akin to strike up the band while the ship is sinking.

By contrast, ASEAN has both strengthened and deepened its engagement with its immediate neighbors. China delivered a huge gift to ASEAN when former Premier Zhu Rongji proposed a free-trade agreement at the 2001 China-ASEAN summit. To demonstrate that it was serious, China even offered unilateral concessions that gave ASEAN an "early harvest" of duty-free access to the Chinese market on 600 agricultural products, including live animals, meat, fish, and dairy produce, other animal products, live trees, vegetables, fruits and nuts. The Chinese leaders then confirmed their seriousness by completing the negotiations in record time. A year after the proposal, the final agreement was signed at the eighth ASEAN Summit in Phnom Penh, in November 2002. According to the agreement, the two sides will establish an FTA within 10 years, first with the six original ASEAN states — Brunei, Indonesia, Malaysia, the Philippines, Singapore and Thailand followed by the less developed ASEAN members, Vietnam, Laos, Cambodia and Myanmar, by 2015. China also accorded the three non-WTO ASEAN members, Vietnam, Laos and Cambodia, most-favored-nation status. The China-ASEAN FTA, when completely implemented, will constitute a common market of 1.7 billion people, with a combined gross domestic product (GDP) of US$1.5 trillion to US$2 trillion.

China's Asian neighbors fully understood the strategic significance of China's grand gesture. A Japanese diplomat told me that Japan saw the China-ASEAN FTA as "a bolt from the blue." The Japanese had complacently assumed that given Japan's longer track record of close trade, economic and political engagement with ASEAN, Japan would always have the edge. Instead, when Japan campaigned for a permanent seat on the UN Security Council, only one ASEAN member, Singapore, openly supported the G-4 (Japan, India, Brazil and Germany) resolution, while another ASEAN member, Vietnam, supported it privately. The first-ever Summit meeting of ASEAN leaders outside the region was also held in China in October 2006.

Both Japan and India have tried to match China's engagement with ASEAN. Japan proposed a free-trade agreement with ASEAN, which is expected to be signed in November 2007. Japan has also offered to help ASEAN establish a computerized system for trade among the group's 10 member countries, and Japan. The proposal is part of Japan's new package of initiatives to help ASEAN achieve its goal of having a European-style single market by 2020 and foster economic integration between Japan and ASEAN. Tokyo has further agreed to provide up to US$ 100 million to fund efforts to set up a comprehensive economic partnership in East Asia.

Not to be left behind, India and ASEAN signed the India-ASEAN Framework Agreement on Comprehensive Economic Cooperation (CECA) in October 2003. The CECA is expected to create a market of 1.5 billion people, and will cover agreements in investments and services, in addition to trade.

So far, the US has not contemplated a grand gesture to upgrade the US-ASEAN relationship. Few in Washington believe that there is a strategic imperative to do so. Instead, Washington has made matters worse by canceling the visit of Bush to the 30th anniversary of the US-Singapore dialogue in September 2007 and in allowing Rice to skip the ASEAN Ministerial meeting. Apparently, US security planners and inside the Beltway thinkers like to focus on the "big stuff" and not waste their time on weak regional organizations like ASEAN. Hence, when EU delegations flock to Washington, all the big names rush to meet them. When an ASEAN delegation comes, they are ignored. Such behavior clearly demonstrates that strategic thinkers in Washington still see the world through the prism of the 19th and 20th century, focusing on the Atlantic when the real geopolitical challenges of the future will emerge from the Pacific.

The 21st century will be the Asian century. All the new major powers will be here. This is where the major geo-strategic action will take place, not in Europe, Africa or Latin America. To be fair, many thoughtful Americans are aware of the challenge coming from the rise of China, but when they think of responses, they think in black-and-white terms. One idea in vogue is to create a new "Gang of Four" — US, Australia, India and Japan — to balance the rise of China. But the new reality of international relations is that old-style Soviet era containment policies will not work. China has already launched preemptive strikes against any possible American policies by sharing its prosperity with its neighbors. The fastest growing trade flows in the world today are those between China and its neighbors, including three members of the new so-called Gang of Four — Australia, Japan and India. Hence, security planners should drop the concept of containment. In a world of greater complexity, they should think of "complex engagement."

A complex engagement with ASEAN would give the US an opportunity to influence the prevailing thinking in East Asia. By demonstrating, both in word and deed that the US intends to remain fully engaged with ASEAN, the US will significantly increase its options in managing the rise of China. The 10 ASEAN countries may be economically weak in a comparative sense, but they played a key role in turning global opinion, especially in the developing world, against the Soviet Union. Today, China is moving ahead of America in winning the hearts and minds of Africa, Latin America and the Middle East. Global surveys show that China is viewed with less distrust than America. The 2007 Pew survey revealed that 26 of the 47 nations surveyed found the US "less favorable;" only nine felt that way about China.

In this globalized world, opinions do matter. At some point in time when America and China begin to compete peacefully for global influence, ASEAN could play a pivotal role. An ASEAN that is perceived to be tilting towards China will help to enhance China's global standing. This is one reason why Japan and India are now working hard to improve their ties with ASEAN. For the same reason, Washington should also make ASEAN a renewed priority.

This will require a huge shift in the prevailing thinking in Washington. Even the more liberal thinkers who are vehemently opposed to the unilateral policies of the neo-conservatives fail to recognize the strategic importance of ASEAN. The Princeton Project on National Security recently came out with an essay entitled, "Forging a World of Liberty under Law" (see the Spring 2007 issue of Global Asia). It has the ambitious goal of matching the strategic vision of George Kennan and having the same impact as his famous "X" essay published in Foreign Affairs (July 1947). The report has many bold recommendations. But it does not mention ASEAN even once in the main essay.

This shows that even if the Democrats gain control of the White House in January 2009, there will likely be no major shift in American thinking on ASEAN. This would be a real tragedy. America would have given up a valuable opportunity to use one of the most influential regional organizations to influence the course of history in the world's most important geostrategic region in the 21st century. To avoid losing this opportunity, American strategic planners should adopt a simple rule whenever they look at any emerging problem across the Pacific. In the midst of their deliberations, they should stop and say, "Think ASEAN." In so doing, they may come up with new strategic approaches. [138]

Mahbubani urges new American administrations heighten their focus on Asia and ASEAN. But even if the new American administration were to take such advice, it is not sufficient to address and manage America's problems. America must do much more. It must collaborate as a win-win partner with Chinese rather than compete with it.

What Mahbubani and other non-Chinese did not call for is, compelling but unthought-of yet, except in China before President Obama indicated on May 24, 2009 that he was launching "a new era of partnership". American policymakers and scholars now must recognize the compelling case for America's new security framework being the partnership of China and America's economic, moral, and military authority. They must collaborate and be aligned to ensure their successes.

American Hubris and Neglect of Asian Affairs

Jonathan Pollack is a professor at the U.S. Naval War College. In 2005 Pollack described the strategic convergence of America's and China's interests in tentative but conventional terms:

In the final analysis, future regional strategic patterns will be driven by events. A collapse in the nonproliferation regime in East Asia, a major conflict over Taiwan, or a breakdown in U.S. regional alliance relations (especially in Korea) constitute the principal nightmare scenarios. Any would likely trigger a longer-term U.S.-Chinese strategic competition, if not outright bipolarity in the region. The parallels with the events of June 1950, which largely established the strategic geography of East Asia for the entirety of the Cold War, are self-evident. As Shi Yinghong has also observed, 'China was a winner [in the Korean War], but winning was very painful, and the long-term cost was considerable...China and the United States were locked in a fierce Cold War confrontation for as long as 20 years, and this indeed played quite a serious negative role in China's international environment and even its internal development....Tremendous difficulties were also created for resolving the Taiwan problem, and there was 'an alliance too tangled to unravel' with DPRK.' Such memories hover over current crises, all of which occupy the very same strategic space as those of a half-century ago.

Alternately, the ability of China, the United States, and other regional powers to achieve noncoercive outcomes to these potential crises would attest to a longer-term strategic convergence between Washington and Beijing. This would likely enable creation of a hybrid security order that constrained major rivalry amidst predominantly convergent security goals. Given the absolute magnitude of China and America's economic, political, and military weight, and the increasing convergence of U.S. and Chinese interests in nonproliferation, energy security, and unrestricted maritime commerce, both countries might ultimately decide to share responsibilities for long-term regional security. But there is a 'to-be-determined' flavor to such possibilities. Even amidst ever-growing regional interdependence, there is nothing foreordained in the region's strategic future, or in the U.S.-China strategic pattern that could underline it.[139]

Many commentators see American leadership in Asia becoming increasingly irrelevant. Some commentators with an Asian rather than an Ameracentic perspective worry less about how to pacify Asia, because China and Japan are pacified already. In contrast, commentators with an Americentric perspective worry about how America can continue to rule Asia as Asian countries progress economically.

There is also another important contrast between an Americentric perspective and the focus of China's policymakers and scholars. While America's leaders were not focused on Asia, China's leaders remain focused on economic development and peace.

The Danger of America Causing an Unnecessary and Catastrophic War

It has been asserted that regardless of who is elected President, America's China policy is "almost certain to be characterized by strategic continuity."[140] However, continuity is the wrong approach.

The *US Quadrennial Defense Review Report* in 2001 stated, without naming China, that "a military competitor with a formidable resource base will emerge in the region" although America will not face "a peer competition in the near future." In 2006, the *US Quadrennial Deference Review* stated: "Of the major and emerging powers, China has the greatest potential to compete militarily with the United States and field disruptive military technologies that could over time offset traditional US military advantages absent US Counter strategies.[141]

To some Americentric observers those zero sum evaluations have compelling moral authority. But the moral authority that American leadership had in Asia in 1945-50 is not the current situation. To many in the rest of the world, China's and deemphasis of military authority stands in sharp contrast to American foreign policy since 1950.

By 2008, America has degraded its economic, military, and moral authority. Being the largest economy and having the largest military does not give America economic or national security. The financial crisis devastating impact showed how dependent America's economic security was on China. Because the administration's military power was fully committed, the reality is that America sought and received China's help in dealing with the North Korean nuclear weapons threat. That reality shows the value of a strategic integration of the interests of America and China.

The success of the partnership will depend on 300 million Americans and their leaders' ability to accept "reciprocal globalization" and "collaborative equilibrium" with 1.5 billion Chinese and their leaders. That partnership has not been recognized and must be accepted by American policymakers.

Hedging or Containing China's Development Militarily

From a moral authority perspective, it would have been better for America not to deny things that neither China nor other observers will believe. For example, the *Financial Times* reported:

> Robert Gates, the US defense secretary, on Wednesday denied that US efforts to boost military relations with India were aimed at creating a "hedge" strategy against the rise of China. I don't see our improving military relationship in this region in the context of any other country, including China," said Mr. Gates, who arrived in Turkey on Wednesday night from India. Speaking to reporters before he left Delhi, Mr. Gates rejected suggestions that efforts to improve relations with other militaries in the region were aimed at China. In the case of India, Mr. Gates said the Pentagon wanted to bolster the ability of the US and Indian militaries to work together on issues such as piracy, terrorism and providing disaster relief.
>
> When you look at the kinds of activities that we are engaged in and the kind of exercises that we conduct...these expanding relationships don't necessarily have to be directed against anybody," said Mr. Gates. "They are a set of bilateral relationships that are aimed at improving our coordination and the closeness of our relationships for a variety of reasons." The Pentagon chief arrived in Delhi from Jakarta where he offered the Indonesian military help with its modernization programme. He also visited Canberra amid concerns that Australia's increasing economic dependence on China could complicate security relations with the US.
>
> One senior Pentagon official traveling with Mr. Gates denied that India was in the middle of a "tug of war" between the US and China. But he suggested the US was attempting to bolster relations with Asian countries to counter China." There is a fundamental commonality of interests between the US and these three democracies that we have visited," he said. "There

are reasons for having interoperable weapons systems…not in an aggressive sense but certainly as a hedge." India had a close military procurement relationship with the Soviet Union but has been seeking in recent years to diversify away from Russian-made defense equipment, a process that has been slowed down by problems of interoperability and by a residual mistrust of US intentions.

Much of this mutual suspicion has fallen by the wayside in the past three years, after the US drive to offer India full civil nuclear co-operation. Like the US, India is looking to take out insurance against China, with which it has an unresolved border dispute and fought a brief but bloody war in 1962. But it is reluctant to be drawn into any crude "containment strategy". Mr. Gates welcomed the recent Indian decision to buy six Lockheed C-130J cargo aircraft. Lockheed Martin and Boeing are competing for a $10bn (€6.75bn, 5.08bn) deal to sell fighter jets to India. Mr. Gates said the US was not looking for "quick results" with India but rather a "steady expansion of our relationship".[142]

America's policymakers and people must ponder the following hypotheses:

1. America's foreign policy and defense strategies operating on the Principles of Conflict will be degraded by hypocrisy, intolerance, bias, arrogance, the pursuit of aggressive dominance and harming others that alienate support among the other nations of the world.
2. America's policies operating on the Principles of Peaceful Coexistence will attract support among the other nations.
3. No nation that alienates or attacks peaceful nations will thrive in the Age of Species Lethal Weapons and Science.

How many American policymakers and scholars, understand or accept these realities?

Expressed in other ways:

1. How can the Principles of Conflict possibly preserve America's economic and national security in the 21st century?

2. How can adopting with China the Principles of Peaceful Coexistence harm America's economic and national security in the 21st century?

3. How can a zero sum game mindset and strategies achieve America's needs in the 21st century?

4. How can a win-win partnership with China harm America's economic and national security needs in the 21st century?

5. How can America, China, or mankind survive in the Age of Species Lethal Weapons and Science if America and China are not partners in implementing and enforcing the Principles of Peaceful Coexistence collaboratively?

These questions and realistic answers support the thesis in the books in this series that:

> America and China, collaborating in a committed genuine permanent global partnership implementing the Principles of Peaceful Coexistence and reciprocally beneficial to the economic and national security of both, must become the permanent policies of both major American political parties and China's political party for the either nation to remain prosperous, and world to be peaceful and thereby governable in the Age of Species Lethal Weapons and Science.

The Long Term Security Alternatives of China and America

Neither these hypotheses nor the New School's thesis is at the heart of American foreign policy or defense strategy, as will be seen from a sampling of conventional American analyses. To further examine that phenomenon, we will examine a collection of essays by the American contributors to *Power Shift: China and Asia's New Dynamics*[143] published in 2005. Unrealistic assumptions are exhibited in the samplings from leading American scholars on American goals in Asia and China. They reflect America's Principles of Conflict-based policies and help shape approaches to foreign policies based on the Principles of Conflict.

Much of conventional American analysis operates at a tactical level, misled by Cold War era preoccupations and unsustainable hegemonic goals, and instead must focus on moral authority or the strategic insights examined in President Washington's Farewell Advice.

Conventional analysis lacks the wise strategic vision examined in chapter 3 of Book 2 that President Kennedy searched for in 1963 and Deng Xiaoping developed and implemented. China's foreign policies and strategies are far sighted and prudent. They must be reciprocated by America.

As the world's most advanced nation, America has suffered from a hardening of attitudes.

However, there are some indications in the following sampling of American views on security interests in Asia of the preludes to a major strategic shift that this and the New School's other books seek to foster.

For example, Jonathan Pollack in "The Transformation of the Asian Security Order" in *Power Shift: China and Asia's New Dynamics* identified longer-term security alternatives to how America and China contemplate their future Asian security options. Four alternative strategic futures seem possible, all linked to longer-term China-America ties:

1. A convergent, more diversified security order largely acceptable to the United States and to China;
2. A mixed security order simultaneously entailing elements of Sino-American competition and collaboration;
3. An overt Sino-American political-military competition; and
4. A Sino-American regional security condominium

Pollack comments that the critical uncertainties are:

1. Will the United States maintain security commitments and military capabilities similar to those of the past?
2. Will Washington and Beijing agree on "rules of engagement" in zones of potential conflict?
3. Will China achieve durable security understandings in all contiguous sub-regions as its military power continues to grow?
4. Will the region avoid a strategic breakdown or major crisis that destabilizes Asia's future?

American Asian Defense Strategies Impact on Asia's Regional Security

Pollack comments:

Despite the desire of nearly all regional states (including China) to realize more autonomous security strategies, U.S. military power retains singular importance in the long-range defense thinking of all regional actors. American military power is in the gestational stages of major change, as posited threats, shifting regional attitudes toward the presence of U.S., and major changes in defense capabilities redefine U.S. strategy options. The predominant thrust of U.S. planning is increasingly contingency- and crisis- driven, with less emphasis on the open-ended presence of U.S. forces long deemed bedrock of regional security. Should the United States again employ major forces in a regional conflict? The primary emphasis would be on achieving declared objectives as decisively and as rapidly as possible, exploiting U.S. technological advantages and denying any presumptive opponent the opportunity to interfere with the conduct of U.S. military operations. Though there are parallels in how other military establishments prepare for war, no other state comes remotely close to the U.S. pursuit of "full-spectrum dominance." U.S. defense strategy therefore presents a potential U.S. adversary with two possible options: (1) to acquire military capabilities that would amply raise the costs, risks, and complications of any major U.S. use of force; or (2) to reconfigure regional security arrangements so as to negate the factors that would lead the United States to use force. China is doing both.

These looming changes in U.S. defense strategy leave unspecified the precise contingencies where the United States might intervene, though crises in Korea or in the Taiwan Strait top the prospective list. U.S. forces would be drawn substantially from those deployed within the region, but also from forces introduced over greater distance. These circumstances reflect the distant theaters, often with minimal warning. The open-ended deployment of major U.S. forces in specific locations (most notably in Korea) is almost certain to change over the next decade. It seems increasingly unlikely that the United States will maintain the 100,000 manpower level in East Asia long deemed a requirement for regional stability. This does not preclude the U.S. capability to deploy massive forces in a crisis. The question is whether a more "over-the-horizon" capability will reshape regional perceptions of U.S. power. To the extent that the United States decides that its military might will only be used in extremis, this affects the incentives of regional states to rely on American power. The looming issue is how the United States persuasively maintains its declared commitment to regional security at lower force levels without regional actors pursing alternate approaches to security that diminish the relevance of U.S. power.

Such circumstances could provide opportunities for a more creative Chinese security strategy. China's advocacy of a "new security concept," though widely dismissed as formulaic and even propagandistic, has growing significance in this context. China's stated (if now somewhat muted) opposition to U.S. bilateral alliances as a residue of the Cold War would seem less challenging to American interests if the United States were already redefining the basis of its alliance ties. For example, should Washington proceed, of its own volition, to more of an 'offshore' strategy in Korea? Then Beijing would likely prove a beneficiary of such as decision, inasmuch as it would reinforce China's predominance on the East Asian mainland. But a more fundamental question persists for both Beijing and Washington: What do these shifts in U.S. strategy imply for a Taiwan crisis?

Pollack comments:

Chinese military planning for a Taiwan crisis constitutes the definitive exception to Beijing's emphasis on a collaborative Asia-Pacific security order. It is the singular example of China's continued pursuit of threat-based military planning. Irrespective of how China would justify a decision to use force against Taiwan (and irrespective of the outcome of such a crisis), the implications of such a decision would be profound. China is acquiring military capabilities that it believes will ultimately enable a short-warning, high intensity attack against Taiwan. These include a growing inventory of short-range ballistic missiles, advanced conventionally powered submarines and other naval platforms, longer-range aircraft, and a host of related capabilities. There is a wide range of scenarios for employing such capabilities. China is also seeking to preempt U.S. involvement in such a conflict, presumably expecting that the crisis could be brought to a speedy and minimally destructive conclusion before Washington could intervene. But China is also building capabilities that would put U.S. military assets at risk and also impart to Japan the potential dangers of contributing to U.S. actions. The risks and consequences inherent in any expanded conflict could hardly be greater.

Are there realistic possibilities for the parties to forestall such as crisis, or (in the event of deterrence failure) to limit its scope. The indications are not encouraging. Policy makers in Taipei, Beijing, and Washington all premise their planning calculations on assumptions that can only be tested fully in armed conflict. Many of these assumptions seem highly questionable, and some are directly contradictory to one another, especially Plus 'the'? divergent judgments in Beijing and Taipei on the likelihood and scale of a U.S military intervention. The respective policy trajectories in all three capitals thus seem largely independent of one another, underscoring the risks of horrific miscalculation.

Though most regional actors would prefer to stand apart from the fray, major hostilities in the Taiwan Strait – even if a military conflict were concluded speedily – would trigger significant reverberations across the region. China would seek to characterize its actions as defending its territorial sovereignty

and national unity, but its willingness to use force would constitute a lasting precedent in Asian security. The likeliest long-term
effects would be on various maritime states, especially where
territorial demarcations with China are still contested. It remains
conjectural whether China's continental neighbors would reassess their prevailing policy assumptions toward Beijing. Much
would depend on the extent of political, economic, and security
investment extant between China and its neighbors at the time
of such a conflict.[144]

The Eclipse of American Dominance in Asia

Pollack's view in 2005 was that:

> A major transition in Asian security is underway in the early
> twenty-first century, with China at the epicenter of this process.
> Depending on future events and policy developments, regional
> security could undergo change that is more profound than at
> any time since the early years of the Cold War. American global
> primacy and the Bush administration's redesign of U.S. national
> security strategy; regional responses to U.S. predominance; the
> economic, technological, and military emergence of major
> regional powers, especially China and India; and a political and
> institutional maturation across Asia are the principal manifesta-
> tions of such change. The possibility of an acute political-
> military crisis in East Asia or in South Asia also hovers over this
> transition process. China and other states remain closely attuned
> to American power and its potential effects on their strategic
> interests. Each seeks to combine enhanced military capabilities,
> restraint in the coercive use of military power, and pursuit of
> collective norms and policies to facilitate larger strategic goals.
> The European balance-of-power system and the Cold War offer
> only limited insight into the security identities and historical
> circumstances shaping these possibilities.
>
> China's ascendance, in conjunction with enhanced
> national power elsewhere in the region, seems likely to dilute
> the singularity of American military predominance and alliance
> relationships evident in Asia during the Cold War. Though
> the U.S. military role remains decisive and American military

primacy is still unchallenged, an unmistakable recalibration of power and influence is underway. Increased regional confidence and competence portend a more indigenously shaped security order in which American leadership will be less pronounced. But these looming shifts raise additional questions.[145]

Pollack focused on key questions:

1. As long-standing security arrangements diminish in relevance, what structures, institutions, and processes will supplant the existing order?
2. Is it possible to reconcile the lack of a larger security structure with the growth of more autonomous military capabilities in China and the other states?
3. What if the new security policies and relationships prove unable to prevent a major regional crisis or heightened strategic competition?
4. How will China's increasing power and enhanced international role redefine regional security as a whole?

In Pollack's view:

At present, three broad objectives shape Chinese security strategy and Beijing's enhanced commitments to security collaboration:

1. China is attempting to limit its exposure in America's strategic headlights, thus deflecting a direct U.S. focus on China's political-military capabilities and strategies.
2. China hopes to prevent any countervailing strategy that could limit the country's future military options and strategic reach.
3. China seeks to forestall or discourage coordinated regional responses to its enhanced economic power, military capabilities, and political influence.

In Pollack's view, all three objectives help define China's regional security strategy and its bilateral and multilateral security alternatives. Pollack asserts:

> China is the only regional power with meaningful security involvement in the four sub-regions of Asia and the Pacific.... The latent potential of a military conflict in the Taiwan Strait, combined with the lack of durable Sino-American political and strategic understandings, reinforces China's centrality in regional security. The country's sustained high growth rate and its ever more prominent position in global trade, energy flows, and natural resource requirements have resulted in regional interdependence unimaginable during decades of domestic upheaval and economic autarky. Sustained double-digit increases in China's defense budget are also contributing to the development of more capable, externally relevant military force. In a word, China has arrived as a regional power. However, its size, strategic weight, and past hegemonic influence generate ample wariness within the region about the longer-term implications of Beijing's economic ascendance.
>
> Numerous international relations theorists and national security specialists first expressed concern about the enhancement of Chinese national power in the 1990s. Many viewed China's rise primarily through the framework of nineteenth-century European balance-of-power politics, with scholars positing that China was the quintessential rising power and that the region was 'ripe for rivalry.' China's burgeoning economic and military capabilities, its presumed geopolitical ambitions, its characterization as an aggrieved power, and its intense wariness of American strategic intentions all contributed to the potential for instability, crisis, and realignment. Strategists foresaw a struggle for domination among Asia's leading states; the denigration of multilateral institutions as peripheral if not irrelevant to international stability; and China's supposed intention to displace American power within the region. A parallel Chinese debate provided a mirror image of these judgments, characterizing China's rise in more benign terms and deeming the United States the primary but diminishing force in long-term Asian security.

However, the warnings contained in many Western and Chinese strategic writings have not materialized. The United States has experienced a strategic resurgence that few anticipated, prompting most Chinese scholars to retreat from earlier claims that multipolarization would constrain the exercise of U.S. power. At the same time, most of Asia...has proven far more stable and resilient than predicted by international relations theorists. Despite intermittent political crises, the region has not experienced war across national borders since the Vietnamese invasion of Cambodia in 1978 and the Chinese thrust into Vietnam in 1979. Equally important, a nascent Sino-American strategic competition has been supplanted by a growing and largely unanticipated accommodation between Beijing and Washington. To some observers, these patterns suggest a regional preference for indirection and informal security norms, a preference that eschews explicit balance-of-power strategies. Others contend that developmental goals provide shared incentives to avoid (or at least obscure) the latent elements of heightened security competition. Some interpret the present calm as prefiguring regional accommodation to Chinese primacy. Still others believe that China's current political-military restraint is intended to defer a longer-term strategic reckoning with the United States until Beijing is better prepared to confront the U.S. political-military challenge.[146]

The prominence of preemption and prevention in the strategic commentaries and defense policies of the United States, Japan, China and Taiwan also reflect these concerns. Any armed conflict that extends to national homelands would hugely disrupt internal and regional stability and would severely impinge on global transactions in commerce, high technology, and energy. There is an inescapable paradox of vastly heightened interdependence, and the parallel vulnerability of these societies to attack....

To date, there has been no regional crisis entailing a major military attack by one state against the capital or industrial and commercial infrastructure of another. Few venture definitive predictions on whether this pattern will hold in the future. Some (including China) are investing heavily in advanced capabilities for deterrence, defense, assertion of sovereign prerogatives, and the use of force. The autonomous, unregulated growth of such capabilities underscores two conclusions: there is no assurance of lasting security in Asia, and China remains pivotal in all futures?

America's Perceptions of Chinese Debate over American Power and Intentions

The New School's perspective is that China's foreign policy and defense strategies are innately win-win for both China's self-interest and China's effect on other nations, rather than zero sum in intent or result. It is useful to compare the views expressed by:

1. China's key policymaker, Deng Xiaoping, as examined in chapter 4 of Book 2 and Chinese scholars examined in chapter 1 of Book 2, with
2. America's four leading presidents examined in chapter 4 of Book 2, recent policymakers' views examined in chapter 7 of Book 2, would-be American presidential policymakers examined in chapter 5 of Book 2, and American scholars examined in this chapter.

The Americentric and Chinacentric perspectives are as different as America and China's foreign policy goals.

Pollack describes the views in China about American power and intentions as:

> Chinese assessments of U.S. power and strategic intentions are closely linked to its regional security policies. Although China has vigorously and successfully pursued an "Asia-based" security strategy, U. S. military power is far too potent and pervasive for any serious Chinese strategic thinker to neglect. Chinese specialist writings on the United States are not a new phenomena none, but their prevailing purposes have broadened, enabling important insights into Chinese national security strategy as a whole. Many participants in these debates are specialists on

international relations and national security policy, not experts on the United States per se. Some focus more narrowly on operational and doctrinal concerns related to future military planning, especially the application of advanced technologies to warfare.

This pattern parallels the U. S. security debate. To U.S. scholars and strategists, China is a principal vehicle in longer-term national security deliberations, much as the United States is a primary vehicle for comparable deliberations in China. U.S. and Chinese assessments reverberate within and between both systems: here is to illustrate how Chinese evaluations of U.S. power and strategic goals are shaping Chinese views of the future of regional security system and Beijing's place in it.

Chinese analysts acknowledge many unsettled questions about the new regional order, with the longer-term U.S. strategy with regard to China being uppermost among these uncertainties. Judgments range, between innovative approaches to the security dilemma to wary optimism about extant trends and possibilities to deep pessimism over longer-term U.S. intentions. Some analysts favor more cooperative security strategies that avoid explicit characterizations of a U.S. threat to China. They argue that a more threat-based approach will only trigger equivalent actions by the United States that would diminish China's security and compel Beijing to allocate additional resources to defense modernization. Others contend that the inexorable growth of Chinese economic power will ultimately trump any presumed U.S. effort to constrain China's larger political and security goals, as well as facilitate regional cooperation as a whole."

A more mainstream assessment seems largely aligned with official policy. It argues for deeper, more diversified relations across the region, pursuit of political-diplomatic collaboration with the United States where feasible (but without excessive expectations of such ties), and the enhanced augmentation of Chinese military power. These mainstream views also highlight U.S. -preoccupations in the greater Middle East and the Persian Gulf and the restraint is intended to defer a longer-term strategic reckoning with the United States until Beijing is better prepared to confront the U.S. political-military challenge.[147]

Pollack asserts:

However, expectations of a cooperative security order seem equally premature. The enhanced military capabilities of various regional powers, including declared or de facto nuclear weapons states in India, Pakistan, and North Korea, loom large in this caution. Wars of territorial conquest may well be an artifact of the past, but major changes in defense technology and military doctrine are redefining national security strategies, especially for states seeking to protect modern industrial and commercial assets that increasingly determine their well-being. Major improvements in the reach, accuracy, and lethality of modern air and naval power and vastly enhanced information and missile capabilities have compressed the warning time available to military planners. These developments have placed major urban and industrial centers across Asia at potential risk of devastating long-range attack, possibly explaining China's recent attention to civil defense and domestic defense mobilization measures.

The prominence of preemption and prevention in the strategic commentaries and defense policies of the United States, Japan, China and Taiwan also reflect these concerns. Any armed conflict that extends to national homelands would hugely disrupt internal and regional stability and would severely impinge on global transactions in commerce, high technology, and energy. There is an inescapable paradox of vastly heightened interdependence, and the parallel vulnerability of these societies to attack...

To date, there has been no regional crisis entailing a major military attack by one state against the capital or industrial and commercial infrastructure of another. Few venture definitive predictions on whether this pattern will hold in the future. Some (including China) are investing heavily in advanced capabilities for deterrence, defense, assertion of sovereign prerogatives, and the use of force. The autonomous, unregulated growth of such capabilities underscores two conclusions: there is no assurance of lasting security in Asia, and China remains pivotal in all regional security futures.[148]

David Shambaugh is a professor at George Washington University, a non-resident fellow at the Brookings Institution and a member of the Council on Foreign Relations. He was of the view in 2005 that:

> The Asian regional order at the outset of the twenty-first century is an increasingly complex mosaic of actors and factors. To be sure, China is one of the principal ones, and its influence is being increasingly felt, but it is far too early to conclude that the regional order has become Sino-centric. Nonetheless, China's growing strength and authority are altering regional dynamics and giving shape to a new Asian order.
>
> Not only is China's power and influence increasing, but Beijing is also exerting its new prowess in ways that seek to stabilize the region and alleviate latent fears about China's intentions. The growing perception that China is a status quo power is especially remarkable when one recalls the earlier era of the 1950s and 1960s, when China sought to destabilize regional governments by supporting armed insurgencies and exporting Maoism, and had border disputes or conflicts with virtually every contiguous country. Today, virtually all the territorial disputes have been negotiated and resolved successfully, result-ing in treaties that delimit 20,222 kilometers of land boundaries, and there is new impetus to resolve the final outstanding dispute between China and India. China is now the exporter of goodwill and consumer durables instead of weapons and revolution. Consider also that merely a decade or so ago China did not even enjoy full-diplomatic relations with South Korea, Indonesia, or Singapore; ties with Vietnam and India were very strained and their borders militarized; and China was ostracized in world because of the events of 1989. At the same time, with the collapse of the Soviet Union and East European party-states, China's leadership was very insecure and insular. Today ties with these countries are robust, and, domestically, a thorough generational transfer of power has brought new leaders to power who brim with confidence and competence. They faced daunt-ing challenges at home, but they are coming to grips with them. Abroad, China's relations with other major powers, including the United States, Russia, and the European Union, have rarely been better, which has only served to further strengthening

Beijing's confidence.

China's new regional posture is reflected in virtually all policy spheres. Overcoming its earlier hesitancy, China is now an involved actor in the vast majority of regional issues, and has become a proactive partner in helping to alleviate or resolve many of them. Beijing's diplomacy has been remarkably adept and nuanced, earning it praise around the region. Concomitantly, fears voiced throughout the region just a few years ago about a Chinese hegemon seeking to impose itself and dominate regional affairs have now become muted. Today China is increasingly seen as a good neighbor, constructive partner, and careful listener. Importantly, it is also increasingly multilateral in its diplomacy. China also seems to be shedding its traditional twin identities of historical victim and object of great power manipulation.

China's new posture has resulted in a blizzard of meetings and exchanges among Chinese officials and their neighboring counterparts, both civilian and military. The sheer volume of diplomacy and discourse is staggering. China now participates in annual heads-of-state summits with virtually all of its neighbors, and there is a constant series of ministerial and sub-ministerial exchanges. China is now posting some of its most seasoned and sophisticated diplomats in key regional embassies, and they are becoming proactive and well known in their local communities. China's new embrace of regional multilateralism was highlighted by its hosting of the 2001 APEC meeting in Shanghai and the attention given President Hu Jintao at the 2003 APEC meeting in Bangkok, although Chinese diplomats are also now deeply engaged in a variety of other regional organizations.

China's growing regional influence derives not only from its hard power—its growing economic weight and military power—but its growing economic weight in ways associated with soft power. While Beijing is certainly not trying to export an ideology today, and does not even seem to possess an ideology to export, even if it were inclined to do so, Beijing does seem to exert some influence in at least two areas.

The first is in the normative realm, where Beijing's enunciation of the "new security concept,' strategic partnerships, and other initiatives to fashion a new set of norms to govern interstate relations and prevent conflict resonates positively among many Asian nations. This is particularly the case in ASEAN, where China's initiatives dovetail very closely with ASEAN's own norms articulated over many years. The second area of potential Chinese soft power lies in the realm of higher education. Training future generations of intellectuals, technicians, and political elites from other nations is a very important form of soft power. This was the role of Great Britain at its imperial zenith and of the United States ever since the 1950s, and now China increasingly fills this role. During the 2003 academic year, there were 77,628 foreign students studying for advanced degrees in China's universities, approximately 80 percent of which came from other Asian countries. South Korea sent by far the largest number of these students (35,363), while Japan sent 12,765, Vietnam 3,487, Indonesia 2,563, Thailand 1,554, and Nepal 1,199.

During that same year there were 3,693 students from the United States. The precise influence that this training will have on future generations of Asian elites is difficult to predict, but these individuals will be sensitized to Chinese viewpoints and interests, and they will have a knowledge of the Chinese language, society, culture, history and politics. Although this form of influence is important, one does not yet find evidence of other traditional forms of soft power—such as Chinese media and popular culture— spreading around the Asian region; if anything, China is increasingly absorbing popular culture, managerial methods, forms of governance, and information from around the region.

To be sure, not all on China's periphery are persuaded by China's "charm offensive." One still occasionally encounters concerns about a looming "China threat" among regional security specialists—notably in Tokyo, Taipei, Hanoi, and New Delhi—but this view is held by a progressively smaller number, even in these capitals. In the economic sphere, China has been able, through a variety of efforts—ranging from responsible management of its currency during the Asian financial crisis, to timely grants of aid omit, and loans, to increased trade, to growing outbound direct investment (ODI), to its stunning proposal to establish a Free Trade Area (FTA) with ASEAN—to similarly assuage *angst* among Southeast Asian countries about the Chinese trade behemoth.[149]

Shambaugh summed up his view of China's "regional posture" in the following terms:

> China's new regional posture is evident. The development of this new posture is still a very fluid and ongoing process, and China remains a long way from achieving preeminence or dominance in the region, but its power and influence are growing steadily.
>
> Although China's posture of late has been largely reassuring to the region, its past behavior has not always been so. Long memories, residual concerns, and irredentist issues remain. Then, of course, there are more traditional, realistic? balance-of-power concerns about a rising power, and, as a consequence, several regional states appear to be practicing various types of "hedging" strategies. Finally, no Asian states (except perhaps North Korea) wish to see the American presence and role in Asia diminished. None wish to be put in the position of having to choose between Beijing and Washington, and all wish to see the United States remain fully engaged, and militarily deployed, in the Asia-Pacific region.
>
> At the end of the day, the future of international politics in the Asian region will rest on the relationship between the United States and China. Asia is certainly big enough for both powers to exercise their influence and power. And although some neoconservative observers in the United States believe that there is an inherent and inevitable structural conflict between the United States and China in the region, and even globally, this is not necessarily the case. On balance the United States and China find themselves on the same side of many of the key issues affecting the future of the Asian region. This argues well for opportunities for tangible cooperation between the two governments. If the two powers have a positive and cooperative bilateral relationship, manage their difficulties well, and keep the Taiwan issue in check, this will only strengthen the stability, security, and development of the region. Conversely, China's integration into the region will condition Sino-American relations and lend powerful forces for stability in that relationship. In short, the relationship between China, the United States, and the other states of the region is a positive sum development.

All nations in the region, including the United States must adjust to the various and complex realities presented by China's ascent. It is not intrinsically something to be feared or opposed, although many may wish to hedge against potentially disruptive consequences. Moreover, China's own preferences may coincide? with those of its neighbors and the United States, which provides ample opportunities for mutual and regional collaboration to resolve problems and challenges. Integrating China into the regional order has been a longstanding goal of ASEAN, China, and the United States. Now that it is coming to pass, the United States should welcome China's place at the regional table and the constructive role that Beijing is "opting in."[150]

Why China's Regional Strategy May Not Be Good For America

Robert Sutter is a professor at Georgetown University and has worked in senior analytic and supervisory positions at the Library of Congress, and with the Central Intelligence Agency, Department of State, and Senate Foreign Relations Committee. Sutter stated in "China's Regional Strategy and Why It May Not Be Good For America:"

> Chinese foreign policy has long focused on Asia, and the Chinese leadership has been developing a relatively pragmatic approach to China's Asian neighbors for more than twenty years.' While China's security concerns have long centered on Asia, its military power has not extended much into the region. China's political and cultural influence has been strongest in Asia, and the largest proportion of its foreign trade has been conducted with Asian neighbors. In the post-Mao period, even though China grew into a global political and economic actor, its foreign policy was still concerned predominantly with Asia.
>
> In the 1980s, Chinese leaders tended to talk a lot about the global international order, but actual Chinese interests were concerned with issues closer to home. Heading the list was ensuring that hostile powers— particularly the United States and the Soviet Union, but also Japan and India—did not establish

dominance around China's periphery. When Chinese leaders discussed these issues, however, they insisted on doing so in a global context, with China positioned as a world leader. Thus, China's conflict with Vietnam in the late 1970s and the 1980s was seen as part of the global struggle against Soviet expansionism, and Chinese opposition to U.S. policies in Taiwan and South Korea was part of worldwide opposition to American imperialism. Such tension between China's regional interests and its global ambitions complicated Western assessments of China's "Asian" policy, as China at the time was seen as "a regional power without a regional policy."[151]

However, Sutter asserted that:

Among the various Chinese moves in recent years toward greater moderation and accommodation in Asian and world affairs, perhaps the most striking has been the abrupt falloff in mid-2001 of the wide-ranging and often very harsh public Chinese criticism of U.S. policy that prevailed throughout the previous decade. For years, and with varying degrees of intensity, the U.S. was portrayed by Chinese polemicists and officials as the "hegemon" and the object of a worldwide struggle. Asia was the primary intended audience for these Chinese criticisms.

The Chinese decision to stop this public campaign contributed markedly to the recent improvement in U.S.-China relations. This decision also raises an important question, debated by U.S. and other analysts, as to whether this shift represents a basic change in China's approach to the United States in Asian and world affairs. Those who see a more confident Chinese leadership tend to believe that there has indeed been a fundamental shift toward "new thinking" in Beijing. Chinese leaders are seen as markedly less prone to react sharply and negatively to U.S. policies and practices that in the recent past would have triggered strident Chinese invective and other assertive actions. Considered a newly "responsible" international player, China is assumed by some to have put aside its efforts—until recently very strong—to work against U.S. influence and power in Asia.

In contrast there are those, including this observer, who find this argument unconvincing for several reasons. First, they see U.S. policies and behavior under the Bush administration as markedly more hegemonic and offensive to long-standing Chinese sensitivities in such areas as Taiwan, missile defense, U.S. defense ties with Japan, U.S. sanctions against China, and the U.S. military posture in Iraq, Central Asia, and Southeast Asia. They find it hard to believe that the Chinese elites' long-standing and deeply rooted suspicion of U.S. policy could change so quickly. Under these circumstances, they consider it more likely that the Chinese government decided to mute anti-U.S. rhetoric and assertiveness for tactical reasons involving China's need to maintain a cooperative relationship with the United States, rather than because of any fundamental change in China's.

Indeed, the Bush administration officials privately warned Chinese counterparts in early 2001 against continuing strident anti-U.S. rhetoric. As the United States seemed to be determined to confront its enemies and likely to remain the dominant power for some time, other power centers, even Russia, were reluctant to confront or seriously challenge U.S. leadership. Under these circumstances, Chinese officials recognized that China was in no position to challenge the United States and attempt to balance U.S. power, even in Asia. This effort would attract few allies and would endanger core Chinese interests in maintaining stability and promoting economic development.

Second, reflecting clear limits on China's accommodation with the United States in Asia, Chinese policy continues to work over the longer term to weaken the predominance of the United States around China's periphery. In the lead-up to the Iraq war, China straddled the fence, privately pledging not to block U.S. military action but siding publicly with France and others in calling for protracted inspections. Beijing's advances in working to resolve the crisis over North Korea's nuclear program still fall short of U.S. expectations that China places more concrete pressure on the government in Pyongyang. A more forceful U.S. stance on North Korea would alarm China, which would very likely take strong measures to block the U.S. pressure. The day-to-day interface of U.S. and Chinese military forces along China's periphery has not been without significant incident, even as the two powers endeavored to resume more normal ties after the April 2001 EP-3 episode. Perhaps of most importance, the PLA buildup targeted at Taiwan and at U.S. forces that might help Taiwan, and U.S. military preparations to deal with Taiwan contingencies, continue unabated. These events suggest that a major breakthrough toward strategic cooperation has not occurred and is unlikely.

Third, constructivist theories regarding learning and change in international relations suggest that Chinese leaders, deeply influenced by nationalistic feelings and anti-American conditioning, will have great difficulty "learning" a more broadly cooperative approach to the United States in Asia.[29] The leaders may also have difficulty refraining from the long-standing tendency to exaggerate the perceived threats posed by the United States or others. Imbued with such a suspicious mindset regarding the United States, Chinese leaders are unlikely to change their minds unless some major event causes them to do so. It is difficult to see such an event in recent Chinese foreign policy.

Fourth, there remains plenty of evidence that Chinese leaders continue to oppose U.S. policy in many areas, notably in U.S. support for Taiwan and U.S. strategic leadership on a number of sensitive issues in Asian and world affairs. Although this opposition has been much less public since mid-2001, it can be seen in a variety of circumstances. A recent book based on files documenting the deliberations of the Chinese leadership shows repeatedly that opposition to U.S. policy in Asia remains a driving force in Chinese policy.

Typical of the negative views of U.S. intentions expressed privately by Chinese leaders was the following statement attributed to Hu Jintao:

> The United States has strengthened its military deployments in the Asia-Pacific region, strengthened the US-Japan military alliance, strengthened strategic cooperation with India, improved relations with Vietnam, inveigled Pakistan, established a pro-American government in Afghanistan, increased arms sales to Taiwan, and so on. They have extended outposts and placed pressure points on us from the east, south, and west. This makes a great change in our geopolitical environment..

To deal with these adverse trends while simultaneously avoiding confrontation with the United States, Chinese leaders have settled on a long-term approach that attempts to balance real or potential adverse U.S. power and influence in non-confrontational ways, implemented so subtly so as not to draw the attention of or irritate U.S. policy makers and Asian leaders, and thereby avoiding adverse consequences for Chinese interests. The competitive and antagonistic aspects of China's stance toward the United States in Asia are more evident in some areas of Asia than others.

Taiwan, as might be expected, is in a class by itself. Official Chinese complaints, though much muted after 2001, repeatedly lay down public markers against U.S. policy and behavior. Chinese rhetoric against Japan is more restrained than it was in the late 1990s, despite Prime Minister Koizumi's repeated visits to the Yakasuni shrine against explicit warnings from top Chinese officials, and much greater Japanese military activism in Asian and world affairs. Nevertheless there are frequent sharp complaints in the Chinese media against Japanese military activism, which is seen as fostered by U.S. policy as a means to enhance U.S. dominance in Asia.

Chinese leaders have been notably restrained in dealing with anti-U.S. themes in Korea. They have generally avoided explicit comment on the anti-American sentiment sweeping South Korea since 2002 and the often sharp U.S.—South Korean differences on relations with North Korea. Presumably they judge that such Chinese rhetoric, which appeared at times in the 1990s, would work against immediate Chinese concerns to avoid military conflict and encourage engagement among the powers concerned with the volatile situation on the peninsula.

In Southeast Asia, Chinese policy and behavior often only thinly veil competition or opposition to U.S. or other powers.36 Chinese officials initially inaugurated their "new security concept" (NSC) at an ASEAN meeting. The moderating effect of the new security concept was offset by the strident Chinese opposition to American power, influence, and policies. The moderation in Chinese policy toward the United States during 2001 was evident when China revised and re-launched its new security concept in meetings in Southeast Asia in 2002, as the NSC was no longer sandwiched between strong anti-U.S. rhetoric.

Nonetheless, Chinese policy and behavior have continued to work, albeit much more subtly, to increase Chinese influence at the expense of the United States and other powers in Southeast Asia. Although the "Shangri-la Dialogue," a high-level security forum convened annually in Singapore by the U.K.-based International Institute for Strategic Studies (IISS), attracted regional defense ministers, China sent only low-level functionaries, instead devoting high-level attention to promoting a new Asia-centered security dialogue (the ARF Security Policy Conference) that marginalized the United States. Greater Chinese flexibility and a willingness to engage in negotiations with the various claimants to South China Sea territories also saw Chinese officials endeavor to use the discussions as a means to restrict U.S. naval exercises in the area. During the multilateral U.S. "Cobra Gold" military exercise in 2001, China conducted its own military exercise in apparent competition. In 2003, lower-level Chinese officials occasionally resorted to strident anti-U.S. rhetoric decrying the occupation of Iraq, which played well in Southeast Asian countries. China also maneuvered in its Free Trade Agreement initiative with ASEAN to shore up China's position relative to the United States, as well as to compete with Japan, South Korea, and India. In 2003 China became the first nation to agree to sign ASEAN's 1976 Treaty of Amity and Cooperation, prompting Russia, India, and Japan to pledge to do the same and placing the United States in a less flattering light.

ASEAN also has been the main arena for Chinese multilateral initiatives that have excluded or tried to marginalize the United States. While cooperating with Japan, South Korea, and other Asian powers in promoting Asia only groups that explicitly exclude the United States, China at the same time also competes with them for leadership in Asian forums.

The ASEAN Plus Three mechanism emerged in the late 1990s as the most important of the regional groupings designed to promote Asian economic cooperation that excluded the United States and other outside powers, and Chinese leaders took a leading role in the group's various initiatives to promote intraregional cooperation and economic safeguards. China opposed Japan's initiative to establish an Asian monetary fund at the height of the Asian economic crisis in 1997, but it came to support a more recent Asian Monetary Fund initiative sponsored by ASEAN Plus Three, which did ease entry into the WTO seen as a driver of Asian growth, Chinese officials and media since 2000 have highlighted China's free trade initiatives with ASEAN, including the "early harvest" concessions dealing with agricultural trade, which have served to undercut concurrent Japanese and South Korean trade initiatives toward Southeast Asia that do not include liberalized agricultural-trade. Chinese leaders for the past year supported efforts to broaden the ASEAN Plus Three dialogue to include salient political and security as well as economic issues.

Beijing also initiated important regional multilateral mechanisms The Boao Forum for Asia (BFA), which meets annually on Hainan Island, as presented by China as the "first annual session" of an Asian version of Davos World Economic Forum. The Boao Forum's goal was to provide a platform for Asian countries to conduct a high-level dialogue about addressing economic and social challenges and promoting economic cooperation in Asia. Working with the Chinese sponsors of the forum, Thailand's prime minister proposed the Asian Cooperation Dialogue (ACD) of foreign ministers as an official counterpart of the BFA, meeting was held in Thailand in June 2002. The foreign ministers of most ASEAN Plus Three members attended and agreed to further meetings.

Elsewhere around China's periphery, the tendency of Chinese leaders to work explicitly against U.S. interests has been muted. In Russia, President Putin has been less willing in recent years to forge a united front with China against U.S. policy, though occasional references to multipolarity and opposition to hegemonism and unilateralism are seen in Russian-Chinese pronouncements. Russia remains willing to supply China with sophisticated weapons for use in a possible Taiwan contingency that could involve the United States, and Russian-Chinese trade is growing from a low level. Chinese commentators in the 1990s envisaged the Shanghai Cooperation Organization (SCO) as excluding the United States from Central Asia. They also often commented negatively on the rapid upswing of the U.S. military presence and U.S. influence in Central and South Asia in 2001, but China adjusted without marshaling a major opposition. China has been in the lead in keeping the SCO moving forward, providing funding and participating in small joint and multilateral military exercises with SCO members— unprecedented steps for the PLA. Beijing has also stressed broadening SCO interests to include economic interchange—steps that may enhance China's leadership role based on the overall strength of the Chinese economy. The United States and other interested powers (e.g., India) are kept out of the SCO deliberations. China has also sought and received Mongolia's pledge not to allow foreign troops in Mongolia.

In South Asia, Chinese leaders have cooperated with the United States, even though their leading position in Pakistan has changed as a result of the strong assertion of U.S. leadership there in 2000. Incremental Chinese efforts to improve relations with India had in the recent past focused on some Sino-Indian common ground against U.S. foreign policy, but this was largely put aside as New Delhi rapidly improved relations—especially military relations—with the United States, even before September 11, 2001. Sino-Indian relations continue to improve, even though they are hampered by key differences, notably the differing stances of the two countries toward Pakistan. India and China have generally eschewed criticism of the United States in their recent interaction.

Sutter concluded:

The post–Cold War Chinese leadership, more focused on domestic issues than on expanding foreign power, have established a strategy that emphasizes conventional nation building and gradually strengthening China's influence. That strategy reflects greater Chinese confidence, which has resulted in a more moderate posture on territorial issues and more initiatives involving bilateral ties and multilateral arrangements.

Because China's approach is to emphasize common ground with neighbors, there is little concrete evidence of how much China's influence has actually increased in Asia—something that would be clearer were China to get neighboring countries to follow policies that China favors, but they do not. Meanwhile, Chinese officials appear to remain highly sensitive to the policies and power of the United States and U.S.-backed allies and associates, especially Taiwan and Japan. North Korea represents another source of uncertainty. The overall rise of U.S. power and assertiveness in post–Cold War Asian and world affairs has many drawbacks for long-standing Chinese interests in Asia. China has viewed negatively or with suspicion greater U.S. support for Taiwan and Japanese military activism, U.S. ballistic missile defense, strengthened U.S. military deployments, closer military cooperation in Central, South, and Southeast Asia, and closer U S military and foreign policy cooperation with India and Russia.

Chinese leaders have learned, after considerable debate over the last twenty-five years, that economic globalization is in China's interests, and they have come to embrace it. On political and security issues, however, China's prevailing pattern is to deal with these questions on a case-by-case basis, taking into account in each instance the costs and benefits for China. In this regard, China is less a "responsible" power, fully embracing international norms in security and political affairs, and more a "responsive" power, carefully maneuvering to preserve long-standing interests despite changing circumstances.

In particular, Chinese leaders have concluded that public opposition to U.S. policies and trends have become counterproductive, especially given the Bush administration's power and firmness against adversaries and the strong opposition of Asian governments to great power contention in the region. Nonetheless, Chinese officials continue to oppose U.S. dominance in Asia and world affairs, and, to work against adverse trends involving the United States in subtle and indirect ways. At the same time, they seem to believe that the overall growth of Chinese power and influence in Asia will secure Chinese interests over the long term, despite the contrary actions and interests of the United States.

Looking forward, Taiwan and North Korea have the ability to take provocative actions that could change the course of China's moderate and cooperative approach in Asia. Of more long-term importance are U.S. power, policy, and behavior, which are likely to remain key determinants in China's regional stance. A more hard-line U.S. posture with respect to sensitive issues like support for Taiwan, military deployments, or closer strategic cooperation with Japan could prompt a reassessment of China's regional stance and a harsh reaction affecting its overall Asian strategy. A weakening of U.S. power through failure in Iraq or U.S. economic decline could prompt more Chinese pressure against U.S. interests, Beijing's probing to roll back recent advances in U.S. support for Taiwan or other recent U.S. initiatives that have worked against Chinese interests.

To hold in check long-standing Chinese tendencies to assertively challenge U.S. interests and developments in Asia that are perceived to be adverse, the United States should carefully manage the U.S.-China relationship from an overall position of U.S. confidence and strength. Alternatively, the United States may over time move away from its insistence on maintaining the dominant strategic position in Asian and world affairs. This could set the stage for a different kind of Sino-American accommodation, with the United States pulling back strategically from Asia as China rises to regional leadership.[152]

China's Rise in Asia Need Not Be at America's Expense

David Lampton is a professor at John Hopkins University and Director of China Studies at the Nixon Center. He was President of the National Committee on United States Relations and was the Director of the China Program at the American Enterprise Institute. David Lampton commented in: *China's Rise in Asia Need Not Be at America's Expense* that:

> ...although China's rising power will certainly present the United States, as well as the PRC's neighbors, with challenges, Beijing's increased capabilities are also becoming a powerful engine for regional and economic growth and essential to meeting current and future transnational challenges. How the outside world responds to China's rise in the short and medium term will importantly influence how China's power is exercised in the long term, notwithstanding the fact that the most important determinant of China's future international behavior will be its people and the domestic system they create. Although suitable hedges against the risks of China's modernization are appropriate, the emphasis of U. S. policy should be placed upon positive integration.[153]

Farewell to verities about China's foreign policy behavior in Asia and beyond. As China's power has increased there have been, and will continue to be, important changes in how Beijing defines its interests, the kinds and mixes of power it employs to achieve its ends, the effectiveness of its policies, and the structure of the East Asian regional system. These changes require alterations in U.S. policy and behavior at the same time that China is developing a stake in a stable yet dynamic status quo in East Asia and beyond. East Asia is not becoming Sinocentric, but it is becoming a place in which Chinese interests and influence cannot be disregarded.

Among the verities receding from view is the notion that China is a nation extensively shaped by a "victim mentality," prickly to deal with because of its attempts to compensate for a hundred-plus years of humiliation. Instead, Chinese leaders now refer to China and the United States as "two influential countries," both of which have "responsibilities", though Beijing still eschews the word "leadership". Also living on borrowed time is the platitude that China is only a "regional power." Indeed, the "region" in which China is active has expanded considerably, now embracing Central Asia, South Asia, and Southeast Asia, with ever more activity in the Middle East and beyond (for more on this, see John Garver's contribution to this volume). China's reach into U.S. financial markets has grown gradually, and it has now achieved significant proportions. Though this chapter focuses on Asia, there are fewer and fewer issues or places in which China has neither interest nor influence.

The reasons these verities are receding are to be found in four variables, one of which is changes in the international system, particularly the preeminence of the United States in the post-Cold War and post-9/11 eras, and China's felt The need to cooperate with others to constrain Washington. China is gaining a certain normative appeal in East Asia and beyond simply by defining a foreign policy paradigm that many nations feel contrasts favorably with that of the Bush Administration in the post-9/11 period. The second factor is China's impressive and sustained economic success, which has provided Beijing with tools and options it never before had, while the third variable is closely connected to the second—interdependence. A new economic order is taking shape in East Asia in which the PRC is becoming a major purchaser of what its neighbors have to sell and a growing investor in their economies. This situation provides the PRC leverage.

Lampton's view in 2005 was:

Cooperation is currently seen in Beijing as more being a more feasible way to protect economic interests and interdependencies than a ruinous drive for military power that Beijing's leaders believe brought the Soviet Union down. And the final set of factors is the changed leadership of China, that the leadership's placement of foreign policy in the context of domestic economic development, and that leaders' greater comfort level with China being an influential country.

The net effect of these variables has been to progressively and fundamentally alter the style and substance of Chinese foreign policy, with the Asian financial crisis of 1997-98 having been a watershed. No single decision was more important than Beijing's policy of holding stable the value of the renminbi (RMB) and contributing to the stabilization funds for Thailand and Indonesia through the International Monetary Fund (IMF). The regional and global praise that China's leadership had received for these moves was important, notwithstanding the fact that Beijing made those decisions out of consideration of its own interests.[2] Reinforcing this positive experience has been the largely favorable outcome of China's accession to the World Trade Organization (WTO) and the accelerated growth and development that has followed. Once the international business community was assured that Beijing was irrevocably committed to joining the global trading system, foreign direct investment (FDI) has surged into the PRC even as investments going to Asia and the rest of the world have declined.

The core of China's contemporary foreign policy is reassurance of neighbors, peacefully securing China's economic lifelines (strategic resources), and building relationships that can constrain the unbridled exercise of U.S. power at the same time that Beijing's influence grows and it continues to draw on the resources of the global system, most importantly the United States. Against this background, this chapter deals with the implications for the United States of China's rise and its evolving foreign policy. Two broad sets of questions animate this chapter: To start, how should we conceive of China's power? What kinds of power are we talking about? For Beijing, what is the preferred mix of power types, now and in the future? And, how are China's neighbors responding to this shifting power mix? Second, what policy issues and challenges does the foregoing development? present to the United States, now and for the foreseeable future?

...although China's rising power will certainly present the United States, as well as the PRC's neighbors, with challenges, Beijing's increased capabilities are also becoming a powerful engine for regional and global economic growth and essential to meeting current and future transnational challenges. How the outside world responds to China's rise in the short and medium term will importantly influence how China's power is exercised in the long term, notwithstanding the fact that the most important determinant of China's future international behavior will be its people and the domestic system they create. Although suitable hedges against the risks of China's modernization are appropriate, the emphasis of U.S. policy should be placed upon positive integration.

THE CHANGING MIX OF CHINESE POWER:
THE DOMINANCE OF REMUNERATIVE POWER

In his classic study entitled *A Comparative Analysis of Complex Organizations*, Amitai Etzioni disaggregated the concept of "power" into three categories: intensive coercive, normative, and remunerative, or, crudely put, the power of guns, ideas, and money. The "open and reform policy" of China (*kaifang, gaige zhengce*) substantially has been about the increase of the PRC's remunerative power. Though China's military power has grown modestly to date (and certainly will grow significantly in the future), and though the attractiveness of China's foreign policy pursuit of multipolalority has contributed to a modest rise in the 'normative' dimension of Chinese power (especially as many around the world have become concerned about U.S. dominance), it is in the realm of remunerative power growth that China's ascent has been most marked.

The expansion of its remunerative power has given China options and avenues for influence that it has not previously enjoyed in the modern era. Beijing's remunerative power is both manifest and latent. China is gaining power as a rapidly growing purchaser of what others throughout Asia have to sell, and the PRC has also become a key part of the global supply chain, producing goods destined for North America, Japan, and Europe. China increasingly is investing throughout Asia while U.S. investment, both monetary and political, have, declined.[154]

Michael Swaine is with the China Program at the Carnegie Endowment for International Peace and has worked at the Rand Corporation. He expressed the view in 2005 that:

> In the case of China, military power has historically been regarded as a pragmatically essential, if not always ethically laudable, requirement for the maintenance of a secure and stable government. One of the primary goals of modern Chinese nationalism has been for the Chinese state to develop a sufficient level of military power to deter future aggression by other states, to support China's long-standing desire to achieve national wealth and power, and to attain international recognition and respect as a great nation. In addition, many outside observers measure the potential threat generated by China's rise as a modern nation-state in large part on the basis of the growing size, capabilities, and configuration of its military forces.
>
> Thus, given China's expanse, its critical geostrategic location astride the Asian land mass, and its overall rapid rate of growth, there is little doubt that its future military posture will exert a decisive impact on the larger security environment and hence on the shape and tenor of those nonmilitary factors mentioned above. This impact will be most keenly felt in Asia. Indeed, china's current and likely near- to medium-term military posture is essentially limited to the Asian region. The only major exception involves those long-range strategic nuclear weapons systems of the People's Liberation Army (PLA) that present a retaliatory, second-strike capability against targets outside Asia, for example, the United States homeland and European parts of the former Soviet Union. The rest of China's strategic forces, as well as all of

its conventional forces, are oriented exclusively toward regional objectives.[155]

Will and Can China and America Avoid a Major Crisis?

Michael Yahuda is Professor Emeritus at the London School of Economics. He commented in 2005:

Historically, rising powers have been regarded as challengers to the existing order and have often precipitated major wars. China's rise has also evoked concern from its neighbors and from other major powers, including the United States. However, China and its neighbors have found ways of mitigating many of these concerns, principally through a process of integrating China into the region through its participation in a number of multilateral institutions based on the principles of cooperation and consensus. To be sure, such institutions do not, in and of themselves, meet all the standard security needs of member states, but they are well suited to improving relations between states that are neither adversaries nor allies. Such institutions facilitate interactions between governments and societies, and they provide the means for leaders to better understand the interests and security concerns of others. Given China's previous relative isolation and its inexperience in institutional cooperation, these institutions have provided mechanisms for China and its neighbors to work together and to mitigate incipient conflicts.

These cooperative multilateral institutions have developed alongside the established series of bilateral alliances long established by the United States with key states along the littoral of the Western Pacific. Although China's leaders have long regarded these alliances as designed at least in part against their country, China's neighbors have seen them and other defense arrangements with the United States as a means of hedging against potential Chinese power. Since the end of the Cold War they have regarded them as a constraint upon China that facilitated their accommodation or engagement with China on terms that were neither those of appeasement nor bandwagoning. At the turn of the century Chinese commentators and officials stopped openly challenging the American security alliances, thereby tacitly accepting that they contributed to regional order, at least for the time being. That of course eased the task of East Asian neighbors, in particular as they accommodate China's growing significance.

Since the end of the Cold War the regional powers have been repositioning themselves. The removal of the bipolar or tripolar order has permitted regional powers various forms of maneuver relative to each other as each has focused primarily on its domestic agenda. Once it was recognized by the mid 1990s that, far from declining, the sole surviving superpower was gathering in strength, the regional great powers accepted that they had more to gain by engaging than by opposing the United States. Some had envisioned that it might be possible to constrain the United States' preeminence by encouraging the emergence of a multipolar world, but as the hopes for that too faded in practice, the regional powers entered the new century both cooperating and competing with each other under the aegis of a not wholly uncontested American hegemony. Thus the Asian order at the beginning of the twenty-first century may be conceived as a pattern of overlapping forms of security. In addition to the long-standing traditional alliance system of the United States, there has emerged a regionally generated system of multilateral institutions based on cooperative security and an incipient complex balance of power involving the regional major states. The U.S.-led alliance system is reasonably well known and understood.[156]

During the Cold War China did not formally address issues of regional order. China's leaders typically tended to direct themselves to universal rather than regional themes. Insofar as China's leaders focused on relations with their neighbors, they did so either in terms of strict bilateral matters, or as a function of Chinese strategic concerns with the two superpowers. This began to change, however, as the Cold War came to an end, partly through China's development of new relations with the USSR and its successor states, and partly through China's reaching out to its neighbors to overcome the diplomatic isolation arising from the Western sanctions after the Tiananmen incident. In the process, the Chinese began to gain more experience in the development of confidence-building measures (CBMs) and in multilateral diplomacy. The latter had begun as a consequence of Chinese attempts to cultivate the more tranquil international environment that was necessary for its new economic policies. Thus China joined the consultative Track II Pacific Economic Cooperation Council (PECC) in the early 1980s, which enabled officials from the foreign affairs and trade ministries as well as associated academics to gain experience in Asian multilateralism. This was a significant advantage when China was invited to join APEC in 1990.

More pertinent, perhaps, was the Chinese experience in developing CBMs with the USSR and its successor states that bordered China. Beginning in the late 1980s, as both the Chinese and Soviet leaders sought to reduce tension and withdraw forces from the borders, they first took separate initiatives and waited for the other to reciprocate. This gradually created sufficient trust for the two sides to cooperate in forming border patrols and to offer mutual assistance when addressing accidents and local incidents. They were then able to coordinate troop withdrawals, military exercises, and other activities. Enhanced confidence led to better demarcation of borders, and even to a settling of past border disputes.

This cooperation soon resumed after the dissolution of the Soviet Union, but this time it operated on a multilateral level, involving the three new Central Asian republics of Kazakhstan, Kyrgyzstan, and Tajikistan. The transition from bilateral to multilateral diplomacy in this case was relatively smooth. Border and security issues were treated multilaterally. The longstanding Soviet-Chinese militarized divide was no more.

New questions arose about the viability and stability of the newly established Central Asian states and what their relations with Russia, as members of the Commonwealth of Independent States (CIS), would be. Afghanistan, with its militant Taliban regime, was potentially subversive of the new regimes. For its part, China had its own reasons for seeking stability in what had suddenly become a highly volatile regime whose instabilities could instigate trouble in adjoining Xinjiang. China's leaders developed policies that sought to assuage Moscow's fears that they were seeking to undermine Russian influence. At the same time, they attempted to assure the new governments of Central Asia that China endorsed their territorial integrity (in light of unstated fears that Russia might seek to redraw their borders) and that China wanted to help their governments to become more effective domestically, so as to gain their cooperation in stopping the movement of militant Uyghurs across the porous borders. China also hoped to gain access to Central Asian oil and natural gas while encouraging cross-border trade in the hope of tying the new states into China's western region in forms of mutually beneficial economic interdependency (albeit on a small scale) .

By 1996 China's leaders and diplomats and branches of the Chinese military had gained experience in multilateralism through participation in a number of regional institutions, notably APEC and the ARF. They felt sufficiently confident to develop a multilateral institution of their own to bolster their interests and address their concerns in Central Asia. The Shanghai Five, soon to be expanded and renamed the Shanghai Cooperation Organization (SCO) when Uzbekistan was added to the original five members, was overtly political in its goal of upholding the existing territorial and political order by opposing the "three evils" of extremist Islam, terrorism, and "splitism." The creation of the SCO was buttressed by the newly announced strategic partnership between Beijing and Moscow. At that point the new regional institution had the additional attraction of its membership being limited strictly to locally resident states, which meant that both the United States and Japan were excluded.

The last situation did not last long, as the events of September 11, 2001, suddenly brought an extensive American presence in Central Asia. At first these events seemed so overwhelming as to make the SCO impotent. Nevertheless, within eighteen months of the deployment of American bases in Central Asia, the Chinese had revitalized the organization by establishing a permanent secretariat in Shanghai, by establishing an antiterrorism center in Bishkek, and by conducting a number of antiterrorism exercises with Kyrgyzstan in October 2002 and with Kazakhstan a year later. Chinese activism here must be assessed alongside the much greater regional military presence of Russia, which has forces deployed in Kyrgyzstan, where it exercises the main responsibility for defense of the country. Russia is also the principal arms supplier to the Central Asian countries. In addition to the CIS, Russia also heads a regional military alliance called the Collective Security Treaty Organization (CSTO), with a NATO-like provision for a joint response to an attack on any of its members. NATO, too, has links with the region through its Partnership for Peace program, and its secretary general has visited Kazakhstan and Kyrgyzstan to enhance practical coopera-tion in countering terrorism and the smuggling of drugs and radioactive materials.

Interestingly, China, too, has expressed an interest in open-ing a dialogue with NATO. This development, like several others mentioned above, is unprecedented and contrary to previous Chinese practice. The significance of these new developments will be explored in greater detail later, but at this point it is suffi-cient to note that they correspond to practical Chinese interests in addressing genuine security concerns affecting Xinjiang and in cultivating goodwill for commercial advantage, as China is the only successful economy in the region capable of satisfying the demand for consumer goods.[157]

Notwithstanding the high degree of activity, including various meetings, conferences, and innovative contributions by Track II institutions, there is no overarching body that brings together the key actors in Northeast Asia on a regular basis. Such multilateralism that does exist in this sub region is too weak and limited in scope to be the basis for order. The one regional meet-ing that brings together the key actors is an ad hoc grouping designed to address the North Korean nuclear issue in a way that is satisfactory to the United States. At the core of the grouping is the U.S. insistence that the North Korean problem should not be seen as a matter to be treated bilaterally between the United States and the North—even though most of the other members of the group would prefer that it were dealt with that way. The fact that there is little multilateralism in evidence in this sub region where the interests of the major powers intersect and where the two most intractable conflicts of Asia are located attests to the absence of a true regional order. Notwithstanding the rise of China, the order that does exist depends heavily on the United States. It is the U.S. alliance with Japan that is central to the Northeast Asian order, and it still lies at the heart of the U.S. security commitment to the region. It is this alliance that has largely underwritten the larger strategic framework that has served nearly all the East Asian states so well in providing the safety net that has facilitated their economic growth and stability in interstate relations. Since the end of the Cold War, as the international security and diplomatic environment has changed, it has been the continuing security arrangements centering on the United States that have enabled the new multilateral cooperative institutions to emerge and flourish alongside the security architecture provided by the United States. This is as true of the ASEAN Plus Three (APT) mechanism, from which the United States is excluded, as it is of the more broadly based APEC and ARF. These regional institutions place a premium on process through consultation and nonbinding agreements reached by consensus at the expense of hard and fast rules, binding commitments, and attempts to address conflict.[158]

America's Taiwan Fairness Hypocrisy: Accidentally or Deliberately Dysfunctional?

Richard Bush is with the Brookings Institution and was with the American Institute in Taiwan, the institution through which the American government conducts substantive relations with Taiwan in the absence of diplomatic relations. He commented in 2005:

> In May 1996, on the occasion of his second inauguration as the president of the Republic of China, Lee Teng-hui offered a unique view on how Taiwan mattered for China. He recalled that China had suffered a series of shocks in its encounters with the West, despite an excellent traditional culture. He expressed the hope that the people of Taiwan would foster a Chinese culture that combined the best of the West with Chinese heritage. He went so far as to draw an analogy between the seminal role that the Wei River valley (the central plains, zhongyuan) had played in the flowering of traditional Chinese culture and the role that Taiwan (which he termed the new central plains, xin-zhongyuan) would play in fostering that new Chinese culture. For Lee, Taiwan represented the best part of China in the modern world, and China would again become a great civilization only if it followed Taiwan's lead.
>
> It is a mark of how rapidly the PRC's wealth and power have grown since Lee's second inaugural that his act of historical

entrepreneurship seems so quaint. Although Taiwan may be on the right side of history in the realm of political values, the other countries in Asia, have had to adjust to the PRC's growing influence as its prowess in other dimensions. And despite growing economic interdependence between the island and the mainland, in most other respects Taiwan has refused to accommodate Beijing's growing influence as its neighbors have. If East Asia is indeed becoming more Sino-centric, Taiwan is in critical ways the exception that proves the rule, for reasons that are unique to Taiwan itself.[159]

Jonathon Pollack commented in 2005:

Chinese military planning for a Taiwan crisis constitutes the definitive exception to Beijing's emphasis on a collaborative Asia-Pacific security order. It is the singular example of China's continued pursuit of threat-based military planning. Irrespective of how China would justify a decision to use force against Taiwan (and irrespective of the outcome of such a crisis), the implications of such a decision would be profound. China is acquiring military capabilities that it believes will ultimately enable a short-warning, high intensity attack against Taiwan. These include a growing inventory of short range ballistic missiles, advance conventional powered submarines and other navel platforms, longer range aircraft, and a host of related capabilities. There is a wide range of scenarios for employing such capabilities. China is also seeking to preempt U. S. involvement in such a conflict, presumably expecting that the crisis could be brought to a speedy and minimally destructive conclusion before Washington could intervene. But China is also building capabilities that would put U.S. military assets at risk and also impart to Japan the potential dangers of contributing to U.S. actions. The risks and consequences inherent in any expanded conflict could hardly be greater.

Are there realistic possibilities for the parties to forestall such a crisis, or (in the event of deterrence failure) to limit its scope? The indications are not encouraging. Policy makers in Taipei, Beijing, and Washington all premise their planning calculations on assumptions that can only be tested fully in armed conflict.

Many of these assumptions seem highly questionable, and some are directly contradictory to one another, especially divergent judgments in Beijing and Taipei on the likelihood and scale of a U.S. military intervention. The respective policy trajectories in all three capitals thus seem largely independent of one another, underscoring the risks of horrific miscalculation.

Though most regional actors would prefer to stand apart from the fray, major hostilities in the Taiwan Strait—even if a military conflict were concluded speedily—would trigger significant reverberations across the region. China would seek to characterize its actions as defending its territorial sovereignty and national unity, but its willingness to use force would constitute a lasting precedent in Asian security. The likeliest long-term effects would be on various maritime states, especially where territorial demarcations with China are still contested. It remains conjectural whether China's continental neighbors would reassess their prevailing policy assumptions toward Beijing. Much would depend on the extent of political, economic, and security.[160]

Unrealistic Assumptions in the Current American Policymakers and Scholars' Mindset on China

The New School's perspectives, in summary, on the sampling of American contributions in *Power Shift: China and Asia's New Dynamics* are:

1. New School's perspective is correct in its hypothesis that a committed genuine global partnership between America and China is the best foreign policy and defense strategy option for America, as well as China, and is the best guarantee of stability in the Asian region.
2. America currently is not a reliable "principal guarantor of order in East Asia" as Americentric observers assert because of American policymakers' unilateralist approach.
3. However, early in the 21st century, these Americacentric

observers realize America cannot solve problems like North Korea's nuclear program by itself or use military authority unilaterally.

4. China and the other countries that border North Korea have great concerns about North Korean refugees fleeing an imploding North Korea. America does not have such borders and these Americentric observers do not give the stability of North Korea the same level of concern as neighboring states do.

5. None of these American scholars even considered a genuine strategic partnership between America and China.

6. Only one of these American scholars addressed the Principles of Peaceful Coexistence that have been the basis of China's policies for 30 years.

7. All of these non-Chinese scholars were operating within the dangerous limitations of the Principles of Conflict, which are manifested in American foreign policy.

8. None of these American scholars examines whether America is a major remaining cause of the Taiwan problem in America-China relations. America encourages Taiwan's independence, perhaps as a way to irritate or destabilize China. China, on the other hand, is steadily and peacefully mitigating its differences with Taiwan. As Deng Xiaoping told the Central Advisory Committee of the Communist Party of China on October 22, 1984.

> The policy of 'one country, two systems' has been adopted out of consideration of China's realities. China is faced with the problems of Hong Kong and Taiwan. There are only two ways to solve them. One is through negotiations and the other is by force. To solve a problem by peaceful negotiation requires that the terms be acceptable to all parties. The solution to the Hong Kong question should be acceptable to China, Britain and the inhabitants of Hong Kong. What for-

mula would they accept? A socialist transformation of Hong Kong would not be acceptable to all parties. Therefore, the formula of 'one country, two systems' was proposed.[161]

But American policymakers, and people will ask: "How do we know that in the future China will not act inconsistently with Deng Xiaoping's "One Country, Two Systems" peaceful solution? Americans do not take into consideration China's conduct in relation to Hong Kong under three leaders, Hong Kong has reverted back to Chinese sovereignty, and this is Hong Kong's case ten years of evidence and in Taiwan's case 30 years of evidence. As will be recalled, Deng Xiaoping stated that:

> In my recent talks with foreign guests, I never failed to assure them that our current policies would not change, that they could rely on their continuity. Still they were not completely convinced....The policy of 'one country, two systems' has been adopted out of consideration of China's realities. China is faced with the problems of Hong Kong and Taiwan. There are only two ways to solve them. One is through negotiations and the other is by force. To solve a problem by peaceful negotiation requires that the terms be acceptable to all parties. The solution to the Hong Kong question should be acceptable to China, Britain and the inhabitants of Hong Kong. What formula would they accept? A socialist transformation of Hong Kong would not be acceptable to all parties. Therefore, the formula of 'one country, two systems' was proposed.[162]

9. We examined America's Taiwan and Cuba Hypocrisy in chapter 2 of Book 2, which is an error in American foreign policy must be correcedt. America' arming of Taiwan contributes significantly to the destabilizing role that America plays in increasing the risk of a confrontation between Mainland China and Taiwan. American policy and arms sales to Taiwan endanger and undermine China's One Country, Two

Systems policy, which seeks peaceful relations with Taiwan.

10. American policymakers Cold War mindset does not allow them to understand that China is earnest about peacefully developing.

11. It is typical of an outdated Cold War mindset to look for military threats from China.

12. Conventional policymakers do not recognize China's peaceful development, now evidenced by *both* Deng Xiaoping's statements and China's policies implementing the Principles of Peaceful Coexistence. That is evidence of the consistent intention, of China's peaceful development strategies.

13. Americans perceive China's peaceful domestic and international development as threatening, because they think in zero sum terms that if China is getting more powerful, it has to be inimical to America's interests and therefore war is inevitable.

14. It is highly unlikely that China will cause or start a war but far too likely that *conventional* American policy in Taiwan, if it had inept leaders, might cause a war that *conventional* Chinese policy in Taiwan tries to avoid.

15. Americentric assumptions grow out of the now over 200-year-old sense Americans have of Americans Exceptionalism. They also grow out of a "sense of honor" that Americans have to support Taiwan against a threat. But China's strategy in dealing with Taiwan is peaceful. It is America's arms sales to Taiwan that is the principle cause of tension between Mainland China and Taiwan.

16. The bullying American Exceptionalism exhibited in the 21st century has degraded America's moral authority. In the administration, America looked like an irresponsible major power while China acted responsibly.

17. America has spent more than a trillion dollars on its Iraq and Afghanistan Wars and has had to borrow money from

foreigners to finance them. China is the largest owner of American Treasury obligations.

18. But the most unrealistic assumption that Americans must change is that although China's political system is different from America's, that does not mean it is a bad system or that it does not enjoy broad support for its success. The reality is that China's political system is different from America's and that its Principles of Peaceful Coexistence-based strategies are not threats to America. The reality is that they protect America's economic and national security.

19. For Americans, intolerance of systems of governments different from their own has enormous moral authority because such systems of government, from an Americentric perspective, are deficient and chosen by foreigners in assumed ignorance or oppression.

20. However, America's long tradition of intolerant rhetoric and regime-change oriented strategies degrade American moral authority.

21. Americentric observers unrealistically project their Cold War mindsets on China's win-win mindset. Having done so, they believe their unrealistic analyses are "realism."

22. Americentric observers are in an illusionary military and geopolitical power struggle with what they view as an innately aggressive China.

23. Meanwhile China is using its ability to peacefully assemble moral authority to accomplish its geopolitical goals of peace and prosperity in a harmonious world.

24. Rather symbolically, China's infrastructure has emphasized submarines rather than aircraft carriers and battle fleets, which are increasingly indefensible. In 2008, as maritime piracy has emerged as a problem, China has announced it will build its first aircraft carrier for defensive purposes. America has eleven aircraft carriers and supporting battle groups.

25. China uses *defensive* military technologies, such as the ability to destroy the satellites the American military uses to manage its assets and target its enemies.

26. That is why China's destruction of a satellite in 2007 was very upsetting to American planners. America objected loudly that China was creating space debris and then promptly destroyed a satellite itself in a projection of power. China did not even announce its destruction of a satellite.

27. American policymakers and scholars perceive China's *defensive* military technologies as *offensive* because they see the world in terms of the Principles of Conflict rather than in terms of the Principles of Peaceful Coexistence. Unfortunately, we must note that a bully perceives resistance, even defensive resistance, as aggressive, threatening, and unfair.

28. A reality Americentric observers refuse to accept is that peaceful development works better, is less expensive, and has more economic and moral authority than America's aggressive use of military authority without moral authority.

29. There is a perception among Asian nations that their problems are of no importance to America, such as poverty, the environment, education, and drug trafficking.

30. America's indifference towards Asia's needs degrades America's moral authority and alienates American allies, and nations that envy America's success.

31. Another unrealistic assumption many Americentric observers have is that new initiatives in China for economic and national security are threatening to American's hegemony and interests, and as such are unacceptable.

Fortunately, when America and China are partners, their security interests will be aligned. Accordingly, many of the issues that the non-Chinese contributors to *Power Shift: China and Asia's New Dynamics* worry about will be eliminated.

Combining the Moral Authority of American and Chinese Exceptionalism in a Harmonious World

Chapter 9

The Charisma of Understanding Other Civilizations' Value

Overview

American and Chinese ways of doing things must complement each other. The diversity currently dividing America and China offers each great opportunities for progress. Recognizing these opportunities and respecting each country's diversity are among the essential conditions for their successful partnership.

American Thought Processes and Values

William Hutton in *The Writing on the Wall: Why We Must Embrace China as a Partner or Face It as an Enemy* asserts that China's internal challenges may derail its economic growth, causing massive shocks to the global economy, which America has a vital interest in preventing, Hutton asserts that China's current economic model is unsustainably "premised on the myriad contradictions and dysfunctions of an authoritarian state attempting to control an economy in transition to capitalism." Hutton makes those classic Americentric assumptions and draws Americentric conclusions from those assumptions. Hutton assumes that the Chinese will have to embrace both the European Enlightenment tradition and "features of the modern Western nations that have spurred the political stability and economic power of the United States and Europe: rule of law, an independent judiciary, freedom of the press," and "authentic representative government that is accountable to the people."

However, he does usefully focus on the real and urgent need for America to manage its relationship with China in a way that persuades the Chinese to accept the virtues of a democratic system like America's. Hutton states:

> China is not such a threat. Rather, it is a sophisticated civilization beset by profound and deepening problems that is making a difficult transition from peasant poverty to modernity. It requires our understanding and engagement—not our enmity and suspicion, which might be self-defeating, creating the very crisis we fear. China's vulnerability is not widely understood. Europe and the United States should stay open to China both in our trade and in the realm of ideas.
>
> Above all, we should be confident. The Enlightenment values and institutions that propelled the west past China in the nineteenth century remain no less important today as sources of competitive advantage and social well-being. They lie at the heart of the emerging "knowledge economy." The problem is that they are being neglected, and in consequence they are fading. In the United States, public institutions, representative government, the media, secondary education, corporations, investment institutions, and especially general supports for developing the individual capabilities of its citizens are simply not working as well as they should. Britain is in a very similar position. And in their preemptive war in Iraq, both countries have actively undermined the system of international law and multilateral governance. If we want to persuade China and the world of the virtues of pluralism, Enlightenment values, and democracy, the United States and Britain have to practice what they preach at home and abroad. At present they do not....

The relationship between the United States and China and that between China and the rest of Asia are delicately poised. Yet there are many problems—most tellingly the environment and global warning, which now threaten ecosystems to the degree that we are fast approaching a tipping point where humanity as a species may be in potential danger—that require an international response and appreciation of our shared fate. Both China and the United States must be part of the solution to these problems. My ambition for this book is that it will help tilt the balance toward more international collaboration, a reappraisal of the so-called Chinese threat, and a recognition of the situation as an opportunity and above all a reaffirmation of Enlightenment values and of the importance of economics and pluralism.

Non-Americans have difficulty in coming to terms with the contradictions and complexity of American nationalism. The United States, because of its special destiny and difference, is felt to have an obligation to lead others; it can also feel no compunction about using its presumed special destiny to justify behaving astonishingly self-interestedly even when there is a clear global interest in collective collaboration. Global warming is one example. Although the United States accounts for about 25 percent of the world's carbon dioxide emissions, George Bush could unblinkingly oppose the Kyoto Protocol in March 2001 because "it exempts 80 percent of the world, including major population centers such as China and India, from compliance, and would cause serious harm to the U.S. economy." The United States could abdicate leadership, pursue its own interests undeterred by an international treaty, and stand aside from concerns that affect humanity. This stance was and is of serious concern to a significant part of the American public and to the United States' allies. Yet Bush suffered little. He was putting America first.

Public opinion and political leadership in the United States are divided between this protectionist, "America first" tendency and an opposing internationalist tendency that favors free trade and a multilateral foreign policy. Under President Bush, the "America first" strain, which was already gaining ground before 9/11, has become predominant. The reaction to 9/11 recalls an analysis by the American political historian Richard

Hofstadter, who identified what he called a `paranoid style' in American politics. There have been periods in American history when conspiracy theories about alien influences, ranging from suspicion of international bankers during the Greenback and Populist era at the end of the nineteenth century to McCarthy's witch hunts in the early 1950s for suspected communists, have given a paranoid, even xenophobic, style to American politics. China is provoking such paranoia as well as the America-first tradition, and the resulting spectacle is not edifying. The anti-China sentiment that has surfaced in the last two or three years is obvious. Some of the twenty bills introduced in this period, aimed at retaliation against China or its imports, would have disastrous consequences. One bill would impose a 27.5 percent tariff on Chinese imports if China does not immediately revalue its currency, the renminbi, significantly. Another bill would set conditions for expelling China from the World Trade Organization, because allegedly China flouts the rules of free trade. Either bill would have an economic impact analogous to a unilateral missile attack. Flows of Chinese finance to support the dollar and U.S. asset prices would collapse; there would be a sell-off in world stock markets; Europe would have to follow the American lead and adopt U.S.-style to head off a flood of cheap Chinese exports being diverted to the European Union; and the Chinese economy would rapidly slow down with incalculable implications for its political stability.

The scope for miscalculation by either the United States or China is huge. These are two nationalist juggernauts, and the Chinese have very limited room to maneuver in responding to the United States' demands, presented with mounting urgency. In the first place a sudden revaluation of the renminbi would have a very depressive effect on the incomes of the 900 million Chinese living in peasant households, because it would lower China's food prices, keyed as they are to world price levels. It would damage savings, arrest export growth, slow down the economy, and raise the specter of a banking crisis. Second, to call for China to comply immediately with western and best Asian standards of corporate governance, transparency, and accountability is to force systemic change on China. Such change is vital and in my view inevitable, but these reforms must be handled with great sensitivity. Change can and will come, and external pressure should be applied, but not to the point that the fallout causes at least as much pain for the west as it does for China.[163]

James Mann in *The China Fantasy: How Our Leaders Explain Away Chinese Repression*[164] goes farther than Hutton and urges that America use more destabilizing, stepped up containment and confrontation strategies against China before China becomes stronger. He asserts that America should confront China and force it to become what we refer to as a Rights Society, Majority Rule Democracy with a Rule of Law System.

Mann recognizes that it may not be America and American companies that are integrating China and Chinese companies into the current international system, but the other way around:

> America has been operating with the wrong paradigm for China. Day after day, American officials carry out policies based upon premises about China's future that are at best questionable and at worst downright false.
>
> With China, the conceptual error the United States is making is in the opposite direction. This time, the failure lies not in America's inability to detect an important change, such as the rise of al Qaeda (I am specifically not arguing, as do some on the political Right, that China will turn into some unimaginable military threat to the United States in the future).
>
> On the contrary, in the case of China the mistake lies simply in the very assumption that change is coming. America hasn't thought much about what it might mean for the United States and the rest of the world to have a repressive, one-party state in China three decades from now, because it is widely assumed that China's political system 'is destined for far-reaching transformation'—that China is destined for a political liberalization, leading eventually to democracy. Yet while China will certainly be a richer and more powerful country a quarter century from now, it could still be an autocracy of one form or another. Its leadership (the Communist Party or whatever it calls itself in the future) may not be willing to tolerate organized political

opposition any more than it does today. That is a prospect with profound implications for America and the rest of the world. And it is a prospect that our current paradigm of an inevitably changing China cannot seem to envision.

The paradigm of a China on the road to political liberalization took hold in the United States because it has served certain specific interests within American society. At first, in the late 1970s and 1980s, this idea benefited America's national security establishment. At the time, the United States was seeking close cooperation with China against the Soviet Union, so that the Soviet Union would have to worry about both America and China at once; it was convenient for the Pentagon to make sure the Soviet Union tied down large numbers of troops along the Sino-Soviet border that might otherwise have been deployed in Europe. Amid the ideological struggles of the cold war, cooperation with China's Communist regime was politically touchy in Washington. So the notion that China was in the process of opening up its political system helped smooth the way with Congress and the American public.

In the 1990s, after the Soviet collapse, the paradigm of a politically changing China attracted a new constituency, in some ways more powerful than the Pentagon: the business community. As President Clinton used trade as a lever for improving human rights in China, he and his administration needed to divert attention from this embarrassing reversal. They did not wish to concede that they had just downgraded the cause of human rights in China; instead, they sought a new, positive-sounding description of their policy. "Integration" gradually became the label of choice, invoked by the president and his top advisers in press conference after press conference. Integration became, above all, the justification for unrestricted trade with China. "We believe it's the best way to integrate China further into the family of nations and to secure our interests and our ideals," declared Clinton in one typical speech.

George W. Bush and his advisers, without ever admitting they were doing so, perpetuated most of the essentials of Clinton's China policy, including the avowed commitment to integration. During Bush's second term, both Secretary of State Condoleezza Rice and former Deputy Secretary of State Robert Zoellick have given speeches about China that have called for integrating China into the international community.

"Integration" has thus become another catchphrase like "engagement," the earlier slogan for America's China policy, which originated during the administration of George H. W. Bush. The connotations of the two words are slightly different. Stripped of its pretensions, "engagement" simply meant that America's top leaders should keep on meeting with Chinese leaders (even if nothing ever happened as a result of those meetings). "Integration" means that the United States should not only talk with the Chinese leadership on its own, but also bring it into meetings with other governments and international organizations.

Despite the slightly different connotations, these two words have the same constituency within the United States: Those among America's elite who favor engagement also favor integration, and vice versa. With both words, the suggestion is the same: With enough engagement, with sufficiently vigorous integration, the United States may succeed in altering the nature of the Chinese regime—although it is not clear exactly how this is supposed to happen. In a way, the American approach is a bit patronizing to China: It sounds as if the United States is a weary, experienced trainer bringing China to a diplomatic version of obedience school. The fundamental problem with this strategy of integration is that it raises the obvious question "Who's integrating whom?" Is the United States now integrating China into a new international economic order based upon free market principles? Or, on the other hand, is China now integrating the United States into a new international political order where democracy is no longer favored and where a government's continuing dictatorship of all organized political opposition is accepted or…

This is not merely a government issue. Private companies —including Internet firms like Yahoo!, Google, and Microsoft— often use slogans like "engagement" and "integration" to explain why they have decided to do business in China, despite Chinese rules and laws that allow continuing censorship. "I think [the Internet] is contributing to Chinese political engagement," Bill Gates told one business gathering. Yet if Microsoft is altering its rules to accommodate China, once again the question is, who's changing whom?

If the world ends up thirty years from now with a Chinese

regime that is still a deeply repressive one-party state but is nevertheless a member of the international community in good standing, will that have been a success for the U.S. policy of integration? If so, that same China will serve as a model for dictators, juntas, and other undemocratic governments throughout the world —and, in all likelihood, a leading supporter of these regimes. China is already serving that function with respect to a number of dictatorships, from Burma to Zimbabwe.

Mann sets out the two current American policy approaches to China and urges a third approach be adopted. Mann ignores the problems in such approaches that Hutton addressed. Mann states:

> What should the United States do to encourage democratic change in China? A detailed list of policies can emerge only after we rid ourselves of the delusions and false assumptions upon which our China policy has long been based. Above all, we have to stop taking it for granted that China is heading inevitably for political liberalization and democracy. George W. Bush has continued to repeat the American mantra about China every bit as much as did his predecessors. "As China reforms its economy, its leaders are finding that once the door to freedom is opened even a crack, it cannot be closed," Bush declared in one typical speech. Such words convey a heartwarming sense of hopefulness about China but do not match the reality of China itself, where doors are regularly opened by more than a crack and then closed again. America's political and corporate leaders also need to stop spreading the lie that trade will bring an end to China's one-party political system. This fiction has been skillfully employed, over and over again, to help win the support of Congress and the American public for approval of trade with China. Trade is trade. It is not a magic political potion for democracy. Its benefits and costs are in the economic sphere; trade has not brought an end to political repression or the Chinese Communist Party's monopoly on power, and there is not the slightest reason to think it will do so in the future, either. In fact, it is possible that our trade with China is merely helping its autocratic regime to become richer and more powerful. America's current China policy amounts to an unstated bargain: We have abandoned

any serious attempt to challenge China's one-party state, and we have gotten in exchange the right to unfettered commerce with China.

What we need now, above all, are political leaders who are willing to challenge America's stale logic and phraseology concerning China. We need politicians who will call attention to the fact that America has been carrying out a policy that benefits business interests in both the United States and China far more than it helps ordinary working people in either country.

The reexamination should apply to both political parties and to both poles of the ideological spectrum On the Democratic Left, we need people who will question the assumptions that it is somehow "progressive" to say that democracy doesn't matter or to assume that it will automatically come to China someday. Such views aren't the least progressive, liberal, or enlightened. Rather they were developed by the Clinton administration to justify policies that would enable Bill Clinton to win corporate support. They were, during the 1990s, other views concerning China within the Democratic Party – those of Nancy Pelosi, for example, and George Mitchell, who took strong stands on behalf of human rights in China. The Democrats rejected those alternative approaches a decade ago and should reexamine them.

Within the Republican Party, we need people who are willing to challenge the Business Roundtable mentality that has dominated the party's thinking on China for so long. If Republicans really care about political freedom, why should they allow American policy toward China to be dominated by corporate interests, while the world's most populous country is governed by a single party that permits no political opposition. George W. Bush was able to conceal his business-oriented approach to hide behind a façade of hawkish rhetoric. Republicans should not allow this to happen again.

Once America finally recognizes that China is *not* moving toward democracy, we can begin to decide what the right approach should be. On the one hand, it is possible that America may seek new measures to goad the Chinese leadership toward democratic change. America also might want to reconsider its doctrinaire adhesion to free trade in dealing with China.

Alternatively, it's possible the American people may decide

that there's absolutely nothing the United States can or should do about a huge, permanently undemocratic, enduringly repressive China. As described in this book, such an entity, a Chinese autocracy persisting into the mid-twenty-first century, would cause large problems for American policy elsewhere in the world. Nevertheless, after weighing the costs and benefits of trying to push for democracy in China, America could opt for a policy of sheer acceptance of the existing order.

The American people are not being given such options now, because the choices are not being laid out. There is virtually no public debate about the Third Scenario. American politicians of both parties talk regularly as if liberalization and democracy are eventually coming to China —that is, that China will follow the Soothing Scenario. Or, occasionally, they raise the prospect of political upheaval in China, the Upheaval Scenario. But the Third Scenario? At the moment, that seems to be outside our public discourse. We need to think about it in order to figure out what we want.

It would be heartening if China's leaders proceed along the lines that America's political leaders predict. It would be wonderful if China opened up, either gradually or suddenly, to a new political system in which the country's 1.3 billion people are given a chance to choose their own leaders. While wishing for such an outcome, I will not hold my breath.[165]

Mann does not explain how America could "goad the Chinese leadership toward democratic change". Such goading is counterproductive and may limit China's desire to implement democratic change. Trade war would easily lead to armed conflict that would prevent any scenario beneficial to America or China. The fundamental issue in the Age of Species Lethal Weapons is that world-engulfing war must be prevented. As we emphasize, basing American foreign policy on the evangelization of America's ideals may reduce the Chinese government's interest in making the political changes that Americans desire. Such changes are a matter for the Chinese as a sovereign nation to decide, not a matter for American government interference. At the same time, American politicians express concern that Chinese investment in America could lead to political interference in America. Again, Fairness Hypocrisy is operating in such.

The problems that Americentric observers, such as Hutton and Mann are concerned with are more complex than Americentric observers can understand. The solutions to their views of China's problems are not self-evident. Americentric observers do not understand that possible solution to the problems Hutton and Mann address is not an Americentric solution.

The Chinese solutions will be Chinacentric for many reasons. China is not and never has been part of America. China has not been conquered by America as Japan and the former Soviet Union were. China has implemented the Principles of Peaceful Coexistence with America and all other nations, which, among other policies, have made China very successful without implementing America's "solutions." None the less, as Robert Zoellick stated in 2008: "It is sometimes hard to change successful models. It is prototypically American to say 'This worked well but now you have to change it.'" Such a "prototypical" American mindset towards China does not work to protect either America's or China's economic and national security.

The Impact of the European Enlightenment on China

The New School perspectives recognize the reality that observers with an Americentric perspective must accept in the circumstances of the 21st century - that there is more under the stars than their European generated Enlightenment philosophy. We must also accept, in order to be enlightened and realistic, that 1.5 billion Chinese have the right to progress socially and economically under what we refer to as a Permission Society, Consensus Democracy and Pre-Rule of Law System. Although 300 million Americans operate under a Rights Society model, it is currently alien to China's culture.

Observers with an Americentric perspective cannot accept the reality that China is very successful in the view of its people, even though it is not a copy of America's Rights Society, Majority Rule Democracy, and Rule of Law System. Hutton has asserted that China must adopt the values of the European Enlightenment for America and China to be partners. He is wrong. Mann has asserted that China will remain an autocracy and urges that America confront China now before it gets stronger. He rejects both the view of some American experts[214] that China will collapse and the view that as China adopts capitalism it will inevitably lead to the development of American style democratic institutions, free elections, an independent judiciary and progressive human rights policies.

Such 21st century observers with intellectual, ideological and emotional commitments that are akin to bias cannot tolerate such hearsay among those who must be saved from themselves. It makes no significant difference to them that the Chinese have their own ways of doing so. They cannot permit the Chinese to place a low priority on accepting the development of American style majority-rule-democracy, human rights and rule of law.

The New School's perspectives recognize that the Chinese, due to their culture and history, place a priority on harmony, desired by Tao, Confucius, and Buddha, rather than the Enlightenment's "dare to think" ethos. From an Americentric perspective, how dare the Chinese think that harmony, order and economic development are more pressing than daring to think and adopting destabilizing American style majority-rule-democracy? How dare the Chinese think having a Permission Society is more suitable than a Rights Society for their sovereignty and order?

It is compelling to many Americentric observers that the Chinese are either ignorant or wrong in accepting a Permission Society and need to adopt immediately a Rights Society model. This passionate Rights Society orthodoxy is strong in Americentric observers in spite of the reality that the Mainland Chinese's indigenous way of doing things *is* working successfully. China's success frightens Americentric observers. From their perspective, the American political system should be as importable into China's culture as Big Macs and blue jeans. But ideology is less importable than cultural influences and material things. If American Rights Society ideology is not automatically adopted, as Big Macs and blue jeans are in China, something is profoundly wrong, such observers assert. At an even more fundamental level, many Americentric observers assume that America must win and therefore China must lose.

Chinese Thought Processes and Values

China's leaders are aware of and admire the European Enlightenment. Premier Wen Jiabao noted during a speech in 2003 at Harvard that:

> On this year's Teacher's Day... I went to see Professor Ji Xianlin of Peking University in his hospital ward. Professor Ji is, is a great scholar in both Chinese and western learning, specializing in oriental studies. I enjoy reading his prose. We talked about the movement of "Eastern learning spreading to the West" and "Western learning spreading to the East". In the 17th and 18th centuries foreign missionaries translated Chinese classics into European languages and introduced them to Europe, and this aroused great interest in some eminent scholars and enlightenment thinkers there. Descartes, Leibniz, Montesquieu, Voltaire, Goethe and Kant all studied the traditional Chinese culture.
>
> In my younger days, I read Voltaire's writings. He said that a thinker who wanted to study the history of this planet must first turn his eyes to the East, China included. Interestingly, one and a half centuries ago, R.W. Emerson, the famous American philosopher and outstanding Harvard graduate, also fell for the traditional Chinese culture. He quoted profusely from Confucius and Mencius in his essays. He placed Confucius on a par with Socrates and Jesus Christ, saying that we read the moral teach-

ings of the Confucian school with profit today, though they were "addressed to a state of society unlike ours". Rereading these words of Voltaire and Emerson today, I cannot but admire their wisdom and farsightedness.

But the Chinese have more to think about than Enlightenment social theory. They must deal with China's indigenous intellectual tradition, and many other realities. China's leaders are far more aware of China's history, traditions and culture than the vast majority of Americentric observers. The Chinese admire America's idealism and achievements, *and in their own Chinese way*, which emphasizes social harmony and economic progress, are emulating them. Wen Jiabao also stated in his speech at Harvard University which he titled: "Turning Your Eyes to China:"

> China and the United States are far apart, and they differ greatly in the level of economic development and cultural background. I hope my speech will help increase our mutual understanding. In order to understand the true China- a changing society full of promises - it is necessary to get to know her yesterday, her today and her tomorrow.
>
> China yesterday was a big ancient country that created a splendid civilization. As we all know, in the history of mankind, there appeared the Mesopotamian civilization in West Asia, the ancient Egyptian civilization along the Nile in North Africa, the ancient Greek-Roman civilization along the northern bank of the Mediterranean, the ancient Indian civilization in the Indus River Valley in South Asia, and the Chinese civilization originating in the Yellow and Yangtze river valleys. Owing to earthquakes, floods, plagues or famines, or to alien invasions or internal turmoil, some of these ancient civilizations withered away, some were destroyed and others became assimilated into other civilizations. Only the Chinese civilization, thanks to its strong cohesive power and inexhaustible appeal, has survived many vicissitudes intact. The 5,000-year-long civilization is the source of pride for every Chinese.
>
> The traditional Chinese culture, both extensive and profound, starts far back and runs a long, long course. More than

2,000 years ago, there emerged in China Confucianism represented by Confucius and Mencius, Taoism represented by Lao Zi and Zhuang Zi, and many other theories and doctrines that figured prominently in the history of Chinese thought, all being covered by the famous term "the masters' hundred schools." From Confucius to Dr. Sun Yat-sen, the traditional Chinese culture presents many precious ideas and qualities, which are essentially populist and democratic. For example, they lay stress on the importance of kindness and love in human relations, on the interest of the community, on seeking harmony without uniformity and on the idea that the world is for all. Especially, patriotism as embodied in the saying "Everybody is responsible for the rise or fall of the country;" the populist ideas that "people are the foundation of the country" and that "people are more important than the monarch;" the code of conduct of "Don't do to others what you don't want others to do to you"; and the traditional virtues taught from generation to generation: long suffering and hard work, diligence and frugality in household management, and respecting teachers and valuing education. All these have played a great role in binding and regulating the family, the country and the society.

China today is a country in reform and opening-up and a rising power dedicated to peace. The late Dr. John King Fairbank used the following words to describe China's over-population and land scarcity. On the land owned by one farmer in the US, there might live hundreds of people forming a village in China. He went on to say that although the Americans were mostly farmers in the past, they never felt such pressure of population density. A large population and underdevelopment are the two facts China has to face. Since China has 1.3 billion people, any small individual shortage, multiplied by 1.3 billion, becomes a big, big problem. And any considerable amount of financial and material resources, divided by 1.3 billion, becomes a very low per capita level. This is a reality the Chinese leaders have to keep firmly in mind at all times.

We can rely on no one except ourselves to resolve the problems facing our 1.3 billion people. Since the founding of the People's Republic, we have achieved much in our national reconstruction; at the same time we have made a few detours and missed some opportunities. By 1978, with the adoption of the reform and opening-up policies, we had ultimately found the right path of development - the Chinese people's path of independently building socialism with Chinese characteristics. The essence of this path is to mobilize all positive factors, emancipate and develop the productive forces, and respect and protect the freedom of the Chinese people to pursue happiness.

In his poem, Malvern Hill, the famous American poet Herman Melville wrote: "Wag the world how it will, Leaves must be green in spring." The youth represents the future of the nation and the world. Faced with the bright prospect of China-US relations in the new century, I hope the young people of China and the US will join their hands more closely.

Chinese forefathers formulated their goals as follows: To ordain conscience for Heaven and Earth, To secure life and fortune for the people, To continue lost teachings from past sages, To establish peace for all future generations. Today, mankind is in the middle of a period of drastic social change. It would be a wise approach for all countries to carry forward their fine cultural heritages by tracing back their origin, passing on the essentials, learning from one another and breaking new ground. My appeal is that we work together with our wisdom and strength for the progress and development of human civilization. Our success will do credit to our forbearers and bring benefit to our posterity. In this way, our children and their children will be able to live in a more peaceful, more tranquil and more prosperous world. I am convinced that such an immensely bright and beautiful tomorrow will arrive!

The Contrasting Ways Chinese and Americans Think, Eat, Govern and Conduct Foreign Policy

The Chinese' consensus-oriented way mindset gives them an advantage in making prosperity and peace their priorities. Americans with zero sum mindsets do not yet realize it is fortunate that one of the world's leading civilizations exhibits a win-win mindset and bases their policies on the Principles of Peaceful Coexistence. It will be fortunate when America adopts more win-win, rhetoric and the Principles of Peaceful Coexistence as the basis of its foreign policy.

It is useful in finding a solution to the Human Extinction Challenge that what some American's describe as China's "Marxist-Leninist Dictatorship," but the New School describes as a "Permission Society" exhibits a more win-win mindset than America's Rights Society.

As we emphasized in Chapters 7, 8, 9, and 10 of Book 1, the power of factions and the dictatorship of the majority are dangerous problems for which America's Founding Fathers struggled to find solutions in America's Constitution. The Chinese have successfully dealt with the danger of factions by using a one-party system.

One of the key cultural patterns among today's Chinese leaders is their emphasis on "win-win" rhetoric that they have aligned with their foreign policies. American policymakers must protect the many benefits of China's foreign policy. "Win-win" policy is not as present in American culture behavior patterns as they are in China.

The Chinese seem more culturally attuned to "win-win" as well as zero sum mindsets than Americans. That difference has a profound consequence: since many Americans do not think the same way as the Mainland Chinese, they do not believe the Chinese are sincere when they speak in "win-win" terms. The Chinese realize that Americans do not understand that their emphasis on the "win-win" approach is not insincere propaganda, but reflective of their way of thinking. It is important that Americans finally understand that the Chinese's "win-win" foreign policy is sincere.

There are two major factors that could shift future Chinese governments away from the Principles of Peaceful Coexistence. The first is American military action against China. The second is the possibility that a successful future China will succumb to arrogance. Deng Xiaoping's policies were designed to counteract the provocation of American aggression or the hubris of future Chinese leaders. It is the responsibility of America's policymakers to prevent the first and it is the responsibility of Chinese policymakers to prevent the second. The partnership will assist in both regards.

The New School's perspectives draw the attention of Americans to the reality that the Mainland Chinese think in win-win terms. Americans, with their rule of law system, have that as the "social glue" that holds their society together. The Mainland Chinese, with their rule by law system use social cohesion oriented behavior (which we refer to as a "win-win mindset and strategies) to provide this "social glue."

Americans and Chinese, think and live in different ways but we believe that they are similar enough to be successful partners. However, the differences between their thought and social processes are essential because there are traits in typical Chinese emotional, thought and behavior processes that are culturally better suited to finding solutions to the Human Extinction Challenge.

For example, eating is a primal instinct. One of the most obvious differences between the behaviors of Americans and Chinese is how they eat. People who habitually share food from common plates, as the Mainland Chinese typically do, are better socially integrated than those who behave in a more individualistic manner. The social processes are manifested in the different approaches of the American and Chinese to sitting down to a table in a group. The Chinese style involves sharing food directly from plates served at the table. The American style typically involves each individual eating his own meal.

This is a particularly striking cultural difference because virtually all of those Chinese middle-age and older know what intense suffering from hunger is and have witnessed people starving to death during the Cultural Revolution. No similar proportion of Americans experienced hunger and witnessed starvation as personally as the vast majority of Mainland Chinese have. Yet the Chinese do not merely eat different food than Americans, they eat food differently. The difference between America and the Chinese styles of "social" as opposed to "solitary" eating habits are as profound as they are striking. Perhaps the example of how Mainland Chinese deal with food is further evidence that will help understand that the Chinese are sincere when they talk of desiring a "harmonious society" and "harmonious world." China's culture emphasize win-win behavior.

The Complementary Genius of the Chinese and American Cultures

A fundamental issue in the Age of Species Lethal Weapons and Science is whether the American government can accept China's Peaceful Coexistence Model As is examined in chapters 1, 2, 4, 6 and 7 of Book 2, Deng Xiaoping's Model of a peaceful economic rise is a win-win model that offers peace and prosperity to both China and other nations. It is compatible with the Responsible Stakeholder Model and James Baker Model.

America and China are capitalist superpowers that must be committed partners to reverse America's decline and preserve China's ascent. America and China must align their economic and national security priorities and synchronize their foreign and domestic goals. To achieve that, American policymakers must evolve beyond their traditional view of China as a threatening foe, "strategic competitor" or merely a "Responsible Stakeholder."

The Baker Model is a step towards accepting China as a major responsible nation or power and equal. We believe that America is making the transition towards a win-win relationship with China. The first step in this shift is the awareness that China's economic success will surpass America's. That is frightening, as are the profound economic crises America has recently suffered. But America is in a transition from arrogance to greater respect for China. American policymakers and people realize that China already has enormous economic resources and potential. Americans realize that China is very important to their economic recovery and future growth. That is a first step toward a new American mindset regarding China.

As Americans adjust their mindset towards China, China's already operating win-win mindset facilitate America's adoption of win-win strategies towards China. China's mindset and strategies exhibit what we refer to as the "genius" of China's culture. That genius has pioneered the Principles of Peaceful Coexistence. What we refer to as the "genius" of America's traditional idealism and respect for the rights of others can be very compatible with China's genius.

What is beginning to erode is the use of economic and military authority without moral authority which we refer to as the hubris of "uncharismatic American Exceptionalism." The next step is the acceptance of the undeniable fact that American economic regulation is not essential for China's economic success. That step is occurring. The necessary step after that is accepting that American Style Majority Rule Democracy is not essential for a society's success. China has been economically successful with the institutions and one-party-state system of government.

America has achieved economic prosperity and world leadership with its genius as a Rights Society. China has achieved them with its genius as a Permission Society. The genius of America's and China's partnership is possible because capitalism with American and Chinese characteristics must remain complementary for either nation to prosper peacefully in the Age of Species Lethal Weapons.

Presidents Jefferson and Hu Jintao are Both Correct

The New School's perspectives focus on President Jefferson's view that: "I know of no safe repository of the ultimate powers of society but the people themselves"[194] It also focuses on President Hu Jintao view that: "Western political systems would be a blind alley for China."[195] How can Hu Jintao be correct, and how can both Jefferson and Hu Jintao be correct, Americans and other observers will ask. The answer is that there is nothing inherently contradictory in these statements. President Jefferson is stating a hypothesis formulated as a universal proposition about human nature. President Hu Jintao was stating a hypothesis that Western political systems would be a blind alley which we take to mean that they would not work effectively to produce the political stability and economic growth that the Chinese people require. The New School's perspective is that in a partnership, America and China can empirically work out the relationship between them. The New School's perspectives are that:

1. Without the successful partnership, President Hu Jintao is correct that Western style political systems are a blind alley for China; and

2. Without the successful partnership, American style democracy would not be sustainable in America itself or in China in the 21st century; and

3. With the successful partnership, President Jefferson may be correct about the American people being a safe repository in the circumstances of the 21st century of the ultimate powers of society; and that

4. With the successful partnership, the type of political system Americans aspired to in Jefferson's lifetime may become universal some day.

Willy Wo-Lap Lam is an advocate of major political change in China. He is a professor in Japan, who was educated in Hong Kong, America, and Mainland China and was a journalist with *Asiaweek* news magazine, the *South China Morning Post* in Hong Kong, and CNN. In *Chinese Politics in the Hu Jintao Era: New Leaders, New Challenges*, published in 2006, his thesis is that:

1. It seems clear that short of cutting the Gordian knot called political liberalization, the Hu-Wen team cannot hope to make much advancement in either restructuring the economy or alleviating sociopolitical woes.

2. Whether the CCP leadership likes it or not, it must initiate

real and substantive liberalization of both the economic and political systems in the rest of this decade. To procrastinate further is to invite the possibility of a lose-lose situation for China and the world. And the globe has become too small and too integrated, and China too important, for any worthy Citizen of the World to afford this outcome.[166]

Willy Wo-Lap Lam does not provide support for either of these assertions. Like many Western observers, his theses are simply assumed to be self-evident correct. He also does not discuss whether the changes he asserts are essential in the four years from 2006 to 2010 would produce chaos or nirvana for China's 1.5 billion people. Although he criticizes President Hu and Premier Wen's policies, Willy Wo-Lap Lam's *Chinese Politics in the Hu Jintao Era: New Leaders, New Challenges*, does indicate that they are making major changes, albeit not the fast changes revolutionizing Mainland China he recommends:

> To date, Fourth Generation leaders such as Hu or Wen have refrained from talking about sensitive issues, such as a time frame for political reform. This is despite the fact that in internal discussions with his aides, Hu often referred to the imperative of timely liberalization of the political structure. For example, in an early 2004 meeting, Hu reportedly told his aides that 'without political reform, we may well get stuck in a cul-de-sac.' This was an echo of former patriarch Deng Xiaoping's famous exhortation in 1992. During his so-called imperial tour of the south in the summer of that year, the late patriarch famously said that 'without reform, there is only one road – to perdition.
>
> However, both Hu and Wen are cautious to a fault in their assessment of far reaching measures such as general elections. In his generally well-received speech at Harvard University in late 2003, Wen claimed that his administration was eager to 'perfect the election system.' However, he went on to say that while elections were already being held in 680,000 villages, 'we do not have the prerequisites for holding higher-level elections.'

He cited the familiar reason that economic development in China was uneven and that 'people's cultural qualities are not sufficient.' Wen asserted that his administration would not stray from the right path if it continued to allow the people to supervise the government.[167]

While recognizing President Hu and Premier Wen's and Deng Xiaoping's desire for political reform after a foundation of economic development and enculturation and (in the New School's view prudent) experiments with elections in 680,000 villages, Wo-Lap Lam nonetheless seems to then ignore the necessity of economic and cultural foundations being put in place from the most local political offices gradually to the highest offices. As we have emphasized in chapter 8 of Book 1, President Franklin Roosevelt in his Four Freedoms Speech recognized Freedom from Fear and Want were essential requirements for preserving Freedoms of Speech and Religion.

From the New School's perspective, Willy Wo-Lap Lam, like many observers, sees the speed rather than the success of political reforms as the key criterion. Speed without sustainable success in economic, social or political reform is not a responsible criterion for those with the daily responsibility for 22% of mankind, in an already economically progressing society.

Willy Wo-Lap Lam is of the view that:

> Moreover, there is a heavy element of noblesse oblige in Hu's approach to democracy: this means that while the ruling party is open enough to consult the divergent views of different sociopolitical groupings, it is not ready to share power with them. This top-down orientation was evident even when Hu was still vice-president. While attending a Chinese People's Political Consultative Conference (CPPCC) meeting in 2001, the Fourth-Generation leader said that the Chinese Communist Party (CPP) must 'take the initiative to accept the supervision of the democratic parties, and it must be able to listen to sharp criti-

cisms. (China has eight so-called democratic parties, which were formed in the early 1950s under the behest of the Communist Party. They are still under the tight control of the CCP United Front Department.) Through 2005, the party chief and president continued to define political liberalization in terms of platitudes such as 'boosting multiparty cooperation under CCP leadership' and 'improving the socialist legal system.'

There is no mistaking the fact that in the first months after the Sixteenth CCP Congress, the Hu-Wen government steered clear of more though-going political-reform measures such as popular elections and power sharing.

Soon after he became party general secretary in November 2002, Hu and Wen started working on what some analysts called Chinese-style glasnost. Hu and Wen started with gestures that are taken for granted in most other countries, for example, announcing the contents of just-ended or forthcoming party and government conferences. From the days of Mao to those of Jiang Zemin, most conclaves of top-level party meeting were shrouded in secrecy–with information made available only a long time afterward. From the Sixteenth CCP Congress onward, Hu and his colleagues made it a point to announce through the New China News Agency (NCNA) meetings of the Politburo as well as the rough agenda of each session. NCNA and other state media also made public the dates of major conferences such as the National People's Congress (NPC) or the plenary session of the Party Central Committee well in advance. For example, it was made known in August 2000 that the third Plenum of the Sixteen Central Committee would be held in October; and that the main theme would be economic reform and revision of the state constitution.

Hu and Wen have also bent over backward to protect the image of benign 'cadres of the masses.' Thus, on the eve of Chinese New Year in 2003, Wen joined miners in northeast Liaoning Province for a subterranean dinner of simple dumplings. On New Year's Day 2005, the premier paid an emotional visit to a child whose father had died in the horrendous coal mine disaster in Tongchuan, Shaanxi, a few months earlier. And while visiting Hong Kong in mid-2003, Wen eschewed the presidential suite – usually de rigueur for CCP leaders – and went about town with his aides in a minivan. Starting with his trip to Russia in

May 2003, Hu abolished send-off and welcome-back ceremonies for senior officials going abroad and coming home. The president later also did away with red-carpet welcome ceremonies when he inspected the provinces.

Yet the Hu-Wen leadership's most dramatic gesture in breaking with the past was the decision to abolish the annual series of top-level meetings at the summer resort of Beidaihe. Given that in the Byzantine world of Chinese politics, symbolism is sometimes as important as the real thing, Hu and Wen have won plaudits on this from liberal cadres and academics. Since the early 1950s, top CCP government, and military officials–as well as party elders–had in the summer of most years repaired to Beidaihe,… to discuss affairs of state. Major decisions on policy as well as personnel were made during 'informal discussion sessions' – often a euphemism for behind-the-scenes skulduggery and backstabbing – in luxurious beachside bungalows. And even though party elders were supposed to have retired from their party or state positions, they still exercised undue influence in Beidaihe's cunning corridors.

The abolition of Beidaihe, which reportedly incurred the ire of expresident Jiang, was much more than a means to save money. As former Chinese Academy of Social Sciences (CASS) sociologist Lu Jianhua indicated, what was more important was a new style of doing things, 'a new effort to regularize [government] procedures and institutions.' Other Beijing-based academics noted that the cancellation of the Beidaihe conferences was testimony to Hu's determination to curtail rule of personality and to run the party and country according to law and institutions.[168]

Willy Wo-Lap Lam also states:

…Hu has tried to base his new order on rule by law. This concept is to be distinguished from the familiar Western ideal of rule of law. What the Hu-Wen leadership has in mind is 'rule by law with Chinese characteristics' because Chinese law will always reflect the decision and spirit of party leadership. When Wen was asked by foreign reporters in early 2004 whether the party is above the Constitution and the law, the premier replied, 'the party leads the people in the formulation of the Constitution,' and said that party leaders and ordinary members would 'set an example in complying with the Constitution. In other words, unlike Western jurist and journalists, party leaders see no contradiction in Chinese-style rule by law on the one hand, and party leadership in the formulation of the constitution and the law on the other. At the very least, however, the Hu-Wen administration must ensure that the statutes are honored by cadres and ordinary people alike.[169]

Premier Wen Jiabao in 2004 stated that experience had cast doubt on its validity of reform that depends on the success in only one aspect of reform. Taking the medium-to-long-term view, the reform of the economic system and that of the political system, which includes people's mindsets, cannot be separated from each other. Premier Wen Jiabao has said:

> Like other countries, the development of democracy [in China] requires a process [of evolution]. …because China is too big and populous and because its development is uneven, we can only have direct elections at the village level.[170]

President Hu Jintao told a group of leading American academics in 2002, when asked about the prospects for grassroots elections, that the experience in many Chinese villages had shown that people voted along 'clan' lines in which voters were more likely to cast their votes for candidates with the same surname as theirs.[171]

Americans must factor into their analysis that in President Jefferson's life time and for many decades afterwards, voting rights were restricted property owners. Note that President Jefferson was not addressing a system that had universal adult suffrage or even a consensus on which adults were entitled to voting rights. Another reality is the difference in American and Chinese history: China today has not developed American style electoral systems and is progressing without them. The New School perspective is that China would not have been able to produce the economic development if it were a Rights Society.

Willy Wo-Lap Lam also states:

> A key to Hu's statecraft is that even without the trappings of Western-style political institutions such as multiparty and parliamentary democracy, the CCP leadership can still get it right –scientifically right – regarding economic and social development....The Hu-Wen leadership has also come up with a 'scientific theory of development'...The post 1978 CCP leadership is dominated by engineers... and believe in the virtues of social engineering.[172]

The New School's perspective is that President Jefferson's hypothesis states both assessments of and hopes about "human nature," the "good society" and "social progress." President Jefferson's hypothesis is compatible with the Chinese President's assessment of where China is in its evolution, its open mindedness and about China's future development. Americans must step back from both the charismatic and uncharismatic forms of American Exceptionalisms' and its hopes and demands for a "big bang" shift from one-party to two-party rule in China. The big bang approach used in the former Soviet Union did not work well for it.

Jefferson's hypothesis and Hu Jintao's assessment of China's current developmental stage are compatible because both countries are works in progress. Only time will tell whether the Chinese will accept Jefferson's universal hypothesis. It is their choice to make.

President Jefferson and President Hu Jintao and Premier Wen Jiabao were and are insightful leaders responsible for guiding their civilizations through the challenges of defining their futures. Only time will tell what arrangements should emerge from the character of the American and Chinese people. President Jefferson was using America's then-fledgling democracy's ethos, which were less advanced than what American majority-rule-democracy would become after Jefferson's death. President Lincoln had to wage a four year civil war in order for American Constitutional majority-rule-democracy to become what it is today.

Even now, American majority-rule-democracy is a work in progress and may be manipulated by organized factional interests. American democracy as it was before George W. Bush entered office may have had liberties that some Americans, such as neo-conservatives and authoritarian Americans, did not think were appropriate for America's circumstances.

President Washington's Farewell Advice also included the following advice:

> The alternate domination of one faction over another, sharpened by the spirit of revenge natural to party dissension, which in different ages & countries has perpetrated the most horrid enormities, is itself a frightful despotism. But this leads at length to a more formal and permanent despotism. The disorders & miseries, which result, gradually incline the minds of men to seek security & repose in the absolute power of an Individual: and sooner or later the chief of some prevailing faction more able or more fortunate than his competitors, turns this disposition to the purposes of his own elevation, on the ruins of Public Liberty.
>
> ...It agitates the Community with ill founded Jealousies and false alarms, kindles the animosity of one part against another, foments occasionally riot & insurrection. It opens the door to foreign influence & corruption...
>
> It is important, likewise, that the habits of thinking in a free Country should inspire caution in those entrusted with its Administration, to confine themselves within their respective Constitutional Spheres; avoiding in the exercise of the Powers of one department to encroach upon another. The spirit of encroachment tends to consolidate the powers of all the departments in one, and thus to create whatever the form of government, a real despotism. A just estimate of that love of power, and proneness to abuse it, which predominates in the human heart, is sufficient to satisfy us of the truth of this position. The

necessity of reciprocal checks in the exercise of political power; by dividing and distributing it into different depositories, & constituting each the Guardian of the Public Weal against invasions by the others, has been evinced by experiments ancient & modern; some of them in our country & under our own eyes. To preserve them must be as necessary as to institute them. If in the opinion of the People, the distribution or modification of the Constitutional powers be in any particular wrong, let it be corrected by an amendment in the way which the Constitution designates. But let there be no change by usurpation; for though this, in one instance, may be the instrument of good, it is the customary weapon by which free governments are destroyed. The precedent must always greatly overbalance in permanent evil any partial or transient benefit which the use can at any time yield.

In China today there are those who propose that a multi-party system replace the one-party system of government. This is not a reform that is likely to preserve China's economic development, Given the enormous economic and military crises that America's two party system has produced, China's one-party system looks far better for China under present circumstances than experimenting with multiparty systems. The issue is not how fast multi-party, majority-rule electoral and legislative systems come to China. The issue is whether they are sustainable for either America or China. The New School's perspective is that it would be catastrophic for America to degenerate into a Permission Society or for China to prematurely adopt a Rights Society model. Each nation must make its own system work successfully.

Mankind has before it the American Experiment, with its Rights Society model, and China with its Permission Society model. Today, America and China restrict voting rights and select their leaders, in their own ways. But in both countries, leaders do not seize power unconstitutionally. As we emphasize in Book 1, there is no uniformly accepted formula that defines "human nature," "the good society," and "social progress." Each society defines these concepts differently but there is one common "law" governing every human being at all time, the laws of physics. In our view, there is another "law" that is sufficiently respected among human beings to be customary moral authority. The diversity of our species and our universal traits are the mix of different numerators that are governed by these common denominators of physics and moral authority.

The New School's perspective is that today America and China are both "governments of the people, by the people, for the people." In China, this has translated into "development for the people, by the people, and its achievements shared by the people." Each system of government is deeply entrenched in its civilization's culture and traditions. The Chinese government and people have generated and accept the one-party state political system, because it has worked successfully since 1978.

The American Experiment as a Rights Society must now respond to the reemergence of China as the wealthiest and most innovative economy in the world. It must do so amid the suffering and chaos of America's badly damaged financial system. America's economic rise occurred in a period of China's political instability and economic weakness, in which it played a very minor role in the global economy. In the 21st century, China's Permission Society is politically stable, has embraced capitalism, and is progressing economically and socially. America's Experiment is not thriving in the ways that it has historically. This dichotomy and the remedies to America's growing economic challenges are examined in Books 1 and 2, *America and China's Emerging Partnership: A New Realistic Perspective* and *America & China's Economic New Partnership Strategy*.

China is a Permission Society, in spite of the popularity of American Exceptionalism. The realities of America's current economic crises and China's GDP growth and successful economic management are strong reasons for the Chinese that China remain a Permission Society. Also the Chinese people see Western political systems as foreign and inappropriate as long as China's political stability and economic development. Finally, China is wise to make Freedom from Fear and Want priorities and to make political changes suited to China's needs rather than America's preferences.

The real contrast is not between America and China, but between Mao Zedong and Deng Xiaoping, Jiang Zemin, Hu Jintao and Wen Jiabao's and their different Chinese models. Americans must recognize this difference, which is profound, and not respond to 21st century China with 20th century American perspectives.

No Need for a Civil War Among Mankind: A Divided World Can Stand

The United States of America defeated the Confederate States of America through military authority. But Lincoln dedicated his Gettysburg address to the dead on both sides of the struggle. That is the difference between foolish partisanship and moral genius. President Lincoln's distillation of the definition of America into the ambiguous phrase "government of the people, by the people and for the people" became shorthand for a form of government that is effective, representative, and seeks the welfare of its citizens. The phase was also defined by the context of Lincoln's time in which European monarchs, later displaced by elected or revolutionary governing bodies, had not been swept away by World War I. Lincoln's use of the phrase is also defined by the contemporary right of people to make other people property, which was controversial enough to require four years of civil war.

There is a way that America's and China's approaches to government can be compatible: through a partnership. The New School's perspectives emphasize that compatibility in a committed genuine partnership is the most likely way to preserve the liberal democratic ideals and security needs of Americans.

The Charisma of Embracing the Impossible When it is the Only Thing that can Work

Genius in leadership requires that both nations make the 21st century's fundamental issue America and China's priority. Can both countries produce leaders with that priority and the genius to ensure collaboration between nations and civilizations? America's and China's leaders and people must combine, and increase their moral, economic and military authority to be able to lead a peaceful world community.

The Power of Moral Military Authority

Gandhi asserted that moral authority was the strongest force known to mankind, that which no weapon was more powerful. America's and China's leaders need not be reticent about asserting the power of moral authority, as even Gandhi was when contemplating the most challenging audience. Here is a letter Gandhi wrote to Hitler:

23/7/'39

Dear friend,

Friends have been urging me to write to you for the sake of humanity. But I have resisted their request, because of the feeling that any letter from me would be an impertinence. Something tells me that I must not calculate and that I must make my appeal for whatever it may be worth. It is quite clear that you are today the one person in the world who can prevent a war which may reduce humanity to the savage state. Must you pay that price for an object however worthy it may appear to you to be? Will you listen to the appeal of one who has deliberately shunned the method of war not without considerable success? I anticipate your forgiveness, if I have erred in writing to you.

I remain,
Your sincere friend,
M. K Gandhi. [173]

Gandhi was asked after World War II whether his non-violent campaigns could have succeeded with Hitler as they succeeded in England. He responded that they would but that many people would be killed in the process. He added that many were killed in the process of stopping Hitler with violence.

The New School's perspective is not asserting that reliance on moral authority alone is sufficient but rather that the combination of moral, economic, and military authority is. Moral authority is about responsibility to others. The prevention of the destruction of mankind is essential to America, and China, perhaps the ultimate source of moral authority transcending the boundaries of civilizations and nations.

Chapter 10

The Charisma of a Rights Society and Permission Society's Harmony

Overview

The charisma of a partnership of America and China that implements the Principles of Peaceful Coexistence is essential for the sustainability of America's and China's Ideals.

The Charismatic Example of a Partnership of a Rights Society and a Permission Society

Capitalism triumphed over communism in the 20th century. American foreign policy must meet a different challenge now. America's Right's Society must align itself with China's successful Permission Society Many nations in need of economic progress, need to align themselves with China's economic success.

It has been possible for America to globalize capitalism, but not as a copy of American capitalism or liberal democracy, as the success of capitalism with Chinese characteristics shows. Pragmatically,

America faces a challenge to their Ideals of human rights which are based on tolerance of the opinions and rights of others, and to the imposition of these Ideals.

There is an inherent contradiction in America's *wishing* and *demanding* that other nations copy it. But that contradiction is reconciled if, instead of demanding that other nations copy them, Americans instead make their behavior the argument for these Ideals. America did that in helping to win World Wars I and II and creating the Marshall and Dodge Plans. Americans must exemplify the Ideals they wish others to emulate: their economic and military authority cannot impose them. To be persuasive about the merit of American Ideals Americans must manifest their value propositions in their thoughts and actions. "Do as I say, not as I do" behavior degrades the moral authority of the idealism that American Ideals have among mankind.

The successful partnership of America and China is essential for many reasons. Among the most important is that America and China, as the mankind's current superpower and emerging mega superpower, have very different cultures, systems of government and powerful capitalist economies. If the world's largest Rights Society and Permission Society cannot be partners it will exacerbate the clashes among the other nations producing conflict between Rights Societies and Permission Societies.

American leaders face challenges in living up to their ideals and their universal applicability that include:

1. America's transition from a Permission Society to a Rights Society took hundreds of years and arose under special circumstances.
2. It is not possible to respect the rights of self-determination of nations, which underpins any hope of the reciprocal respect of rights that a peaceful world requires, and
3. It is not possible for American military and economic author-

ity to impose its Ideals that are not indigenous to the nations, such as China.

4. The fate of mankind will be determined by whether majority-rule-democracies can accept the right of self-determination of non majority-rule-democracies and whether the nations that are not majority-rule-democracies will accept the success of majority-rule-democracies.

5. Only if America and China can respect their different one and two-party ways of governing themselves, by their example, and with the combination of their economic, military and moral authority, will they be able to limit and ameliorate conflict within, between, and among Rights Societies and Permission Societies and civilizations.

6. America must align its economic success with China's in order not to be economically dwarfed.

China is not making the evangelization of its Permission Society Model a priority since the death of Mao Zedong.

Will America Become a Permission Society Before China Can Become a Rights Society?

There are appalling scenarios in which America's Rights Society Model fails by competing unsuccessfully with China's Permission Society economy:

1. America could devolve into a Permission Society with weakened rule of law, human rights and majority-rule-electoral features inconsistent with America's Constitution's Ideals. That is intrinsically a horrible prospect, and would prevent China's evolution into a Rights Society. That is examined in chapters 7, 8, and 9 of Book 1.

2. America could degrade into a Permission Society with weak-

ened rule of law, human right, policymaking and electoral features inconsistent with America's Constitution's ideals and requirements as they have been defined in America's development phase as China evolves into a Rights Society.

3. China's growing wealth and educational achievements might result in China evolving rule of law and human rights protections. But America's deterioration into a Permission Society could stop China's evolution into a Right Society.

America, China and Mankind at the Crossroads to Prosperity and Peace or War and Ruin

The current international system was developed in a world in which China was not participating. It remains one of the poorest nations and is not benefiting from the existing international system. It is unrealistic to expect that the current system is merely going to recognize new "stakeholders" now that China has become the world's fastest growing economy in the world's most populated nation. That the global financial crises has destroyed the status quo supports what Michael Mandelbaum asserted in *The Case for Goliath: How America Acts as the World's Government* examined in chapter 3 of Book 1. Too many nations have been harmed by the existing international system. The readjustment could be fractious as well as traumatic. The redesign of the international system requires the collaborative equilibrium only achievable with a successful partnership of America and China.

Fortunately, China's culture and behavior emphasizes win-win value propositions that have come from the implementation of the Principles of Peaceful Coexistence. That offers America an important role in achieving a Harmonious World. Americans must now accept China's peaceful development that focuses on economic development and peaceful relations as a responsible great power. America must help lead in implementing China's harmonious world model.

America's Hemgemony Model is not sustainable.

It is hard to understand things that are outside one's own mindset. Americans typically do not understand the Chinese mindset developed in Permission Society contexts which are so different from American and European mindsets developed in Rights Society contexts. Americans must move beyond projecting their mindset onto China and viewing China's escape from hunger as a threat and challenge to America. *China's policy is to not be a threat to America.*

What President Kennedy referred to as "Pax Americana" remains America's agenda. Michael Mandelbaum examines the Pax Americana Model in *The Case For Goliath: How America Acts As The World's Government In The 21st Century.*[174] President Kennedy realized in 1963 that a Pax Americana could not work. That is why we have examined Presidents Washington, Lincoln, Franklin Roosevelt and Kennedy's genius for peace and compared their advice with the conventional perspectives of America's presidential candidates, policymakers, and scholars on the perpetuation of the 20th century international system that America dominates.

The advice of the four presidents who saved America from failure is different from the conventional American perspective but it is similar in many ways to Deng Xiaoping's advice. Deng Xiaoping realized that resisting a Pax Americana should not be allowed to distort China's priorities. It is precisely played an increasingly influential role in implementing the Principles of Peaceful Coexistence that the interests of America and China can be aligned successfully, so long as America, like China, makes prosperity and peace its priorities and progresses beyond:

1. the Pax Americana Model;
2. the Principles of Conflict among nations; and
3. its sum mindset and conventional strategies.

Americans need to reflect on the hypothesis that China's Harmonious World Model presents a better agenda for America and the new international system than its conventional Pax Americana Model. American policymakers and a people must adopt China's Harmonious World Model and emulate its behavior because:

1. The other 190 nations are considering China's model and approach.
2. The Chinese are *sincerely* committed to prosperity and peace and recognize that they must be shared with nations to be expanded within China.
3. China's economic, military, and moral authority has established the foundation of its Harmonious World Model.
4. China wants to partner with America in providing a Harmonious World Model to the dangers that the global financial system, international system, and Pax Americana are struggling with.
5. America can protect its global leadership, Ideals, and economic interests far better in a partnership with China than with a zero sum mindset in a declining economic, Pax Americana Model.
6. As the realities of the 21st century unfold, the Pax Americana Model will cost more than Americans can spend.
7. America can either lead with China in forming a Harmonious World based on the Principles of Peaceful Coexistence or let the Principles of Conflict undermine its economic and geopolitical security.

The view of most of other nations is that although China's rapidly increasing economic authority is alarming its unprecedented economic leap is beneficial to all other nations and consistent with its Harmonious World Model. This is reassuring to many nations that are affected China's success and gives China increasing moral authority. China will ensure that it has sufficient military authority to defend itself but also that its ambitions are peaceful. That makes all the difference in the rise of a great power and makes perfect sense in the Age of Species Lethal Weapons and Science. China's vision of a harmonious international system is attractive to many nations. It offers greater respect and fulfillment of the needs of other nations than America's more selfishly focused use of economic and military authority. The Harmonious World Model has charisma similar to that of the Pax America Model from 1945 to 1950. Americans need to implement the advice of the four presidents to whom they are most indebted in order to embrace the advice of Deng Xiaoping.

Chapter 11

The Unique Potential of Human Rights in a Harmonious World

Overview

The moral authority of America's and China's partnership and the charisma of American and Chinese Exceptionalism that must police and pacify mankind is essential for the successful operation of a new international system.

No nation or group of nations can rule or run the world using the Principles of Conflict in the Age of Species Lethal Weapons and Science. The successful, permanent partnership of America and China, operating on the Principles of Peaceful Coexistence is essential for either America or China or the other 190 nations to successfully safeguard their own economic and national security needs.

The new international system emerging in 21st century is driven by the emergence from poverty and growing influence of many developing nations, which that did not participate in the designing or dominate the of the international system designed and dominated by America and the other developed nations in the 20th century.

The New School's perspective is that American attempts to "tinker" with the 20th century international system cannot adequately serve the interests of other nations, particularly in the aftermath of the 2008 global financial crisis. As a result, these attempts will not meet the needs of America. America must adopt the Principles of Peaceful Coexistence as the basis for its foreign policy, as China has.

America will find that if it offers more win-win value propositions to other nations that the United Nations will become a valuable means of safe guarding American national security. It is America's conventional foreign policy that makes the United Nations ineffective. America's changes will not solve all other nations' behavior, but they will improve stabilization and give America enhanced moral authority. The United Nations will be a more effective means of safe guarding America's national security needs when America's priorities become ensuring economic development and peace. America will not preserve its security if it continues with its conventional the goals of seeking to sustain superpower hegemony.

America and China, as genuine partners, must ensure that the United Nations operates as an effective forum for developed and developing nations. America and China must also ensure that the United Nations effectively polices the enforcement of the Principles of Peaceful Coexistence. As the Age of Species Lethal Weapons and Science evolves the world's nations need the stability and economic progress that America's and China's collaborative leadership roles in the United Nations. The developed and developing nations need the example and benefits of collaboration rather than the clash of the American and Chinese civilizations and America's Rights and China's Permission Societies.

In addition, these nations need the examples of both models of government. The two models have different perspectives on "human nature" and how to provide their respective citizens with "good government," a "good society," and "social progress." The Permission Society Model suits some societies and the Rights Model others. Some societies will shift between models. Sometimes such shifts will be successful innovations and sometimes they will be the indict of "failed states." Each nation's shifts should be determined the nation "by itself, for itself, of itself" pursuant to the principle of self-determination.

America's and China's successful partnership may facilitate the integration of the Ideals of American and Chinese Exceptionalism. The stable foundation of Harmonious World Exceptionalism is essential for any sustainable adoption of American Exceptionalism. It is not possible for either country's charismatic Exeptionalism to be realized except in the successful partnership of America and China.

The Relationship of Nations is Innately both a Zero Sum and Win-Win Game

Individuals, groups of people (i.e. factions), factions, nations and civilizations compete with each other. Some people and nations lose and others win. The results to date of experiments by nations, such as the adoption of Marx's economic theories, to eliminate or ameliorate or manage the zero sum game features in human nature have largely been economically unsuccessful and therefore unsustainable. The New School's perspectives, enlightened by the recognition of the need to solve the Human Extinction Challenge, addresses the problem that we currently live in a Principles of Conflict based on zero sum game world that requires win-win outcomes in the Age of Species Lethal Weapons and Science.

The creation of the United Nations, with its Charter seeking to operate and institutionalize the Principles of Peaceful Coexistence among mankind was, like the creation of the Age of Species Lethal Weapons and Science, a result of the last World War. But, the Principles of Conflict in human nature lessen its effectiveness of the United Nations in fulfilling the goals of its Charter. China is the only large nation that has been able to transcend the Principles of Conflict in its economic and foreign policies and defense strategies to date.

America's relationship with the United Nations and its Charter needs to be "realistic". To do so, Americans must be realistic in understanding the *limitations* on America military and economic authority. During the first eight years of the 21st century America has not acted appropriately in its relationship with the United Nations.

The United Nations Charter is patterned on the American Constitution in many ways. America's relationship with the United Nations manifests both the *win-win value propositions and the zero sum game decision making processes* found in the American Constitution. Both within America and within America's and its role in the United Nations, the reciprocal rights enshrined in the American Constitution and the United Nations Charter clash with and are vulnerable to the majority-rule and the veto powers of powerful minorities found in both America and the United Nations. In other words, the ideals and missions of the American Constitution and of the United Nation's Charter seek to protect and promote can be either furthered or negated by the outcomes of majority-rule-decisions and vetoes of determined, powerful factions pursuing their own subjective assessments of what is in their self-interest. Within America, presidential vetoes can be overridden, by majority rule decisions of the Senate and House of Representatives if the political will on a particular issue is sufficient. However, within the United Nations, America's veto, and four other nation's vetoes, can block things a particular American government of the day does not like or which any of seven other powerful nations do not like.

Under Article 27 of the UN Charter, Security Council decisions on all substantive matters require the affirmative votes of nine members. A negative vote, or veto, by a permanent member prevents adoption of a proposal, even if it has received the required 9 affirmative votes. Abstention is not regarded as a veto. Since the Security Council's inception, China has used its veto 6 times; France

18 times; Russia/USSR 123 times; the United Kingdom 32 times; and the United States 82 times. The majority of Russian/Soviet vetoes were in the first ten years of the Council's existence. Since 1984, China (ROC/PRC) has vetoed 3 resolutions; France 3; Russia/USSR 4; the United Kingdom 10; and the United States 43. Procedural matters are not subject to a veto, so the veto cannot be used to avoid discussion of an issue.

The Security Council had five permanent members who were originally drawn from the victorious powers after World War II:

1. The French Republic
2. The Republic of China
3. The Union of Soviet Socialist Republics
4. The United Kingdom of Great Britain and Northern Ireland
5. The United States of America

Before the establishment of the Security Council, USSR and UK were against the Republic of China ("ROC") membership, but the USA insisted that the ROC be on the Security Council. President Roosevelt recognized the importance of China, with its population of then four hundred million. He preferred a rising friend rather than enemy in the future, and hoped that including China would make the Security Council more representative. Deng Xiaoping advised the Chinese to always remember this and other American acts of respect for China. After the 1949 Revolution, the Peoples Republic of China was recognized as a successor state and replaced the Republic of China as a permanent member of the Security Council.

Ten other members of the Security Council are elected by the General Assembly for two-year terms, with five replaced each year. The members are chosen by regional groups and confirmed by the United Nations General Assembly. The African bloc chooses three members; the Latin America and the Caribbean, Asian, and Western European blocs choose two members each; and the Eastern

European bloc chooses one member and one of these members is an Arab country, alternately from the Asian or African bloc.

America's veto power is powerful but cannot build consensus for things that an American government wants, but other nations on the Security Council do not accept. In the experience of the Presidency of George W. Bush, Americans have the lesson of what America has aspired unsuccessfully to do at the United Nations. America's first presidential administration in the 21st century made a deplorable contribution, by showing serious dangers within both the frameworks of the American Constitution and the United Nations Charter. In the 21st century, the first President viewed it as desirable to mislead the United Nations in the attempt to gain approval of the regime-change War in Iraq, and sought to ignore the United Nations when it would not endorse America's self-interest. That American administration sought to undermine the effectiveness of the United Nations in many ways, such as the appointment of John Bolton as American Ambassador to the United Nations, who was consistently hostile to the United Nations. That Administration was able to circumvent submitting John Bolton for approval as America's Ambassador to the United Nations by the Senate and House of Representatives. The American President knew John Bolton's appointment would not be confirmed and used a Congressional recess appointment to avoid the congressional approval process in 2005 and 2006. Such a choice of ambassador and the method of his appointment exemplify the principle of what we term "might is right." In an international system based on the principle of might is right, rather than right is might, no nation, is safe.

As the world's sole superpower, America's behavior is either an inspiring or terrible example to other nations that endanger to mankind's survival. The sometimes misconceived self-interest of America, undermines the United Nations and International law. The behavior of America makes the United Nations ineffective in solving many dangerous international problems.

If the United Nation's Charter cannot be made to operate successfully by its sovereign nation members, then its mission cannot operate successfully. The consequences in the Age of Species Lethal Weapons and Science include human extinction.

The United Nations was created to respond to the dangers of the Age of Species Lethal Weapons and Science. It can be said that what is at stake is whether there is a safe repository for the ultimate powers of mankind. If a democracy cannot manage the nations of the world based on the Principles of Peaceful Coexistence, then no power on earth can operate a stable international system in the new economy.

A Dilemma Americans Face

The preambles of the American Constitution and the United Nations Charter differ. The purpose set out in the American Constitution is the American peoples' pursuit of life, liberty and happiness. The purpose set out in the United Nations Charter is avoiding further world wars, which have become far too dangerous to mankind's survival. If the pursuit of life, liberty, and happiness cannot align with the pursuit of prosperity of mankind under the United Nations Charter, then the life, liberty and the pursuit of happiness of the American people will not be sustainable.

The American people and each Presidential administration face that dilemma. Americans face the choice of what potential definitions of what "life, liberty and the pursuit of happiness" mean, and whether such definitions are more important priorities than preventing another world war. The American people and each new Presidential administration must recognize this dilemma and solve it by accepting the primacy of purpose set out in the United Nations Charter. It was largely crafted by American policymakers who had experienced two world wars.

The Moral Authority of American Ideals of Human Rights in China's Ideal of a Harmonious World

America led in the creation of the United Nations and the drafting of its Charter and mission. Its wisdom in doing so must be revitalized so it can protect the world's economic and national security in the post 9/11 Age of Species Lethal Weapons and Science.

The Charter of the United Nations opens with the Preamble:

WE THE PEOPLES OF THE UNITED NATIONS DETERMINED

To save succeeding generations from the scourge of war, which twice in our lifetime has brought untold sorrow to mankind, and

To reaffirm faith in fundamental human rights, in the dignity and worth of the human person, in the equal rights of men and women and of nations large and small, and

To establish conditions under which justice and respect for the obligations arising from treaties and other sources of international law can be maintained, and

To promote social progress and better standards of life in larger freedom

AND FOR THESE ENDS

To practice tolerance and live together in peace with one another as good neighbors, and

To unite our strength to maintain international peace and security, and

To ensure, by the acceptance of principles and the institution of methods, that armed force shall not be used, save in the common interest, and

To employ international machinery for the promotion of the economic and social advancement of all peoples,

HAVE RESOLVED TO COMBINE OUR EFFORTS TO ACCOMPLISH THESE AIMS

Accordingly, our respective Governments, through representatives assembled in the city of San Francisco, who have exhibited their full powers found to be in good and due form, have agreed to the present Charter of the United Nations and do hereby establish an international organization to be known as the United Nations.

The first six Articles in the United Nations Charter state the purpose and criteria for membership in the United Nations:

Article 1

The Purposes of the United Nations are:

1. To maintain international peace and security, and to that end: to take effective collective measures for the prevention and removal of threats to the peace, and for the suppression of acts of aggression or other breaches of the peace, and to bring about by peaceful means, and in conformity with the principles of justice and international law, adjustment or settlement of international disputes or situations which might lead to a breach of the peace;

2. To develop friendly relations among nations based on respect for the principle of equal rights and self-determination of peoples, and to take other appropriate measures to strengthen universal peace;

3. To achieve international co-operation in solving international problems of an economic, social, cultural, or humanitarian character, and in promoting and encouraging respect for human rights and for fundamental freedoms for all without distinction as to race, sex, language, or religion; and

4. To be a centre for harmonizing the actions of nations in the attainment of these common ends.

Article 2

The Organization and its Members, in pursuit of the Purposes stated in Article 1, shall act in accordance with the following

Principles.

1. The Organization is based on the principle of the sovereign equality of all its Members.
2. All Members, in order to ensure to all of them the rights and benefits resulting from membership, shall fulfill in good faith the obligations assumed by them in accordance with the present Charter.
3. All Members shall settle their international disputes by peaceful means in such a manner that international peace and security, and justice, are not endangered.
4. All Members shall refrain in their international relations from the threat or use of force against the territorial integrity or political independence of any state, or in any other manner inconsistent with the Purposes of the United Nations.
5. All Members shall give the United Nations every assistance in any action it takes in accordance with the present Charter, and shall refrain from giving assistance to any state against which the United Nations is taking preventive or enforcement action.
6. The Organization shall ensure that states which are not Members of the United Nations act in accordance with these Principles so far as may be necessary for the maintenance of international peace and security.
7. Nothing contained in the present Charter shall authorize the United Nations to intervene in matters which are essentially within the domestic jurisdiction of any state or shall require the Members to submit such matters to settlement under the present Charter; but this principle shall not prejudice the application of enforcement measures under Chapter VII.

The original Members of the United Nations shall be the states which, having participated in the United Nations Conference on International Organization at San Francisco, or having previously signed the Declaration by United Nations of 1 January 1942, sign the present Charter and ratify it in accordance with Article.

Article 4

1. Membership in the United Nations is open to all other peace-loving states which accept the obligations contained in the present Charter and, in the judgment of the Organization, are able and willing to carry out these obligations.
2. The admission of any such state to membership in the United Nations will be effected by a decision of the General Assembly upon the recommendation of the Security Council.

Article 5

A Member of the United Nations against which preventive or enforcement action has been taken by the Security Council may be suspended from the exercise of the rights and privileges of membership by the General Assembly upon the recommendation of the Security Council. The exercise of these rights and privileges may be restored by the Security Council.

Article 6

A Member of the United Nations which has persistently violated the Principles contained in the present Charter may be expelled from the Organization by the General Assembly upon the recommendation of the Security Council.

The United Nation's Charter is based upon the Principles of Peaceful Coexistence, but the United Nation's mission must contend with the Principles of Conflict in human nature.

The No Surrender Approach to America's Definition of its Self-interest

John Bolton's appointment as America's Ambassador to the United Nations, is a classic example of an attempt by America to reduce the influence of the United Nations, which is a sort of democracy of nations and court of international opinion that deliberates on mankind's issues, problems, needs and goals.[175]

Eric Shawn is a Fox News Reporter and the author of *The U.N. Exposed: How The United Nations Sabotages America And Fails The World*. He states that the United Nations was created to promote peace and international understanding, but has failed to achieve its original mission, which was to address the most dangerous threats facing the civilized world, to condemn terrorist acts, as well as encouraged America's enemies, and some of the world's most oppressive governments. Shawn states that America's allies' selfish economic interests drive United Nation's challenges to America's sovereignty. The criticisms have validity.

However, their criticisms is that democracy among nations leads to inaction. But America's domestic history is a monument to overcoming such tendencies in democracy by respecting the rights of others. In addition, an important feature of critiques of the United Nations, as it currently operates, is that America itself exemplifies the Fairness Hypocrisy and other Principles of Conflict that make the United Nations ineffective at achieving its mission. America's approach to the United Nations asserts is self-interest that seeks to benefit the interests of America rather than what is beneficial for mankind.

Stephen Walt, a professor at Harvard, asserts in *Taming American Power* that:

> The United States is the strongest and most influential Great Power in modern history. It also remains a remarkably immature Great Power – one whose rhetoric is frequently at odds with the reality of its own conduct and one that often treats the management of foreign affairs as an adjunct to domestic politics....the United States brings in a new team every time the White House switches parties. Americans remain remarkably ignorant of the world they believe it is their obligation and destiny to run, and the topic of foreign affairs captures public attention only when major mistakes have already been made.

If the United States wants to make its privileged position acceptable to others, then the American body politic must acquire a more serious and disciplined attitude toward the conduct of foreign policy. In the past, seemingly secure behind its nuclear deterrent and oceanic moats, and possessing unmatched economic and military power, the United States allowed its foreign policy to be distorted by partisan sniping; hijacked by foreign lobbyists and narrow domestic special interests; blinded by lofty but unrealistic rhetoric; and held hostage by responsible and xenophobic members of Congress. Even after the dramatic wake-up call on September 11, 2001, efforts to reform U.S. intelligence services, to corral loose nuclear materials, and to improve U.S. homeland security have been half hearted at best. And even though the country faced a new and very real enemy in al Qaeda, the Bush administration was able to persuade Congress and the American people that preventive war against a country that had nothing to do with 9/11 was still the best way to fight Osama bin Laden and his followers. Is this the way that a mature Great Power behaves?

The problem, alas, goes deeper than that. Despite its pretension as the world's only superpower, the United States has starved its intelligence services, gutted its international-affairs budget, done little to attract the ablest members of its society to government service, neglected the study of foreign languages and cultures, and basically behaved as though it simply didn't matter whether U.S. foreign policy were run well or not. This policy might have been sufficient in the past (though it is hard to be proud of it), but it will not serve us well in today's world.

What is needed, instead, is greater confidence in America's fundamental principles and institutions and greater wisdom in understanding what U.S. power can and cannot accomplish. America' core values of liberty and opportunity unleashed the energy upon which our economic prosperity is built. That prosperity, in turn provides the sinews of our military power and the hard core of our international influence. But the ability to defeat other armies and our influence over the world economy do not give the United States either the right or the ability to impose these principles on others, and it hardly gives 5 percent of the world's population the obligation, capacity, or right to govern vast areas of the world by force. Instead of telling the world what to do and how to live –a temptation that both neoconservative empire-builders and liberal internationalists find hard to resist – the United States should lead the world primarily by example. If we have faith in our core principles; we will expect to win hearts and minds first and foremost because others will see how we live, and see what we have, and they will want those things too.

Despite the missteps the United States has made in recent years, it still retains enormous material power and considerable global influence. The question is whether its future choices will draw others closer, drive them into sullen resentment, or provoke them into open resistance. The United States can use its power and wealth to compel others to do what it wants, but this strategy will surely fail in the long run. In most circumstances, the key is not power but persuasion.

There is a lesson here. More than anything else, the United States wants to retain its position of primacy for as long as it can. To do this, it must persuade the rest of the world that U.S. primacy is preferable to the likely alternatives. Achieving that goal will require a level of wisdom and self-restrain that has often been lacking in U.S. foreign policy – largely because it wasn't needed. But it is today. Although geography, history, and good fortune have combined to give the United States a remarkable array of advantages, it would still be possible to squander them. And if the United States ends up hastening the demise of its existing partnerships and giving rise to new arrangements whose main purpose is to contain us, we will have only ourselves to blame.[176]

Walt summarizes the ways in which America used its power after the Cold War to serve American interests rather than deal with specific security threats. He focuses on the broad gap between Americans' perceptions of their global role as positive and the negative ways in which America is perceived abroad. Walt asserts that other states fear, resent, or hate America partly because it is the world's most powerful country, but also because of its behavior. Other states use delegitimization strategies to resist America. The delegitimization strategy accuses America of being a morally bankrupt society whose actions abroad are generally selfish, capricious, cruel to others. If America's behavior in fact has those faults, they will make it hard for America to win support internationally.

Nations that choose to accommodate American penetrate the American body politic and give individual politicians strong incentives to favor closer ties. Walt cites the Israel lobby as the most successful nation that uses the American political system to gain influence over American foreign policy.

Walt focuses on the questions of:

1. How can America encourage states to see its dominant position as beneficial?
2. How can America convince other nations that its foreign policy deserves broad international support?
3. How can America ensure that it is not exploited by nations that appear to embrace American values and goals but are trying to manipulate American power for their own purposes?
4. How can America make its global position more legitimate in the eyes of others?

Walt asserts that America's position in 2005 required greater knowledge, wisdom, and self-restraint than ever before, and that achieving this level of wisdom requires fundamental changes in the ways Americans approach the world. He states:

> This it's the true paradox of American primacy: Instead of enabling the United States to act however it wishes, America's dominant position encourages other states to fear our unchecked power and look for ways to constrain it. If we want the rest of the world to welcome U.S. primacy, therefore, we must convince them that American power is not something to be tamed, but rather something that will be used judiciously and for the boarder benefit of mankind.

Walt's views are the mirror those of President Washington in his

Farewell Address of 1796.

How realistic is conventional American "realism"? In 2008, then Secretary of State Rice's published the article "Rethinking the National Interest: American Realism for a New World," in *Foreign Affairs:* [177]

> What is the national interest? ...
>
> We recognize that democratic state building is now an urgent component of our national interest. And in the broader Middle East, we recognize that freedom and democracy are the only ideas that can, over time, lead to just and lasting stability...
>
> The United States has long tried to marry power and principle---realism and idealism. At times, there have been short---term tensions between them. But we have always known where our long---term interests lie. Thus, the United States has not been neutral about the importance of human rights or the superiority of democracy as a form of government, both in principle and in practice. This uniquely American realism has guided us over the past eight years, and it must guide us over the years to come.
>
> By necessity, our relationships with Russia and China have been rooted more in common interests than common values...
>
> The last eight years have also challenged us to deal with rising Chinese influence, something we have no reason to fear if that power is used responsibly. We have stressed to Beijing that with China's full membership in the international community comes responsibilities, whether in the conduct of its economic and trade policy, its approach to energy and the environment, or its policies in the developing world. China's leaders increasingly realize this, and they are moving, albeit slowly, to a more cooperative approach on a range of problems...
>
> China needs to do much more on issues such as Darfur, Burma, and Tibet, but we sustain an active and candid dialogue with China's leaders on these challenges.
>
> The United States, along with many other countries, remains concerned about China's rapid development of high-tech weapons system. We understand that as countries develop,. They will modernize their armed forces. But, China's lack of transparency about its military spending and doctrine and its

strategic goals increases mistrust and suspicion. Although Beijing has agreed to take incremental steps to deepen U.S.-Chinese military-to-military exchanges, it needs to move beyond the rhetoric of peaceful intentions toward true engagement in order to reassure the international community.

Our relationships with Russia and China are complex and characterized simultaneously by competition and cooperation. But in the absence of workable relations with both of these states, diplomatic solutions to many international problems would be elusive. Transnational terrorism and the proliferation of weapons of mass destruction, climate change and instability stemming from poverty and disease---these are dangers to all successful states, including those that might in another time have been violent rivals. It is incumbent on the United States to find areas of cooperation and strategic agreement with Russia and China, even when there are significant differences...

Although the United States' ability to influence strong states is limited, our ability to enhance the peaceful political and economic development of weak and poorly governed states can be considerable. We must be willing to use our power for this purpose-not only because it is necessary but also because it is right. Too often, promoting democracy and promoting development are thought of as separate goals. In fact, it is increasingly clear that the practices and institution of democracy are essential to the creation of sustained, broad-based economic development -and that market-driven development is essential to the consolidation of democracy. Democratic development is a unified political-economic model, and it offers the mix of flexibility and stability that best enables states to seize globalization's opportunity and manage its challenges. And for those who think otherwise: What real alternative worthy of America is there?

Democratic development is not only effective both to wealth and powers, it is also the best way to ensure that these benefits are shared justly across entire societies, without exclusion, repression, or violence...

For the United States, promoting democratic development must remain a top priority. Indeed, there is no realistic alternative that we can---or should---offer to influence the peaceful evolution of weak and poorly governed states. The real question is not whether to pursue this course but how.

We first need to recognize that democratic development is always possible but never fast or easy. This is because democracy is really the complex interplay of democratic practices and culture. In the experience of countless nations, ours especially, we see that culture is not destiny. Nations of every culture, race, religion, and level of development have embraced democracy and adapted it to their own circumstances and traditions. No cultural factor has yet been a stumbling block-not German or Japanese "militarism," ort Latin America's alleged fondness for caudillos, not the once-purported preference of eastern Europeans for despotism.

The fact is, few nations begin the democratic journey with a democratic culture. The vast majority create one over time-through the hard, daily struggle to make good laws. Build democratic institutions, tolerate differences, resolve them peacefully, and share power justly. Unfortunately, it is difficult to grow the habits of democracy in the controlled environment of authoritarianism,. to have them ready and in place when tyranny is lifted. The process of democratization is likely to be messy and unsatisfactory, but is absolutely necessary. Democracy, it is said, cannot be imposed, particularly by a foreign power. This is true but beside the point. It is more likely that tyranny has to be imposed.

The story today is rarely one of peoples resisting the basics of democracy---the right to choose those who will govern them and other basic freedoms. It is, instead, about people choosing democratic leaders and then becoming impatient with them and holding them accountable on their duty to deliver a better life. It is strongly in our national interest to help sustain these leaders, support their countries' democratic institutions, and ensure that their new government are capable of providing for their own security, especially when their nations have experienced crippling conflicts. To do so will require long—term partnerships rooted in mutual responsibility and the integration of all elements of our national power---political ,diplomatic, economic, and, at times, military...

Investing in strong and rising powers as stakeholders in the international order and supporting the democratic development of weak and poorly governed states---these broad goals for

U.S. foreign policy are certainly ambitious, and they raise an obvious question: Is the United States up to the challenge, or, as some fear and assert these days, is the United States a nation in decline?...

We, should also be confident that the foundations of the United States' economic power are strong, and will remain so. Even amid financial turbulence and international crises, the U.S. economy has grown more and faster since 2001 than the economy of any other leading industrial nation. The United States remains unquestionably the engine of global economic growth...

Perhaps of greater concern is not that the United States lacks the capacity for global leadership but that it lacks the will...

The old dichotomy between realism and idealism has never really applied to the United States, because we do not really accept that our national interest and our universal ideals are at odds. For our nation, it has always been a matter of perspective. Even when our interests and ideals come into tension in the short run, we believe that in the long run they are indivisible...

How to describe this disposition of ours? It is realism, of a sort. But it is more than that---what I have called our uniquely American realism. This makes us an incredibly impatient nation....This has led our nation to make mistakes in the past, and we will surely make more in the future. Still, it is our impatience to improve less-than-ideal situations and to accelerate the pace of change most enduring achievements, at home and abroad...

An international order that reflects our values is the best guarantee of our enduring national interest, and America continues to have a unique opportunity to shape this outcome. And if we remain confident in the power of our values, we can succeed in such work again...That's part of the indeed, we already see glimpses of this better world...

Anatol Lieven's evaluation in *American Right or Wrong: An Anatomy of American Nationalism* of what he the "realist philosophy" is that:

The central flaw in the Bush administration's realism is not particular to that administration, but is characteristic of the realist philosophy as a whole. This flaw lies in a certain innate tendency to see the world as characterized by opposition and actual are potential hostility between states, rather than by a potential for cooperation, generated by a common stake in the capitalist world system, and finally, to see this opposition as the most important single element in the international system. This element in the thinking of the U.S. establishment was tremendously fuelled by the Cold War and the military, economic, bureaucratic, and academic structures that it created.

The malign consequences of this are twofold. In the first place, while the realist approach may find ample room for pragmatic cooperation with individual states, it contains a built in bias against thinking of the international system as a whole in terms of cooperation. Second, this approach tends to be utterly blind to threats to the international order and indeed to modern civilization which stem from the outside traditional realist categories, global warming being the most notable example. In this sense, contemporary American realism might be compared to that of Metternich and his school – sometimes technically brilliant, but incapable of understanding the new world growing up around them.[177]

The New School's perspective is that the only way America can persuade other nations that its power will be used judiciously is for America to use its power for the broader benefit of mankind. There is no synthetic deception that will fool all of mankind. Americans either take or do not take President Washington's advice that they should:

> "Observe good faith & justice towards all nations. Cultivate harmony with all. Religion and morality enjoin this conduct; and can it be that good policy does not equally enjoin it? It will be worthy of a free, enlightened, and, in no distant period a great nation, to give to mankind the magnanimous and too novel example of a people always guided by an exalted justice & benevolence"

At this point, in considering the lack of realism in conventional

American Principles of Conflict Realism, it is important to note what President Washington said immediately following his advice:

> Who can doubt that in the course of time and things the fruits of such a plan would richly repay any temporary advantages which might be lost by a steady adherence to it? Can it be that providence has not connected the permanent felicity of a nation with its virtue? The experiment, at least, is recommended by every sentiment which ennobles human nature. Alas! Is it rendered impossible by its vices?

The results produced in his own time endorse the pragmatic and enduring realism of his advice. President Washington stated in his Farewell Address that he gave his advice because of:

> ...a solicitude for your welfare which cannot end but with my life, and the apprehension of danger, natural to that solicitude, urge me on an occasion like the present, to offer to your solemn contemplation, and to recommend to your frequent review some sentiments; which all the result of much reflection of no inconsiderable observation, and which appear to me all important to the permanency of your felicity as a people.

One of the most important reasons that America cannot get the United Nations to protect America's security interests is that American administrations do not implement President Washington's advice. Worse still, some nations follow America's example.

In the themes of President Washington's advice there is a more broadly based vision of America's interests than is found in post 1950 conventional American foreign policy "American Principles of Conflict Realism" exhibit the "War Mindset" rather than the "Peace Mindset" examined in chapter 4 of Book 2.

President Washington's advice is consistent with the Principles of Peaceful Coexistence. We will refer to his advice as "American Principles of Peaceful Coexistence Realism." President Washington's advice to Americans, like Deng Xiaoping's advice to the Chinese, seeks to rise above the characteristics in human nature that the New School's perspectives term the "Principles of Conflict". China is following "China's Principles of Peaceful Coexistence Realism."

President Washington's "realism" works. President George W. Bush's administration's "realism" does not work. America has not been following President Washington's advice in the 21st century. The consequences of America's manifestation of President Washington' vision of America's needs will be more beneficial, than the consequences of implementing Bush's more narrowly focused vision.

President Washington's ideals helped at America's creation to tame a generation of exceptionally strong leaders, diverse economic and political interests, and clashing factions with passionate beliefs in the United States of America's. Each of those thirteen states, had its own leaders, agenda, and fears. President Washington's American Principles of Peaceful Coexistence Realism successfully tame the same centrifugal force as exist in the United Nations. President Washington's ideals and behavior have the realism of working both in the America of the 18th century and even more so in the 21st century with. Human nature has not changed and President Washington's ideals are even more essential in the Age of Species Lethal Weapons than in his lifetime.

The United Nation's ineffectiveness in fulfilling its mission is are rooted in the Fairness Hypocrisy in which nations demand fairness while seeking to treat others unfairly. President Washington was an example of an American leader eschewing Fairness Hypocrisy. In the future, every American government must ensure that America is such an example in the United Nations.

The consequence of America's choice to implement foreign policies based on American Principles of Peaceful Coexistence Realism is a successful method whereas the consequences of implementing American Principles of Conflict Realism is failure.

What we term the American Principles of Peaceful Coexistence Realism and Chinese Principles of Peaceful Coexistence Realism will align in a "more perfect union" than Chinese Principles of Peaceful Coexistence Realism and American Principles of Conflict Realism.

George Washington and Deng Xiaoping had similar experiences and led developing nations, albeit with different forms of government.

America's 44th president and Vice-President lead the world's most developed economically. China's President and Premier can do so much more to assist America if its President and other leaders embrace the partnership of America and China. The solutions to America's dangers require its collaboration and moral authority. The collaboration of these civilizations is essential for the survival of the respective ideals of America and China.

The Solution to America's Problems and Dangers is to Change America's Conventional Goals Which are Inconsistent with America's Ideals and Economic and National Security

As noted in chapter 1 of Book 1 Machiavelli is thought of as a "realist" and as expressing the view that might is right. But his advice in *The Prince*, although asserting that might is right, was qualified. Machiavelli recognized the power of what he termed "greatness and nobility of character," such as that later exhibited by General and President Washington to lead in America's birth. Machiavelli addressed his advice to a Prince. But substitute the word "America" for the word "Prince" and paraphrase Machiavelli; consider what Machiavelli advised:

> ...what ought to be the conduct and bearing of [America] in relation to [its] subjects and friends...it seems to me better to

follow the real truth of things than an imaginary view of them. For many Republics and Princedoms have been imagined that were never seen or known to exist in reality. And the manner in which we live, and that in which we ought to live, consider what are things so wide asunder, that [a nation which] quits the one to betake [itself] of the other is more likely to destroy than save [itself]; since any [nation which] would act up to a perfect standard of goodness in everything, must be ruined among so many that are not good. It is essential, therefore, for [America which] desires to maintain [its] position, to have learned how to be other than good, and to use or not to use [its]goodness as necessity requires...[America] need never hesitate, however, to incur the reproach of those vices without which [its] authority can hardly be preserved; for if [it] well consider the matter. [it] will find that there may be a line of conduct having the appearance of virtue, to follow which would be [its] ruin, and that there may be another course having the appearance of vice, by flowing which [its] safety and well-being are secured.[178]

To solve the problem of the ineffectiveness of the United Nations in serving America's security needs let us further consider Machiavelli's advice. He also stated:

And here comes in the question whether it is better to be loved rather than feared, or feared rather than loved. It might perhaps be answered that we should wish to be both; but since love and fear can hardly exist together, if we must choose between them, it is far safer to be feared than loved. For men it may generally be affirmed that they are thankless, fickle, false, studious to avoid danger, greed of gain, devoted to you while you are able to confer benefits upon them, and ready, as I said before, while danger is distant, to shed their blood, and sacrifice their property, their lives, and their children for you; but in the hour of need they turn against you. [America, therefore, [which] without otherwise securing [itself] build wholly on their professions is undone. For the friendships which we buy with a price, and do not gain by greatness and nobility of character, though they be fairly earned are not made good, but fail us when we have occasion to use them.

Moreover, men are less careful how they offend him who makes himself loved than him who makes himself feared. For love is held by the tie of obligation, which because men are a sorry breed, is broken on every whisper of private interest; but fear is bound by the apprehension of punishment which never relaxes its grip.

Nevertheless, [America] should inspire fear in such a fashion that if [it] do not win love [it] might escape hate. For a man may well be feared but not hated....[179]

How is America to be feared and loved? America cannot fool all of mankind: it must convince mankind that it is a benevolent leader which cannot do if the Principles of Conflict remain the basis of its foreign policy.

When Deng Xiaoping made China's goals prosperity and peace the results were entirely different for China than when Mao Zedong implemented different priorities and goals.

To the degree that America is not following President Washington's advice, it is the example of the change it does not want to see in the world. As examined in chapter 4 of Book 1, America's War on Terror and conventional foreign policy and goals exacerbate the mistakes it makes when it departs from President Washington's advice.

America will still live in a dangerous world if it follows President Washington's advice, but will be a better part of that world, will evoke more support, and will perform its leadership role with moral authority. It cannot lead with military and economic authority bereft of moral authority.

Arthur Schlesinger noted in *War and the American Presidency*:

Democracy in the twenty-first century must manage the pressures of race, of technology and capitalism, and it must cope with the spiritual frustrations and yearnings generated in the vast atomicity (not a word in the dictionary) of global society. The great strength of democracy is its capacity for self-correction. Intelligent diagnosis and guidance are essential.

> 'Perhaps no form of government' said Bryce [in the *Common-wealth of Nations*] needs great leaders so much as democracy.' Yet even the greatest of democratic leaders lack the talent to cajole violent, retrograde, and intractable mankind into utopia. Still, with the failures of democracy in the twentieth century at the back of their minds, leaders in the twenty-first century may do a better job than we have done of making the world safe for democracy.[180]

Schlesinger did not have before him the New School's perspectives, agenda and plan and he concluded that: "even the greatest of democratic leaders lack the talent to cajole violent, retrograde, and intractable mankind into utopia." However, wasn't it utopian for Gandhi to think that he could stop a civil war among 300 million Hindus and Muslims? But Gandhi's moral authority was sufficient to achieve that feat. How much greater than the moral authority of a single private citizen of India is the moral authority of America's 44th President leading a nation with historic moral authority?

As President Obama stated in his essay in *Foreign Policy*:

> There are compelling moral reasons and compelling security reasons for renewed American leadership that recognizes the inherent equality and worth of all people. As President Kennedy said in his 1961 inaugural address "To those people in the huts and villages of half the globe struggling to break the bond of mass misery, we pledge our best efforts to help them help themselves, for whatever period is required - not because the communists may be doing it, not because we seek their votes, but because it is right. If a free society cannot help the many who are poor, it cannot save the few who are rich.' It will show the world that America remains true to its founding values. We lead not only for ourselves but also for the common good...
>
> It was not all that long ago that farmers in Venezuela and Indonesia welcomed American doctors to their villages and hung pictures of JFK on their living room walls, when millions, like my father, waited every day for a letter in the mail that would grant them the privilege to come to America to study,

work, live or just be free...

We can be this America again. This is our moment to renew the trust and faith of our people – and all people – in an America that battles immediate evils, promotes an ultimate good, and leads the world once more.

Ultimately, no foreign policy can succeed unless the American people understand it and feel they have a stake in its success – unless they trust that their government hears their concerns as well. We will not be able to increase foreign aid if we fail to invest in security and opportunity for our own people. We cannot negotiate trade agreements to help spur development in poor countries so long as we provide no meaningful help to working Americans burdened by the dislocations of a global economy. We cannot reduce our dependence on foreign oil or defeat global warming unless Americans are willing to innovate and conserve. We cannot expect Americans to support placing our men and women in harm's way if we cannot show that we will use force wisely and judiciously. But if the next president can restore the American people's trust – if they know that he or she is acting with their best interest at heart, with prudence and wisdom and some measure of humility – then I believe the American people will be eager to see America lead again.[181]

William Bryce asserted in the *The American Commonwealth*:

'Perhaps no form of government needs great leaders so much as democracy.'

The reason that there is an America is because its people have been able to find leaders who know that they and America must: Observe good faith & justice towards all nations. Cultivate harmony with all. America must always find *and support such leaders*.

What would solve the Deadlock at the United Nations and Enable it to fulfill its Mission?

The United Nations will only be able to work effectively and fulfill its mission when the survival of mankind is recognized by America and China as the fundamental issue of the Age of Species Lethal Weapons and Science. Let us pray that this does not occur after a catastrophic events that kills millions or billions.

Imagine that:

1. Iran destroys Israel, and Iran is destroyed. Both enemies cease to exist as a result of the clash of civilizations and the aggression that results. Oil prices skyrocket as Middle East production stops. The economies of developing and developed nations collapse. Food stops being produced and distributed. Anarchy and chaos reign; or
2. North Korea attacks the United States killing 100 million American and North Korea ceases to exist. The global economy collapses and the economies of developed and developing nation collapse. Food stops being produced and distributed. Anarchy and chaos reign;
3. A terrorist attack somewhere nations using Species Lethal Weapons and Science. Imagine unimaginable scenarios....

The American Senate Foreign Relations Committee predicts a 70% chance of experiencing a major biological, chemical, or nuclear attack in the next seven years. It may be too late then. Will any government be able to function after a Species Lethal Weapons and Science catastrophe? The United Nations must work at least as well in governing mankind as the United States of America, after a civil war, was able to govern itself. World Wars I and II were such "civil wars among mankind." As the 21st century's first global financial crises have made astonishingly clear, we live in a fragile, interdependent, and vulnerable system.

Flaws in the Moral Authority and Management of the Dream of the American Ideal of Human Rights

There are fundamental weaknesses in the use of might is right strategies that seek to universalize American Ideals of human rights, rule of law, and majority-rule-democracy. Perhaps the questions focused on in the New School's perspectives will reveal such weakness. But much depends on American and Chinese presidential visions, collaborative problem-solving abilities and the support for the new partnership of America and China.

China's leaders, have long wanted such a partnership. They, like Deng Xiaoping and even Mao Zedong, recognized the exceptional kindness of Americans and admire America most among all other nations.

Can peace, prosperity, and the universal acceptance of the American Ideals be achieved by:

1. America appointing itself or acting as de facto "government of the world"?
2. By self-determination in each of mankind's nations in the United Nations if America and China are not committed partners?
3. An alliance of the majority rule democracies in a "League of Democratic Nations," a "Concert of Democracies" or "Atlantic civilizations" alliance that seeks to clash on behalf of the defense of liberal democracy?

America appointing acting as de facto government of the world is what we have seen in the George W. Bush Presidency. American ideals cannot be based upon or be obtained by the Principles of Conflict. They can be pursued and evangelized by their example among Americans if they adopt the Principles of Peaceful Coexistence.

A "League of Democratic Nations," Concert of Democracies,

or alliance of Atlantic civilizations that seeks to defend American interests is the road to war and ruin. That road must not be chosen by Americans.

The use of might is right strategies to achieve the universality of American ideals is arrogant and self-defeating and endangers the viability of these Ideals.

The Moral Authority and Management of China's Dream of a Harmonious World

Can peace, prosperity, and the universal acceptance of China's ideals be achieved? It must be recognized by American policymakers, and people that:

1. China's dream of a Harmonious Society accommodates the hubris of America's evangelization of its ideals.
2. The Chinese government's ability to keep America's and its prosperity aligned depends on American policy choices.
3. The Chinese government's ability to accommodate America evangelizing its ideals and exercising its hegemony is not infinite.
4. America can go too far, and the more aggressively America evangelizes its Ideals the more America harms its charisma and undermines its hegemony.
5. It is not in America's self-interest nor within the ambit of its moral authority for its government to aggressively interfere in China's sovereignty, self-determination, and internal affairs by demanding China adopt American definitions of human rights, supporting dissent in Tibet and selling upgraded missile systems to Taiwan.
6. America does not have the authority to ignore the views of other nations within the United Nations while is evangelizing the universal acceptance of American Ideals.

7. An alliance of majority-rule-democracies led by America won't work and is a road to war and ruin.

Can America's leadership become more win-win than zero sum based? American Presidents must compensate for the "winner take all" deficiencies of American majority-rule-democracy, as Presidents Washington, Lincoln and Kennedy sought to do, by forming bipartisan Administrations that embrace different opinions and insights.

Chinese One-Party State Socialist Capitalism, and American Two-Party Four Freedoms Capitalism

The power and influence of the successful new Chinese model of capitalism comes from it, involving:

1. 22% of mankind rather than a less populated country;
2. A large rather than a small country;
3. Asia rather than America or Europe;
4. An Asian rather than American or European people;
5. An Asian rather than a European or American culture; and
6. By an Asia rather than the European or American civilizations.

Wealth is power. Europe and America had unequaled wealth and power in the 17th through 20th centuries and claimed much of the world outside their homelands as theirs. That process defined their political, social and economic histories and deeply affected less advanced nations such as China. The economic, military, intellectual and imperialistic components of Europe and America's success produced arrogance that was supportable in the world led by Europe and then America. But in the 21st century, the uncharismatic form of American Exceptionalism has become hubristic.

The American Peoples' Choice in Defining China and America's Future

Charismatic American Exceptionalism has lost its inspiring meaning and degraded into unsustainable economic and military authority. Can the American people produce leaders capable of crafting the solutions to the problems mankind creates? The danger is in the way the American electoral and legislative decision-making processes are too domestically focused, or unable to adapt to the challenges within and outside of America. There is a danger that the evangelizing of American Ideals that was able to work when America was a developing country may not work in a world where other developing countries surpass America's achievements economically. If America cannot always select successful leaders it will leave America's militarily poorly managed. Destabilizing economic challenges and catastrophic events await America and mankind. If the character of the American people and their decision making processes are not able to cope, America will become a failed civilization.

America's Responsibility to Its Ideals, China and Mankind

An unstable America can destabilize many other nations, with other perspectives on the nature of man, of "a good society" and of "social progress", which reject America's Ideals. The American people bear the responsibility of selecting presidents who are able to protect America and China simultaneously, and stabilize other nations. Are America's leaders and people equal to the challenge they face?

Chapter 12

America's Choice of Failure or Success

Overview

The key issue in American-Chinese relations is what choices Americans will make. America's China policy is critical because of the weakening of American and strengthening of Chinese. The economic and political results of the wealth and competitiveness of nations is shifting from benefiting America to resulting in new economic superpowers that could dwarf America's economy. The possible responses that will be attractive politically to many Americans but not effective, include:

1. Trade protectionism
2. Evangelizing America's Ideals and political systems;
3. Aggressive confrontation of China as a nation Americans perceive as an enemy.
4. War

The protectionism and evangelization moves will be politically attractive to some Americans, but protectionist moves misalign America and China's success. China, not America, is likely to be the world's main driver of economic growth in the future. Evangelizing American Ideals is not going to work, and will not change China into a copy of America. The possible move that hopefully will not be attractive politically, but will stop China's economic development is war.

America and China as Responsible Great Powers

The New School's perspectives emphasize that America must change its priorities because they are inconsistent with its Ideals and security.

China's policymakers and scholars recognized 30 years ago that collaboration was an essential requirement and in the 21st century adopted the Principles of Peaceful Coexistence.

However, American policymakers are focused on America's 20th century foreign policy traditions and are not correctly addressing the 21st century's fundamental issue. As a result, the global economy and the international system are increasingly unstable.

Among the new realities facing America are:

1. The globalization of America's economy has led less developed nations such as China, that were the targets of extending American economic power to develop economic power. It has resulted the empowerment of developing nations that were able to generate governments capable of achieving economic development without copying America's Ideals. That was not the outcome of economic globalization Americans intended.
2. America can only interrupt the peaceful rise of China by using military aggression to destabilize it.
3. But in the Age of Species Lethal Weapons and Science the tactics of economic and military aggression are not sufficient

to protect America.

4. China's strategy since 1978 does not confront America militarily. In the past, a great power's economic growth was usually accompanied by military aggression. China's priorities are an exception to the violent rise of new great powers.

5. China is in a multi-decade process of eclipsing America economically without challenging it militarily. The major potential conflicts between America and China are: Taiwan, Tibet, and human rights in China and are all matters of China's internal affairs and sovereignty.

6. China is using its successful adoption of capitalism and resulting economic authority, to obtain the natural resources and cooperation it requires from other nations.

7. China's military strategy and tactics are defensive. It has focused on more cost effective strategies than America. China has built submarines rather than aircraft carriers and battle fleets, and focused on high tech systems, such as those capable of disabling the satellites America relies on to operate.

China's peaceful development is nonetheless perceived by as a threat and somehow improper or unfair. America's pride in its Ideals has conventionally evoked a desire to confront China militarily or ideologically to try to change China to a majority-rule-democracy.

Americans have been focused on a backward rather than a forward looking focus on how to contain or destabilize China. Various approaches have not been successful in trying to:

1. Intimidate or defeat China with America's military authority in Korea from 1950 to 1953 and Vietnam from 1959 to 1975;

2. Contain China's economic growth and global influence;

3. Use sanctions and ostracize China, which worked with the USSR;

4. Use conditional acceptance strategies, which are naïve given

China's size and importance, to change China into an American client nation as a "responsible stakeholder;"

5. Change China's political system by evangelizing human rights and political reform and encouraging unrest in Tibet and tension between Mainland China and Taiwan;

6. Change China's stable political system and successful economic sovereignty by massive investment by American companies, which has not been successful as China will not allow American interests to take over China's economy.

7. Use a zero sum game mindset against China which cannot be successful and does not align America's economic success and national security with China's.

Reciprocal Globalization in the 21st Century

What we term "reciprocal globalization," driven by the need to preserve China's economic sovereignty, entered a new phase with the leadership of Hu Jintao. One of his first policy innovations was the call in 2002 for Chinese companies to "go global." China's leadership recognized that Chinese companies would only be able to compete successfully if Chinese companies could compete successfully with foreign companies. American and European economic arrogance between 1978 and 2008 began to become hubris as China deployed its "go global" and "Innovative Economy of the World" developmental policies.

The "Scramble for China" turned into what Japan, America and Europe might term "Chinese economic imperialism" in the 21st century, or what we refer to as "China's reciprocal globalization response to the Japanese, American and European led Scramble for China." The Scramble for China sought to take control of China's economic sovereignty using the authority of money. It sought to control China's domestic and foreign policies just as European and American nations sought to between 1860 and 1949 period. But the military and economic superiority of Japan, Europe, and America from 1860 to date was undermined by the Chinese in the 1949 revolution. China first ensured its Freedom from Fear by safeguarding sovereignty and becoming a nuclear power, then pursuing China's Freedom from Want with unprecedented speed and success.

Economic Authority Wars

With typical "Do as I say, not as I do" immoral authority, America and European nations demand again that China open up to foreign competition, which is a euphemism for domination. But America and European nations block Chinese corporations from achieving control positions in American or European corporations. The solutions to these problems are examined in *New China Business Strategies: Chinese and American Companies as Global Partners*.

Capitalism's arbiter of power is money and, military authority. One school of thought in America relies on economic means to contain and compete with China. Another favors the use of military authority and war with China before China becomes too strong. But China is already too strong for either approach because it is one of the major engines of global economic success, and because this is the Age of Species Lethal Weapons and Science. If the equalizing factor weapons of mass destruction did not exist, and America had not had failed experiments with limited conventional "testing wars" with China in Korea and Vietnam, America might use its investment in military assets to crush China's economic growth or destabilize its politically. But in the Age of Species Lethal Weapons and Science wars can be fought with money. Money can destroy foreign countries' economies or make, them vulnerable to foreign intervention. The Asian Financial Crisis of 1997-1998 is a classic example of that. But by 2008, if not before, while America was focusing on Arab-generated terrorist rejection of American values China has become far too strong for America or Europe to crush it economically. China in 2008 is not Indonesia in 1998.

In 2008, capitalism with American or European characteristics is in crisis, and capitalism with Chinese characteristics may be harmed as a result. In 2008, with a per capita income that is only 1/12th of America's, China , which achieved annual GDP growth of 11% to 13%, is witnessing the mismanagement of American capitalism on a scale that was almost unimaginable, except by persons such as George Soros and Warren Buffett. American capitalism is suffering because of failures it did not prevent. America now must make reforms to protect itself from economic failures. In doing so, the differences between capitalism with America and Chinese character-istics are reducing.

Which system is more sustainable: capitalism with American characteristics or with Chinese characteristics? The objective results indicate capitalism with Chinese characteristics works better for China than capitalism with American characteristics works for America. It follows that capitalism with American characteristics does not have much credibility as the form of capitalism that China should adopt.

Support for a conventional war fought against China is likely nil. Support for war with nuclear weapons is also likely nil. But if a war could be fought economically against China it might be waged. But economic war against China is not winnable and likely not supportable by Americans. Fortunately, "the new face of war," in discovering unwinnable new ways to fight, is strengthening the pragmatism, necessity, and achievability of peace.

America's Mindset and Strategy Change Challenge

The plan presented in Books 1 and 2 for the creation of a future for mankind requires an unconventional new agenda and grand strategy for coordinating American and Chinese policies and align-ing their economic and national security.

In 1978, after China's Cultural Revolution, a vast majority of the Chinese recognized the need for profound change in a 5000 year-old culture. That is what the selection of Deng Xiaoping, Jiang Zemin, Zhu Rongji, Hu Jintao and Wen Jiabao expressed. With such a broadly felt need for change it was possible. The success of the changes the Chinese have made since 1978 was impossible, but is now a reality that has changed China and mankind.

After 200 years of success, America is undergoing its own sort of "cultural revolution" after the experiment with economic theories and neoconservative authoritarian practices. After America's experiment with an authoritarian administration, a vast majority of Americans in both political parties is ready for profound change.

America's President and people must reach out to the Mainland Chinese and form a more perfect union as committed, genuine partners.

The American People's Fundamental China Question

An essential solution to America and China's security challenges is "the America-China Partnership" required for "reciprocal globalization" and "collaborative equilibrium" examined in the next book in this series: *China & America's New Economic Partnership*. What we term the "Fundamental China Question" is whether America's leaders people, and Constitutional majority-rule-democracy will take the road to prosperity and peace? As 21st rather than 20th century Americans, we must align our economic and foreign policies, and economic success with China's and adopt the "Harmonious World" goal, as well as implement a win-win mindset, strategies, and goals.

Endnotes

1. Zhang Yunling and Tang Shiping, David Shambaugh ed., *Power Shift: China and Asia's New Dynamics*, 2005, 48

2. Zhang Yunling and Tang Shiping ibid, 56-7

3. Zhang Yunling and Tang Shiping, ibid, 48

4. Zhang Yunling and Tang, ibid, 59-60

5. Want Jisi, "China Search for Stability With America," *Foreign Affairs*, September/October 2005, 39

6. Wang Jisi, "America in Asia: How much does China care?, *Global Asia*, Fall 2007, 28

7. Ibid 24-25

8. Ibid 25

9. Ibid

10. Ibid 25-26

11. Ibid 25-26

12. Ibid 25-26, 27-28

13. George Washington Farewell Address, John Grafton ed., *The Declaration of Independence and other great Documents of American History 1775-1865*, Dover, 2000, 56-57

14. "Unity Depends on Ideals and Discipline," Selected Works of Deng Xiaoping, Vol. III, 116 15"For The Great Unity of the Entire Nation", ibid,165

15. Mahatma Gandhi, Speech at the Inter-Asian Relations Conference, April 2, 1947

16. Speech at Harvard University, 2003, Wen Jiabao

17. Xinhua News, April 13 2006

18. Julia Lovell, *The Great Wall: China Against the World 1000 BC – AD 2000*

19. Geoff Mulgan, *Good and Bad Power: The Ideals and Betrayals of Government*, 2006, 46-47

20. Sung Chul Yang, "Arbitrator or Antagonist: A new American Dilemma, "*Global Asia*, Fall 2007, 30

21. Ibid.

22. Ibid.

23. Laurence Brahm ed., *China's Century: The Awakening Of The Next Economic Powerhouse*, p 58

24. Selected Works of Deng Xiaoping, III, 344-345

25. Laurence Brahm, "Media and Communications," *China's Century: The Awakening of the Next Economic Powerhouse*, 2001, 367

26. Selected Works of Deng Xiaoping, , III 90-91

27. Selected works of Deng Xiaoping, III, 93

28. Ibid,93-4

29. Zhang Zhiming, *The Communist Party of China and China's Political Democracy*, China International Press, 2007, 10

30. Vincent Wilson Jr., *The Book of Great American Documents*, American History Research Associates, 1967, 4

31. Ibid

32. Alexis de Tocqueville, Democracy in America, Bantam Classics, 2000, 198-199

33. Ibid.

34. Ibid.

35. *USA Today*, "Reclaiming America's promise," July 7, 2008

36. Ibid.

37. Joyce Hawkins, ed, *The Oxford Reference Dictionary*, Clarendon Press 1986

38. *USA Today*, "Reclaiming America's promise," July 7, 2008

39. Kishore Mahbubani, "Wake up, Washington: The US risks losing Asia, *Global Asia*, Fall 2007,

40. Andrew Kramer, "Deals With Iraq Are Set To Bring Oil Giants Back," *New York Times*, June 19, 2008,1

41. Thomas Hobbes, *The Leviathan*

42. George Washington Farewell Address, John Grafton ed, *The Declaration of Independence and other great Documents of American History 1775-1865*, Dover, 2000, 56-57

43. Selected Works of Deng Xiaoping, III, 116.

44. Selected Works of Deng Xiaoping, III, 165

45. David Herszenhorn, "Estimated, costs of Iraq war were not close to Ballpark,"*New York Times*, March 19, 2008, A9

46. Stephen Fidler, "War's spiraling cost inspires shock and awe, *Financial Times*, March 18, 2008, 10

47. Vincent Wilson J., The Great Book of American Documents, History Research Associates, 1967

48. Alexis de Tocqueville,*Democracy in America*, Bantam Classics, 2000

49. The Collected Works of Abraham Lincon, edited by Roy P. Basler

50. Ibid

51. Ibid

52. The Inaugural Address of the U.S. Presidents. Central Compilation & Translation Press, 142

53. Ibid, 298

54. Arthur Schlesinger Jr., *War and the American Presidency*, 2005, 133-4

55. Ibid

56. John F. Kennedy, *Commencement Address at American University*, June 10, 1963

57. Selected Works of Deng Xiaoping, III, Foreign Language Press, 376

58. "Hold High the Banner of Mao Zedong Thought and Adhere to the Principle of Seeking Truth from Facts" Selected Works of Deng Xiaoping, II, 138

59. Selected Works of Deng Xiaoping, II, 369-72

60. Selected Works of Deng Xiaoping, II,407- 408

61. Selected Works Of Deng Xiaoping, III, 59

62. Selected Works Of Deng Xiaoping, III, 102-3

63. Selected Works Of Deng Xiaoping, III, 107-9

64. Selected Works Of Deng Xiaoping, III, 110-2

65. Selected Works Of Deng Xiaoping, III, 131-3

66. Selected Works Of Deng Xiaoping, III, 230-1

67. Selected Works Of Deng Xiaoping, III,245-6

68. Selected Works Of Deng Xiaoping, III, 274-6

69. Selected Works Of Deng Xiaoping, III, 284-7

70. Selected Works Of Deng Xiaoping, III, 309-11

71. Selected Works Of Deng Xiaoping, III, 318-9

72. Selected Works Of Deng Xiaoping, III, 320-2

73. Selected Works Of Deng Xiaoping, III, 335-7

74. Selected Works Of Deng Xiaoping, III, 338-9

75. Selected Works Of Deng Xiaoping, III, 341-3

76. Selected Works Of Deng Xiaoping, III, 350-1

77. Selected Works of Deng Xiaoping, III, 59

78. Jed Babbin and Edward Timperlake's book: *Showdown: Why China Wants War With The United States*, Regency Publishing Inc, 2006,1-3

79. Wikipeadia

80. John F. Kennedy, *Commencement Address at American University*, June 10, 1963

81. James Taub, The Unfreedom Agenda, *New York Times Magazine*, May 2008;

82. Gerald Seib and John Harwood, "America's Race to the Middle, *Wall Street Journal*, May 10, 2008, A1

83. Barrack Obama, "Renewing America's Leadership, *Foreign Affairs*, January/February, 2008

84. Coleman-Obama To Lead New Senate China Working Group, Press Release Senator Coleman

85. John Edwards, "Reengaging with the World: A Return to Moral Leadership," *Foreign Affairs*, September/October 2007, 19

86. Fareed Zakaria, The Rise of the Rest, *Newsweek*, May 12, 2008, 24

87. Hillary Rodham Clinton, "Security and Opportunity for the Twenty-first Century," *Foreign Affairs*, November/December 2007, 2

88. John McCain, "An Enduring Peach Built on Freedom: Securing America's Future," *Foreign Affairs*, November/December 2007, 19

89. Elizabeth Holmes and Neil King Jr. "Will McCain's Hawkish View Play on the National Stage," *Wall Street Journal*, March 6, 2008, A6

90. Anatol Lieven, "Why we should fear a McCain presidency, Financial Times, March 26, 2008, 9

91. Mitt Romney, "Rising to Global Challenges," *Foreign Affairs*, January/February, 2008, 142

92. Bill Richardson: New Realism: A Realistic and Principled Foreign Policy, Foreign Affairs, January/February, 2008, 142

93. Rudi Giuliani essay: *"Towards a Realistic Peace Defending Civilization and Defeating Terrorists by Making the International System Work"* Foreign Affairs, September/October 2007, 2-4

94. Michael Hukabee Americas Priorities in the War on Terror, *Foreign Affairs*, January/February, 2008, 155-158

95. *The Economist*, America at its best, June 7-13, 2008, 15

96. John Bolton, *Surrender is Not an Option*, Threshold Editions, 2007

97. Gerald Seib, "Clinton, Obama and a Difference That Matters," *Wall Street Journal*, February 26, 2008, A2

98. Tom Mitchell, Mure Dickie and Demetri Sevastopulo, "Kitty Hawk left at sea by China's refusal of Thanksgiving reunion", *Financial Times* November 22, 2007, 1

99. Remarks By Chinese President Hu Jintao to the US-China Business Council, The US Chamber of Commerce and the National Committee on U.S.-China Relations, April 20, 2006 © Federal News Service Inc

100. Samuel Huntington, ibid, 258, cites Hans-George Betz, "The New Politics of Resentment: Radical Right-Wing Populist Parties in Western Europe," Comparative Politics, 25, July 1998, 413-427

101. Anatol Lieven, *America Right or Wrong: An Anatomy of American*

Nationalism, Harper Perennial, 2004

102. Laurence Brahm, *China's Century: The Awakening of the Next Economic Powerhouse*, John Wiley & Sons, 2001, 365-367

103. Ibid, 217

104. Victor D Cha, "Winning Asia: Washington's Untold Success Story," *Foreign Affairs*, November/December 2007, 98

105. Ibid,100

106. Robert Zoellick "Whether China: From Membership to Responsibility." National Committee on United States China Relations, September 21, 2005 1- 4

107. Ibid, 4-7

108. Ibid.

109. Robert Zoellick, "A global mission for China and America" in the *Financial Times*, January 23, 2007, 13

110. Stephen Glain, "Why America's Point Man on China Is Running Into a Wall," *Newsweek*, December 17, 2007, 4

111. Paulson worried 'bazaar open' on Senate stimulus bill," *Reuters*, February 6, 2008

112. Selected Works Of Deng Xiaoping, III, 310

113. John F. Kennedy, Commencement Address at American University, June 11, 1963

114. Selected Works of Deng Xiaoping, III, 59

115. Edward Wong, "Booming China Faults US Policy on the Economy, *New York Times*, June 17. 2008, 1

116. Krishna Guha, "US calls for clarity on China oil stocks, *Financial Times*, June 17, 2008, 2

117. Azar Gat, "The Return of Authoritarian Great Powers," Foreign Affairs, July/August 2007, 59-60:

118. Ibid

119. Wu Miagfa, "China playing a key role as UN member," *China Daily*, December 24, 2007, 4

120. Julia Lovell, ibid

121. John Ikenberry, "The Rise of China and the Future of the West," *Foreign Affairs*, January/February 2008, 23

122. Ibid 27

123. Ibid 24-25

124. Ibid 23-24

125. Ibid 30

126. Robert Zoellick, Wither China: From Membership to Responsibility 2

127. Robert Zoellick's Third Annual Barnett Oksenberg Lecture Constantine

128. Zhang Yunling and Tang Shiping, "China's Regional Strategy," *Power Shift: China and Asia's New Dynamics*, Ibid 110-111

129. Clive Prestowitz, "The Purpose of American power in Asia," *Global Asia*, Fall 2007, 10-11

130. Ibid

131. Ibid, 14

132. Ibid,10-11

133. Ibid

134. Ibid

135. Kishore Mahbubani, "Wake up, Washington: The US risks losing Asia, *Global Asia*, Fall 2007, 16

136. Ibid

137. Ibid

138. Ibid

139. Jonathan Pollack. 343 in David Shambaugh ed, *Power Shift: China and Asia's New Dynamics*, University of California Press, 2005

140. Gerald Curtis, The US in East Asia: Not Architecture, But Action, *Global Asia*, Fall 2007, 43

141. Ibid 32

142. Demetri Sevastopulo and Jo Johnson, "US denies strategy against China," *Financial Times*, February 28, 2008, 3

143. David Shambaugh, 49-50

144. Jonathan D. Pollack, "The Transformation of the Asian Security Order," Shambaugh, Ibid. 329

145. Ibid, 230

146. Ibid, 330-1

147. Ibid, 336

148. Ibid, 332-333

149. David Shambaugh, 24-26

150. Ibid

151. Robert Sutter, "Chin's Regional Strategy and Why It May Not Be Good For America," *Power Shift: China and Asia's New Dynamics*, David Shambaugh, ed., University of California Press, 2005, 293

152. Ibid.

153. David M.Lampton, "China's Rise in Asia Need Not Be at America's Expense," David Shambaugh ed, *Power Shift: China and Asia's New Dynamic*, 2005, 308

154. Ibid, 307

155. Swaine, Shambaugh ed., ibid 266

156. Michael Yahuda, "The Evolving Asian Order, Shambaugh ed., ibid, 347-8

157. Ibid, 351-353

158. Ibid, 357-8

159. Richard Bush David Shambaugh ed, *Power Shift: China and Asia's New Dynamic*, 2005

160. Pollack, ibid, 339-340

161. Selected Works Of Deng Xiaoping, III, 91

162. Ibid

163. William Hutton, *The Writing on the Wall, Why We Must Embrace China as a Partner of Face It as an Enemy*, Free Press, 2006.

164. James Mann, The China Fantasy: How Our Leaders Explain Away Chinese Repression, Viking 2007

165. Ibid,110-112

166. Willy Wo-Lap Lam, *Chinese Politics in the Era of Hu Jintao*, East Gate Books, 2006, 108-109

167. Ibid

168. Ibid, 108-109

169. Ibid, 109-110

170. Ibid, 271

171. Ibid, 117

172. Ibid

173. Gandhi

174. Michael Mandelbaum, *The Case For Goliath: How America Acts As The World's Government in the 21ˢᵗ Century*, Public Affairs, 2005

175. Eric Shawn, *The U.N. Exposed: How The United Nations Sabotages America's Security And Fails The World,*, Sentinel, 2006

176. Stephen Walt, *Taming American Power: The Global Response U.S. Primacy*, Norton,2005, 245-247

177. Condoleezza Rice, Rethinking the National Interest, American Realism For a New World, *Foreign Affairs*, July/August 2008, 2

178. Niccolo Machiavelli, The Prince, Dover Books, 1992, 40

179. Ibid, 43-44

180. Arthur Schlesinger Jr., *War and the American Presidency*, 2005, 119

181. Barrack Obama , "Renewing America's Leadership," *Foreign Affairs*, January/February, 2008

www.ingramcontent.com/pod-product-compliance
Lightning Source LLC
Chambersburg PA
CBHW081345280326
41927CB00042B/3070